EASTERN WAYS TO THE CENTER

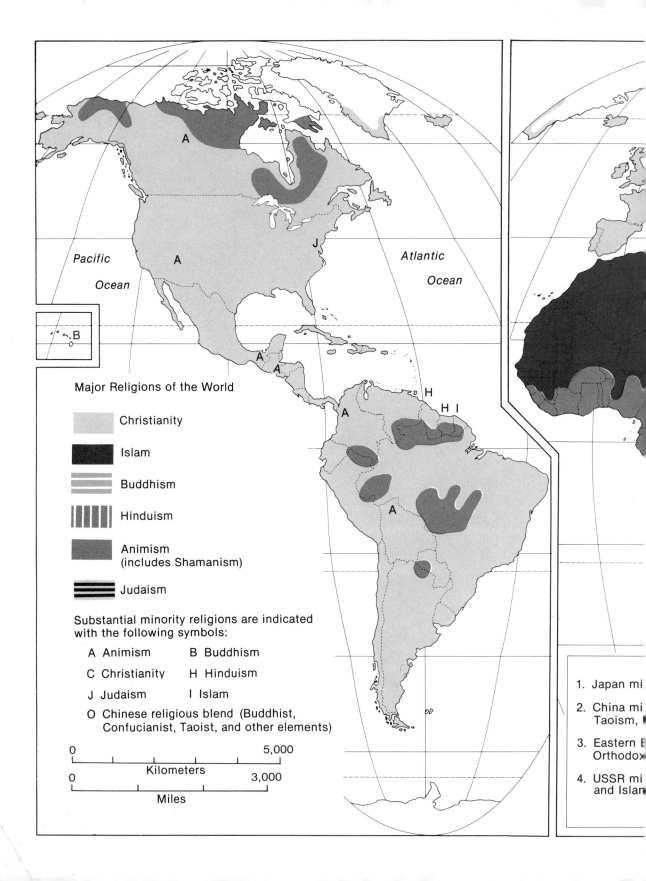

Major Religions of the World

	Christianity
	Islam
	Buddhism
	Hinduism
	Animism (includes Shamanism)
	Judaism

Substantial minority religions are indicated with the following symbols:

A Animism   B Buddhism

C Christianity   H Hinduism

J Judaism   I Islam

O Chinese religious blend (Buddhist, Confucianist, Taoist, and other elements)

Pacific Ocean

Atlantic Ocean

0   5,000
Kilometers
0   3,000
Miles

1. Japan mi

2. China mi
   Taoism,

3. Eastern E
   Orthodox

4. USSR mi
   and Islan

4

3

B

1

Pacific Ocean

2

I

C

C

C

H

C

C

I

A

I

C

C

C

O O

C

C

C

C

C

C

C

C

C

C

C

C

I

Buddhism and Shinto.

Buddhism, Confucianism,
, and Marxism.

e mixes Marxism and
stianity.

Marxism, Orthodox Christianity,

Religions	North America	South America	Europe	Asia	Africa	Oceania	World
		Approximate Population of the Major World Religions (1980)					
Total Christian	237,096,500	175,114,000	342,630,400	95,987,240	128,617,000	18,058,500	997,503,640
Roman Catholic	133,489,000	162,489,000	177,087,300	55,077,000	47,024,500	4,395,500	579,562,300
Eastern Orthodox	4,750,000	516,000	55,035,600	2,428,000	13,306,000	409,000	76,444,600
Protestant	98,857,500	12,109,000	110,507,500	38,482,240	68,286,500	13,254,000	341,496,740
Jewish	6,250,340	595,800	4,045,120	3,192,860	176,400	76,000	14,336,520
Muslim	376,200	251,500	14,945,000	428,266,000	145,214,700	90,000	589,143,400
Zoroastrian	1,250	2,100	10,000	256,000	650	1,000	271,000
Shinto	60,000	90,000	—	57,003,000	1,200	—	57,154,200
Taoist	16,000	10,000	—	31,260,000	—	—	31,286,000
Confucian	97,100	70,000	—	155,887,500	1,500	14,000	156,070,100
Buddhist	185,250	193,200	193,000	254,241,000	20,000	35,000	254,867,450
Hindu	88,500	850,000	400,000	475,073,000	1,179,800	400,000	477,991,330
Totals	244,171,140	177,176,600	362,223,520	1,501,166,600	275,211,250	18,674,500	2,578,623,610
Population	369,759,000	245,067,000	750,198,000	2,557,562,000	469,361,000	22,775,000	4,414,722,000

Adapted from *Historical Atlas of the Religions of the World* by Ismael R. Al Faruqui and David E. Sopher. Copyright ©
1974 by Macmillan Publishing Company, Inc. Reprinted by permission of Macmillan Publishing Company, Inc.

Of related interest . . .

The Religious Life of Man Series   Frederick Streng, editor

EASTERN WAYS TO THE CENTER
AN INTRODUCTION TO ASIAN RELIGIONS

Denise Lardner Carmody
Wichita State University

John Tully Carmody
Wichita State University

Wadsworth Publishing Company
Belmont, California
A Division of Wadsworth, Inc.

Religious Studies editor: Sheryl Fullerton
Production editor: Judith McKibben
Managing and cover designer: Cynthia Bassett

Printed in the United States of America
1 2 3 4 5 6 7 8 9 10—87 86 85 84 83

ISBN 0-534-01342-2

Library of Congress Cataloging in Publication Data
Carmody, Denise Lardner, 1935–
    Eastern ways to the center.
    Bibliography: p.
    Includes index.
    1. Religions. 2. Asia—Religion. I. Carmody,
John, 1939–   II. Title.
BL1032.C37   1982   291′.095   82-15911
ISBN 0-534-01342-2

In Memory of

Catherine R. Carmody
Stephen J. Carmody
Denis Lardner
Martha Comen Lardner

Contents

Contents

Preface

This book derives from the numerous courses we have taught, singly and together, in the world religions. The following observations will indicate our intentions in writing it.

First, our main audience is college students. We do not assume prior courses in religion, and we have tried to use direct, clear prose.

Second, we have emphasized history and structural (philosophical and comparative) analysis, which seem to us the richest beginning approaches to the religions. The introduction explains our rationale, which we hope will give our work a distinctive character.

Third, a textbook has a secondary audience—the teachers who use it. For them (and the more adventurous students) we offer a sizable number of references, usually to recent sources. Because the journals *History of Religions* and *Journal of the American Academy of Religion* are easily available, we have frequently referred to articles in these journals, which we abbreviate in citations as *HR* and *JAAR*. The annotated bibliography at the back of the book, intended for students, emphasizes interesting works that are nontechnical.

Fourth, we explicitly discuss women's experiences with the Eastern religions, because most treatments give short shrift to the female population. Religion has been a major influence on women's cultural roles everywhere, so such neglect can impede liberation.

Fifth, the book revises and expands the materials on Eastern religions in our comprehensive world religions text, *Ways to the Center* (Wadsworth, 1981). The main blocks of new material are set in boxes, so that they may be used as enrichment studies.

Last, our deepest hope is that the book invites the reader to the mysterious center of human experience, where authentic religion offers all of us our best names.

We take pleasure in gratefully acknowledging help from the following persons and institutions: Robert L. Cohn, Thomas V. Peterson, John Pickering, the Institute for the Arts and Humanistic Studies of the Pennsylvania State University, the Institute for Ecumenical and Cultural Research (Collegeville, Minn.), the Mabelle McLeod Lewis Memorial Fund, the Office of Research and Sponsored Programs of Wichita State University, and the Research Office of the College of Liberal Arts of the Pennsylvania State University.

We are also indebted to the scholars who reviewed our manuscript at various stages and provided valuable suggestions. Willard Johnson, San Diego State University; M. Gerald Bradford, University of California at Santa Barbara; Gene R. Thursby, University of Florida; Robert F. Streetman, Montclair State College; Thomas V. Peterson, Alfred University; Nancy K. Frankenberry, Dartmouth College; Gary Davis, Northwest Missouri State University; W. Richard Comstock, University of California at Santa Barbara; Richard Paulson, Fresno City College; William B. Huntley, University of Redlands; R. Lanier Britsch, Brigham Young University; Robert S. Michaelsen, University of California at Santa Barbara; Glenn Yocum, Whittier College; Jeffrey Broughton, California State University, Long Beach; J. Patrick Olivelle, Indiana University; James Fennelly, Adelphi University; Francis H. Cook, University of California, Riverside; and Nathan Katz, Williams College.

Symbols Used on Chapter-Opening Pages

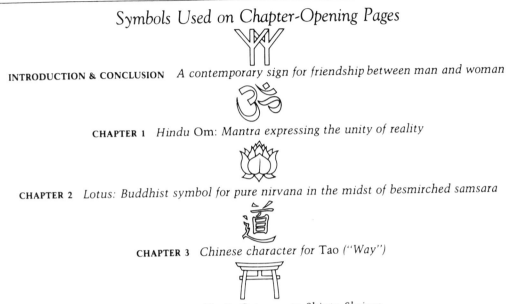

INTRODUCTION & CONCLUSION   *A contemporary sign for friendship between man and woman*

CHAPTER 1   *Hindu Om: Mantra expressing the unity of reality*

CHAPTER 2   *Lotus: Buddhist symbol for pure nirvana in the midst of besmirched samsara*

CHAPTER 3   *Chinese character for Tao ("Way")*

CHAPTER 4   *Torii: Gateway to Shinto Shrines*

Introduction

EASTERN WISDOM: TWENTY-FIVE KEY DATES

CA. 1500 B.C.E.	HINDU VEDAS
800–400	HINDU UPANISHADS
536–476	BUDDHA
500	OLDEST PARTS OF CONFUCIAN *ANALECTS*
500–200	HINDU EPIC POETRY: *MAHABHARATA, RAMAYANA, BHAGAVAD GITA*
350	CHINESE *TAO TE CHING*
236	RISE OF MAHAYANA BUDDHIST LITERATURE
100 B.C.E.–100 C.E.	RISE OF HINDU BHAKTI LITERATURE
5 C.E.	BUILDING OF JAPANESE NATIONAL SHRINE AT ISE
200	NAGARJUNA, LEADING BUDDHIST PHILOSOPHER
430	BUDDHAGHOSA, LEADING BUDDHIST PHILOSOPHER
550	INTRODUCTION OF BUDDHISM TO JAPAN

700	GOLDEN AGE OF CHINESE POETRY
712–720	COMPLETION OF JAPANESE SHINTO CHRONICLES
749	FIRST BUDDHIST MONASTERY IN TIBET
788–820	SHANKARA, LEADING HINDU PHILOSOPHER
1000	FLOURISHING OF CHINESE PAINTING AND CERAMICS
1017–1137	RAMANUJA, LEADING HINDU PHILOSOPHER
1130–1200	CHU HSI, LEADING CHINESE NEO-CONFUCIAN
1175	HONEN, LEADER OF JAPANESE PURE LAND BUDDHISM
1485–1533	CHAITANYA, LEADER OF HINDU KRISHNA-BHAKTI
1646–1694	BASHO, LEADING JAPANESE BUDDHIST POET
1730–1801	MOTOORI NORINAGA, LEADER OF JAPANESE SHINTO RENAISSANCE
1869–1948	MAHATMA GANDHI, LEADER OF INDIAN FREEDOM MOVEMENT
1893–1977	MAO TSE-TUNG, LEADER OF COMMUNIST CHINA

The religious life of humanity is a vast spectacle that is hard to keep in perspective. Therefore, we should make our goals and methods clear from the outset. Our primary goal is to make clear how the East's religious traditions have oriented billions of human lives. Our primary method is to place the study of religion in the context of the humanities and approach the traditions with a consistent format. Let us explain these notions in more detail.

THE NATURE OF RELIGION

Picture yourself in New Delhi. You are outside *Rajgat*, the memorial to Mahatma Gandhi, the politician and holy man who led India to freedom from British colonial rule. Before you, squatting on the broken sidewalk, are three small boys with wooden flutes. They are piping tunes directed toward round wicker baskets, and when they lift the baskets' covers, three silver cobras slowly weave their way out. You watch for several minutes, fearful but entranced. Then the boys shove the cobras back under their arms and approach you for their fee. A few rupees seem fair enough—you don't want to upset those cobras.

Does this picture shine a light on the exotic East? Is it a minor revelation of Indian culture? Yes, but only if you know a little background. In India, as in many other countries with ancient cultures, serpents have been potent symbols (think of the story in Genesis, chapter 3). Perhaps because they appear menacing or phallic (penislike), they have stood for something very basic, something very close to the life force. For centuries, groups of Indians have specialized in snake handling, and the skills have been passed along from father to son. Their profession has combined show business and a bit of crude religion. It has been both entertainment and an occasion to shiver about the implications of death and life.

Now picture yourself in medieval England. In 627 C.E. ("common era" = A.D.)

the monk Paulinus came to King Edwin in northern England and urged him to convert his people to Christianity. After some debate, one of Edwin's counselors stood up and said: "Your majesty, on a winter night like this, it sometimes happens that a little bird flies in that far window, to enjoy the warmth and light of our fire. After a short while it passes out again, returning to the dark and the cold. As I see it, our human life is much the same. We have but a brief time between two great darknesses. If this monk can show us warmth and light, we should follow him."[1]

For medieval Europe, the warmth and light that made life seem good radiated from Jesus Christ. At the core of Europe's complex and in many ways crude culture at that time, there was a faith that a personal father God so loved the world that he had given his son to heal and enlighten it. When they shared that faith, European monks, kings, and kings' counselors largely agreed on their conception of life. Monks, for instance, were willing to give up family life in order to bear witness to God's love. Kings tried to show that their rule derived from what God had done through Jesus, and counselors tried to show commoners how the kings' rule mediated God's will. Often, of course, monks and kings and counselors did things that we find hard to square with Jesus, pursuing wealth and power by means of guile. But their culture forced them all to confront Christian warmth and light, as Indian culture forced Indians to confront sex, death, and life.

Our two pictures are not quite compatible. The modern Indian scene stressed rather primitive sexual or vital energies, while the medieval English scene stressed lofty love and vision. Westerners have tended to view Indian and European life in that way, as the writings of early Christian missionaries to India suggest. However, the past century of scholarship in religious studies has shown the deficiencies of such an attitude, so we must add a few comments on the two scenes.

First, drawing a picture of medieval Europe that is raw and primitive would not

and *The Virgin Spring*, death and sex and life are jammed together like serpents in a basket. Because of the Black Death, the plague that killed about three-quarters of the late medieval European population, monks and commoners marched in processions while they beat themselves, scourging their flesh with whips to do penance for their sins and to keep death away. The harshness of medieval life also led to brutal wars and brutal rapes. The knight and the squire of *The Seventh Seal*, who watch the procession of penitents, have kept company with death since they went to war as Crusaders. The young girl who is raped and killed in *The Virgin Spring* sums up medieval primitiveness. Sex and death pour out in her blood, and only after her father has slain the rapists do we see hope for new life trickle forth in a fresh spring. Medieval Europe, Bergman suggests, was as raw as India has ever been.

Second, were we to go inside the memorial to Gandhi and look at the scene at his commemorative stone, the sublimity of Indian culture and its visions of warmth and light would rise up and parallel those of Christian Europe. *Rajgat* blends green grass, elegant black marble, and fresh flower petals of orange and pink. They symbolize the beautiful spirit of the Mahatma, the little man of great soul. Gandhi was a politician who moved people by *satyagraha*—the force of truth. Without military arms, much money, or even much respect from British leaders, he forced the whole world to take notice. When he vowed to take no food until India's just claims were met, the world held its breath. When he led groups of nonviolent *satyagrahis* into the midst of club-swinging soldiers, he upset the conscience of the world. By the simple rightness, the sheer justice, of his cause, Gandhi showed how his Hindu conception of God could be very powerful. His God was "Truth," and it finally shamed the British into withdrawal.

Snakes and scourges, love and truth—they have shot through India, Europe, and most other parts of the world. In contemporary America, they or their offspring live with us yet. For instance, our nuclear mis-

Figure 1   Buddha Image, Northwest India, Gupta Period (300–620). Nelson Gallery-Atkins Museum (Nelson Fund).

be hard. In Ingmar Bergman's movies of the medieval period, such as *The Seventh Seal* siles are for many citizens and analysts eerie phallic symbols. Like cobras we are trying to get back in their baskets, the missiles give us shivers. Many people see the missiles' thrust, their destructive power, and the claims that they give us security or economic life as brutalizing and raping our culture. From Hiroshima to Three Mile Island, nuclear power muddles our wellsprings and hope.

So too with the ways that we whip ourselves for guilt, the ways that we still crave love, the ways that we search after light. Our guilt keeps psychiatrists in business. Our searches for light fill churches and schools. Clearly we are sisters and brothers to religious Indians and Europeans. Clearly their snakes and saviors relate to our own.

Religion is the issue of ultimate meaning that this discussion of cobras and monks spotlights. It is the part of culture—Eastern, Western, or contemporary American—that we study when we ask about a people's deepest convictions. For instance, Hinduism is the animating spirit, the soul, the way of looking at the world, that has tied snake handling and *satyagraha* together for most Indians. Christianity is the way of looking at the world that has joined scourging to Jesus for most Europeans. Religion, then, is what you get when you investigate striking human phenomena to find the ultimate vision or set of convictions that gives them their sense. It is the cast of mind and the gravity of heart by which a people endures or enjoys its time between the two great darknesses.

STUDYING RELIGION

Certain attitudes should be cultivated in all study, but the study of religion demands more self-awareness and personal engagement with its materials than most other disciplines do. For instance, although reducing physical science to "objective" observing and testing is simplistic, since all knowledge is ultimately personal,[2] physical science does not make great demands on a student's inner experiences of suffering or love. The humanities (those disciplines that study our efforts at self-expression and self-understanding) involve more of such inner experiences, because suffering and love shape so much of history and literature, yet even the humanities seldom deal with direct claims about ultimate meaning. Only in philosophy and religion does one directly encounter systems about God, evil, and humanity's origin and end. Philosophy deals with such concepts principally in their rational forms, while religious studies meet them more concretely in the myths, rituals, mysticisms, behavior patterns, and institutions through which most human beings have been both drawn to ultimate meaning and terrified of it.

More than in any other discipline, the student in a religious studies course is confronted with imperative claims. The religions are not normally warehouses where you pay your money and take your choice. Rather, they are impassioned heralds of ways of life. More than most people initially like, the religions speak of death, ignorance, and human viciousness. However, they also speak of peace and joy, forgiveness and harmony. Whatever they discuss, though, they are *mystagogic*, which etymologically means "mystery working." The religions work mystery. Their preoccupations, when they are healthy, are nature's wonder, life's strange play of physical death and spiritual resurrection, and the possibility of order in the midst of chaos. The religions say that the kingdom of God is in your midst, because you are a being who can pray, "Abba, Father." They say that the *Tao* ("the Way") that can be named is not the real *Tao*. Above all, they say that the person who lives divorced from the mysteries of rosy-fingered dawn and wintery death is less than fully human. So Sioux Indians revered the East, because dawn symbolizes the light of conscience. So Jewish scripture speaks of love as strong as death. So, finally, Islam speaks for all religions when it says that Allah—Muslim divinity—is as near as the pulse at our throats. Clearly, then, we cannot study the religions well if we are afraid of mystery or in flight from death and life.

We also cannot study the religions well if we insist on forcing them into the categories of our own faith. We must first take them on their own terms, giving their experiences and problems a sympathetic hearing. After we have listened to the wisdom of a scripture such as the Hindu *Bhagavad Gita*, we may and should compare it with the wisdom of our Western faiths. Unless we then say with the Christians' Saint Peter, "I see now how true it is that God has no favorites, but that in every nation the person who is God-fearing and does what is right is acceptable" (Acts 10:34), we risk acting with prejudice and condescension.

A second reason for remembering life's mystery, then, is that it helps us clear away prejudice. Talk of the New Testament superseding the Old or of revealed religion besting paganism—without strong qualifications— is self-serving and naive. Used as a word of God, Jewish scriptures open onto a divinity ever new, ever fresh, and ever free. Taken in its experiential vividness, a Zen Buddhist's enlightenment *(satori)* tears the veil of ignorance and comes as revelation and grace.[3] As Thomas Aquinas insisted, we do not know what God is. As John Calvin knew, the mind without mystery is a factory of idols. The most authoritative Western theologians have counseled against prejudice.

It is worth pointing out that the religious studies course offered here is not theology, at least not the theology of a church. Church theology tends to be a search for an understanding of one's own faith that is directed by the particular creed or commitment of an individual or group. Spontaneously the search spreads to a probing of all life's dimensions in terms of such a commitment. So, there develops a theology of art, a theology of history, and even a theology of the world religions.[4] In these theologies, however, a goal is to square data with one's own faith or religious group. Moreover, a church theology's ultimate goal is to promote its own faith. It studies art, history, or the world religions in order to beautify, advance, or defend its own vision of things, whether the church be Muslim, Buddhist, Jewish, or Christian. The understanding that theology seeks in such study is not necessarily distorted, but it is in the service of preaching, ministering, and counseling. When it is not in such service, church theology becomes divorced from the life of its community.[5]

In a university, however, neither students nor teachers are expected to confess their faith (or nonfaith). We, the authors, have argued elsewhere[6] that it is proper and healthy to make clear one's position on the *implications*, for thought and action alike, to which a course's studies lead. In other words, there is nothing wrong and much right with teachers and students becoming personal—dealing with concrete, practical implications. There is much wrong, however, in university courses that place their own values on other people's art, history, or religion and thereby distort them. One must listen with an open mind before judging and deciding.

So we urge you to get inside the religions' experiences and values and to compare them with your own. In fact, we very much hope that your study will enrich your appreciation of nature, increase your wonder about life's meaning, and increase your resources for resisting evil. But we do not set these hopes in the framework of any one faith. We are not, in other words, doing church theology. You may be Christian, Jewish, Buddhist, agnostic, atheistic, or anything else. To us such labels do not matter. What matters is that you be human: a man or woman trying to hear the Delphic oracle's "know thyself," a person humble with the Confucian virtue of sympathy or "fellow feeling" *(jen)*.

What benefits will this effort to study humanistically bring you? At least two spring to mind. First, you will be able to grapple with some of the most influential and wisest personalities of the past. Second, you will better understand the world of the present, in which all peoples on the globe are much closer than they have ever been before.

To illustrate the first benefit, let us call on the Chinese sage Confucius. In his time (551–479 B.C.E.) people were advancing the dictum that it is better to pay court to the stove (to practicalities) than to heaven (to ideals) (see *Analects* 3:3). Confucius batted their dictum back. If you do not pay court to heaven, he said, you will have no recourse when practicalities fail to bring you good life. In other words, the mystery of life is more than food and drink, more than shelter and pleasure. Important as those things are, they do not make truly good life. Only moving in the Way *(Tao)* of heaven makes us humans what we ought to be and what we most deeply want to be. If we settle for the stove, we halve our potential riches.

To illustrate the second benefit of the humanistic study of religion, we must comment briefly on current history. Today it is a commonplace observation that the world is becoming one. That does not mean that all peoples are agreeing on a common government, economy, or philosophy. It does mean that communications, transportation, economics, and other forces are tying all nations together. Thus, commentators speak of a "global village" or a "planetary culture." They remind us of the novelty of the twentieth century, the only time when it could have happened that when Gandhi fasted, the world held its breath; that when Mao died, his funeral reached every capital. Further, in our nuclear age all curtains can be raised. In our age of escalating population and hunger, all the silos of Kansas cast shadows on East Africa.

All the implications of the current state of affairs are too numerous to detail. We may be on the verge of a new phase of evolution; the human sciences may just be approaching their maturity. Or the outer complexity of human affairs may just be developing a self-consciousness among humans so that they can cope with these affairs. In either case, religion acquires an added significance, because we cannot learn much about the evolution or self-consciousness of the global village unless we listen to its members' deepest perceptions and convictions. Religion shows a people's deepest perceptions and convictions. Hinduism, Buddhism, Christianity, and Islam form the souls of a majority of the world's population today. To live together in the future, humans will have to understand the world religions very well.

THE ANCIENT EASTERN MIND

In this book we are trying to understand the Eastern religions. To understand them well, we must appreciate the antiquity of many of the notions underlying their world views. A good way to begin is to focus on the shaman, the central figure of prehistoric (nonliterate) religion, East and West.

According to Mircea Eliade,[7] the shaman is a specialist in archaic techniques of ecstasy. Specifically, tribes of Siberia and central Asia (which scholars consider the most purely shamanistic) often select their shamans for psychological features and capacities that render them apt for ecstasy— for going outside themselves. The typical prospect is sensitive, introverted, inclined to solitude, and perhaps sickly (perhaps epileptic or given to fainting). By adolescence he (males predominate in Siberian shamanism) is thought different—peculiar, brooding, religious. If he has an emotional crisis or if something strange happens to him (such as getting very sick or being struck by lightning), elders will consider him appropriate for initiation into shamanism. That will entail learning tribal lore and ecstatic techniques and then passing an initiatory ordeal.

In Siberia the initiatory ordeal amounts to a ritualized experience of suffering, death, and resurrection. The candidate's body is dismembered; he dies and is transported to the realm of the gods. There his organs are replaced or renewed, sometimes with special stones or other tokens of his visit added. Depending on the beliefs of his tribe, he may fly to heaven as a bird, climb a sacred pole or tree (the *axis mundi* connecting earth to heaven), or travel up the rainbow. Which organ is replaced seems to depend on what his tribe thinks is the organ that ultimately quickens us. Bone and blood are popular choices. The constant feature of the ordeal is bodily sundering and death. As noted, the death usually takes place in the realm of the gods, after a flight or ascent, and a benefactor god or ally typically reconstitutes the candidate's body (replaces the removed organ) and returns him to life.

This experience takes place while the candidate is in ecstasy, standing outside his normal consciousness. If the initiation is public, the community gets a running narration of how it is going, with descriptions of the ascent, the celestial realm, the dismembering, and sample voices of the gods. A modern Westerner would probably call the proceedings imaginary, but ancient peoples tend to equate the real with the vividly experienced, so they consider it quite real.[8] Further, studies show shamans to be the healthiest members of their tribes psychologically, not the most schizoid, hysterical, or neurotic. Performing his duties makes the shaman feel good and heals him of his ills, so whenever he is out of sorts, the shaman will sing or drum and go out of himself to the gods.

When the candidate has passed his initiatory ordeal, he is usually accepted by his community and can start functioning as a shaman. His principal functions are healing, guiding the dead to the afterworld, and acting as a medium between the living and the dead. These functions show much of what a shaman's tribe believes, which is essentially that the universe and the human being are both dualistic. The universe is dual because it includes the human realm, where the shaman's body remains, and the spiritual realm, to which his spirit travels. The human being is dual because he or she has both a bodily and a spiritual part. The spirit's "travel" is the shaman's colorful experience of ecstasy.

Ordinarily, a shaman goes into ecstasy in order to gain knowledge or power. He must find out from the gods what is ailing a patient or what the right medicine is. (For ancient peoples, illness is as much a spiritual matter as a physical one.) Similarly, to find where the game has gone, the shaman must be able to go to the gods who keep the game. For example, to the coastal Eskimos, this meant swimming to the depths of the sea, where the goddess Sedna, who ruled the seals and the fish, had fenced them in. To guide the souls of the departed, the shaman must also be able to travel to the land of rest. If a tribal member suffers soul loss (which causes sickness), the shaman must be able to trace the soul and retrieve it.

Wherever he goes, the shaman reports on his progress. His functioning therefore recreates the community in two senses: (1) He helps his people reassert their view of the world, and (2) he gives them an entertaining account of his plunge to the bottom of the sea, his fight to get past Sedna's vicious watchdog, and so forth. When he returns from a mission, he often requires the community to renew itself. Sedna may be withholding the fish because someone has broken a taboo—a hunter may have mistreated a seal, two brothers may have had a violent fight, or spouses may have aborted a fetus. Such a violation of the tribe's ethic must be atoned, for it has ruptured their harmony with nature. Thus, the skillful shaman creates a forum in which his people can confess their guilts and express their regrets and fears. He tries to reconcile enemies and convince the whole tribe to reaffirm its ethical ideals.

How do shamans gain their tribe's confidence to do this? Some develop paranormal powers, including clairvoyance and clairaudience (seeing and hearing beyond the normal range). Others possess an impressive knowledge of herbs, drugs, tribal traditions, or special vocabulary. Probably the shamans' greatest success, though, comes from their mastery of techniques of suggestion, which are especially effective with peoples of vivid imagination.

Eliade's description of shamanism stresses ecstasy and the shaman's ability to go into a trance and travel to the realm of the sacred powers. Other scholars interpret shamanism more loosely, stressing its social dynamics.

Some functionaries in ancient societies give guidance by taking in a spirit. In other words, rather than going out to the gods, the gods come into them. That is the case for much of the shamanism in China and Japan. Typically shamans there sing songs and go into a trance as a way of being taken over, being temporarily inhabited or possessed. Significantly, such shamanism has been practiced more by women than by men. In China, the female shaman's song to her guiding spirit has a romantic tone, as though a beloved were pining for her lover.[9] In Japan, the *kami*, or spirits, who come are erotically intimate. In both places, the possessed shaman performs divination, discerning what the spirits want or what the future will require. Additionally, the Japanese shamans used to band together and walk a regular beat through the local villages, offering personal advice and medical healing. In performing this work, they developed teaching techniques that contributed to Japanese theater and dance.[10]

I. M. Lewis's anthropological study of spirit possession and shamanism[11] reveals important sociological aspects. Lewis finds that many of the spirit-possessed live on the margins of society. This contrasts with Eliade's theory, in which the shaman is a key social figure. Part of the contrast may lie in the fact that Lewis deals more with modern societies, whose power structures are more differentiated and complex. Another part may lie in Lewis's concentration on the "enthusiasm" of "little people" (marginals) in highly developed religious traditions (including Islam and Christianity).

Etymologically, *enthusiasm* means "being filled with the god." In Lewis's study it tends to mean emotional exaltation, as we can observe in rural American religion, where the devout may swoon, sing ecstati-cally, or dance. Interestingly, societies that grant women little status tend to have a substantial number of female enthusiasts. Most likely, such women use their religious experience to gain a little respect and influence. So, too, with the powerless people prominent among other groups of ecstatics. Their religion may be genuine, but the attention they receive can be very welcome.

If shamanism is to be considered in general terms, the phenomena of visions and tutelary spirits must be considered. Among Native Americans the vision quest is a regular feature of an adolescent's passage to maturity. This quest is especially clear for men (it is less clear for women), and some of its most famous examples are in *Black Elk Speaks*.[12] There we read that even before adolescence and without a quest, Black Elk was taken into the air on a cloud, saw groups of prancing horses, was told by "grandfathers" about his people's sad future, and finally was taught the sacredness of his nation's hoop—the circle representing all the Sioux.

This vision stayed with Black Elk throughout his life, dominating his interpretation of all that he observed and experienced. After he had grown old and witnessed many sadnesses, he climbed Harney Peak (for the Oglala Sioux the center of the world), prayed to the grandfatherly spirits, and confronted for the last time the broken hoop, the withering of the tribal tree. As if in answer to the tearful conclusion of his life, a raincloud appeared in the clear sky—a dramatic expression of the Great Spirit. Perhaps a majority of Native Americans were shamans in this way (though not necessarily in such dramatic fashion), for many of them lived by a personal vision and spirit.

Not all shamanist figures are exalted personalities or seers. Some are charlatans who perform for applause or money, and some are "black" shamans, who solicit the powers of evil to inflict harm. In fact, shamans run the full gamut: from holy persons, expert in venerable lore, stooped from bearing the tribe's burdens, to quacks and half-mad mutterers. (Films show Nepalese shamans performing the crudest of cures, with filthy fetishes [objects believed to have protective power] and the blood of cocks. No doubt they offer some psychological comfort to their people, but they must be hygienic disasters. Similarly, films of Yanomamo shamans, who practice among the fierce people living at the border of Venezuela and northern Brazil, indicate that their visions come from ingesting hallucinogenic snuff. The snuff induces visions of *hekura*, tiny humanoid figures who may be used for healing friends or making enemies sick. The Yanomamo shaman's vocation demands some dedication—periods of celibacy, for instance—but most Yanomamo shamans practice in order to ingest snuff and fight.)[13]

Whether he ingests snuff or goes in trance to the bottom of the sea, the shaman's world is very ancient. Indeed, it is continuous with the worlds of Paleolithic hunters and gatherers, who also tried to gain the help of benign spirits, ward off the influence of evil spirits, and keep their tribes on good terms with mother nature.

The great religions of India, China, and Japan all represent significant breaks with this shamanic world view. Shamanic elements remained in Hinduism, Buddhism, Chinese religion, and Japanese religion, but new experiences, insights, and symbols proved more powerful. We must never forget, however, the general shamanic background from which Hinduism, Buddhism, Confucianism, Taoism, and the other Eastern religious innovations stepped forth. These innovations were part and parcel of the military, economic, political, and scientific movements that gave rise to an India, China, and Japan considerably different from their prehistoric forebears, but even the most venerable of the Eastern cultures are less than five thousand years old. For perhaps ninety-five thousand years before these cultures arose, Eastern peoples followed leaders like Eliade's Siberian shaman. It is likely they still feel his touch.

THIS BOOK

In this book we introduce the great Eastern traditions that will be our main focus by showing their relation to the ancient nonliterate mentality. In India, for example, the ancient religious mind has long remained vital. The veneration of life forces, sex, and natural phenomena has long been popular. Similarly, a keen sense of the sacred and a rich body of rituals and mythology link Hinduism and Buddhism to oral traditions. Neither of these great Indian religions took a predominantly shamanist turn, but through the early literature of both shines the magic of the spoken word. Thus, both employ oral elements in a new synthesis rather than casting them away or leaving them behind.

From the Vedas (the Hindu scriptures) and the Tripitaka (the Buddhist scriptures), though, we can sense that Indian religion early distinguished itself from the Western traditions of Egypt, Iran, and Greece. Although Iranians, Greeks, and Indians share the same Indo-European ethnic and linguistic origin, only the Indians developed a strong tradition of yoga. (Whether this means that yoga first derived from the Dravidian peoples, the non-Indo-Europeans replaced by the Indo-European invaders, is not wholly certain. However, the hypothesis seems well-founded.) *"Yoga"* means "discipline," especially the interior discipline of meditation. Since prehistoric times, Indian yogis have given their culture an appreciation of spirituality and a profound hunger for peace by going deep into their own consciousnesses.

To some extent, Indian interiority paralleled that of Iran and Greece. Zoroaster and Plato, for instance, both clarified the structure and light of consciousness. However, Indian yoga took a somewhat different path. Though some Indian meditators and philosophers studied psychology and epistemology (the structure of human awareness and knowledge), most pursued wisdom lying beneath the rational mind. Sitting in a stable position, such as the lotus, most yogis tried

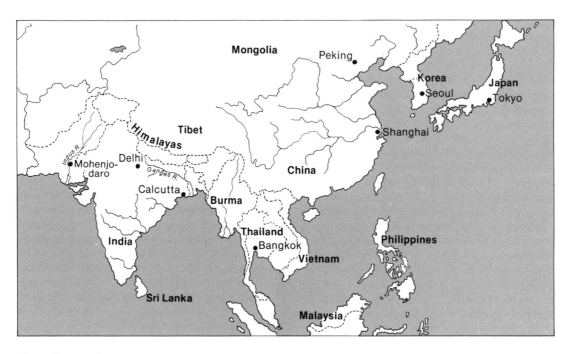

Figure 2   Asia.

to bring their consciousnesses to "one-point-edness"; that is, they focused on mental awareness itself rather than on its images, thoughts, or feelings. Heightening their sense of psychosomatic unity through regular breathing and other techniques, they strove for what Mircea Eliade has called *enstasis*—self-possession.

Etymologically, enstasis is the opposite of ecstasis. Where ecstasis goes out, enstasis goes in. Thus, the shaman and the yogi present an extreme contrast. The former specializes in techniques that take the spirit out to travel, the latter in techniques that settle the spirit down at home. The religion of civilized India seems to have stepped away from the ancient religious mind through a disciplined search for spiritual autonomy or self-possession. Instead of wild singing and hair-raising flights of imagination, it emptied the mind of imagination to achieve tranquility and trance. Probably from these states Indians got their intuitions of Hindu *moksha* or Buddhist *nirvana*—of release from the burdensome human condition.

We will be able to justify this hypothesis in two fairly long chapters, thereby assuring that our contrast between ancient and Indian religion is not simpleminded. In its bhakti or devotional religion, for instance, India was quite ecstatic. In its mythology of the gods and heroes, it was quite imaginative. Still, you might begin your move from ancient to Indian religion by paying special attention to the yogic strain. For after all due qualification, yoga remains a distinctively Indian concept, a characteristic feature of the Hindu-Buddhist religious mind.

The chapters on Chinese and Japanese religion present an analogous situation. From prehistoric times, shamanism and a concern for the sacred prevailed in both lands. Both the Chinese and Japanese were ritualist, and both generated full mythologies. In Confucianism and Taoism, though, China discarded the ancient religious mind somewhat. By stressing ethics and nature's "Way" *(Tao)*, respectively, these two Chinese traditions forged the foundation of a vast civilized religion. (Buddhism's arrival in China strengthened this foundation.) The result was a culture that was quite formal, socially stratified, and yet aesthetic. More than Iran and Greece, China, like Egypt, developed a culture of apparent permanence, surviving numerous social upheavals through its blend of religious and ethnic spirit.

The case is somewhat different with Japan, because the native Japanese religion, Shinto, has a quite ancient point of view. In it nature bulks large, and shamanist elements are strong. However, Japan, like China, adopted Confucian, Taoist, and Buddhist strands. Together with the articulate, self-conscious Shintoism, Japan developed another civilized religion that is both formal and aesthetic. Thus, formalism and aesthetics distinguish the East Asian religions from ancient religion.

The East Asian sage is a quite elegant figure. If the shaman is an impressive ecstatic and the Indian yogi an impressive enstatic, the East Asian sage is a sober, worldly, yet graceful dancer to the *Tao*—to nature's song. That, too, is impressive.

After we have surveyed the major Eastern religious traditions, we shall at the end pause again to take stock. First, we will look back at the religions' unity and diversity. Second, we will have some thoughts on the uses of religion—on the services Eastern religion has tendered through the centuries. Third, we will reflect on being an American citizen of the religious world—a contemporary at least somewhat tutored by the mysterious humanity of the past. In that way, perhaps, our book will complete its circle and make a *mandala*—a symbol of wholeness.

Our material content is as comprehensive as our space allows. To organize all this information, though, we have employed a format that has three aspects. First, wherever possible, we will describe how the religion under consideration appears. In other words, we will try to describe what it looks like and its atmosphere. From travel and study, we will offer vignettes of Hindu temples, Buddhist monasteries, Confucian government, and Japanese art. Ideally, these vignettes will launch you into each religion briskly, engaging your interest and whetting your taste.

The second aspect of the format is history. Having dealt with the religion's appearance, we will tell its story—trace how it evolved. Historical explanation is now a staple in Western studies. You use its cause-effect reasoning every day. There are problems in analyzing ancient and Eastern religious traditions historically, because they frequently have not recorded their pasts nor conceived of their identities as Westerners do. Nevertheless, we can describe Eastern traditions fairly well.

The last aspect of our format is structural analysis: asking how a religion puts together its world view.[14] For example, how does it tend to think and feel about the physical world? As you will see, Hinduism tends to think about the physical world differently than Japanese Buddhism does. Similarly, if we investigate a religion's sense of society, self, or divinity, we will find illuminating likenesses and unlikenesses. Structural analysis and comparison, then, enable us to sharpen differences and discern similarities.

Finally, a few pedagogical comments. Our three-aspect format stems from what we have discovered about the mind's patterns of inquiry. In inquiry, the mind regularly moves from experience, through understanding and judgment, to decision.[15] That is, human knowing begins in wonder, from information that teases and beguiles. Then it works to grasp and affirm reality—to achieve an understanding of how the information makes sense, to achieve an insight or "click." Finally, this understanding leads to a decision: What am I going to do about this insight; what action does it command? Thus, our format moves from soliciting your interest in a religion, to explaining how it arose, to analyzing it structurally so you can decide what it might mean for your own life.

Our job, finally, is to structure the material so that you may understand it and decide well. Your job is to be attentive, intelligent, reflective, and decisive. If you do so, you will make progress toward your center. If we do our job well, you will see how the Eastern religions themselves are but ways to the Center. The coincidence of your center and the Center is that peak experience which T. S. Eliot described as being "at the still point of the turning world." We human beings are so made that all our significant times, good and bad, take us into mystery. Mystery is more intimate to us than we are to ourselves. Mystery is closer than the pulse at our throats. Centering in mystery and recognizing that only ultimate reality can give us our lives, religious persons the world over have been paramount humanists. To follow their ways, even just in one's mind, is therefore a great chance for liberal—freeing—education. We will be happy if we increase your likelihood of seizing such a chance.

Study Questions

1. What would it mean for you to say, "Religious studies are integral to liberal education"?

2. Suggest why the world religions are more significant today than they were a generation ago.

3. How would you relate the history of religious traditions to their comparative analysis?

4. Describe your mind's movement from experience to understanding to judgment to decision.

5. Why would you like or not like to be a shaman?

Chapter One

HINDUISM: TWENTY-FIVE KEY DATES

CA. 2750 B.C.E.	GROWTH OF CIVILIZATION IN INDUS VALLEY
CA. 1500	ARYAN INVASIONS; VEDIC LITERATURE
800–400	UPANISHADS
600–500	CHALLENGES OF MAHAVIRA AND BUDDHA
CA. 500	ARYANS AS FAR SOUTH AS CEYLON
500–200	EPIC POETRY: *MAHABHARATA, RAMAYANA, BHAGAVAD GITA*
322	CHANDRAGUPTA FOUNDS MAURYAN EMPIRE
100 B.C.E.–100 C.E.	RISE OF BHAKTI LITERATURE
480 C.E.	FALL OF GUPTA EMPIRE
680	FLOURISHING OF TAMIL BHAKTI MOVEMENT
788–820	SHANKARA, LEADING PHILOSOPHER
800–900	RISE OF HINDU ORTHODOXY

Hinduism

Hinduism has been central to Indian culture from prehistoric times to the present. Its traditions have existed for thousands of years, yet, through constant adaptation, they have continued to be contemporary. Hundreds of millions of people have organized their lives through Hindu traditions, showing that Eastern religion has been a force well worth our trying to measure.

APPEARANCE

Imagine yourself in the departure lounge of the Tehran airport, waiting for a night flight to Delhi on Air India. Most of your fellow passengers wear turbans or saris. The plane is running on time, and after you board, you notice that the hostesses are graceful creatures wearing saris and nose rings, with spots of vermilion on their foreheads. The voice over the address system speaks colonial British with a tight Indian inflection. The food is a spicy curry, and the woman beside you tries to get it past her cranky baby, explaining that they have already been traveling two days from Washington on their way home for a visit in Bombay. The flight goes smoothly, but it is still a relief to stagger off the plane, stretch, and start the customs gauntlet. There you meet the first of dozens of bureaucratic forms, all backed by carbon paper, that will trace you across the subcontinent.

Delhi is quiet at dawn. The ancient cab careens down wide streets with wild grass growing along the edges. In the fields stand a few cows and water buffalo. The two boys sitting in the front of the cab look about fifteen. They are slight, dark, and very alert. Obviously they are used to this racing entrance to their capital. When they have left you off at your modest hotel, you pause to test the dusty, humid air. At 6 A.M. it is 90° F.—the monsoon should arrive within the week. From experience you know that you are too keyed up to recover your lost sleep now, so you wash quickly and take to the streets. Often the first hours of immersion in a new country are the richest. It is high adventure just to walk the city.

The city is coming to life. Vendors stir by their wooden stands, where many of them have slept for the night. Cars zoom around traffic circles belching exhaust, beginning their noisy concert. Along broken sidewalks come Indians of all sizes and shapes, most in traditional garb, but a few in business suits or slacks and short-sleeved shirts. Two barefoot women kneel on the sidewalk and begin their day's work: breaking up the old brick so that the sidewalk can be rebuilt. As you approach Connaught Circus, the shops are opening—bookstores, clothing stores, restaurants. Outside these shops, under a shady portico, shoeshine men and food vendors are setting up. They smile and beckon you to inspect their goods. You smile back your "no thanks" and opt for a city tour by the government agency bus.

On the city tour your favorite stop is the Birla Temple (Figure 3), a yellow and pink sandstone enclave built by a wealthy family in the 1930s. Through the main gate pour dozens of people, mainly families with small children. The temple grounds are apparently a favorite spot for picnics and holiday outings. The first impression you have of the temple proper is "Perfect—could have been designed by Disney." It is all alcoves, extensions, niches, and wings jutting at oblique angles. In the main section, opposite the entrance, you find a cool interior. There the people wander slowly, talking and laughing but keeping a respectful atmosphere for those who bow, join their hands, and pray at one of the shrines. A priest attends the shrine for Krishna. He sits reading with head shaved and the colorful folds of his robe draping to the floor. A worshiper calls him and makes a contribution. The priest then sprinkles flower petals before the image of Krishna and utters low, rhythmic prayers for several minutes.

In the next chapel you read in English

Figure 3   Birla Temple, modern Hindu temple in New Delhi, replete with statues of gods and animals. Photo by J. T. Carmody.

verses from the *Bhagavad Gita* and admire the wall murals that depict scenes from this scripture. Going outside, you wander between marble elephants into the grassy park. Behind the temple is a reflecting pool, a miniature of the famous one before the Taj Mahal, so you climb a rocky hill to see the temple mirrored in the lambent waters. The people around the park and pool are clearly very much at home. They love the cool, shady trees, the unkempt grass on which the children run barefoot.

All in all, the temple is a very colorful place: elephants and the elephant god Ganesha, Krishna, Buddha, Shiva, and numerous buxom consorts. In the monks' quarters, annexed to the temple, study is a serious business, but most of the temple has a rather light-hearted atmosphere. Overhead the sky is clear and the sun is blazing. Yet the very clarity of the air seems to intensify the murkiness of the temple's meaning. The colors and shapes of the sandstone buildings say it could only have been built in recent times, yet something prehistoric smiles from the statues in the alcoves. Verses from the *Dhammapada* that decorate the Buddha's temple blend with verses from the *Gita* singing Krishna's praise. Is it all one? To what does it tally in the mind of that small, plump woman there, lost in prayer before a statue of Vishnu? What do her three children make of it, as they wiggle and squirm down the steps onto the grass? The only thing really clear to you is that you have no clarity. Too much runs together.

HISTORY

Pre-Vedic India

Before the first invasions of Aryans from the northwest around 2000 B.C.E., an impressive Indian culture already existed. Its beginnings stretch back to the second interglacial period (400,000–200,000 B.C.E.), and its earliest religion, on the basis of ancient peoples living in India today, was shamanist, focusing on the worship of nature—especially on the life force. In 1924 excavations at two sites along the Indus River, called Harrapa and Mohenjo-daro, furnished the first extensive evidence of a high ancient Indian culture. This culture, called the Harrapan, stretched over about 500,000 square miles[1] and was distributed in small towns between the two "capitals" of Harrapa and Mohenjo-daro. Other excavations in what is now Pakistan have disclosed cultures predating the Harrapan, but this Indus Valley culture is the largest source of information about pre-Aryan Indian ways. Carbon dating suggests that the Harrapan culture flourished about 2150–1750 B.C.E., and some evidence indicates that the culture was remarkably stable throughout that period.

Harrapa and Mohenjo-daro seem to have had populations of thirty to forty thousand. Both were about one mile square. That few weapons have been found suggests that their people were not very warlike. Outside each city was a citadel—a construction somewhat like the tiered Babylonian ziggurat—which was probably used for worship rather than for military defense. There were large granaries in the cities, two-room apartments nearby for the granary workers, and high city walls. Most building was done with kiln-dried bricks, which were standardized at 3 by 10 by 20 inches. Through the city ran an excellent sewage disposal system, with terra-cotta pipes and manholes through which workmen could enter to clean the pipes. The houses were multistoried dwellings with thick walls and flat roofs. Outside stairways to the roofs suggest that people slept there on hot nights.

The entire city plan suggests orderliness: Streets were wide and rectilinear, houses had chutes for sliding trash down into collection bins, and apartments had bathrooms and toilets. Larger buildings included a bathhouse 108 by 180 feet, with a tank 20 feet wide by 39 feet long by 8 feet deep. If this tank was used like similar ones outside Hindu temples today, its likely purpose was ritual bathing.

Some of the most significant remains from the Harrapan culture are small sandstone seals, engraved with a pictorial script and apparently used to mark property. They are decorated with various animals, both real and imaginary, and indicate a modest economic and artistic life. Other interesting finds include a small bronze statue of a dancing girl, lithe and graceful, and a red sandstone sculpture of the torso of a young man, also artistically impressive. Some scholars hypothesize that these finds indicate creative potential that was stifled by conservative forces, but others logically suggest that these artifacts are the only remains we have of a rather vigorous art whose other products perished. The first scholars, in their interpretations of pre-Aryan culture, believed that the artistry of the Harrapans was static and even monotonous, and it changed little over 400 years. The uniformity in the bricks and buildings suggests a strong deterrent to innovation, and the people were likely ruled by autocratic priests, who insisted on conformity to a theopolitical tradition based on worship at the religious citadels and lavatory tanks. Since the mid-1960s, however, this interpretation has been disputed by other artifacts and cross-cultural comparisons. Though much of what we know of the Harrapan culture does suggest stability, it probably had its ups and downs like most other cultures.

Beginnings of Hinduism

R. N. Dandekar, who refers to the Harrapan culture as "protohistoric Hinduism," has commented extensively on one religious artifact that has excited great scholarly interest—a seal depicting a three-faced nude male deity.[2] The deity has horns, sits on a stool, has an erect penis, and places his heels in a yogic position. Around him are an elephant, a tiger, a rhinoceros, a buffalo, and some antelope. He wears bangles on each arm, a chest decoration hangs round his neck, and a fan-shaped headdress rises between his horns. All these features are associated with the classical Hindu god Shiva, who rode a bull, was lord of yoga, and often appeared both nude and ithyphallic (with penis erect). This correspondence argues that the fertility associations of the classical Shiva go back to Indus Valley religious culture. Since the headdress of the sealed figure is like Shiva's hunting costume and his matted ascetic's hair, it is also likely that Indus Valley culture considered its proto-Shiva a wild yet ascetic force. Since the classical Shiva was Lord of the Animals, the representation of the animals on the seal makes the relationship almost indisputable.

A variant of this seal shows the Indus Valley god with just three symbols: a bull, a trident, and a phallus—all symbols of the classical god. Other remnants from Harrapan culture suggest that the prime aspect of the proto-Shiva was fertility, for archeologists have found a number of cylindrical cones that almost surely represent the male sexual organ (linga) as well as rings that represent the female (yoni). Fertility worship may have originally been independent of the worship of the Lord of the Animals, but by Harrapan times they clearly had joined: proto-Shiva was the god of the sexual life force. However, the yoni remains suggest that there was also a fertility cult of the mothers or of a mother goddess. Many female figurines discovered in the Indus Valley support this hypothesis. Often they carry smoke-stained cups, which suggest a practice of burning oil or incense. Other seals carry engravings of trees, animals, and water—more evidence of a sensitivity to nature's fertility.

Precisely how this fertility religion related to the apparently sedate city culture of Harrapa or Mohenjo-daro awaits explanation. The fertility emphasis continued in later religion, however, indicating that Aryans as well as the natives considered sexual powers sacred. By about 1500 B.C.E. the Harrapan culture was destroyed, after perhaps a millennium and a half of existence. (Most scholars postulate a long growth period before the 400 years of prosperity.) The destructive Aryan conquerers were a pastoral and nomadic people who loved fighting, racing, drinking, and other aspects of the warrior life. They probably came from the north, where the cooler climate favored such vigor, and they thought of themselves as the salt of the earth—their name means "from the earth" or "noble." (This name survives in *Iran* and *Eire*; in addition, all European languages save Finnish, Hungarian, and Basque are related to the Aryans' language.)

*The Aryans had fair skin and pointed noses, a fact responsible for their hostile reaction to the dark, snub-nosed Dravidians (as the natives were called). They moved by horse, ate meat, and hunted with bow and arrow. There is no evidence that they ever learned to navigate or sail, and they produced no striking art, although they did know iron and fashioned good weapons. Like many other warrior, nomadic peoples (for example, the Celts), they loved story telling and singing. Indeed, their culture and religion were highly verbal. Their society was male dominated, with a primarily patriarchal family structure, priesthood, and cast of gods.[3] Above all, they were mobile, pushing through Greece, Italy, Iran, and India. After 2000 B.C.E. they were strong enough to dominate the native Indians, but they may have started trickling into India from the northwest as much as 2000 years previously.

Troy Wilson Organ suggests that the Aryans' favorite god, Indra, whom we shall study when we turn to the *Rig-Veda*, was a projection or personification of their own sense of character.[4] He was exuberant and warlike—a boaster, a thunderbolt thrower, a big drinker, a slayer of dragons. He ruled by seizure rather than inheritance, loving action rather than stability. Indra aggressively seized the waters of heaven, released them, and fashioned the earth. Some have suggested that Indra was first a culture hero and only later a leading god, but from their earliest time in India, the Aryans undoubtedly looked to him as the source and model of their prowess in war. Even in his fondness for drinking Indra was a great model, for what hardy people has not sanctioned its love of drink?

Two peoples thus contributed to the beginnings of Indian (Hindu) culture. If the Harrapan culture was representative, the people who preexisted the Aryans in the Indus Valley were stable, even conservative city dwellers who nevertheless developed (or took from earlier peoples) fertility rites devoted to such gods as the wild proto-Shiva. The Aryans were a rough, fighting people who had a much simpler technology than the Harrapans but whose poetry and religion were more imaginative. These Aryans became the dominant force militarily and politically, imposing their will and their gods on the subjugated Dravidian natives.

However, Indian culture never lost its Dravidian features. At most they were dormant for a while. After the demise of Vedic culture, Dravidian interests in fertility reemerged (the Aryans had their own fertility interests). These interests focused on the established god Shiva, but the complex devotionalism of later Hinduism is best explained in terms of many non-Aryan factors. Since the Indians have tended to keep old practices by incorporating them into their existing ones, the persistence of the Harrapan Lord of the Animals is typically Hindu.

Vedic India

By Vedism most scholars mean the culture resulting from the mixture of Aryans, Harrapans, and other peoples of the Indus and Ganges valleys. This culture expressed itself in the earliest Indian writings, which are a collection of religious songs, hymns, spells, rituals, and speculations called the Vedas. It is convenient to consider them as representing the first stages of Hinduism, for although later India abandoned many of the Vedic gods and practices, the Vedas retained scriptural status throughout the later centuries, weaving themselves deeply into India's fabric.

The word *veda* means "wisdom" (cognates are the English *wit* and the German *wissen*). The Vedic pieces were originally oral. In fact, the proto-Hindus considered human speech divine, so singing and praying to the gods became sacred actions. Scholars have found that the Aryans composed some of the hymns found in the oldest Vedic literature before they entered India. The hymns honoring the sky and the dawn, for instance, are remarkably like the religious literature of other Indo-Europeans, indicating that they go back to the time before the Aryans split into the Iranian and Indian branches.

To the traditional Hindu, the Vedic literature represents the highest intuitive knowledge that the *rishis* (holy persons or seers) had attained.[5] The technical term denoting such a state of wisdom is *shruti*, which translators often render as "revelation." *Shruti* does not connote that divinities outside the human realm broke through the veil separating heaven and earth in order to impart light from above; as we shall see, Hinduism does not have such an exalted view of the gods. Rather, *shruti* implies that the eminent holy person has perceived certain things in peak experiences (often induced by the ritual drink soma). Therefore, Vedic literature, representing what the *rishis* had seen, was considered the best and holiest presentation of knowledge.

The Vedas consist of four separate collections of materials. Together, these four collections are known as the *Samhitas*. *Samhitas* therefore is a synonym for Vedas. The individual collections are called the *Rig-Veda*, *Sama-Veda*, *Yajur-Veda*, and *Atharva-Veda*. The *Rig-Veda* is the oldest, largest, and most important. It contains more than a thousand *suktas*, or individual units, which are hymns to the gods, magical poems, riddles, legends, and the like. They show considerable learning and poetic skill,

which argue against their being the spontaneous poetry of free-wheeling warriors or
rude peasants. More likely, they represent
the work of priestly leaders—the careful creation of an educated class concerned with
regulating contact with the gods and maintaining its own social status.

Most of the *Rig-Veda*'s hymns have
two purposes. First, they praise the god being
addressed; second, they ask the god for
favors or benefits. For instance, the *Rig-Veda*
praises Agni for deeds that show the splendor of his status as the god of fire. (These
deeds appear to be not so much mythical
allusions to feats that the god performed in
the beginning as similes drawn from human
experience. For example, Agni's flame is like
the warrior's battle rush: As the warrior
blazes upon the enemy, so the god of fire
blazes through the brush or woods.) Then,
having fattened the god's ego, the hymn
singer makes his petition. In *Rig-Veda* 6 : 6
he asks for wealth: "wealth giving splendor,
. . . wealth bright and vast with many
heroes."

Though this praise-and-plead purpose
is the most usual, the *Rig-Veda* has other
functions. For instance, it includes petitions
for forgiveness of sins, such as having
wronged a brother, cheated at games, or
abused a stranger, which indicate a developed moral sense. Although the *Rig-Veda*
may not separate itself completely from an
ancient world view, where being out of
phase with the cosmic processes is almost
physically dangerous, it provides solid evidence of religion centering on free, responsible choices made for good or evil. As well,
some of the hymns of the *Rig-Veda* are philosophical, wondering about the first principle behind the many phenomena of the
world. A famous philosophical text is
10 : 129, where the poet muses about the
creation of the world. At the beginning there
was no being and no nonbeing, no air and no
sky beyond. It was, in fact, a time before
either death or immortal life had begun.
Then only the One existed, drawn into being
by heat that interacted with the primal
waters and the void. However, from desire

the One started to think and emit fertile
power. Thus, impulse from above and energy
from below began to make the beings of the
world. But, the hymn asks in conclusion,
who knows whether this speculation is valid? Even the gods were born after the world's
beginning, so who can say what happened?
Only one who surveys everything from the
greatest high heaven knows, if indeed even
that being knows.

Such deep musing, culminating in a
skepticism about the human capacity to
fathom creation's ways, anticipates the
more philosophical portions (the Upanishads) of the Vedic literature, which we shall
consider below. It is not typical of the *Samhitas*, however, for they are usually more
concrete. For instance, both the tenth book
of the *Rig-Veda* and the entire *Atharva-Veda*
contain numerous spells and charms, indicating that the earliest Hindu mind tried to
ward off forces of evil and commandeer
forces of good. By contrast, the *Sama-Veda* is
largely a religious songbook, while the
Yajur-Veda is a priestly work of instructions
for performing sacrifices.

In all these works, words have a more
than literal intent—they have a power and
force to effect what they express. Therefore,
the entire Vedic literature is in a certain,
modern sense magical. The *Atharva-Veda*,
though, had considerable secular impact,
since much of it entered Hindu medical lore,
furnishing the beginnings of the extensive
repertoire of incantations by which doctors
tried to heal. (*Atharva* 6 : 136, for instance,
has spells for growing thick hair and curing
baldness.)

✳Ancient India assembled three other
collections, which are included in what is
called the Vedic literature. These are the
Brahmanas, the *Aranyakas*, and the *Upanishads*. The *Brahmanas* are principally directions for sacrifice—books of ritual for
priests. The *Aranyakas* are interpretations
and defenses of the sacrifices—books of
"theology" explaining what was done and
why. The Upanishads, finally, are a collection of speculations on the ultimate order of
things. They represent a departure from the

magical and sacrificial mentality (though not a break). Along with the four Vedas, these three other collections also merit the rank of *shruti*. Thus, they, too, are part of the foundation of orthodox Hinduism, part of the *rishis'* legacy.

In his classical training, a noble Hindu youth memorized these four collections.[6] (However, tradition defended Vedic materials against profane use. A lower-class person who even heard their reading was to have hot wax poured into his or her ears.) After memorizing them, advanced students analyzed the Vedas with the help of revered commentaries. In that way, the Vedic literature spawned philosophical and scientific discussion. Considered alone, the Vedas represent the convictions and practices of the first thousand years or so of Aryan-Hindu culture.

The Vedic Gods

A study of the Vedic gods shows what the earliest Hindus thought about the deepest forces in their world. The gods are many and complex (tradition said there were 330 million), but of course a few stand out as the most important. They are all *devas* (good divinities), as distinguished from *asuras* (evil divinities). (In Iran the terminology is just the reverse, suggesting that the Iranian-Indian split may have been theological.)[7] The Vedas cast most *devas* in human or animal form. Since the main feature of the *devas* was power, we may consider them functional forces: the warmth of the sun, the energy of the storm, and so on. To express these larger-than-life qualities, later Indian artists often gave the *devas* supernumerary bodily parts. An extra pair of arms, for instance, would indicate prowess in battle; an extra eye would indicate ability to discern events at a distance. Typically, a *deva* was a male deity associated with a female consort, who represented his energetic force *(Shakti)*. (In developed Hindu speculation, the male principle was passive, or cool.) Later Tantrist

Hinduism focused on *Shakti*, often through the practice of ritual sex.

Scholars have described the worship of the many Vedic gods and *Shaktis* as *henotheism*. This word indicates that at the moment of praying or concentrating on a particular god, the worshiper tends to elevate that god to primacy without denying the existence of the other gods, who have their claims to importance. Thus, the devout Vedist placed the god he or she was addressing on center stage, but only for the moment. Psychologically, henotheism was a convenient sort of forgetting or bracketing, allowing one to elevate Agni today and Indra tomorrow, depending on whether fire or storm was more relevant. Further, the Vedic worshiper sometimes blended the attributes of one god with those of another. So a prayer for justice might address Varuna, the god of order and judgment, first, but thinking about Varuna's blazing face might bring Agni to mind. The concluding petition, then, might be to Agni.

By textual analysis, scholars have uncovered different generations of the Vedic gods. The oldest group consists of the gods of the sky and the earth that the Vedas share with other Indo-European religious texts. For instance, the Vedic Father Sky (Dyaus Pitar) is related to the Greek Zeus and the Roman Jupiter. Like them, he is the overarching power that fertilizes the receptive earth with rain and rays of sun. The Vedic earth is the Great Mother, the fertile female.[8] These deities are not the most prominent Vedic gods, but they echo in the background as the oldest.

The second oldest group, whose age is confirmed by Iranian parallels, includes Indra, Mithra, Varuna, Agni, and Soma. We have seen that Indra was the warrior god of the storm much beloved by the Aryan conquerors. Mithra was the god of the sun. (In Iran he became the great helper of Ahura Mazdah, while in the Hellenic world he became an important mystery god.) Varuna was the god of cosmic and moral order, and Soma was the god of the exhilarating cultic drink. Known in Iran as *haoma*, soma gave visions so dazzling that it became integral to the sacramental cult (scholars dispute whether the drink was hallucinogenic). Agni, finally, was the god of fire, whose importance increased as the sacrifice focused more and more on fire. It is worth noting that most of the deities in this second generation represent earthly and especially heavenly forces. Perhaps the storm, the sun, and the sky were all originally joined in Dyaus Pitar, but later they became separate objects of devotion.

The third generation of gods includes Brahma, Vishnu, and Shiva, who are not true Vedic gods but rather developments of Vedic *devas* on Indian soil. In other words, they arose after the Aryans arrived in India (and so perhaps indicate Dravidian influences). We shall consider them more fully below.

Finally, the fourth generation, which comes to the fore in the Upanishads, comprises abstract deities such as One God, That One, Who, and the Father of Creation (Eka Deva, Tad Ekam, Ka, and Prajapati).[9] Upanishadic seers had become dissatisfied with the concrete, world-affirming outlook at the core of the *Rig-Veda* and searched for simpler, more spiritual notions.

The Vedic priests divided the gods according to the three realms: celestial, atmospheric, and earthly. During much of the Vedic period, the sun was the chief celestial god, Indra was the chief atmospheric god, and Agni presided over the earthly gods. Among the celestial gods, Varuna came to eclipse the sun, for his association with order attracted to him much of the awe felt for the old Dyaus Pitar.

A Dravidian god associated with Indra in the atmospheric realm was Rudra, who originally seems to have been the god of the monsoon but in Vedic times grew close to Shiva and became rather demonic.[10] As the Vedic fire sacrifice developed, Agni became more important, taking on aspects of the sun (celestial fire), lightning, and ascetic energy (inner heat). We have mentioned Soma, another earthly god. In time Indians thought that taking soma would guarantee immortality. Sarawasti, wife of Brahma, became most important in post-Vedic times, but in the scriptures she functions as the gracious goddess of music, scholarship, and speech.

Brahmanism

In the early Vedic period, the sacrifice was quite simple. It required no elaborate rituals, no temples, no images—only a field of cut grass, some ghee (clarified butter) for the fire, and some soma (some poured onto the ground for the gods and some drunk by the participants). Later the sacrifice became more elaborate, involving the chanting of magical sounds, reenacting the world's creation, and slaying a variety of animals.[11] Since this elaboration went hand in hand with the increasing importance of the priest (*brahmin*, or brahman), commentators often refer to sacrificial Vedic religion as Brahmanism.

The *Atharva-Veda* shows the magical aspects that Brahmanism developed. At their most powerful, the priests thought that their chants and sacrifices controlled the world. Whereas originally one prayed to the gods because they ran the world, in Brahmanic days the priests considered sacrificial speech and action efficacious in their own right: If one executed the ritual properly, it could not fail to obtain its object. Properly uttered, the words of prayer compelled the gods. As a result, ritual magic almost overshadowed all social life, and the cult grew more and more complicated. Not surprisingly, many people soon found this complexity intolerable. Before it lost control, however, Brahmanism made a permanent impact on Hinduism. Subsequent reinterpretations of Vedic scriptures, including that of the *Bhagavad Gita*,[12] showed great effort to retain the concept of sacrifice.

Brahmanism reached its greatest elaboration with the horse sacrifice, a ceremony that lasted more than a year. In the first step of this complicated ritual, attendants bathed a young white horse, fed it wheat cakes for three days, consecrated it by fire, and then released it and let it wander for a year. Princes and soldiers followed the horse, conquering all territory through which it traveled. After one year, servants brought the horse back to the palace. During the next new moon, the king shaved his head and beard. After an all-night vigil at the sacred fire, the queens went to the horse at dawn, anointed it, and decorated it with pearls. A sacrifice of 609 selected animals, ranging from the elephant to the bee (and sometimes a human), followed.

The sacrifice reached its climax after attendants slaughtered the horse itself and placed a blanket over it. The most important queen then slipped under the blanket to have (simulated?) sexual intercourse with the horse, while the other queens and the priests shouted obscene encouragements. After this, participants ate the horse in a ritual meal. The entire ceremony fits the pattern of ancient celebrations of the new year, which often involved sacrifices and orgies designed to renew the world's fertility.

The Upanishads

Before the end of the Vedic period, Brahmanism declined for at least two reasons. First, common sense dictated that society had more to do than listen to priests chant all day. The texts imply that even during the times of the *Rig-Veda*, people were unhappy with the priests' constant prating. A satire in 7 : 103, for instance, likens them to frogs croaking over the waters. Second, intellectuals desired something more satisfying than magic. The Upanishads reveal the intellectuals' turn to interiority, which resulted in sacrifice becoming less a matter of slaughter, ritual, and words and more a matter of soul cleansing and dedication to the divine powers.

The word *Upanishad* connotes the secret teaching that one receives at the feet of a guru. Out of hundreds of treatises (over the period from 800 to 300 B.C.E.), a few Upa-

nishads came to the fore.[13] They show that the intellectuals embraced a variety of styles and ideas and that their movement was poetic as much as philosophical. Whether poetic or philosophical, though, the movement's goal was quite religious: intuitive knowledge of ultimate truths.

Scholars have cited three progressions in the intellectual development of the Upanishadic movement.[14] First, belief moved the many Vedic deities into a unified conception of how the world came to order. In part, this was a shift away from the nature forces that dominated the early Vedas, a search for a single explanation for all phenomena (this search extended the idea developed in *Rig-Veda* 10 : 129). The desire for such an explanation is a spontaneous, natural urge of the human intelligence, for, given sufficient leisure and tradition, people everywhere wonder about the world's origin. In such wondering, many find a plurality of explanations to be unsatisfactory.

Thus, the writers of the Upanishads pushed beyond henotheism, which temporarily accorded an individual god such as Agni all power and might, towards monism, the notion that all entities share in and manifest a single primal reality or stuff. In the Brihad-Aranyaka Upanishad (3.9.1), for instance, a pupil asks the sage Yajnavalkya how many gods there are. Yajnavalkya begins by answering, "3,306," but the pupil keeps pushing him, and Yajnavalkya finally answers, "One." This move toward monism characterizes many Upanishads and thus much of later Hindu philosophy. Vedanta, perhaps the most famous of the orthodox philosophical schools, pushed Upanishadic monism to the point where *only* the one ultimate reality existed, everything else being illusion.

The Upanishads themselves do not agree as to whether the unity behind everything is personal, impersonal, or a mixture of the two. However, they do tend to use two words in discussing it, both of which are more impersonal than personal. The first word is *Brahman*, which generally means the first principle, cause, or stuff of the objective world. Brahman, in other words, is the final answer for the Upanishadic thinkers who wondered about how things are founded—especially things in the material world.

The second progression in Upanishadic thought shifted from concern for external matters to concern for internal matters—from objectivity to subjectivity. Whereas the Vedas resonated with the energy of storm and fire, the Upanishads discovered the world of mind and spirit. From this new world emerged the second word relating to the unity behind all things, *atman*. This word means the vital principle or deepest identity of the subject—the soul or self. Third, probing this reality by thought and meditation, the Upanishadic seers moved away from Vedic materiality to spirituality. The internal world, the world of atman and thought, was a world of *spirit*.

Combining these progressions and the new concepts of Brahman and atman, some of the Upanishadic seers found a coincidence—the basic reality within and without, of self and the world, is the same. Atman is Brahman. So in the Chandogya Upanishad (6.1.3), the father Uddalaka teaches his son Shvetaketu that Shvetaketu himself *is*, most fundamentally, Brahmanic ultimate reality: *Tat tvam asi* ("That thou art"). The soul and the stuff of the world are but two sides of the same single "be-ing" or "is-ness" that constitutes all existing things.

For the Upanishadic thinkers, this realization was liberating because it avoided the Brahmanistic multiplicity, externalism, and materialism that had sickened their souls. Though sacrifice and the gods continued to have a place in Upanishadic religion, they were quite subordinate to monism.

In addition, the Upanishadic thinkers felt an urgent need for salvation, unlike the Vedists. Perhaps echoing Buddhist beliefs, the writers of the Upanishads worked with experiences that they found more dismal, depressing, and afflicting than the first Aryans had. Whereas those vigorous warriors had fought and drunk, living for the moment, these later meditative sages examined the human condition and found it sad. To express their beliefs, they fashioned the doctrines of samsara and karma, which did not appear in the early Vedas.

Samsara (the doctrine of rebirths) implies that the given world, the world of common sense and ordinary experience, is only provisional. It is not the ultimate existence. To take it as ultimate or fully real, therefore, is to delude oneself and thus to trap oneself in a cycle of rebirths. Only when one penetrates Brahman, the truly real, can one escape this cycle. Otherwise, one must constantly travel the scale of animal life (up or down, depending on one's advances or backslidings in wisdom).

Karma is the law that governs advancement or regression in the samsaric life of deaths and rebirths. Essentially, it is the belief that all acts have unavoidable consequences. In an almost physical way, they determine one's personality. Karma also explains one's status: A person's present life is shaped by that person's past lives. The only way to escape the round of rebirths, the pain of samsara, is to advance by meritorious deeds and be saved or freed.[15] (Hinduism chooses to live with the illogic of a law both necessary and capable of being undercut by freedom.)

If samsara and karma represent the problem that confronts human beings, *moksha* represents the solution. For the Upanishads, one who is free of desire escapes the bondage of karma and so the samsaric cycle of rebirths. *Moksha* is this state of freedom from desire, this escape or "salvation." The Upanishads principally conceive of attaining *moksha* by an intuitive insight into the nature of reality. Realizing that Brahman is the inmost essence of everything, the enlightened person stands free of the beguilements that illusory appearances can arouse. By uniting herself to Brahman, the enlightened person partakes of Brahman's changelessness. Whereas samsara means constant change—birth, aging, death, rebirth—*moksha* means serene stability in union with Brahman.

THE ISA UPANISHAD

The Isa Upanishad, one of the shortest, offers a good specimen of the Upanishadic style. Robert Hume, the famous translator of the Upanishads into English, divides the Isa into eighteen stanzas.[16] The strong emotions the stanzas display remind us that the Upanishadic seers were *religious* philosophers—people pursuing a vision that would bring them *moksha*. The Isa's passionate quest for a single principle to explain the diversity of the world's many phenomena also reenforces the impression that many of the Upanishadic seers had grown soul-sick from the complexity of Brahmanic religion.

The first stanza of the Isa announces the monistic theme: Unless we see that the Lord (*Isa*) envelops all that exists, we misunderstand reality. There must be a stable principle giving rest to all the moving things. The religious person renounces all these moving things and so comes to enjoy human life. Such renunciation takes him away from coveting the wealth or possessions of other people, which so frequently is a cause of sadness.

Stanza two develops this basis of freedom. It is possible to live in the world, performing the duties of one's station, without being attached to one's deeds. In that case, the deed (*karman*) does not adhere to the personality or weight it down. Detachment therefore is the antidote to karma. If one is free from concern about the effects of one's actions, one can work for *moksha.*

But, as stanza three emphasizes, those who do not detach themselves receive a stern punishment after death. If they have slain the Self (the presence of Brahman within) by desirous, badly motivated deeds, they will go to dark worlds ruled by devils.

Stanza four shifts back to a positive viewpoint. The One that does not move, that stands free of the changing things of the world, is swifter than the human mind and senses. Wisdom is placing one's action in this One, reposing one's self in what is so swift it is stable.

Human life therefore faces a paradox, as stanza five shows. The principle underlying everything that exists seems both to move and not to move. Insofar as it is the inmost reality of whatever exists, it moves in all things' move-

ment. Insofar as it gives all these things their basis, it is free of their movement, self-possessed rather than dependent on another. So, too, the One can be both far and near, both outside and within any being of the samsaric world.

Stanza six suggests a focus to bring this blur into clarity. By looking on all beings as though they reposed in the Self (the world's soul), and looking at the Self as though it were present in all things, the wise person stays close to the Brahman that is the world's ultimate significance.

According to stanza seven, the profit in this focus is the freedom from delusion and sorrow it brings. The person who perceives the unity of reality, seeing the single Self everywhere, achieves a knowledge and joy that the ignorant, mired in the world's multiplicity, never know.

This leads, in stanza eight, to an imaginative flourish. Picturing the world-ruler, the human being who has realized his full human potential, the Isa unfurls a flag of glowing attributes: wise, intelligent, comprehensive, self-sufficient. By dealing with what is bright, bodiless, pure, and unaffected by evil (by dealing with the Self), this person has reached the summit, come to stand close to eternity.

Stanzas nine and ten are quite mystical, probing the nature of religious enlightenment. If those who worship ignorance (who neglect the Self) go into a blind darkness, those who delight in true knowledge go into a greater darkness or mystery, a state beyond the dichotomy between knowledge and nonknowledge. The wise people who have handed down Vedic wisdom confirm this: Enlightenment and *moksha* are mysterious.

Stanza eleven adds another dimension: The wise person, holding knowledge and nonknowledge together, passes over death and gains immortality.

The "beyond" or transcendent character of true enlightenment appears even more clearly in stanzas twelve and thirteen. Both nonbecoming (changelessness) and becoming (change) can be illusory. The ultimate truth of Brahman transcends such oppositions. So too it transcends the opposition between origin (being the source of everything) and nonorigin (not being the source). The saving intuition that brings *moksha* takes the perceiver to another realm, where the dichotomies and antagonisms thrown up by ordinary human intelligence do not pertain.

According to stanza fourteen, this saving intuition also conjoins becoming and destruction. If one understands their relation, he can ride destruction across the chasm of death, ride becoming to the far shore of immortality.

The Isa concludes prayerfully, in stanza fifteen praising the sun as a cover of reality and asking divinity to uncover its face, so that we might fulfill our primary human obligation, which is to grasp reality. Stanza sixteen calls divinity the nourisher, the sole seer, the controller of fortunes, the one who is yonder yet the inmost reality of the personality. Stanza seventeen prays that while our body ends in ashes, our breath may take us to the immortal wind. This will happen if we remember our purpose, grasp the import of our deeds. The Isa's last prayers, in stanza eighteen, are addressed to Agni: Lead us to prosperity by a godly path, you who know all the ways. Keep us from the crooked ways of sin, for we want to offer you ample adoration.

The Period of Native Challenge

From about 600 B.C.E. to 300 C.E. the Vedic religion, including its Upanishadic refinements, was seriously challenged by some Indians. We have already seen that the Upanishads represent an adverse reaction to sacrificial Brahmanism.[17] However, even the Upanishads themselves, the final fruits of the Vedic tradition, were eventually contested by materialist, Jain, Buddhist, devotionalist, and other religious views. As well, the entire Vedic tradition of *shruti* grew through commentaries and instructions. Hindus refer to these materials collectively as *smriti* (memory or tradition).

Some Hindus remained loyal to the early Vedic gods and sacrifices, but the strong challenges decisively changed the religion of the majority. In fact, during the period of contest, the blend of Aryan and Dravidian traditions developed in a variety of directions. As a result, Hinduism became an umbrella religion—a shelter over India's great diversity of beliefs and customs.[18]

Materialistic, Jain, and Buddhist challenges to Vedism first arose in northeastern India, where warrior tribes were more than ready to contest the priests' pretensions to cultural control. By this time (600 B.C.E.), the Aryans had settled in villages, and India was a checkerboard of small kingdoms, each of which controlled a group of such villages. Some intellectuals, radically opposed to the Vedas, strongly attacked the Vedic belief that there is a reality other than the sensible or material. It is hard to know precisely what these materialists taught, because few of their writings have survived, but Buddhist literature reports that Ajita, a prominent materialist thinker, said that earth, air, fire, and water are the only elements—the sources of everything in the universe. According to Ajita, the differences among things just reflect different proportions of these elements. Human beings are no exception, and at death they simply dissolve back into these four elements. There is no afterlife, no reincarnation, no soul, and no Brahman. During the brief span of one's life, a person should live "realistically," enduring pain and pursuing pleasure. Nothing beyond the testimony of the senses is valid knowledge, and what the senses reveal is what is real.

Jainism was a very different challenge that grew from the struggles for enlightenment by Vardhamana, called the Jina (conqueror) or Mahavira (great man). He was born to wealth but found it unfulfilling, so he launched a life of asceticism. After gaining enlightenment by this self-denial, he successfully preached his method to others.

The Jina opposed both the ritualism and the intellectualism of the Vedic tradition. The only significant sacrifice, he said, is that which conquers the self. Similarly, the only worthy knowledge is that which enables the personality to escape karma and samsara.[19]

The Jina's followers became opponents of all forms of violence and pain. Consequently, they opposed the Vedic sacrifice of animals, calling it an assault on life that opposed true religion. Also, Jains became critical of matter. Their "karma" was a semisolid entity that attached itself to the spirit through acts involving material objects.[20] In memory of the Jina, whom they considered to be a great *tirthankara* ("crosser of the stream of sorry life"), Jains eschewed eating meat, harming anything believed to have a soul, and physical activity. Since total avoidance of these activities was practically impossible, Jains tried to balance any injury that they inflicted or bad karma that they generated with acts of self-denial or benevolence.

The popularity of Jainism and of Buddhism, which arose only slightly later, testifies to the dissatisfaction with Vedism that many Indians experienced during the sixth century B.C.E. At the time of the Mahavira's death (due to voluntary starving), his followers have been estimated at more than half a million. There were more women than men, and many more laypeople than monks and nuns. For laypeople and monks alike, however, Jainism developed guiding vows, similar to commandments, which have been a principal reason for the persistence of Jainism in India to the present.

The lay vows include commitments not to injure living beings, not to lie or steal, not to be unchaste, not to accumulate large sums of money, not to travel widely or possess more than what one needs, not to think evil of others, and not to pursue evil forms of livelihood. There are also positive vows to meditate and to support the community of ascetic monks.

Today there are about 2 million Jains in India (the largest cluster is in Calcutta), who, through their discipline and their spe-cialization in business, have become quite prosperous. In their temples one can see pictures of nude, ascetic saints who represent an ideal of complete detachment, and the Jain doctrine of *ahimsa* (noninjury) has made a permanent impression on Indian culture.[21]

Since we shall discuss Buddhism at length in the next chapter, we need only note here that, from a Hindu perspective, Buddhism arose, much like Jainism, as an anti-Vedic protest in the sixth century B.C.E. It was another stimulus to Hindu reform, another attack on both the Vedic sacrifices and their Brahmanistic rationale.

Bhagavata

Especially in western India, movements arose that, unlike materialism, Jainism, and Buddhism, forced changes from within Hinduism. A collective word for these movements is Bhagavata (devotionalism), which connotes an emotional attachment to personal gods such as Krishna and Shiva. Devotees *(bhaktas)* continue to claim that such devotion is a way of salvation or self-realization that is superior to sacrifice or intellectual meditation.[22]

In the central Indian city of Mathura, devotion was focused on the god Krishna. There has been much debate about the background of this god (his name means dark blue or black and was a common one). Some have claimed that Krishna originally was a solar god, others that he was a vegetative god, and still others that he was a mythical hero. Organ suggests that the Krishna cult may have appropriated five minor religions that flourished in the Mathura area.[23] All these religions related to a solar deity, whom the local people worshiped as a personal god and petitioned for gifts.

Whatever its origins, the Krishna cult became very popular, and it developed a wealth of legends about Krishna's birth and adventures that ultimately made Krishna the most beloved of the Indian deities.

In one legend, demons tried to kill the baby Krishna, but he was stronger than they.

When the demoness Putana, who had taken the form of a nurse, tried to offer him a breast covered with poison, Krishna took it and sucked out all her milk and blood. When another demon approached him, Krishna kicked the demon so hard that the demon died. Another cluster of legends describes the child Krishna's pranks (he was always stealing his mother's butter, for which he had a great appetite)[24] and the young man Krishna's affairs with young girls. Consequently, Krishna became the object of love—the love for an infant and the romantic and sexual love for a handsome young lord.[25]

The premier work of the Bhagavata tradition is the *Bhagavad Gita*, in which Krishna is the featured god. The *Gita* offers ways of salvation to all types of persons, but *bhakti* (devotional love) appears to be its highest teaching.[26] This is especially so if one reads the *Gita* as the progressive instruction of a pupil (Arjuna) by his guru god (Krishna). The *Gita* is set in the context of a great battle (the subject of the epic poem the *Mahabharata*), and it deals successively with (1) the ethical problem of war (one must do one's caste duty; there is no killing of the soul), (2) the valid ways to wisdom and realization (these are sacrifice, meditation, and action without attachment to its results), and (3) the divinity's unveiled countenance (the dazzling vision that is recounted in chap. 11). Then, in what seems to be the work's climax, Krishna tells Arjuna that the best "way" (*marga*) is love of Krishna and that he, Krishna, loves his devotee in return. In other words, there is a divine love for humanity as well as a human love for divinity (chap. 18). This final teaching, probably even more than the *Gita*'s catholic offering of many religious ways, has made it Hinduism's most influential text.

In later Hindu theology, Krishna became an avatar, or manifestation, of Vishnu, whom we shall discuss shortly. However, we should first describe the beginnings of a devotional cult to Shiva. This cult, too, was a reaction against the Vedic religion, and one of its fascinating texts is the Shvetashvatara Upanishad. For the devotees of Shiva, this text serves much as the *Bhagavad Gita* serves Krishnaites—as a gospel of the personal god's love. It is unique among the Upanishads for its theism (focus on a personal god), yet it shares with the monistic Upanishads an effort to think logically.

The author begins by asking momentous questions: What is Brahman? What causes us to be born? Then the author rejects impersonal wisdom, materialism, and pure devotion as being inadequate answers. His own answer is to interpret Brahman (the ultimate reality) as a kind of god, who may become manifest if one meditates upon him. In the Shvetashvatara Upanishad, the preferred designation for Brahman is Rudra-Shiva. Rudra probably was the Dravidian form of Indra and Shiva a god of fertility.[27] In the post-Dravidian combination of these gods, the accent was on slaying and healing, destroying and creating—the lord of the two rhythms of life.

According to this Upanishad, Shiva is in everything. He has five faces and three eyes, which show his control of all directions and all times (past, present, and future). The devotee of Shiva therefore deals with a divinity as ultimate and powerful as Krishna but whose destructive capacities are more accentuated. Rudra is a god whom one has to appease. The Vedic attitude toward him was "Go away, please." Shiva is more welcome, but his life power is nothing with which to fool. It plays when the earth quakes and when the lion tears the lamb. It weaves a net of illusion around the dance of life, making it both beguiling and dangerous.

Devotion to Krishna (Vishnu) or Shiva, then, satisfies the person who wants religious feeling and a personal god with whom to interact. Probably this sort of person predominated in Hindu history. From the legends about the gods and from the epics (especially the *Mahabharata* and the *Ramayana*), the *bhaktas* found models for religious love and for faithful living as a good child, husband, wife, and so on. Theologically, these models imply monotheism, personalism, and free self-giving rather than legalistic obligations. To the *bhaktas*, they meant finding peace by surrendering oneself in faith—making the god one's refuge and hope. In sum, bhakti was complete emotional dedication to one's god.

Smriti

During this period of challenge to Vedic authority, one other development merits attention because it was responsible for a great deal of Hindu religious literature. This movement was commentary on the Vedic literature which was intended to make it more comprehensible, practicable, and contemporary. The authority of this commentary movement is described by the word *smriti* (tradition). *Smriti* provided such diverse literatures as the *Dharma Shastras*, or law codes (of which the Laws of Manu are the most famous); the writings of the six orthodox schools of philosophy; legendary works such as the *Mahabharata* and the *Ramayana*; the *Puranas* (more legendary materials, often from folk or aboriginal sources); commentaries appended to the Vedas (for example, the *Ayur-Veda*—the "Life-Veda," devoted to systematic medicine—which tradition added to the *Atharva*); tantric writings on occult and erotic matters; writings ("Agamas") peculiar to sects such as the Vaishnavites and the Shaivites; and writings on logical or ritualistic forms of thought.

STORIES FROM THE *MAHABHARATA*

Two stories from the *Mahabharata* illustrate not only the popular forms that *smriti* took but also the ambivalent status to which the brahmins had fallen by the time of the native challenges.

The first story might be called "The Curse of a Brahmin."[28] It shows the power attributed to brahmins and also the colorful world of supernatural forces that Vedic religion bequeathed later India.

Once the great King Parikshit went hunting. Wounding a deer, he chased it deep into an unfamiliar forest. There he came upon a hermitage with an old ascetic priest sitting near some cows. The king approached the brahmin, told him who he was, and asked him whether he had seen the wounded deer. But the brahmin gave the king no answer, for the brahmin had taken a vow of silence. The king repeated his question, and when he again received no reply, he got very angry. Gazing around, he spied a dead snake, lifted it with the end of his bow, and hung it round the priest's neck to shame him. The brahmin still did not utter a sound, so the king gave up and returned home empty-handed.

The old brahmin had a son, and when the son's friends heard of the incident, they teased the boy about his father's disgrace. The son asked his friends how his father had come to have a dead snake hung round his neck, and the friends told him the story of King Parikshit's visit. The son reacted angrily, cursing the king: "May Takshaka, the king of the serpents, kill this wretch who placed a dead snake upon the shoulders of my frail, old father."

When he returned home, the son told his father how he had cursed the king. The old brahmin was not pleased. Ascetics, he said, should not behave so impetuously. The son had forgotten that they lived under the protection of King Parikshit, who defended all the priests of his realm. The king had not known of the father's vow, so he should be forgiven much of his anger and bad behavior.

To try to repair the damage of his son's action, the brahmin promised to send a messenger to warn the king. Both the father and the son knew, though, that the curse of a brahmin could never be thwarted.

When the old brahmin's messenger told the king of the curse, he was saddened by how he had abused the priest. He was also worried about his life, so he took counsel with his ministers about how to protect himself. They advised him to build a high platform, standing on tall posts, so that no one could approach him unobserved, and to remain there for seven days. The king followed this advice, and moved his living quarters to the platform.

Toward the end of the seven-day period, the serpent king Takshaka sent several of his servants to King Parikshit disguised as ascetics. Not sensing any danger, king Parikshit allowed the ascetics to mount his platform and accepted their gifts of water, nuts, and fruit. When the ascetics had departed, King Parikshit invited his counselors to enjoy the gifts with him. But just as he was about to bite into a piece of fruit, an ugly black and copper-colored insect crawled out. The king looked at the setting sun, which was ending the seventh day, gathered his courage, and dared Takshaka to assume his true form and fulfill the brahmin's curse. No sooner had he said this than the insect turned into a huge serpent and coiled itself around the king's neck. Bellowing a tremendous roar, Takshaka killed the king with a single mighty bite.

The story has several morals. First, it teaches the exalted status of priests. Dealing with holy things and marshaling great spiritual power by their ascetic practices, priests can perform marvels that ordinary humans can barely conceive. Therefore ordinary humans, including kings, ought to deal respectfully with priests.

Second, however, a brahmin's very power imposes on him the responsibility to stay above petty emotions that might lead him to abuse this power. Thus the old father was deeply disturbed by his son's intemperate curse. A brahmin's power ought to serve the people around him, improving their lives. The many Hindu stories in which priests do not act as ideally as they should suggest that the common people often found their priests wanting.

Third, the story piquantly illustrates the intimacy with nature that popular Hinduism retained. Even though the Upanishads were pressing toward a purely spiritual conception of reality, in which a single Brahman would relativize the reality of both human beings and snakes, the popular religion that came out of the period of native challenge stayed deeply immersed in the cosmological myth. (The cosmological myth is the assumption that all things that exist live within physical nature, the span from heaven to earth. With this assumption, gods and human beings, serpents and kings, become more alike than unlike one another.) This made for a very lively and imaginative "reality," in which curses

such as the brahmin's were plausible enough to teach both priests and commoners a religious lesson.

The second story from the *Mahabharata* might be called, "The Well of Life."[29] It offers a dramatic picture of the dangers of samsaric existence.

Once there was a brahmin who wandered into a dark forest filled with wild animals. Indeed, so ferocious were the lions, elephants, and other great beasts of this forest that even Yama, the god of death, would only enter it when absolutely necessary. The brahmin only came to sense the wicked nature of the dark forest gradually, but then he grew more and more fearful. Panicking, he found himself running in circles, becoming more and more confused.

Finally the brahmin looked about on every side and saw that the forest was caught in a huge net held by a giant woman with outstretched arms. There were five-headed serpents everywhere, so tall that their heads nearly reached the heavens. Then the brahmin came to a clearing, with a deep well covered by vines and underbrush. Running frantically from a wild elephant that was pursuing him, he stumbled into the well, fell through the brush, and lodged halfway to the bottom, held upside down by a few vines.

At the bottom of the well was a huge snake. Above him waited the great elephant, which had six faces and twelve feet. To the side, in the vines that held him, were many bees that had built hives and filled them with honey. When the honey dripped toward him, the brahmin reached out to catch it in his mouth. The more honey he ate, the more he could not satisfy his thirst for it. Meanwhile, black and white rats gnawed at the vines holding him. Though the elephant stood guard above, the serpent stood guard below, the bees buzzed on all sides, and the rats gnawed at his lifeline, the brahmin continued to grope for more honey.

As many Hindu commentators have made clear, the story is an allegory for the human condition. The forest is the limited sphere of our life, dark and filled with dangers. The woman holding a net over the forest is the process of aging, which allows no human life to escape. The beasts of the forest are the diseases and other forces that can destroy us, while the serpent at the bottom of the well is time, which eventually receives all living things. The six-faced elephant with twelve feet is the year, with its twelve months, while the black and white rats are night and day, the devourers of our life spans. Finally, the honey is the pleasures of life, for which our thirst seems unslakable.

The allegory, then, paints human life as tragic. Despite danger on all sides, we persist in pursuing transient pleasures. This is samsara with a vengeance. It is attachment making us oblivious to the great questions of what direction we should be taking and how we ought to be battling death. If we are ever to escape the painful circle of rebirths, which ensures that life after life we will suffer fear and pain, we must realize our self-imposed bondage. Plunging heedlessly into a dangerous life, we are soon fleeing in panic. We have gotten in over our heads, and before long we are upside down in an inescapable pit. Above and below, the many forms of time wait like jailers, ensuring that we stay in terrible danger. Meanwhile, day and night nibble our life span away.

Clearly, the story wants to impress upon its hearers the fearsome nature of unreflective living. If we simply live instinctively, pursuing the pleasures of the senses and fleeing the pains, we will end up in the most trying of circumstances.

Only by estimating correctly the lay of the land and refusing to get trapped in life's forests or to fall into time's snares can we escape a tragic ending. Only by avoiding the whole battlefield of time can we enter into true freedom.

The Hindu keys to true freedom, therefore, are attention and detachment. We must watch where we are going, and we must stay free of worldly desires. The brahmin is pathetic because his calling or station especially should have educated him in these virtues. Were he noble in substance rather than just noble in name, he would not have wandered into the forest aimlessly. Similarly, he would not have abandoned himself to the sweet honey, forgetting his mortal peril. By meditation, sacrifice, austerities within and austerities without, he would have had hold of his time and been powerful in spirit. Then the beasts would have held no terrors, the well would have gaped to no avail. Then nothing so slight as sensual pleasure would have distracted him from his fight with time. Detached and self-possessed, he would have given time no toehold, nothing by which to keep him in thrall. But, the story implies, few priests or few people of any station are true brahmins, strong in spirit, so most people find aging a fearsome process.

The basic form of the *smriti* was the sutra, an aphorism or short sentence designed to expose the pith of a position.[30] By the end of the third century C.E., the *smriti* tradition had developed some very important and common ways of understanding the Vedic heritage.

For example, the *smriti* tradition developed the central trinity of Hindu gods (Trimurti) called Brahma-Vishnu-Shiva. Through history, many Hindus have believed this trinity to be an essential format of divinity. Brahma is an impersonal creator god, rather distant. Tradition depicts him as red and having four hands and four arms. He has a beard and holds a bow, a scepter, a drinking cup, and a Veda.[31] He rides on Hamsa, a white goose, and his consort is the lovely Sarawasti, whom we have mentioned as the goddess of music and scholarship.

Vishnu is a much more popular god, whom the *Puranas* and the Vaishnavite literature consider supreme. He is associated with water, and according to tradition the Ganges flows from under his feet while he rests on the coils of the great serpent Shesha. He is a gracious god, sending many avatars of himself to help humans in need. His vehicle is the great bird/giant Garuda, and he is depicted as blue. Like an ancient monarch, he carries a conch shell, a battle discus, a club, and a lotus. He has four arms, signifying his power to fight evil, and his consort is the much beloved Lakshmi.

Shiva, as we have seen, was originally a storm and fertility god. His vehicle is the bull and he has five faces, three eyes, and four arms. His hair is matted (as befits a yogic ascetic), and his clothing is a tiger skin held by a serpent. His many consorts *(Shak-*

tis), which are different forms that his quiet wife Parvati assumes, are important cosmic energies. The most important ones are all menacing: Uma, an ascetic; Durga, a ten-armed demon slayer; and Kali, a black goddess who drinks blood and feeds on corpses. Shiva is the destroyer, as Brahma is the creator and Vishnu the preserver.

The commentaries also developed Vedic notions of time and extended the doctrines of karma and samsara. Time was measured in great cycles (kalpas) that stretched for 4,320,000 human (solar) years (12,000 divine years, each of which was 360 human years). Each kalpa divides into four yugas—ages having different religious qualities.[32] The krita yuga is the golden age, four times the length of the worst age (the kali yuga, which is the present time). In the golden age humans live long and happy lives that are close to perfection. In the kali yuga religion declines, sickness and sin prevail, and lives are short. After each sequence of the four ages, another kalpa begins. A thousand kalpas make a Brahma Day, the span from the universe's creation to its destruction, which is followed by a Brahma Night of the same duration. This is a period of universal rest, after which another Brahma Day follows, and so on.

Karma and samsara have enormous roles in this universal scheme. Indeed, they represent a condition of cause and effect, death and rebirth, that has antecedents and consequences without measure. As a result, moksha is all the more impressive.[33] The smriti literature does not explain how human freedom (which it asserts) operates within karma to work moksha, but it does claim that one can end suffering and mortality by penetrating the veils of illusion that conceal the cosmic process.

The great social development of the smriti period was the caste system. The Vedas (for example, Rig-Veda 10:90) had spoken of the creation of humanity in terms of the four ranks: priests, warriors, merchants, and workers. In the original sacrifice Purusha, the primal man, gave his mouth, arms, thighs, and feet to make those four ranks.

However, law codes such as Manu's were required to justify casteism.[34] Apparently, casteism precedes the Aryan subjugation of the native Indians, but whether it was first based on color, occupation, tribe, or religious beliefs is unclear.[35]

In practice castes subdivide into about 25,000 occupational jatis, which have made Hindu social life a jigsaw puzzle. These societal distinctions have spawned some social customs peculiar to the eye of the outsider. For instance, fishermen who weave their nets from right to left do not speak to fishermen who weave from left to right, and coconut harvesters do not associate with coconut cultivators. Further, members of one jati often cannot marry members of another. Modern India has tried to deemphasize these customs, but they remain influential. Modern India has also tried to improve the lot of the untouchables, who lie outside the caste system, but they still exist. Even now, only certain groups of people carry garbage, clean homes, work in banks, and so on.

Personal Life

During the smriti elaboration of Vedic tradition, another influential doctrine was that of the four legitimate life goals. These were pleasure (kama), wealth (artha), duty (dharma), and liberation (moksha). Kama was the lowest goal, but it was quite legitimate. Kama meant sexual pleasure but also the pleasure of eating, poetry, sport, and so on. Artha was also a legitimate goal, and around it developed learned discussions of ethics, statecraft, manners, and the like.[36] Because the person of substance propped society, wealth had a social importance and was thus more significant than pleasure.

Dharma, or duty, was higher than pleasure or wealth. It meant principle, restraint, obligation, law, and truth—the responsible acceptance of one's social station and its implications. So in the Bhagavad Gita, Krishna appeals to Arjuna's dharma as a warrior: It is his duty to fight, and better one's own duty done poorly than another's done well. Moksha meant liberation, freedom, and escape. It was the highest goal of life, because it represented the goal of one's existence: self-realization in freedom from karma and ignorance. The concept of *moksha* meant that life is samsaric—precarious and illusory. It also meant that pleasure, wealth, and even duty all could be snares.

As a complement to its exposition of life goals, *smriti* also analyzed the stages in the ideal unfolding of a life.[37] For the upper classes (excluding the workers), the four stages, or *ashramas*, were student, householder, hermit, and wandering mendicant. In a 100-year life, each would last about 25 years. In studenthood, the young male would apprentice himself to a guru to learn the Vedic tradition and develop his character. Depending on his caste, this would last 8 to 12 years and dominate the first quarter of his life. Then he would marry, raise children, and carry out social responsibilities. Hindu society honored marriage, and the economic, political, and social responsibilities of the householder gave him considerable esteem.

When the householder saw his children's children, however, *smriti* urged him to retire from active life and start tending his soul. He could still give advice and be helpful in secular affairs, but he should increasingly detach himself from the world. Finally, free of worldly concern, seeking only *moksha*, the ideal Hindu would end his life as a poor, wandering ascetic. Thereby, he would be an object lesson in the true purpose of human life, a teacher of what mattered most.

In effect, this scheme meant an ideal development (not often realized but still influential) of learning one's tradition, gaining worldly experience, appropriating both tradition and experience by solitary reflection, and finally consummating one's time by uniting with ultimate reality. From conception to burial, numerous ceremonies paced the Hindu through this cycle. The most important were adornment with the sacred thread (signaling sufficient maturity to begin studying the Vedas), marriage, and funerary rites. Women fell outside this scheme. During most of Hindu history, their

schooling, such as it was, took place at home, and they were not eligible for *moksha*.[38]

The Period of Reform

From about 300 to 1200 C.E., the various movements that criticized or amplified the Vedic heritage resulted in a full reform of Hinduism. Of course, it is difficult to distinguish additions, such as those of the *smriti* writings, from revisions, but we can see in the growth of the six orthodox philosophies (described below) and the rise of the major Hindu sects developments that effectively revamped Hinduism.

A convenient distinction in the discussion that follows is that between those who reject the Vedas (for example, materialists, Jains, and Buddhists), called *nastikas* ("those who say no"), and those who accept the Vedas, or *astikas* ("those who say yes"). The orthodox philosophies, or *darshanas*, originated with *astikas*. In other words, the orthodox philosophies were conceived as explanations of *shruti* (revelation). There are six such philosophies or schools: Mimamsa, Samkhya, Yoga, Nyaya, Vaisheshika, and Vedanta.[39] We can content ourselves with explaining Vedanta, the most celebrated *darshana*, although we will explain some practical implications of Samkhya and Yoga.

Before reviewing Vedanta, though, we should note that none of the orthodox *darshanas* is philosophy in the modern Western sense. Rather, they are all systems of reasoning and categorizing that defend the Vedas or help bring people to *moksha* through understanding the Vedas. Thus, the soul of Vedanta is not scientific detachment or uncovering the structures of reality for their own sake—or even uncovering truth for its own sake. Rather, Vedanta brings the student to an intuitive, liberating encounter with the sacred that will validate tradition and make one wise. For that reason, Vedanta is thoroughly religious.

Shankara, the greatest of the Vedanta thinkers, was a Malabar brahmin of the ninth century who tried to systematize the

Upanishads in terms of "unqualified non-dualism" *(advaita)*. In other words, he tried to explain the basic Upanishadic concepts of Brahman and atman with consistency and rigor. To do this, Shankara first established that there are two kinds of knowledge, higher and lower. Lower knowledge is under the limitations of the intellect, while higher knowledge is free of such limitations.

The limitations of the intellect include its reasoning character, its dependence on the senses, and its dependence on the body to act. These limitations are all subjective, since they are limitations of the knower, or subject. The objective limitations to knowledge, due to aspects of the known thing, are space, time, change, and cause-effect relationships. Because of objective limitations, we tend not to see or grasp reality in itself.

Higher knowledge comes by a direct perception that is free of either subjective or objective limitations. In practice it is the direct vision that the seers who produced the Vedas enjoyed—*shruti.* Quite likely, therefore, Shankara assumed that the Vedanta philosopher practices a yoga like that of the ancient sages. If so, he assumed that the Vedanta philosopher experiences a removal of the veil between the self and Brahman (with which the self is actually identified).

Shankara then applied this theory of higher and lower knowledge to *hermeneutics,* the study of textual interpretation. According to Shankara, all passages of the Upanishads that treat Brahman as *one* derive from higher knowledge; all references to Brahman as *many* or dual derive from lower knowledge. We can paraphrase this by saying that Brahman in itself is one and beyond all limitations, while Brahman for us (as we perceive it through sensation and reasoning) appears to be multiple—to be both in the world and beyond it, both material cause and prime mover.

With the subtlety of a great philosopher, Shankara wove the two edges of Brahman-in-itself and Brahman-for-us into a seamless whole. With the religious hunger of a mystic, he sought to correlate within and without. (Rudolf Otto has shown the similarity of Shankara's dynamics to those of the Western mystic philosopher Meister Eckhart.)[40] Shankara's core affirmation in his philosophical construction was that reality within is identical with reality without: Atman is Brahman. In other words, when one realizes through revelation, or higher knowledge, that there is no change, no space-time limitations, no cause-effect qualifications to the real, one then discovers that there is no self. Rather, there is only the Self, the Brahman reality that one directly perceives to be the ground of internal and external being.

From the perspective of lower knowledge, there is, of course, a personal, separate, changing self (an atman, or *jiva*). In absolute terms, though, there is one indivisible reality that is both subjectivity and objectivity, that is atman-Brahman. Since we rarely perceive directly, we often live and move in maya (illusion). The world of maya is not unreal in the sense that there are no elephants in it to break your foot if you get in the way of a circus parade. The elephants in the world of maya are substantial, their dung is mighty, and their step will crush your foot. But this viewpoint has limited validity. From a higher viewpoint, all that goes on in maya has no independent existence. The elephants' movement is a "play" of the only reality that exists independently—that is uncaused, unconnected, sovereign, and fully real.[41]

Vaishnavism

In the period of reformation, keen speculative minds tried to rehabilitate the Vedic heritage by showing the reasonableness of *shruti*. It is doubtful that they directly converted more than a few intellectuals, but they did impressively demonstrate that orthodox Hinduism, through Vedic revelation, could enable one to make powerful interpretations of reality. The more popular reformations of Vedism were theistic movements that brought the energies of Bhagavata (devotionalism) back into the Vedic

MA JNANANANDA

Advaita Vedanta can seem a rarefied system, unrelated to most people's daily lives. It can seem merely a web of lofty ideas. On occasion, however, one meets a teacher of Advaita Vedanta who turns the insights of Shankara toward a powerful practice. Ma Jnanananda of Madras is such a teacher, and describing her personality and message may suggest how Shankara's philosophy lives on in present-day India.

Ma is a familiar form of *Mother.* Jnanananda is a spiritual mother (also a physical mother) to numerous followers in present-day Madras. She is both a *guru* and a *sannyasi.* A guru is a religious teacher. A sannyasi is "one who has taken a formal vow renouncing all worldly life, including family ties and possessions. Such a vow, in effect, means death to one's former life. This renunciation allows full-time pursuit of spiritual goals and fosters spiritual development. Such vows have been common in India from ancient times to the present."[42]

Ma gained her lofty position as a guru because one of the leading Advaita Vedanta figures of contemporary India, Shankaracharya of Kanchipuram, recognized that she had penetrated the deepest truths of Hinduism, through mystical absorption with Brahman. Jnanananda had done this while living in the world, married and raising five children. That probably accounts for her great ability to relate the teachings of Vedanta to her disciples' daily problems at work or in family life.

Photographs of Ma taken before she became a guru show a lovely woman, well dressed and well groomed. The beauty still lingers, but now it seems a reflection of her inner peace. She has traded her fine clothes for a simple sari of ochre cloth, cut her hair short, and painted on her forehead and arms horizontal stripes of a thick paste made from ashes, to symbolize her death to vanity and worldly desires.

Ma's teaching is rooted in her profound experiences of *samadhi. Samadhi* is a state of deep trance, an experience of the basic consciousness that has no form yet relates the person to all other things. Here is Ma's description of her earliest experiences. "In that state I used to ask myself, 'Where am I?' Then I would try to think of myself at some point, but I immediately felt myself to be at the opposite point."[43] The result of such *samadhi* is a profound conviction that all things are one, that the world at bottom is a simple unity.

To help her disciples gain this perception, from which flows great peace and integration, Ma Jnanananda stresses four principles or virtues, all of which have venerable roots in traditional Hinduism. First, she insists on absolute truth, on trying always to stand in the light of conscience and the light of objective reality. One who would seriously pursue the Advaita Vedanta path toward enlightenment has to employ lightsome means. Second, she urges purity. This means clearing the inner waters, letting all immoral thoughts and desires sink toward the bottom, like useless silt. Third, the disciple must develop his or her *dharma*, the righteousness that comes from fulfilling the duties of one's state in life. Last, Ma stresses *ahimsa* or nonviolence, the attitude of trying to do no injury to any fellow creature.

Together, these four virtues compose a spiritual program that Ma calls "action without desire." It is at least as old as the *Bhagavad Gita*, yet completely practical in the contemporary world. Essentially, it means self-surrender, so that one's life more and more stands free of either worries about the past or troubling anticipations of the future.

The end result of such a self-surrender should be a complete focus on God. In the regime Ma would have a disciple follow, the day begins with some prayer or meditation to the deity of the disciple's choice. After this, the disciple turns to the work of the day, trying to perform her duties in such a way that they do not distract her mind from God. The ideal is always to surrender completely to God. When distracting thoughts enter the mind, one should return to God by substituting a prayer or *mantra* (sacred sound). The goal always is "realization" of God, experiential awareness of the divinity in everything.

As this realization increases, worldly things lose their allure. Bit by bit one is skirting the dark forest of fearsome desires, moving away from the powers of samsara and time. We can never control all the events of our lives, but we can control our attitude toward them. If we regard what happens to us as intended for our detachment from samsaric things, intended for our attachment to God, all things will become profitable.

The final state of realization brings a great love of God. As one's union with divinity increases, one's fulfillment overflows. In this conviction, Ma Jnanananda is a sister to the great mystics of other religious traditions. East and West, they agree that union with God or ultimate reality is the greatest success a human being can attain. Ma Jnanananda therefore shows that Shankara's stress on the sole reality of Brahman is neither eccentric nor ethereal. As it works in her own life, and the lives of many of her disciples, it is a source of great fulfillment and love.

---

fold. Two principal such movements centered on Vishnu and Shiva. Although these two movements fought for the common person's allegiance and presented quite different versions of divinity, they both advanced Vedic tradition and made a religion that combined some intellectual clout with much emotional enthusiasm.

The theistic religion centered on Vishnu (Vaishnavism) got its impetus from the patronage of the Gupta kings in the fourth century C.E., and it depended on interpretations of the Trimurti (the Brahma-Vishnu-Shiva trinity) that placed Vishnu in the foreground. Perhaps the most winning aspect of Vaishnavite doctrine, though, was its notion that the god is concerned about human beings, fights with them against demon enemies, and sends incarnations of himself (avatars) to assist humans in troubled times. Traditionally there are ten avatars, the most important being Rama (the hero of the epic *Ramayana*), Krishna, Buddha(!), and Kalki (who is yet to come).

Vaishnavism promoted itself in several ways. Two of the most effective tied Vishnu to the bhakti cult. Between the sixth and the sixteenth centuries, the *Puranas* (legendary accounts of the exploits of gods and heroes) pushed Vishnu to the fore.[44] The *Bhagavata Purana*, perhaps the most influential, was especially successful in popularizing the avatar Krishna. In fact, the tenth book of the *Bhagavata Purana*, which celebrates Krishna's affairs with the girls who tended cows *(gopis)*, mixes erotic entertainment with symbolism of the divine-human relationship. As the cowgirls were rapt before Krishna, so could the devotee's spirit swoon before god. When one adds the stories of Krishna's extramarital affairs with Radha, his favorite *gopi*, the religious eros becomes quite intense. The *Puranas* were thus the first vehicle to elevate Vishnu and his prime avatar to the status of bhakti (devotional) gods.

The second way in which Vaishnavite bhakti was promoted occurred in southern India during the seventh and eighth centuries.[45] There Tamil-speaking troubadours called *alvars* ("persons deep in wisdom") spread devotion to Vishnu by composing religious songs. However, their wisdom was simply a deep love of Vishnu, a love that broke the bonds of caste and worldly station. The constant theme of the songs was Vishnu's own love and compassion for human beings, which moved him to send his avatars. The *alvars* were so successful that they practically ousted Buddhism from India, and they were the main reason that Vishnu-Krishna became the most attractive and influential Hindu god.

A third way that Vaishnavism prospered was more intellectual—it had the good fortune of attracting the religious philosopher Ramanuja,[46] who is now second only to Shankara in prestige. Ramanuja lived in the eleventh century, and his main accomplishment was elaborating upon the

Upanishadic doctrine in a way that made divinity compatible with human love. This way goes by the name *vishishtadvaita*—"nondualism qualified by difference." It opposed the unqualified nondualism of Shankara, whom Ramanuja regarded as his philosophical enemy. For Ramanuja, Brahman consisted of three realities: the unconscious universe of matter, the conscious community of finite selves, and the transcendent lord Ishvara.

Further, Ramanuja held that the Upanishadic formula "This thou art" meant not absolute identity between atman and Brahman but a relationship: the psychological oneness that love produces. The highest way to liberation was therefore loving devotion to the highest lord who represented Brahman. Knowledge and pure action were good paths, but love was better. By substituting Vishnu or Krishna for Brahman or Ishvara, the Vaishnavites made Ramanuja a philosophical defender of their bhakti. For those who wanted to reformulate revealed doctrine through love, Ramanuja was the man.

Shaivism

Contending with Vaishnavism was Shaivism—devotion to Shiva. Shankara had been a Shaivite, but his intellectualism hardly satisfied the common person's desires for an emotional relationship with divinity. As we have seen, Shiva was a somewhat wild god of fertility and destruction. He was the Lord of the Dance of Life and the destroyer who terminated each kalpa of cosmic time. From the earliest available evidence, Shaivism was a response to this wild god. It was frequently a source of emotional excesses, and its tone always mixed love with more fear and awe than Vaishnavism did.[47]

For example, one of the earliest Shaivite sects, which the *Mahabharata* calls Pashupati, taught that in order to end human misery and transcend the material world, one had to engage in such rituals as smearing the body with cremation ashes; eating excrement, carrion, or human flesh; drinking from human skulls; simulating sexual inter-

course; and frenzied dancing. Members of other sects, such as the eleventh-century Kalamukha (named for the black mark they wore on their foreheads), became notorious as drug addicts, drunkards, and even murderers.[48] Even when Shaivites were thoroughly respectable, their religion was more fiery and zealous in its asceticism than that of the love-struck but more refined Vaishnavites. Shaivite priests tended to come from the lower, nonbrahmin classes, and Shaivite followers often regarded the *lingam* (phallus) as Shiva's main emblem. Parallel to the Vaishnavite *alvars* were the Shaivite *adiyars*, whose poetry and hymns were a principal factor in Shiva's rise to prominence, especially in southern India.

The Shaivite movement also received royal patronage in southern India from the fifth to the tenth centuries. During those centuries the Shaivites waged war against both the Buddhists and the Jains. After winning that fight they turned on the Vaishnavites, singing of Shiva's superiority to Vishnu. In their theology they stressed not only the Lord of the Cosmic Dance and the god of fertility and destruction but also the hidden god. Even the worship of the phallus they enshrouded in mystery by placing it behind a veil. In addition, they often substituted representations of Nandi, Shiva's bull, or one of his *Shaktis* for the god Shiva himself.

Thus, the worshiper of Shiva grew conscious that he or she was a sinner through the mysterious ritual and Shiva's own symbols of fire and a skull. As a result, there was little equality, little of the lover-beloved relationship, between the devotee and Shiva. The Shaivite deprecatingly referred to himself or herself as a cur. That the god would come to such a person was pure grace. Worship, then, was essentially gratitude that the tempestuous god chose to forgive rather than destroy.

Shaktism

A last reformulation of the Hindu tradition came through movements that scholars group as Shaktism or Tantrism.[49] This sort of Hinduism focused on secret lore whose prime objective was to liberate the energies of sex and magic. Insofar as Shiva's *Shaktis* represented the energy of female divinity, they exemplified Tantrist powers. It is hard to know exactly what *Shakti* sects believed and practiced, because most of their rites were secret, but one of their main beliefs was that the union of coitus is the best analogy for the relationship between the cosmos and its energy flow. This belief seems to have spawned a theory of parallels or dualisms, in which male-female, right-left, and positive-negative pairings all had magical aspects. (In this belief Tantrism resembles Chinese yin-yang theory, which we will consider in Chapter 3.)

One of the many Tantrist rituals for gaining *moksha* was called *chakrapuja* (circle worship). In it men and women (Tantrist groups tended to admit members without regard for sex or caste) used a series of elements (all having Sanskrit names beginning with the letter *m*) that might facilitate union with *Shakti*: wine, meat, fish, parched rice, and copulation. In right-hand Tantrism these elements were symbols. Left-hand Tantrism used the actual elements (not hedonistically but with ritual discipline, to participate in *lila* [reality's play]). Other Tantrist practices involved meditation to arouse the *kundalini*—the snake of energy lying dormant at the base of the spine.[50]

Overall, then, the reformation of the Vedic tradition meant expanded roles for the Vedic gods and a shift of popular religion from sacrifice to devotional, theistic worship. The reformers tried to defend and extend their ancient heritage, allowing people to respond to any part of it that they found attractive. In this way, the reformers created an eclectic religion that is very tolerant of diversity in religious doctrine and practice.

The Period of Foreign Challenge

From about 1200 C.E. on, Hinduism increasingly contended with foreign cultures, rulers, and religions. Islam and Christianity both made serious impacts on Indian life, and their presence is felt to this day. Islam, a factor in India from the eighth century on, first affected Indians of the Sind and Punjab regions in the northwestern part of ancient India, where Muslims traded and made military conquests. Invasions in the eleventh century put much of the Indus Valley region under Muslim control, and by 1206 Islam had conquered most of northern India. By 1335 Muslims controlled the south as well, and their final dynasty, the Mogul, did not end until 1858.

The policies of Muslim leaders toward Hinduism varied. Many were tolerant and allowed the Indians freedom to practice their traditional ways. Others, such as the Mogul zealot Aurangzeb (ruled 1658–1707), attempted to establish a thoroughly Muslim state and so tried to stop drinking, gambling, prostitution, the use of narcotics, and other practices that were prohibited by Islamic doctrine. Aurangzeb destroyed over 200 Hindu temples in 1679 alone, and he discriminated against Hindus in the collection of taxes and custom duties and in various other ways.

The permanent changes that Islam made in Hinduism and that Hinduism made in Indian Islam are hard to determine because the two faiths are intertwined. Islamic architecture and learning influenced Hinduism deeply, while Hindu casteism affected Indian Muslims as well. Muslim fundamentalism, based on the belief that the Qur'an is God's final word, probably upgraded the status of the Hindu Vedas, and many Hindus found *Sufism*, the devotional branch of Islam, quite compatible with their native bhakti practices.

One definite result of Islam's presence in India was a new, syncretistic religion, Sikhism. Traces of it were found among Hindus who considered aspects of Islam very attractive, but it actually began as a result of the revelations of the prophet Nanak, a Punjabi born in 1469. Nanak's visions prompted him to sing the praise of a divinity that blended elements of the Muslim Allah and the Hindu Trimurti. This god he called the True Name. The religious prescriptions for serving the True Name that he set for his followers were rather severe and anticeremonial, steering away from Hindu pilgrimages and devotions and favoring compassion and neighborly good deeds. The Sikhs developed into a small but hardy religious band, and on numerous occasions they proved to be excellent warriors. They number about 6 million in India today, and their great shrine remains in Amritsar in the northwest. Many of the other holy Sikh sites, however, are now in Pakistan because of the 1947 partition.[51]

Christianity has been present in India since the first century C.E. according to stories about the apostle Thomas's adventures there. It is more certain that a bishop of Alexandria sent a delegation to India in 189 C.E. and that an Indian representative attended the Council of Nicaea (325 C.E.). Only in the sixteenth century, however, did the Christian missionary presence become strong, in the wake of Portuguese (and later Dutch and English) traders. The British East India Company, founded in 1600, increasingly controlled the Indian economy and trade, and after the Sepoy Mutiny in 1857 the company, which had become a sort of government, gave way to direct colonial rule. When India became independent in 1947, after almost a century of British colonial rule, it had some experience with the political ideas and social institutions of the modern West.

The Christian impact, as distinguished from the Western impact, has not been impressive statistically. According to 1964 census figures, only 2.4 percent of all Indians considered themselves Christians. Nevertheless, Christians opened hundreds of charitable institutions, especially schools, and were responsible for the first leprosaria. They also promoted hospital care for the tuberculous and the insane. In fact, Christianity's greatest impact was probably the rousing of the Hindu social conscience. The tradition of dharma as social responsibility had not resulted in the establishment of institutions for the poor and sickly. While

Western culture opened India to modern science, technology, and democratic political theory, Western religion drove home the ideal of social concern. Mother Teresa of Calcutta continues that tradition today.

The native Hindu movements during the past seven centuries have not been particularly social.[52] After the reformation of the ancient tradition, Hinduism directed itself toward the further development of bhakti. Islamic Sufism stimulated this tendency, as we suggested above. In the religious poetry of Kabir, a forerunner of the Sikh founder Nanak, the love of God became the heart of a religion that ignored distinctions between Muslims and Hindus, priests and workers.[53] For Kabir this love correlated with a pure heart only.

For Ramananda, a follower of the philosopher Ramanuja, the important thing was to adore God, whom Ramananda called Rama, with fervent devotion. Rama considered all persons equal. In southern India, especially among the people who spoke Tamil, the Lord Vishnu increasingly appeared as a god of pure grace. Self-concern is useless and distracting, the Tamils told their Sanskrit Vaishnavite brethren. Not works but love is redeeming.

In west central India, from the thirteenth to the seventeenth centuries, a poetic movement called the Maratha renaissance carried the message of bhakti. Tukaram, the greatest poet of this movement, stressed God's otherness and the sinfulness of human beings. His god was not the Brahman who was identical with one's innermost self but a free agent and lover whose goodness in saving sinners was the more impressive because of their distance from him.

Modern Bhakti

In these and other movements, modern Hinduism increasingly focused on bhakti, moving away from Vedic orthodoxy. The singers of bhakti cared little whether their doctrines squared with the Upanishads or the great commentators. The notions of *shruti* or *smriti*, in fact, meant little to them.

They thought that the love they had found undercut traditional views of social classes, sex, and even religions. The god of love was no creator of castes, no despiser of women, no pawn of Hindus against Muslims. With little concern for intellectual or social implications, the singers and seers who dominated modern bhakti gave themselves over to ecstatic love.

Perhaps the greatest representative of bhakti was Chaitanya, a sixteenth-century Bengali saint whom his followers worship as an avatar of Krishna.[54] Chaitanya, originally a brahmin, converted to Vaishnavism and spent his days worshiping Lord Krishna in the great Bengali temple of Puri. Increasingly his devotions became emotional, involving singing, weeping, dancing, and epileptic fits. He died in delirium in the surf off Puri, where he was bathing. Somewhat typically for modern bhakti, Chaitanya repudiated the Vedas and nondualistic Vedanta philosophy as opposing a gracious god. All were welcome in his sect, regardless of caste, and he even sanctioned worship of a black stone, thinking that it might help some followers' devotion. He stressed the followers' assimilation with Radha, Krishna's lover, arguing that the soul's relation to God is always female to male.

Yet Chaitanya also stressed the necessity to toil at religious love and opposed those who argued that grace was attained without effort. His followers deified him, seeing his unbounded religious ecstasy as the ideal communion of divinity and humanity. He was the major figure in the devotional surge toward Lord Krishna that produced some remarkable Bengali love poetry during the sixteenth and seventeenth centuries.[55] His movement continues, with a rather high profile, in the United States through the work of Swami Prabhupada, founder of the International Society for Krishna Consciousness and of the Bhaktivedanta Book Trust. The swami's monks in saffron robes who chant on street corners and his numerous publications[56] have made "Hare Krishna" part of our religious vocabulary.

Partly in opposition to the excesses of bhakti and partly because of the influence of Western culture, a group of Bengali intellectuals in the early nineteenth century began to "purify" Hinduism by bringing it up to the standards that they saw in Christianity. The first such effort was the founding of the group Brahmo Samaj by Rammohan Roy in 1828. Roy was a well-educated brahmin whose contacts with Islam and Christianity led him to think that there should be only one God for all persons, who should inspire social concern.

God should, for example, oppose such barbarism as suttee (*sati*), the Hindu practice in which a widow climbed on her husband's funeral pyre and burned with him.[57] In 1811 Roy had witnessed the suttee of his sister-in-law, whom relatives kept on the pyre even though she was screaming and struggling to escape. He knew that in Calcutta alone there were over 1,500 such immolations between 1815 and 1818. Roy pressured the British to outlaw the practice, and in 1829 a declaration was issued that forbade it (though it did not completely stamp it out). Members of the Brahmo Samaj thought this sort of social concern was essential to pure religion.[58]

Another movement to modernize Hinduism that originated in Bengal in the nineteenth century was the Ramakrishna Mission. Its founder, Ramakrishna, was an uneducated brahmin who became a mystic devotee of the goddess Kali, a *Shakti* of Shiva, whom he worshiped as a divine Mother. After visions of Kali and then of Rama, the epic hero, Ramakrishna progressed through the Tantrist, Vaishnavite, and Vedanta disciplines, having the ecstatic experiences associated with the traditions of each. He even lived as a Muslim and a Christian, learning the mystic teachings of those traditions. From such eclectic experience he developed the joyous doctrine that we can find God everywhere: Divinity beats in each human heart. Ramakrishna's teachings achieved worldwide publicity through his disciple Vivekananda, who stressed the theme of worshiping God by serving human beings.

Figure 4   *Raj-ghat, memorial to M. K. Gandhi in Delhi. Photo by J. T. Carmody.*

The Ramakrishna Mission has sponsored hospitals, schools, and cultural centers, and it keeps an American presence through the Vedanta Society, which has chapters in many American cities.[59]

Tagore and Gandhi

In the twentieth century, these currents of domestic and foreign stimuli to religious and social reform inevitably affected the controversies over Indian nationalism and independence. The controversies themselves largely turned on the assets and liabilities of the British and Indian cultures. Not all Indians opposed the British, largely because they did not have a single national tradition themselves. Rather, Indians tended to think of themselves as Bengalis or Gujaratis or Punjabis—natives of their own district, with its own language and traditions.

What the Indian tradition meant, therefore, was far from clear. This fact emerges in the lives of two of the most intriguing modern-day personalities, Tagore and Gandhi.

Rabindranath Tagore (1861–1941), modern India's most illustrious writer, won the Nobel Prize for literature in 1913. His life's work was a search for artistic and educational forms that would instill Indians with a broad humanism. For this reason, he was leery of nationalism, fearing that it would crush individual creativity and blind Indians to values outside their own country. In the West, Tagore found a salutary energy, a concern for the material world, which seemed to him precisely the cure for India's deep cultural ills. However, he despised the Western industrial nations' stress on machinery, power politics, and democracy. In Tagore's renewed Hinduism, India would give and receive—give resources for individual creativity and receive Western energies for using that creativity to improve society.

Mohandas Gandhi (1869–1948) was a political genius who made some of Tagore's vision practical. He trained as a lawyer in England and found his vocation as an advocate of the masses in South Africa, where he represented "colored" minorities. In India Gandhi drew in part on a Western idealism that he culled from such diverse sources as the New Testament, Tolstoy's writings on Christian socialism, Ruskin's writings on the dignity of work, and Thoreau's writings on civil disobedience. He joined this Western idealism with a shrewd political pragmatism of his own and Indian religious notions, including the *Bhagavad Gita's* doctrine of karma-yoga (work as a spiritual discipline) and the Jain-Hindu notion of *ahimsa* (noninjury). Gandhi's synthesis of these ideas resulted in what he called *satyagraha* (truth force). To oppose the might of Britain he used the shaming power of a simple truth: Indians, like all human beings, deserve the right to control their own destinies.

Gandhi was a genius at symbolizing truth force. In Joan Bondurant's study,[60] one can see how he worked out *satyagraha* campaigns of civil disobedience, striking, marshaling public support, and so on. In Erik Erikson's study of Gandhi at middle age,[61] one can see the psychological roots of *satyagraha* and something of its promise as an instrument for sociopolitical change in the nuclear age. In Gandhi himself one can see the conflicts, confusions, and riches of the Hindu tradition in the mid-twentieth century, for he called himself just a seeker of *moksha*, just a servant of the one God found whenever we harken to truth.[62]

CONTEMPORARY HINDUISM

As we have already stressed, Hinduism is an umbrella for a great variety of different religious ideas and practices. Of necessity, we have concentrated on the ideas and practices that stand out when one attempts a historical overview. The outstanding ideas, however, tend to be the possession of intellectuals, at least in their reflective form. For the common people, it tends to be the many rituals of the Hindu religious year that mediate the sense of at-one-ment with the world that religion seeks to inculcate. To conclude this historical survey, we concentrate on a few of the rituals that fill popular Hinduism today. Let us begin with an anthropologist's description of how a village of central India celebrated *Naumi*, a high point of a festival devoted to nine goddesses.[63]

Naumi occurs in the fall, in either September or October. It is the ninth day of the festival of the nine goddesses—a sort of arithmetic highpoint. In the afternoon of Naumi, the main activity is a procession of men possessed by gods. Throughout the entire festival of the nine goddesses mediums are constantly making contact with the supernatural world, so the procession of possessed men is a kind of climax to their work.

In this village, the two principal mediums were a weaver and a carpenter. The weaver claimed that his tutelary spirit was the mother goddess (*Mata*), while the carpenter claimed that he was directed by the spirit of a local incarnation of Vishnu. The weaver's behavior was the more elaborate of the two. For the entire nine days of the festival, he fasted, living in a small hut adorned only with a picture of Mata, five baskets of sprouting wheat, and a few ritual objects. People visited him during these days, asking for help with their personal problems. For example, a woman asked the weaver what she should do for pains in her back. He gave her some grains of sorghum to eat and told her to offer a gift to the goddess.

The carpenter claimed that he could not afford to spend the whole nine days away from his work, so he held only limited sessions for clients. However, the carpenter's sessions had the strong support of the local headman (and so drew the wealthier people), because the headman had once consulted him about obtaining a son and had had his request granted by the carpenter's guiding spirit.

On the afternoon of Naumi, at the climax of the feast, both mediums held rites in their houses. The followers of the carpenter sacrificed rice and ghee to his god, while the followers of the weaver sacrificed a goat. Both mediums then led their followers to the center of the town, where they processed to the pounding of drums. On this occasion some magicians enlivened the proceedings. Indeed, one magician continually excited the weaver, who was in trance, by sleight-of-hand tricks with limes. The magician would make the limes appear and then disappear. Since limes are thought to accompany the mother goddess, each time the limes appeared the weaver would become beside himself with expectation, thinking his special god had drawn near. The procession also had a fertility aspect, for some of the men carried seedlings which they finally sunk in a well outside the village, to "cool" them for the best growth.

In the evening the people sacrificed a goat at each of the three principal shrines, trying to assure the town's good fortune in the coming year. They also purified themselves with fire, walking between two flames and passing through the flames their tools, butter churns, swords, and the like. The anthropologist reporting these customs was advised to pass across his everpresent pen and camera.

Although the afternoon procession was the most popular part of Naumi (in large measure because it drew magicians and other showmen), the evening sacrifices, performed for the welfare of the whole village, were no less important. In fact, in the evening someone visited all forty-four of the village's shrines, praying for all the gods' help during the coming year. (Since there were only about 900 people in the village, there was one shrine for about every twenty people.) The order of visitation shows how the village ranked these shrines: mother goddess, smallpox goddess, Vaishnavite Temple, another mother goddess, lord of the south village gates, Shaivite Temple, local small god, god of the nath caste, temple where a treaty was signed with some marauders, local mother goddess, temple of the brahmin caste, another Vaishnavite Temple, and more.

The anthropologist reporting this bevy of temples did not always know precisely what function a given god was thought to perform, and his mention of so many *castes* (occupational groups) shows the splintered character of village Indian society even in recent times. The temples concerned with smallpox, cholera, and leprosy are a sad commentary on rural Indian health, while the several temples dedicated to the mother goddess show that recent folk Hinduism has continued India's millennial adoration of the Great Mother, the primal source of life and comfort.

The rituals of folk Hinduism vary from geographical area to geographical area, depending on local gods and customs. Among Hindus of the Himalayas, a strong shamanistic influence remains. Many of these people's religious ceremonies involve a shaman's possession (much like the possession of central Indian mediums such as the weaver and carpenter). More often than not, a family calls upon a shaman because of some misfortune: "Most supernatural beings make their presence felt by imposing difficulties or troubles upon people—usually disease or death to people or animals, and sometimes other troubles such as hysteria, faithless spouses, sterility, poor crops, financial loss, or mysterious disappearance of belongings."[64] When such things happen, people usually ask a shaman to hold a seance. Thus, a goodly number of ad hoc ceremonies supplement the annual cycle of ceremonies similar to Naumi.

The shaman may be from any caste, and he tends to make his living by acting as the medium of a particular god. Usually he opens a consultation by singing prayers in honor of his god, to the steady beat of a drum. As he enters into trance, often he becomes impervious to pain, as he demonstrates by touching red-hot metal. When the god has taken full possession of the shaman, the god usually uses the shaman's voice to tell the client what is troubling him and what should be done to cure it. The god may also identify thieves or harmful articles that have brought the misfortune. If the client does not like the god's diagnosis or advice, she simply goes to a different shaman.

More often than not, the treatment the god suggests is performing a *puja* (short ceremony) in honor of the being that is causing the trouble. (In the case of a ghost, the *puja* amounts to an exorcism.) Other popular treatments are making pilgrimages or removing harmful objects causing disease. If the case is impossible to cure (for example, a person deranged beyond healing), the god may prescribe an impossible treatment (for example, the sacrifice of a cow; since the cow is sacred to Hindus, sacrificing a cow is unthinkable).

If the suggested cure is performing a *puja*, other religious specialists generally enter the scene. Their job is arranging and executing a ceremony in which the god can enter a human body, ideally that of the victim, dance in it, and make known any further demands. These *puja* specialists usually come from the lower castes, and their basic method of inducing the god's possession of the victim is playing percussion instruments.

The ceremony tends to unfold in three parts: the dance, the *puja* or prayer proper, and the offering. Usually the ceremony takes place in the shrine of the god who is concerned. The shrine itself is very simple, generally consisting of one to four iron tridents about eight inches high. The people place these in a niche in the wall, if the shrine is indoors, or at the base of a large stone, if it is outside, in effect marking off a sacred space. During the ceremonies the shrine is lighted by a small oil lamp, and often a container of rice and small coins hangs near it, as an offering to the god.

The dance, which begins the ceremony, is intended to attract the god (or any other spirit or ancestor who likes to dance in the bodies of humans). The gods are thought to like dancing because it gives them a chance to air their complaints and needs. Dancing most often occurs in the evening, but sometimes it is repeated the following day. As the drummers increase the intensity of the beat and the room fills with onlookers, smoke, and heat, the rhythms become more compelling, until someone, either the victim or an onlooker, starts to jerk, shout, and dance, first slowly but then more wildly. The possessed person is honored with incense and religious gestures, and fed boiled rice, because for the moment he or she is the god.

After the god has danced his fill, he usually speaks through the possessed person, telling the cause of his anger (the source of the misfortune) and detailing what it will take to appease him. The victimized person and his or her family then make a short prayer to the god, expressing

reverently their desire to comply with his requests, after which they make the offering the god has demanded.

The most frequent offering is a young male goat. The people place the goat before the shrine and throw rice on its back, while the ritual specialist chants mantras. When the goat shakes itself, the onlookers believe the god has accepted their offering. An attendant (usually from a low caste; higher caste people tend to consider this defiling) takes the goat outside and beheads it. The attendant then places a foot and the head of the animal before the shrine, as an offering to the god, along with such delicacies as bread and sweet rice. The ritual specialist eventually gathers these up, as part of his fee, and the family and guests share the rest of the goat.

The anthropologist describing this kind of ceremony found that the villagers strongly believed in its efficacy. Thus one teenage boy attributed his father's recovery from pneumonia to a possession ceremony, while another informant opined that the gods are like lawyers: The more you give them, the more they will do on your behalf. Clearly, therefore, the villagers of the Himalayas, as much as the villagers of central India, have continued to supplement the more official festivals of the Vedic gods with many local folk practices.

A third sort of ritual common in contemporary Indian religion deals with a stage of the life cycle, helping a person cope with puberty, marriage, parenthood, or widowhood. The *habisha* ritual performed by middle-aged women in the eastern province of Orissa illustrates this sort. To begin, the anthropologist making the report notes that the *habisha* ritual is a *brata* or vowed observance: "Historically, vows have been an important part of Hindu ritual life for centuries. People make vows mainly to secure something in this world, such as progeny, wealth, good fortune, health, fame, or long life; sometimes people make vows to secure something in the next world; and occasionally, as in the *habisha* rites, people make vows to gain something both in this world and in the next."[65] The vows may last as short a time as a day, or as long as the rest of one's life, but whatever their time, they are serious business. As the stories of the *Puranas* emphasize, failure to fulfill a vow can lead to dire consequences.

Consequently, the person who makes a

vow usually prepares assiduously to fulfill it, by fasting, worshiping gods, taking frequent purificatory baths, abstaining from sexual relations, refraining from drinking water or chewing betel nuts, and not sleeping during daylight hours. From this asceticism, as well as the fulfillment of the vow itself, the vower gains spiritual power. In the case of the *habisha* ritual, the spiritual power focuses on preventing the death of the woman's husband. Most *habisha* participants, in fact, are menopausal women trying to protect their husbands from death (and trying thereby to protect themselves from the sad fate of the Hindu widow).

For the women whom our source studied, participating in the *habisha* ritual, and especially going on pilgrimage to the holy town of Puri, had been the high point of their lives. Typically, the women dedicated a thirty-five day period in October-November to purificatory rituals and fasts in honor of Jagannatha, a local version of the young god Krishna. The imaginative context of these devotions was the legendary scene of the young Krishna among his female devotees (gopis). Krishna was the cow herdsman and the gopis were the milkmaids. The *habisha* women reproduced scenes from this legend in rice powder, churned milk in imitation of the gopis, offered coconuts and cowrie shells to a replica of Krishna, and danced ecstatically to express their great love of the god. If possible, they concluded their season of devotions with a forty-mile trip to the temple of Lord Jagannatha in Puri.

The elaborate preparations of one informant show the seriousness with which Indian women can enter upon rituals like *habisha*. This informant, a fifty-five-year-old married woman named Tila, was a member of the confectioner caste. Six days before the beginning of *habisha* in 1971, she had a barber trim her fingernails and toenails. Then she took a ritual bath and summoned the brahmin who usually performed ceremonies for her family. He further purified Tila by sprinkling cow-dung water on her head. Ideally, he said, people would purify themselves for *habisha* by drinking *panchagavia*, as in the old days, but nowadays few people were so thorough. *Panchagavia*, it turned out, is the five holy sub-

stances of the cow: milk, curds, clarified butter, urine, and dung. Tila apparently forewent this treat, promising, however, that she would be the brahmin's disciple for the full month, that she would listen to his daily recitation from a sacred book, and that she would fulfill her vows of fasting, purification, and sexual abstinence.

The typical day of the votive period began with a chilly predawn bath at the village pond. Facing in each of the four directions, the women involved prayed to the gods, to their ancestors, and to other sources of help, dipping into the water and purifying themselves. Then they made mud-pictures of the god Vishnu as a child, offered prayers to the rising sun, and took burning wicks to the village temple, where they chanted and prayed. These ceremonies, as well as their common dedication, bonded the women together, so that for the *habisha* month they put aside their rivalries, jealousies, and gossip. From the village temple they retired to their individual homes, where they cooked the one meal they were allowed to eat each day at sundown. Tila was allowed to eat only rice, lentils, green plantain, taro, cucumber, ginger, and custard apple—foods considered pure. She could have no spices, but each of her meals had to contain clarified butter, a holy substance from the cow.

During the *habisha* days, Tila was especially careful to avoid such defiling contacts as stepping on animal feces or touching a person from a low caste. She would join the other women for ritual baths, prayers, drawings, and above all dances reenacting the legends of Krishna. The psychosocial explanation for these ceremonies is the upper-caste Hindu woman's fear of an early widowhood. The younger the widow, the worse her fate, because widowhood means marginal status as a financial dependent, a potential source of sexual disturbance, and a being polluted by contact with death. The religious explanation is the devotional satisfaction that immersion in the theistic cult of Krishna, loving communion with Krishna, sponsors. Insofar as Krishna becomes the center of the women's emotional lives, the chance *habisha* offers them to concentrate on Krishna intensely for a whole month is a high opportunity.

STRUCTURAL ANALYSIS

Nature

For the most part, Hinduism considers nature (the physical cosmos) to be real, knowable, and orderly. The cosmos is a continuum of lives; consequently, human life is seen as an ongoing interaction with the lives of creatures above and below it. Finally, most Hindus consider divinity to be more than physical nature and human self-realization (*moksha*) to entail release from the laws of karma. Let us develop these ideas.

The statement that the physical cosmos is real requires some qualification. Through history, the average Hindu, concerned with making a living and caring for a family, has had little doubt that the fields, flocks, and other physical phenomena are real. Also, the hymns of the Veda that revere the sun and the storm express a vivid appreciation of nature. Even many of the philosophers spoke of the world as *sat*—having being or reality. Only the idealistic thought of the Upanishads, as the Vedanta developed and somewhat organized it, called the physical world into question.

Furthermore, because of the Vedic notion of *rita* (order, duty, or ritual) and the later notion of karma, Hinduism found the natural world quite orderly. *Rita* presided over such phenomena as sunrise and sunset and the seasons. Karma expressed the Hindu belief that all acts in the cosmos result from previous causes or choices and produce inevitable effects. To be sure, there are various religious paths (*margas*) for escaping karmic inevitability, and we shall discuss those paths below. Nonetheless, *rita* and karma suggest that the world is patterned, regular, and dependable. This does not mean that flood, famine, earthquake, sickness, or war cannot occur, but it does mean that none of these calamities makes the world absurd.

Karma, as we have seen, was connected with the notion of transmigration and rebirth. *Rita* is involved with the vast space-time dimensions in which Hindu cosmology delights. Together these concepts give nature a gigantic expanse that is replete with connections. The connections that most interested the average Hindu linked the myriad living things. Astrology and astronomy brought some people in contact with planetary forces, but the average Indian was more interested in other people and animals. Shaivites expressed this interest by venerating the powers of fertility. Ancient rites honoring the Great Mother and other rites stressing Shaktism reveal other Hindu responses to the wonders of life. The symbolism surrounding Shiva and his consorts (such as Kali) explicitly links life with death. At a level above the ancient mentality's concerns with the vegetative cycle of death and rebirth and the taking of life by life, Hinduism placed the connection between death and life in the context of the great cycles of creation and destruction: the Brahma Day and Brahma Night, Shiva's dance of life and death, and the sportive play of *lila* or maya.

The Jain notion of *ahimsa*, which many Hindus adopted to varying degrees, implied the connectedness of all lives through its practice of not harming any living thing. Many Indians refused to eat meat out of the desire not to harm animals. Nonviolence toward the cow, which one might not kill even to help the starving (but which might itself starve), epitomized for many Hindus a necessary reverence for life. Taking karma and transmigration (the passing of the life force from one entity to another) seriously, the Hindu thought that life, including one's own, was constantly recasting itself into new vegetative and animal forms. Such life was not an evolutionary accident or something that ended at the grave. The inmost life principle continued on.

Hinduism had negative as well as positive aspects. Certainly maya and samsara can carry negative overtones. In fact, the whole thrust toward *moksha* suggests that the natural sphere is of limited value. For more than a few Indians, the natural sphere has been a prison or place of suffering. Yogis of different schools, for instance, have tried to withdraw from materiality in order to cultivate enstasis.[66] Other Hindu mystics have sensed that there was something more ultimate than the ritual sacrifice, the play of natural processes, and even the emotions of the devout worshiper of the bhakti god.[67] In this sense samsara opposed the freedom suggested by *moksha*, which meant exit from what one had known as natural conditions.

Another negative view of the natural world results from Hinduism's relative disregard for social improvements. However, it is misleading to label Hinduism as world denying or life denying, since India's culture has produced warriors, merchants, artists, and scientists—a full citizenry who took secular life seriously.[68] Nonetheless, Hindu culture was seldom secular or materialistic in our modern senses, usually stabilizing society by referring to a god or Brahman transcending human space and time. (We may say the same of traditional premodern societies generally.) In addition, Hinduism's reference to metaphysical concepts retarded its concern with health care, education, and economic prosperity for the masses. (Again, we could say this of many other traditional cultures.) When he argued for a secular state and a turn to science rather than religion, Nehru spoke for many modern, educated Indians. Even today, the religion of the villages, which is often quite primitive, hinders the improvement of agriculture, family planning, housing, and health care.

Thus, Hinduism's Aryan beginnings, which were so bursting with love of physical life, and Dravidian beginnings, which were tantamount to nature and fertility worship, were negated over time. The most serious blows came from intellectual Hinduism and bhakti, which found life good by spiritual exercises and thus were not concerned with transforming nature or social justice.

In Eric Voegelin's terms, neither the early Hinduism that began close to nature nor that which withdrew from nature to human spirit escaped the cosmological myth. In Israel, Greece, and European Christian culture, such a withdrawal made nature less than divine. Unlike the religions of these Western cultures and the prophetic theology of Islam, Hinduism tended to keep gods and humans within the cosmic milieu. *Moksha* is an exception, but *moksha* was seldom articulated clearly. It primarily proposed that human self-realization comes by escaping the given world.

One confirmation of the view that Hinduism did not differentiate the realms of nature, divinity, and society is that the concept of creation from nothingness never became a dominant Hindu belief. In Hindu cosmology the universe goes its rhythmic way of Brahma Days and Brahma Nights; it has always existed and always will. Insofar as the concept of *moksha* suggests that we may transcend this cosmic rhythm, it carried seeds of a doctrine of creation from nothingness. However, the Hindu explanation of creation involves gods molding the world from preexisting stuff.[69] Thus Hinduism differs from Western religion by considering the world divine. It always remained somewhat under the cosmological myth.

Society

As we have seen, Hinduism structured society by caste and numerous occupational subclasses. In addition, families traced themselves back through their departed ancestors.[70] Outside the four castes were the untouchables, and there were also occasional instances of slavery. The basic structure of the four castes received religious sanction in the *Rig-Veda* (10 : 90), where the priests, warriors, merchants, and workers emerged from the Great Man's body after he was sacrificed.

The Laws of Manu, expanding the doctrine of casteism, specified the castes' social duties. The brahmin, for instance, had six required acts: teaching, studying, sacrificing for himself, sacrificing for others, making gifts, and receiving gifts. Brahmins also were to avoid working at agriculture and selling certain foods (such as flesh and salt). Were they to do these things, they would assume the character of the persons of the other castes. In a similar way, Manu set duties and prohibitions for the warriors, merchants, and workers, giving the entire society a comprehensive dharma. As a result, Hindus considered their dharma to be a given rather than a matter of debate or free choice. Indeed, it was the basic cement of Hindu society.[71]

Nonetheless, various religious inspirations and movements introduced some flexibility. Many of the bhakti cults rejected caste distinctions, contending that all persons are equal in the god's sight. The possibility of stepping outside the ordinary organization of things in order to become a full-time ascetic or seeker of liberation loosened the stranglehold of both dharma and caste. Throughout history, the patchwork organization of the Indian nation also added to social flexibility. Since most of the people lived in villages, and most of the administrative units were local rather than national, local customs were very strong.

Thus, Hindu society was remarkably diverse and tolerant despite its official rigidity. The complexity of social stations and religious allegiances meant that there were many legitimate ways through life. In the family, which was usually quite large, or extended, the chief figure was the father. Family organization was usually patriarchal, as was property administration. Women had some property rights, according to some legal schools, but their position was generally inferior. In fact, the place of women in Hindu society illustrates well the overall Hindu social and religious outlooks.

Women's Status

We know little about the earliest Indian women's social status. There is evidence of fertility rites among the pre-Aryans, as we have seen, suggesting a cult of a mother goddess or a matriarchal social structure. In Vedic times women clearly were subordinate to men, but in earlier times they may have held important cultic offices, created canonical hymns, and been scholars, poets, and teachers.[72] In the Brihad-Aranyaka Upanishad, the woman Gargi questions the sage Yajnavalkya, indicating that wisdom was not exclusively a male concern. It therefore seems likely that in early India at least some girls of the upper castes received religious training like the boys'.

However, between the first Vedas (1500 B.C.E.) and the first codes of law (100 C.E.), women's religious role steadily declined. A major reason for this was the lowering of the marriage age from fifteen or sixteen to ten and even five. This both removed the possibility of education (and consequently religious office) and fixed women's role to being wife and mother. In fact, in later Hinduism being a wife was so important that a widow was prohibited from mentioning any man's name but that of her deceased husband. Even if she had been a child bride or had never consummated her marriage, the widow was not to violate her duty to her deceased husband and remarry. If she did, she would bring disgrace on herself in the present life and enter the womb of a jackal for her next rebirth.

Thus, the widow was the most forlorn of Hindu women. Without a husband, she was a financial liability to those who supported her. If menstruating, she could be a source of ritual pollution. If barren, she was useless to a society that considered women essentially as child producers. In such a social position, many widows must have felt that they had little to lose by throwing themselves on their husband's funeral pyre.[73] (Even suttee, though, was not simple. If the widow did not burn herself out of pure conjugal love, her act was without merit.)

Women were sometimes admitted as equals into the bhakti and Tantrist sects. However, two circumstances in Tantrism minimized the social liberation that the open admission might have effected. First, the Tantrist sects tended to be esoteric, or secret, which made their public impact minor. Second, the Tantrist interest in tapping *shakti* energies often led to the exploitation of women by men. Thus, the males tried to gain powers of liberation (*moksha*) by symbolic or actual sexual intercourse, with the result that the females became instruments rather than equal partners.

Nevertheless, the Tantrist image of perfection as being androgynous tended to boost the value of femaleness. How much this ideal actually benefited Indian women is difficult to say, but it probably did very little. In Hindu society, women were not generally eligible for *moksha*; the best that a woman could hope for was to be reborn as a man. There is little evidence that Tantrism eliminated this belief.

In fact, the overall status of women in Hinduism was that of wards. They were subject, successively, to fathers, husbands, and elder sons. As soon as they approached puberty, their fathers hastened to marry them off, and during their wedded lives they were to honor their husbands without reservation. According to the *Padmapurana*, an influential text, this held true even if their husbands were deformed, aged, debauched, lived openly with other women, or showed them no affection. To ritualize this attitude of devotion, orthodox Hindu authors counseled wives to adore the big toe of their husband's right foot, bathing it as they would an idol, and offering incense before it as they would to a great god.[74]

Worse than ward status, however, was the strain of misogyny (hatred of women) running through Hindu culture. The birth of a girl was not an occasion for joy. Hindus attributed it to bad karma in a previous life and frequently announced the event by saying, "Nothing was born." A girl was a financial burden, for unless her parents arranged a dowry there was small chance that she would marry, and the Vedic notion that women are necessary if men are to be complete (which the gods' consorts evidence) lost out to Manu's view that women are as impure as falsehood itself. In fact, Manu counseled "the wise" never to sit with a woman in a lonely place, even if that woman be one's mother, sister, or daughter.[75]

Consequently, Hindu religious texts frequently imagine a woman as a snake, hell's entrance, death, a prostitute, or an adulteress. In Manu's code, slaying a woman was one of the minor offenses. In the Hindu family, the basic unit of society, woman was therefore the negative charge. The high status of the householder did not extend to his wife or female children. India only honored women for giving birth and slavishly serving their husbands. (In a study of the emotional attitudes that this pattern has inculcated in modern India, Aileen Ross found the following intensity ratings for the listed relationships [the higher the number, the more intense the relationship]: mother-son, 115; brother-sister, 90; brother-brother, 75; father-son, 74; husband-wife, 16; sister-sister 5. She gives no rating for the mother-daughter relationship.)[76]

THE HINDU CHILD

The Hindu child was subjected to religious ceremonies well before birth. For devout Hindus, there were rituals to ensure conception, to procure a male child, and to safeguard the child's time in the womb. Birth itself involved an important ceremony, which ideally took place before the cutting of the umbilical cord, that included whispering sacred spells in the baby's ear, placing a mixture of ghee and honey in its mouth, and giving it a name that its parents were to keep secret until its initiation. Birth made both parents ritually impure for ten days, which meant they were not to take part in the community's ordinary religious rites. Ten days after birth the child was given a public (as contrasted with the secret) name. Some households also solemnized an early ear-piercing and the first time the parents took the child out of the house and showed it the sun.

A. L. Basham, from whose book *The Wonder That Was India* we are taking this description of Hindu childhood, lists some of the other rituals that devout parents included in a child's first years:

More important [than the first vision of the sun] was the first feeding (annaprasana). In the child's sixth month he was giv-

*en a mouthful of meat, fish, or rice (in lat-
er times usually the latter) mixed with
curds, honey, and ghee, to the accompani-
ment of Vedic verses and oblations of
ghee poured on the fire. The tonsure (cu-
dakarma) took place in the third year, and
was confined to boys; with various rites
the child's scalp was shaved, leaving only
a topknot, which, in the case of a pious
brahmin, would never be cut throughout
his life. Another ceremony, not looked on
as of the first importance, was carried out
when the child first began to learn the
alphabet.*[77]

There was a pressing motive for parents to
have sons, in that at least one son was thought
necessary to perform the parents' funeral rites,
without which they could not be sure of a safe
transit to the other world. Adopted sons were better than nothing, but they were nowhere near so
good as natural sons. Girls were of no use what-
soever, because girls could not help their parents
in the next world, and at marriage girls passed
into the families of their husbands. Although
Indian history shows some evidence of female
infanticide, this practice seems relatively rare.
Despite their lesser desirability, many girls were
cared for and petted like sons.

Indeed, Indian literature shows few instances of such maxims as "Spare the rod and
spoil the child," and one gathers that most Hindus had relatively happy, indulged childhoods. In
Indian poetry, for example, children are often
shown laughing, babbling, and being welcomed
onto their parents' laps, even when it was likely
they would leave those laps quite soiled. On the
other hand, poor children were set to work soon
after they were able to walk, and wealthier children started their studies as young as four or five.
Thus boys usually were set to studying the alphabet by their fifth year. Richer families engaged
tutors for their children, and through the Indian
Middle Ages (prior to the Muslim invasions)
many village temples had schools attached. The
education of girls was considered much less pressing than that of boys, but most upper class
women became literate. Prior to his initiation,
when he was invested with the sacred thread and
set to studying the Vedas, an upper-class boy usually concentrated on reading and arithmetic.

The initiation of brahmin boys usually
occurred when they were eight. For warriors the
ideal age was eleven, and for merchants twelve.
The key element in this initiation was hanging a
cord of three threads over the boy's right shoul-
der. The cord was made of nine twisted strands
(cotton for brahmins, hemp for warriors, and wool
for merchants). To remove this thread anytime
during his subsequent life, or to defile it, involved
the initiate in great humiliation and ritual im-
purity.

Another important element in the initiation was whispering the *Gayatri*, the most sacred
verse of the *Rig-Veda* (3:62:10), in the ear of the
initiate. Whereas previously he had been a child,
not really a member of the Aryan people, this
access to the Vedas began his spiritual, fully
human life. The Gayatri is addressed to the old
solar god Savitr, and it functions in Hindu ceremonies much as the Lord's Prayer functions in
Christian ceremonies, as a basic and privileged
expression of devotion. In Basham's translation it
runs: "Let us think on the lovely splendour of the
god Savitr, that he may inspire our minds."

In later times initiation and investment
with the sacred thread became limited mainly to
brahmins, but in Vedic times the other upper
classes initiated their children, often including
their girls. The initiation made the child an
Aryan, a member of a noble people, opening the
door to his first serious task, that of mastering the
sacred Aryan lore. Accordingly, soon after initiation the child was apprenticed to a brahmin in
order to learn the Vedas. During this period he
was to be celibate, to live a simple life, and to
obey his teacher assiduously. There were no sexual overtones to the initiation rite, and other ceremonies took care of the passage to physical
maturity.

Conclusion

The rewards of Hindu religion were in the hands of a relative few. By excluding women, untouchables, and workers, Hinduism told well more than half the population that their best hope was rebirth in a better station sometime in the future. (For the most part, only a member of a high caste could reach *moksha*.) However, in the family and the different trades, dharma gave all castes some legitimacy. Nonetheless, if the fundamental belief of Hinduism is considered to be the struggle for self-realization, these honors were rather tainted. For instance, in the ideal life cycle men of the upper three castes were to leave their families in middle age and retire from social life. A husband might take his wife into retirement with him, but he had no obligation to do so. If anything, tradition probably encouraged him to go off alone. What a person intent on self-realization did for children, servants, or the lower classes in his city was secondary to what he did for his own atman. In the Brihad-Aranyaka Upanishad (2.4.5), Yajnavalkya praised his wife Maitreyi for wanting his help in gaining immortality rather than in gaining wealth. This made her dear to him, not because he loved her earthly self but because he loved her atman.

The smaller units of Hindu society were less honored religiously than they were in other cultures. For instance, although Hindu marriage involved a sacramental rite, it was not regarded as highly as Jewish marriage, which is one of life's three great blessings (the Torah, good deeds, and marriage). The larger social organizations in India never approached the unity of a nation or empire, so one does not find the analogies between earth and heaven that one finds in Mesopotamia or Egypt, where the king was the mediator of divine substance, or *maat*—the mediator between the above of the gods and the below of the human realm. Indians may have sometimes pictured the realm of the many gods as a sort of government with superiors and subordinates, but this imagery is not so strong as it was in Greece or China.

Indian society was simply too diverse and too fragmented to reflect the macrocosm.

Thus, Hindu society is very complex. Dharma meant that religion supported a responsible attitude toward society, and the law treatises specified these responsibilities. On the other hand, *moksha* and bhakti militated against taking worldly life too seriously. For those absorbed in religious liberation or religious love, political, economic, and even family structures must have seemed of negligible importance.

Understandably, many of the great religious figures of Indian history left the social scheme. The Mahavira and the Buddha both left high-caste homes (the Buddha, in fact, left a wife and small child). Shankara urged celibacy and skipping the two middle stages of the life cycle so that one could pursue liberation wholeheartedly. The wandering minstrels of bhakti clearly did little for their families' or towns' social stability. Since pleasure and wealth meant less than duty and liberation, they were less effective ties to temporal pursuits than they have been in other cultures. Thus, Hindu society was remarkably "unhistorical"—not simply in the sense that it kept relatively few records of temporal affairs but in the deeper sense that it defined itself by a striving for something that was not temporal.

Self

Obviously, the average Hindu did not think about the self in isolation from nature and society. The social caste-system and the cosmic samsara-transmigration system were the framework of any studious self-examination. Within this framework, however, an individual might set about the task of trying to attain *atmansiddhi*, the perfecting of human nature. This was another way, more concrete perhaps, of posing what *moksha* or the *mahatma* (the "great soul") meant.

In the *Rig-Veda*, *atmansiddhi* was the pious man who faithfully recited the hymns and made sacrifices to the gods.[78] The *Brahmanas* changed the ideal to the priest who could faultlessly conduct the expanded ritual. The Upanishads shifted perfection toward the acquisition of secret knowledge about reality. The *smriti* literature valued more worldly achievement. There the most excellent man was he who could rule public affairs and lead in community matters. The *Bhagavad Gita* spoke of love as the highest attainment, but it described the realized human personality as being stable in wisdom and having overcome the desires of both the flesh and ambition. Recently Indian saints such as Ramakrishna and Gandhi have stressed, respectively, the mystic loss of self in God and the service of Truth. Clearly, therefore, Hindu tradition allows the self many forms. Generally speaking, though, the ideal implies emotional, intellectual, and spiritual maturity and honors the social side of a human being as well as the solitary.

Hinduism's ideal self can also be analyzed by reviewing the stages of the life cycle. Studentship was a time for learning both tradition and self-mastery. From the guru the student learned what the scriptures and classics *meant*—how one could take them to heart and practice them. As well, living in poverty and practicing celibacy and obedience were intended to develop self-control, so that in later life one could do what one should and be master of one's passions.

The householder applied this education in experience and assumed responsibilities. Many Hindus have complained bitterly about child marriage,[79] arguing that it inhibited their ability to mature in a healthy fashion. This is certainly true for girls, and most boys as well. When they married at sensible ages, however, Indians had the chance to assume the responsibilities of being spouses, parents, and contributing members to society. They could pursue the lower goods, pleasure and prosperity, but within the higher dharma of their caste. If the emotional intensity profile of the family described earlier held true throughout history, the husband and wife were evidently not the prime relationship in the Hindu household. Rath-

er, marriage was intended more for raising children, continuing the family line, providing a place for the aged, and revering the departed ancestors than for the romantic fulfillment of the man and woman.

In the third stage of the life cycle, occurring after about twenty years of householdership, the self was to step away and reflect on what it had experienced. This custom reminds one of the Chinese saying "In office a Confucian, in retirement a Taoist." The "Confucian" mentality of the householder, concerned with practicalities, ought in the third *ashrama* (stage) to slowly yield to the "Taoist" mentality of contemplating nature's ways and nourishing one's poetic spirit. This corresponds to psychologist C. G. Jung's view that in the second half of life the personality tends to grow more reflective as it prepares for death and tries to accept what its life has amounted to thus far. In such reflection the lessons of youth are reviewed. As a youth one could hear the guru and try to take his teaching to heart, but that effort was bound to be shallow, because one did not have enough experience to know what the superficially simple precepts really meant. By the age of retirement, though, the reflective person could see that dharma really was necessary for personal and social order, because he had witnessed the chaos that follows when people do not fulfill their responsibilities.

However, we can only fully analyze the ultimate point to "forest dwelling," as the third stage was often called, by linking it with the final stage. The lessons of reflection were not part of an abstract or objective science of human behavior. Rather, one retired in order to care for the personal soul—to gain deliverance. Indians pictured the sage that emerged in the fourth stage, at the end of life, as a wandering ascetic. Stripped of goods and concerns, he moved freely in pursuit of *moksha* (or demonstrating its achievement). If, as a beggar, he was a social burden, he more than recompensed society by his example and teaching.

As we mentioned earlier, this final stress on *moksha* made Indian society "unhistorical." For more so than the West, India placed religion before all else. To be sure, *moksha* has parallels with the Western "unitive way," which ideally followed periods of penance and intellectual awakening. (And, to be sure, not all Indians were wholeheartedly religious.) But this Western scheme was intended primarily for monks and priests, not for laypersons as the four Hindu stages were.

The Upanishads jostled the classical life cycle for many. As we have seen, the Upanishadic self was the atman identified with Brahman. For this revered part of the Hindu tradition, then, the most important aspect of the self was the spiritual core. More than the body, this spiritual core was the key to escaping rebirth. If one was serious about escaping rebirth, why wait for the final stages of the life cycle? Why not cultivate the atman full-time? Some such reasoning surely prompted those who became wanderers long before old age. Whether through study or meditation, they pursued a way that implied that the self's needs or aspirations could outweigh social responsibilities.

To be sure, the sage or liberated person ultimately was a boon to society, which recognized this through its support of beggars and yogis. Still, there was a conflict between the freedom to pursue *moksha* full-time and the social expectancies of marriage and procreation. The Buddha's "great renunciation" crystallizes this tension. He wanted to pursue enlightenment, but his father wanted him to continue the family rule. So he had to sneak away in the night, renouncing social obligations.

Bhakti, too, jostled the serene four-stage life cycle in its assertion that love of the god was the ultimate value. Such love was apparently available to women and outcastes, as well as to men of high social status. The conceptions of heaven and hell of the bhakti sects varied and were often unclear, but the love of the personal god definitely became the way to both his grace and a happy afterlife. However, how this meshed with the traditional view of reincarnation is rather obscure.

For our interests, however, it seems clear that the bhakti movement indicated to individuals that the most important thing in their lives was not an ascetic withdrawal to achieve *moksha* but a passionate immersion in emotional love. Often this must have seemed like recompense to women for their having been left outside the official structure of the life cycle. By fasting, pilgrimages, prayers, and the performance of devotion *(puja)* in the home, women and others outside the structure could accomplish the essence of *moksha*—uniting themselves with a reality beyond samsara. When they took up bhakti, then, many Indians had good reason to reject the traditional ways. Their new treasure more than cast the elitist *moksha* in the shade.

In the last thousand years or so, the individual Hindu has therefore had a variety of ways of viewing his or her life journey. The four stages, the Upanishadic or bhakti wandering, the household devotions—any of these concepts could give their lives meaning. Hinduism explicitly recognized that people's needs differed by speaking of four *margas* that could lead to fulfillment and liberation. Among intellectuals, the way of knowledge was prestigious. In this *marga* one studied the classical texts, the Vedic *shruti* and commentators' *smriti*, pursuing an intuitive insight into reality. Shankara's higher knowledge is one version of this ideal. If one could gain the viewpoint where Brahman was the reality of everything, one had gained redeeming wisdom.

The Samkhya philosophical tradition had a dualistic viewpoint. By its elaboration of matter *(prakriti)* and spirit *(purusha)*, Samkhya gave sense experience more validity than Vedanta did. The reality of matter meant highlighting the three *gunas*, or constituent qualities, that comprise everything.[80] *Sattva*, *rajas*, and *tamas* tended toward virtue, passion, and dullness, respectively. The self was thus to strive for *sattva*'s rule.

So to strive, the self had to realize that there are only three reliable means of knowledge: perception, inference (reasoning), and

Figure 5   Dancing Krishna (Krishnagopal), thirteenth century, Chola period. Nelson Gallery-Atkins Museum (Nelson Fund).

outside the closed system of material nature or *prakriti* there is a contentless, transparent realm of spirit or *purusha*. The more one moved into the realm of *purusha*, the closer one came to *moksha* or deliverance from the entrapments of *prakriti*. From the fourth century c.e. on, numerous Indians pursued salvation according to these Samkyha guidelines.

But philosophy patently did not attract everyone, and many whom it did attract could not spare the time to study. Therefore, the way of *karma* (here understood as meaning works or action) better served many people. The *Bhagavad Gita* more than sanctioned this way, which amounted to a discipline of detachment. If one did one's daily affairs peacefully and with equanimity of spirit, then one would not be tied to the world of samsara. Doing just the work, without concern for its "fruits" (success or failure), one gave *karma* (here meaning the law of cause and effect) nothing to grasp. Gandhi, who was much taken with this teaching of the *Gita*, used spinning as an example of *karma-marga* or *karma-yoga* (work discipline). One just let the wheel turn, trying to join one's spirit to its revolutions and paying the quantity of production little heed. When *karma-yoga* was joined to the notion that one's work was a matter of caste obligation, or dharma, it became another powerful message that the status quo was holy and meaningful.

A third *marga* was meditation (*dhyana*), which meant some variant of the practices that Patanjali's *Yoga Sutras* sketch.[81] Contrasted with the way of knowledge, the way of meditation did not directly imply study and did not directly pursue intuitive vision. Rather, it was usually based on the conviction that one can reach the real self by quieting the senses and mental activity in order to descend without thinking to the personality's depths. In this progression, one approached a state of deep sleep and then went beyond it to nondualism. "Seedless *samadhi*" (pure consciousness) was the highest of the eight branches of yogic progress, but to enter *moksha* one had to

the instruction of gurus based on the Vedic texts. Using these three sources, the adherent of Samkyha tried to clarify the differences between pleasure and pain. Pleasure (quiet fulfillment, certitude) is the experiential effect of *sattva*. Pain (discomfort) is the experiential effect of *rajas*. Delusion (error) is the experiential effect of *tamas*. By analyzing these experiences, the adherent could lessen the influence of *tamas* and increase the influence of *sattva*. This in turn could help him come to realize that there is a solid basis for freedom, for it would suggest that leave even it behind. Along the way to *samadhi* one might acquire various paranormal powers (such as clairvoyance or telepathy), but these were of little account. Below even the subconscious one wished to rest without desire on the bottom of pure spirit. For the many who meditated, the way of *dhyana* usually meant peace, a great sensitivity to body-spirit relationships (through, for example, posture and breath control), and a deepening sense of the oneness of all reality.

Finally, bhakti had the status of a *marga*, and, according to the *Bhagavad Gita*, it could be a very high way. Of course, *bhaktas* ran the gamut from emotional hysteria to lofty mysticism. The *Gita* qualified the self-assertiveness justified by bhakti, however, by making its final revelation not human love of divinity but Krishna's love for humans. On the basis of such revelation, the *bhakta* was responding to divinity as divinity had shown itself to be. In other words, the *bhakta* was realizing human fulfillment by imitating God. (That was true of the yogi as well, which suggests that in India, as in other religious cultures, the self was finally an image of divinity.)

Divinity

Our final consideration is how Hinduism experienced and conceptualized divinity. This is no less complex than the dimensions of nature, society, and the self. In the early Vedic literature, the gods are principally natural phenomena. It is the wondrous qualities of the storm or fire that elevate Indra and Agni to prominence. By the time that the Brahmanic emphasis on sacrificial ritual dominated, the gods had come under human control. The final stage of Brahmanism was the view that the ritual, if properly performed, inevitably attains its goal—it compels the gods to obey. When we couple this subordinating view of the gods with the notion of samsara, the gods become less venerable than human beings. Human beings have the potential to break with samsara and to transcend the transmigratory realm in *moksha*. The gods, despite their heavenly estate, are still within the transmigratory realm and cannot escape into *moksha*.

The Upanishads, as we saw, moved away from the plurality of gods toward monism. One can debate whether this view is atheistic or religious, but the debate turns on semantics. However, both the Upanishads and the Vedanta philosophers stated that the knowledge of Brahman or atman is redemptive. Such knowledge, in other words, is not simply factual or scientific but has the power to transform one's life—it is light out of existential darkness. Therefore, from the side of the one who experiences Brahman's dominance, we can surely speak of "religious" (ultimately concerned) overtones.

As well, the place that Brahman has in the world view of the Upanishads and the Vedanta correlates with the place that God has in monotheism. Brahman is the basis of everything, if not the creator. It is the supreme value, because nothing is worth more than the ultimate being, which, once seen, sets all in light and order.

THE PROBLEM OF EVIL

For many Western observers, Indian philosophy has seemed strangely silent about the problem of evil. In these observers' eyes, the Hindu doctrine of rebirth shifted the problem of evil away from the Western orientation, in which an individual (like Job in the Bible) can accuse God of having dealt with her unjustly, having caused her to suffer through no fault of her own. Rebirth, coupled with the notion of karma, meant that one existed through long cycles of time whose overall justice was beyond human calculation, and that one's fate in a given lifetime was the result of one's actions in a previous existence. Thus there was no unmerited punishment and consequently no "problem" of evil. The gods did not have to justify themselves before innocent sufferers and evil was not a surd, irrational force corroding human sanity.

Recently Wendy Doniger O'Flaherty has challenged the simplicity of these Western assumptions:

> *Philosophers and theologians may set up their logical criteria, but a logical answer to an emotional question is difficult both to construct and to accept. The usual example of extraordinary evil given in Indian texts is the death of a young child. If one says to the parents of this child, "You are not real, nor is your son; therefore you cannot really be suffering," one is not likely to be of much comfort. Nor will the pain be dulled by such remarks as "God can't help it" or "God doesn't know about it." It is only the ethical hypothesis that is emotionally dispensable: God is not good, or God does not wish man to be without evil (two very different arguments). And this is the line most actively developed by Hindu mythological theodicy.*[82]

By "Hindu mythological theodicy" O'Flaherty means the effort one can find in the Hindu epics and devotional literature to justify God's ways, or the way things occur in the world. One of the early reasons why Hinduism developed an articulate response to the problem of evil was the attacks of the Buddhists, who found evil a soft spot in Hinduism's armor. Thus Buddhist texts satirically ask why the Hindu gods do not set the world straight. If Brahma, for instance, is lord of all things born, why are things so confused and out of joint? Why is there such unhappiness and deception? If we are honest, it seems as though Brahma ordained not dharma (a good working order) but adharma (chaos).

Hindu thinkers struggled to meet this challenge. In trying to understand evil, they tended to regard natural disasters, such as earthquakes, and moral wrongs, such as murder, as but two aspects of a single comprehensive phenomenon. Thus the Sanskrit term *papa* (evil) embraced both natural and moral evil. In the *Rig-Veda*, probably the moral sense prevails: People are evil-minded, committing adultery or theft. Still, the *Rig-Veda* does not necessarily see such evil as freely chosen. Moral evil or sin may occur without the sinner willing it. Therefore, one finds few prayers of personal repentance in the *Rig-Veda*, though numerous prayers for deliverance from the bad things other people can do. The *Atharva-Veda* also tends to blend natural and moral evils, and to see moral evil as an intellectual mistake rather than a culpable flaw in character. There are exceptions to these tendencies, such as the *Rig-Vedic* hymn of repentance to Varuna (5:85), but the overall inclination of the Vedic texts is to regard evil not as something we humans do but as what we do not wish to have done to us.

Although Hinduism tried out many different responses to the problem of evil, in O'Flaherty's opinion it favored myths that blamed God for evil (in contrast to the West's favorite myths, which blamed human beings). This gives Indian mythology a rather tragic tone. When it moves from the drama of creation to the pathos of creation's defects, the Indian imagination is inclined to picture reality as intrinsically misbuilt. The result is a world view in which evil is an integral factor. In the comprehensive system of this world, as enlightened minds perceive it, there is both the purity of healthy-minded people and the dirt of sick-minded people.

We can turn to the Vedas as a source of optimism, stressing healthy-mindedness, or to the Upanishads as a source of pessimism, stressing sick-mindedness. The Vedas emphasize benevolent gods whom one can invoke as aids in attaining heaven, while the Upanishads emphasize inadequate or even malevolent gods who are a central cause of our human problems.

In the subsequent tradition, through the epics and *Puranas*, one finds an integration of both emphases, a sort of dualism or unity of opposites: "Evil is recognized as horrible, death terrifying, heresy wicked, but these are accepted and integrated with the healthy goals of the Vedic lifeview."[83]

In our opinion, this traditional tendency would have enhanced the attraction of proposals to undercut the entire dualistic realm. *Moksha* would then have become an escape from a world in which tragedy was inevitable because evil was as aboriginal as good. The sages could say very little about the sort of life that *moksha* would bring, because all expressible experience was mottled by suffering. They intuited, however, that *moksha* was full of being, bliss, and awareness—an existence beyond evil's reach.

The two aspects of Brahman, finally, approximate what monotheistic religions have made of their God. Being beyond the human realm *(nirguna)*, Brahman recedes into mystery. This parallels the Christian God's quality of always being ineffable and inconceivable. But being within the human realm *(saguna)*, Brahman is the basis of nature and culture. In this way it approximates the Christian conception of the Logos, in whom all creation holds together.

Brahman, of course, is impersonal, whereas most monotheistic religions conceive their deities on the model of the human personality. If we free personality of its human limitations, however, Brahman might qualify as personal. Either way, it is the functional equivalent of the most comprehensive realities of other religions. Like the Chinese *Tao* it cannot be named, yet it mothers the ten thousand things. Like the Buddhist Suchness or Buddha-nature, it must be described in both absolute and relative terms.

The bhakti cults revered still another form of Hindu divinity. For the followers of Vishnu-Krishna or Shiva, the older type of henotheism (elevating one god to primacy of place) returns with a vengeance. Vaishnavites do not strictly deny the reality of Shiva or Brahma, nor do followers of these other gods deny the reality of Vishnu or Krishna. The mere fact that bhakti sects devoted to different gods contend among themselves shows that they take the other gods seriously. But the emotional ardor of the devoted *bhaktas* suggests that they grant their gods the ultimate value of a monotheistic God. The same holds for devotees of goddesses, who may actually outnumber devotees of the male gods. The Devi-mahatmya writings, for instance, have fashioned a warrior queen who is the equal of Vishnu.[84]

In Krishna's manifestation to Arjuna in the *Bhagavad Gita*, we can see how this monotheistic value took symbolic form. Krishna becomes the explosive energy of all reality. In the *Gita*, his theophany (manifestation of divinity) is the ultimate revelation of how divinity assumes many masks in space and time. Whatever reality is, Krishna is its dynamic source. Much like the Upanishadic Brahman, he is the one source capable of manifesting itself in many forms. But whereas the atmosphere of Brahman is serene and cool, the bhakti-prone Krishna is turbulent and hot. When J. Robert Oppenheimer, one of the developers of the American atom bomb, saw the first nuclear explosion, Krishna's dazzling self-revelation came to his mind. Thus, the Hindu divinity, like the Hebrew divinity of the chariot or the Zoroastrian divinity of the sacrifice, could be a refining fire.

This refining fire makes the world rise from and fall back into formlessness. As we have seen, the Trimurti of Brahma, Vishnu, and Shiva stands for creation, preservation, and destruction. Shiva himself, however, presides over life and death as the Lord of the Dance of Creation. The Shaivites, in this belief, indicate more clearly than the Vaishnavites how many Hindus retain a quite ancient notion of divinity.[85] Shiva is a complex reality, to be sure, but his ascetic and destructive aspects reflect quite ancient encounters with spiritual forces.

Through his *Shaktis* Kali and Durga, Shiva relates to grisly cults trafficking in corpses and skulls. Through his association with basic life forces, he is a link between *bhaktas* and the rude snake worshipers who still populate rural India. There is manifest in this wild god, therefore, another version of divinity's energy. In contrast to the Vedantic Brahman, Shiva is turbulent and hot, and his energy is as concrete and intrusive as its symbolic phallus. (There are equally concrete female deities. Unfortunately, scholars have not studied them as thoroughly.)[86]

KALI

One female deity whom scholars have studied thoroughly is Kali, the mistress of death. Part of the fascination Kali has evoked stems from her dreadful appearance. Usually she is portrayed in black, like a great storm cloud. Her tongue lolls, reminding the viewer that she has a great thirst for blood, and she shows fearsome teeth. Her eyes are sunken, but she smiles, as though enjoying a terrible secret. Round her neck is a garland of snakes, a half-moon rests on her forehead, her hair is matted, and often she licks a corpse. In her hand is apt to be a necklace of skulls. She has a swollen belly, girdled with snakes, and for earrings she has corpses. Her face projects a calm contentment, as if the savage realities of life, its evil and deathly aspects, suit her just fine.

Moreover, certain historic associations have besmirched Kali's name, linking her with some of the most loathsome, degenerate streams in Hindu culture. For example, she has been linked with blood sacrifices, including those of human beings, and she has served as the patron goddess of the Thugs, a vicious band of criminals that flourished from ancient times until the late nineteenth century and devoted themselves to strangling carefully selected victims as a way of honoring the goddess of death. (It is from this group that our English word *thug* has come.) Nonetheless, a careful study of Kali's full history as a major Hindu deity suggests that she has functioned as more than simply a lodestone for the soul's blacker passions.

First, Kali does not appear in the earliest Hindu texts, but comes on the scene fairly late. Second, throughout her history it is largely peripheral people, marginal groups, that populate her cults. Third, the geographic areas most devoted to Kali have been Bengal and the Vindhya Mountain region of south-central India. Fourth, when Kali became associated with the tantric cults her appearance changed, for a potential benevolence more clearly emerged.

Tantrism's concern with tapping libidinal energies led to the rise of many female deities from the seventh century C.E. on, and by the sixteenth century Kali was intimately connected with the more adventurous, "left-hand" tantric sects. For some important left-hand tantric sects, religion became a dramatic effort to conquer the fractured world and gain *moksha*. An indispensable ally in this effort was the *shakti* power of female divinity.

> *In his attempt to realize the nature of the world as completely and thoroughly pervaded by the one Sakti, the* sadhaka *(here called the hero,* vira) *undertakes the ritual known as* panca-tattva, *the ritual of the five ("forbidden") things (or truths). In a ritual context and under the supervision of his guru, the* sadhaka *partakes of wine, meat, fish, parched grain, and sexual intercourse. In this way he overcomes the distinction (or duality) of clean and unclean, sacred and profane, and breaks his bondage to a world artificially fragmented.*[87]

Kali is a personification of the most forbidden or truthful thing, death. Therefore, the tantric hero presses on to confront Kali, trying to transform her (death) into a vehicle of salvation. Consequently, the hero is apt to go to Kali's favorite dwelling place, the cremation grounds, meditate on each terrible aspect of her appearance, and try by penetrating her fearsomeness to pass beyond it. Translating the hero's rationale we might hear him say: "By embracing death with my every pore and synapse, I will make Kali rid me of all fear of death, all alienation from this death-infiltrated world."

It is doubtful that the average Hindu worshiper of Kali had such an adventurous, or highly conscious, rationale as that of our tantric hero, but the devotionalism of many followers, especially those from the Bengal area, shows a similar effort to make worship of the goddess a way to come to grips with life's worst features. Thus the poetry of Ramprasad (1718–1775), one of the most influential Bengali singers of Kali's praises, speaks of a mother who makes those attached to her as mad as she is. Ramprasad begs Kali to deal with him as a mother and help him accept her wild, incomprehensible behavior. As the *Bhagavad Gita* swells the figure of Krishna, so that he becomes coextensive with the whole of mysterious creation, so Ramprasad swells the figure of Kali, so that she becomes coextensive with the whole of mysterious creation. By remaining devoted to her, despite her forbidding appearance, the poet expresses a blind faith that somehow, sometime, life will show itself to have been worth living.

Ramakrishna (1834–1886), another very influential Bengali devotee of Kali, taught much the same message, but in more ecstatic and joyful terms. Going out of himself in adoration of the goddess, Ramakrishna pointed to a realm beyond good and evil, beyond all the dichotomies we make in everyday life. This is a realm where the deepest forces of death and life intermingle, moving the world to a rhythm only divinity can comprehend.

Figure 6   Nrtta-Ganapati (Dancing Ganesha) from Rajasthan, North Central India, tenth century. Nelson Gallery-Atkins Museum (Nelson Fund).

Indian divinity thus has many levels and many facets. It follows that Hinduism itself has many forms and many values, since the concept of divinity is the heart of any religion. In our opinion, the dimensions of nature, society, and the self are subordinate to the dimension of divinity, since the last determines the places of the first three. In other words, Hindus arrange nature, society, and the self in view of the Agni, Brahma, or Krishna who centers their lives in mystery. If Brahma is the divinity, then nature, society, and the self are all versions of maya, are all illusion and play. If Agni, the god to whom one directs the fire sacrifice, is the divinity, then nature stands by divine heat, society stands by priestly sacrificers, and the self strives after *tapas* (ascetic heat) or lives by ritual mantras (verbal formulas for controlling the divine forces). Finally, if Shiva is the divinity, then divinity destroys castes, is the arbiter of life and death, and reduces the self to a beggar for grace.

Nevertheless, one could begin with the view of nature, society, or the self and develop what divinity and the other two subordinate dimensions meant. In other words, cosmology, sociology, and psychology have their legitimate places in religious analysis.

However, historians of religion believe that no system of interpretation can truly substitute for the system that the religion itself implicitly uses. In other words, we cannot reduce the religions to their cosmological, sociological, or psychological factors. They must remain essentially what they claim to be: ways emanating from and leading to the divine. For this reason, the concept of divinity in a religion will always be the most crucial concept. God or ultimate reality is by definition the ultimate shaper of a world view, because divinity determines the placement of the other dimensions and thus the world view. Having had many forms of divinity, Hinduism has had many world views.

Study Questions

1. What does the Harrapan proto-Shiva suggest about pre-Vedic Indian religion?
2. Why did Vedic religion come to stress sacrifice?
3. How could Upanishadic knowledge bring salvation?
4. Can you translate *moksha* into terms that your contemporaries would find attractive?
5. In what sense did *bhakti* personalize Hindu divinity?
6. Does the status of Indian women through the ages wholly discredit Hinduism?
7. To what extent could we adapt the classical Hindu life cycle to the needs of Americans today?
8. Does Indian religion show that ultimate reality is at least as much impersonal as personal?
9. Explain the significance of Kali.
10. Why would you like or not like to be a disciple of Ma Jnanananda?
11. How satisfactory is the Hindu view that evil is an intrinsic part of this world?

Chapter Two

BUDDHISM: TWENTY-FIVE KEY DATES

536–476 B.C.E.	BUDDHA
519	GAUTAMA'S ENLIGHTENMENT
473	FIRST BUDDHIST CONGRESS
363	SECOND BUDDHIST CONGRESS
273–236	REIGN OF BUDDHIST EMPEROR ASOKA
236	RISE OF MAHAYANA TRADITION
160	*PRAJNA-PARAMITA* LITERATURE
80	LOTUS SUTRA; BUDDHIST DECLINE IN INDIA
CA. 200 C.E.	NAGARJUNA, LEADING PHILOSOPHER
220–552	MISSIONS TO VIETNAM, CHINA, KOREA, BURMA, JAVA, SUMATRA, JAPAN
430	BUDDHAGHOSA, LEADING PHILOSOPHER
594	BUDDHISM PROCLAIMED JAPANESE STATE RELIGION

Buddhism

Buddhism arose in India when a strong, enlightened personality, Siddhartha Gautama, persuasively proposed a better way to structure individual and social life than did contemporary Brahmanistic Hinduism. Moreover, his contemporaries were sufficiently impressed to institutionalize his teaching and assure its survival. Where Buddhism survived and most prospered, however, was not the Enlightened One's native land; in India Hindu devotionalism and then Islam proved more powerful than Gautama's "middle way." Missionary Buddhism kept the Way alive and developing. Consequently, we will begin with a description of Buddhism in Thailand and Japan today.

APPEARANCE

Bangkok is a lovely city of Buddhist temples. Both its past history and its present culture reflect the deep influence of the Buddha. Similarly Kyoto, the ancient Japanese capital, is still a living example of Buddhist culture.

Were you to visit the Imperial Compound in Bangkok (Figure 7), you might well consider your air fare a bargain. The vivid blue sky sets off a complex of shrines and government buildings whose beauty is so overwhelming that one can only call the compound a jewel. First of all, it is brilliantly colorful. The slanted roofs of the buildings, which seem midway between Indian and Chinese styles, are of orange, blue, and green enamel tile. Their sharply angled gold peaks and corners represent Garuda, the giant bird who flies Buddhas and emperors on their celestial journeys. In some portions of the compound many small shrines run together, connected by porticoes. The shrines contain relics of holy persons or worthy benefactors. At their entrances, two fierce protector spirits usually stand guard; they can be ten feet tall and have the bulging eyes and ready swords of folk mythology. They are at once amusing and instructive, three-dimensional cartoons and object lessons in religious imagination.

In other corners of the compound delicate spires curlicue skyward, like gold-dipped cones of soft ice cream. Within the most celebrated Thai shrine, that of the Emerald Buddha, dozens of monks, devout laity, and slightly confused tourists kneel or pad softly in stocking feet. The Emerald Buddha is perhaps four feet high and carved in jade. He is dressed according to the season, being naked in the summer and covered with a little shawl when the weather is cool. The devotion to him is a mixture of aesthetic appreciation for his artistic rendering in precious stone and genuine religious veneration of the light and fulfillment that he represents.

In Kyoto many temples vie for the tourist's favor. The Moss Temple first beckons as a respite from the summer heat and city turmoil. Many shades of green vegetation slow one's pace, encouraging a return to the simple beauties of natural growth. Passing the small tea cottage near the first bend in the green stream prompts one to think of the exquisite ceremonies that Buddhism nurtured. Taking tea in a disciplined, simple ceremony acts out the immediacy and the flow of the world made apparent through enlightenment. Delighting in bamboo and rough stones, Japanese have venerated nature since prehistoric times, joining this attitude to their Buddhist sense for the unity of life, the cycles of the samsaric wheel.

Kyoto's Zen Rock Garden is likewise an education in Buddhism. The empty space around the rocks (the expanse of raked sand) teaches as much about emptiness as most sutras can. Indeed, even Westerners contemplating the angular rocks learn of the relation between the bare and the penetrating. Such contemplation recalls Zen master Ikkyu's response to a layperson who asked him how to make progress: "Attention."[1] Close attention to the sand and the rocks works a peculiar purification.

The rival for the Rock Garden's preeminence in Kyoto is probably the Golden Pavilion Temple (Figure 8). There the pond

Figure 7   Temples of the Imperial Compound, Bangkok. Photo by J. T. Carmody.

characteristic of Buddhist temple grounds perfectly mirrors a three-story frame structure gilded with gold. On a clear day it produces a double image of peaceful beauty. Perhaps recalling Hua-yen Buddhism's use of mirror imagery to show the connectedness of all things, the visitor at the Golden Pavilion starts to wonder about image and reality, about how things appear and what they really are. The pond is so pleasing yet varies so with the seasons that it joins beauty and change in a yearly ballet. When the cherry blossoms bloom around the pagoda, Buddha-nature (ultimate reality) dons pale pink. When the snow settles on the frozen pond, Buddha-nature is pure white. Gardeners can manipulate the blossoms and the snow, but much in the present is out of human hands. The Golden Pavilion teaches this lesson very gently.

HISTORY

The Buddha

The Buddha was born about 560 B.C.E. in the town of Kapilavastu in what is now a part of Nepal just below the Himalayan foothills. His people were a warrior tribe called Sakyas and his clan name was Gautama. The religious climate in which he grew up was quite heated. Some objectors were challenging the dominance of the priestly brahmin class. As we saw in the last chapter, the writers of the early Upanishads reveal the dissatisfaction with sacrifice that was burning among intellectuals, while the accounts of the Mahavira are evidence of the ascetic movement that also challenged the priestly religion of sacrifice. In secular culture, the sixth century B.C.E. saw a movement from

Figure 8   The Golden Pavilion Temple, Kyoto. Photo by J. T. Carmody.

tribal rule toward small-scale monarchy, a growth in urban populations, the beginnings of money-based economies, the beginnings of government bureaucracies, and the rise of a wealthy merchant class.[2] Thus, the Buddha grew up in a time of rapid change, when people were in turmoil over religion and open to new teachings.

Pious myth heavily embellishes the accounts of the Buddha's birth and early life, so it is difficult to describe this period of his life accurately. Legend has it that his father, Suddhodana, was a king, and that he received a revelation that his child would be a world ruler if the child stayed at home but a spiritual saviour if the child left home. According to other legends, the Buddha passed from his mother's side without causing her any pain, stood up, strode seven paces, and announced, "No more births for me!"[3] In other words, the child would be a spiritual conquerer—an Enlightened One.

As the Buddha grew, his father surrounded him with pleasures and distractions in order to keep him in the palace and away from the sights of ordinary life. When the Buddha came of age, the father married him to a lovely woman named Yasodhara. So Sakyamuni ("sage of the Sakyas") lived in relative contentment until his late twenties. By the time of his own son's birth, however, the Buddha was restless. (He named the child Rahula [fetter].)

What really precipitated Sakyamuni's religious crisis, though, was an experience he had outside the palace. On several outings he met people who were aged, diseased, or dead. They shocked him severely, and he became anxiety ridden. How could anyone take life lightly if these were its constant dangers? Meditating on age, disease, and death, the young prince decided to cast away his round of pleasures and solve the riddle of life's meaning by becoming a wandering beggar. Renouncing his wife, child, father, and goods, he set off to answer his soul's yearning.

The teachers to whom the Buddha first apprenticed himself specialized in meditation and asceticism. Their meditation, it appears, was a yogic pursuit of enlightenment through *samadhi* (trance). From them the Buddha learned much about the levels of consciousness but was not fully satisfied. The teachers could not bring him to dispassion, tranquillity, enlightenment, or nirvana (a state of liberation beyond samsara). In other words, the Buddha wanted a direct perception of how things are and a complete break with the realm of space, time, and rebirth.

To attain these goals, Sakyamuni turned to asceticism to such a degree that he almost starved himself. The texts claim that when he touched his navel, he could feel his backbone. In any event, asceticism did not bring what Sakyamuni sought either. (Because of this, he and his followers have always urged moderation in fasting and bodily disciplines. Theirs, they like to say, is a middle way between indulgence and severity that strives to keep the body healthy, as a valuable ally should be, and to keep the personality from excessive self-concern.)

What liberated the Buddha, apparently, was recalling moments of peace and joy from his childhood, when he had sat in calm but perceptive contemplation. According to the traditional accounts, Mara, the personification of evil or death, tried to tempt Buddha (who sat meditating under a fig tree) away from this pursuit.[4] First, he sent a host of demons, but the Buddha's merit and love protected him. Then, with increased fear that this contemplator might escape his realm, the evil one invoked his own power. However, when Mara called on his retinue of demons to witness his power, the Buddha, who was alone, called on mother earth, which quaked in acknowledgement. As a

last ploy, Mara commissioned his three daughters (Discontent, Delight, and Desire) to seduce the sage. But they, too, failed, and Mara withdrew. (Psychological interpretation can illuminate the details of this legend when they are considered as symbols of dramatic changes in the personality—the challenges, fears, resistance, and final breakthrough.)

Enlightenment

The *enlightenment* (realization of the truth) itself occurred on a night of the full moon. According to tradition, Buddha ascended the four stages of trance. In later times these four stages were considered as a progressive clarification of consciousness: (1) detachment from sense objects and calming the passions; (2) nonreasoning and "simple" concentration; (3) dispassionate mindfulness and consciousness with bodily bliss; and (4) pure awareness and peace without pain, elation, or depression.[5]

According to tradition, then, one progressed in a contemplative sitting by moving from confusion and sense knowledge to pure, unemotional awareness. The assumption was that this progress facilitated direct perception of reality—seeing things as they really are. It might bring in its train magical powers (the ability to walk on water, to know others' minds, or to remember one's previous lives, for instance), but its most important achievement was to eliminate desire, wrong views, and ignorance, which are the bonds that tie one to samsara. To break them is therefore to free consciousness for nirvana.

Another traditional way of describing the Buddha's enlightenment is to trace his progress through the night. During the first watch (evening), he acquired knowledge of his previous lives. This is a power that some shamans claim, so it is not Buddha's distinguishing achievement. During the second watch (midnight), he acquired the "divine eye" with which he surveyed the karmic state of all beings—the dying and rebirth cycle that is their destiny. With this vision

The Eightfold Path outlines the lifestyle that Buddha developed for people who accepted his teaching and wanted to pursue nirvana. As such, it is more detailed than a description of what Buddha directly experienced in enlightenment—something that he probably elaborated on later. The explanation of reality that Buddha developed out of enlightenment, which became known as the doctrine of dependent coarising, also came later. It explains the causal connections that link all beings.

Enlightenment seems to have been the dramatic experience of vividly perceiving that life, which Sakyamuni had found to consist of suffering, had a solution. One could escape the terror of aging, sickness, and death by withdrawing one's concerns for or anxieties about them—by no longer desiring youth, health, or even life itself. By withdrawing in this manner, one gave karma nothing to which to cling, for desire was the means by which karma kept the personality on the wheel of dying and rebirth. Removing desire therefore took away karma's hold. To destroy desire for karmic existence, though, one had to penetrate the illusion of its goodness. That is, one had to remove the ignorance that makes sensual pleasures, financial success, prestige, and so on, seem good. Buddha designed the Eightfold Path and the doctrine of dependent coarising in order to remove ignorance and rout desire.

Figure 9   Head of Buddha, third to fifth century, c.e. *Nelson Gallery-Atkins Museum (Nelson Fund).*

he realized that good deeds beget good karma and a move toward freedom from this destiny, while bad deeds beget bad karma and a deeper entrenchment in samsara. The second achievement made Buddha a moralistic philosopher, insofar as he saw the condition of all beings as a function of their ethical or unethical behavior.

During the third watch (late night), the Buddha reached the peak of perception, attaining "the extinction of the outflows" (the stopping of desire for samsaric existence) and grasping the essence of what became the Four Noble Truths: (1) All life is suffering; (2) the cause of suffering is desire; (3) stopping desire will stop suffering; and (4) the Eightfold Path (explained below) is the best way to stop desire.

Dependent Coarising and the Eightfold Path

Often Buddhists picture dependent coarising as a wheel with twelve sections or a chain with twelve links (the first and the last are joined to make a circuit).[6] These twelve links explain the round of samsaric existence. They are not an abstract teaching for the edification of the philosophical mind, but an extension of the essentially therapeutic analysis that the Buddha thought would cure people of their basic illness.

The wheel of dependent coarising turns in this way: (1) Aging and dying depend on rebirth; (2) rebirth depends on becoming;

(3) becoming depends on the appropriation of certain necessary materials; (4) appropriation depends on desire for such materials; (5) desire depends upon feeling; (6) feeling depends upon contact with material reality; (7) contact depends on the senses; (8) the senses depend on "name" (the mind) and "form" (the body); (9) name and form depend on consciousness (the spark of sentient life); (10) consciousness shapes itself by karma; (11) the karma causing rebirth depends on ignorance of the Four Noble Truths; and (12) therefore, the basic cause of samsara is ignorance.

One can run this series forward and back, but the important concept is that ignorance (of the Four Noble Truths) is the cause of painful human existence, and that aging and dying are its final overwhelming effects and the most vivid aspects of samsara. Thus, the chain of dependent coarising is a sort of practical analysis of human existence. It mingles concepts of physical phenomena (for example, aging and dying depend on rebirth) and concepts of psychological phenomena (for example, appropriation depends on desire). The result is called *dependent coarising* (or origination) because it is a doctrine of mutual causality.

In the Buddha's enlightenment, as he and his followers elaborated upon it, there is no single cause of the way things are. Rather, all things are continually rotating in this twelve-stage wheel of existence. Each stage of the wheel passes the power of movement along to the next. The only way to step off the wheel, to break the chain, is to gain enlightenment and so detach the stage of ignorance. If we do detach ignorance, we stand free of karma, karmic consciousness, and so on, all the way to aging and rebirth.

The result of enlightenment, then, is no rebirth, which is the implication of nirvana. Nirvana is the state in which the chain of existence does not obtain—in which desire is "blown out" and one escapes karma and samsara. Thus, nirvana begins with enlightenment and becomes definitive with death. By his enlightenment, for instance, the Buddha had broken the chain of dependent co-

arising; at his death his nirvana freed him from rebirths.

The Eightfold Path (which is the Fourth Noble Truth) details how we may dispel ignorance and gain nirvana[7] by describing a middle way between sensuality and extreme asceticism that consists of (1) right views, (2) right intention, (3) right speech, (4) right action, (5) right livelihood, (6) right effort, (7) right mindfulness, and (8) right concentration. "Right views" means knowledge of the Four Noble Truths. "Right intention" means dispassion, benevolence, and refusal to injure others. "Right speech" means no lying, slander, abuse, or idle talk. "Right action" means not taking life, stealing, or being sexually disordered. "Right livelihood" is an occupation that does not harm living things; thus, butchers, hunters, fishers, and sellers of weapons or liquor are proscribed. "Right effort" avoids the arising of evil thoughts. In "right mindfulness," awareness is disciplined so that it focuses on an object or idea to know its essential reality. "Right concentration" focuses on a worthy object of meditation.

The first two aspects of the Eightfold Path, right views and right intention, comprise the wisdom portion of the Buddhist program. If we know the Four Noble Truths and if we orient ourselves toward them with the right spiritual disposition, then we are wise and come to religious peace. Tradition groups aspects three, four, and five under morality.[8] To speak, to act, and to make one's living in wise ways amount to an ethics for nirvana, a morality that will liberate one from suffering. Finally, aspects six, seven, and eight entail meditation. By setting consciousness correctly through right effort, mindfulness, and concentration, one can perceive the structures of reality and thus personally validate the Buddha's enlightened understanding.[9]

The three divisions of the Eightfold Path compose a single entity, a program in which each of the three parts reinforces the other two. Wisdom sets up the game plan, the basic theory of what the human condition is and how one is to cope with it. Morality applies wisdom to daily life by specifying how one should speak, act, and support oneself. Regular meditation focuses one on the primary truths and the reality to which they apply. In meditation the Buddhist personally appropriates the official wisdom, personally examines the ethical life. As a result, meditation builds up the Buddhist's spiritual force, encouraging the peaceful disposition necessary for a person to be nonviolent and kindly.[10]

The Dharma

Buddhists have seen in Sakyamuni's enlightenment the great act founding their religion. The Buddha is worthy of following because in enlightenment he became flooded with knowledge *(bodhi)*. What he saw under the Bodhi Tree in the third watch was nothing less than the formula for measuring life and curing its mortal illness. The Four Noble Truths and dependent coarising are two favorite ways of presenting the essential truths of Buddha's knowledge.

Buddha himself apparently debated what to do after achieving enlightenment. On the one hand, he had this dazzling light, this potent medicine, to dispense. On the other hand, there was dreary evidence that humanity, mired in its attachments, would find his teaching hard to comprehend and accept.[11] Legend says that the god Brahma appeared to the Buddha and pleaded that the Enlightened One teach what he had seen for the sake of wayward humanity. Out of compassion (which became the premier Buddhist virtue), the Enlightened One finally agreed to Brahma's request.

According to tradition, his first sermon occurred in Deer Park near Benares, about five days' walk from Gaya, where enlightenment took place. He preached first to some former ascetic companions who had rejected him when he turned away from their harsh mortification, and his calm bearing won them over. What Buddha first preached was the Four Noble Truths, but he apparently prefaced his preaching with a solemn declaration of his authority as an immortal enlightened one. From this preface Buddhists have concluded that one must have faith in the authority behind the *dharma* (the teaching) if the dharma is to have its intended effect.

THE FIRE SERMON

Opening ourselves to the Buddha's authority, let us imagine that we are listening to his famous Fire Sermon.

The Buddha was following his customary pattern, dwelling in one place as long as seemed profitable and then moving on to the next. So, having finished a stint in Uruvela, he set out for the town of Gaya Head. With him went a great band of priests. When they got to Gaya Head, the Blessed One addressed the priests as follows:

O priests, all things are on fire. The eye is on fire, as are the forms the eye receives, the consciousness the eye raises, the impressions the eye transmits, the sensations—pleasant, unpleasant, or indifferent—that the eye's impressions produce.

All that has to do with our seeing is on fire.

And in what does this fire consist? It consists in the flame of passion, the burning of hate, the heat of infatuation. Birth, old age, death, sorrow, lamentation, misery, grief, and despair are all expressions of the fire that comes into us through our eyes.

In the same way, the ear is on fire with burning sounds. The nose is on fire with burning odors. The tongue is on fire with flaming tastes. The whole body is on fire with flaming touches. Even worse, the mind is on fire: hot ideas, burning awareness, searing impressions, smoldering sensations. Again I say, the fire of passion, birth, old age, death, sorrow, lamentation, misery, grief, and despair is burning you up.

What, then, should you do? If you are wise, O priests, you will conceive an aversion for the eye and the eye's forms, the eye's consciousness, the eye's impressions, and the eye's sensations, be they pleasant, unpleasant, or indifferent. If you are wise, you will conceive an aversion for the ear and its sounds, the nose and its odors, the tongue and its tastes, the body and the things it touches, the mind and all that passes through it.

If you conceive this aversion, you will divest yourselves of passion. Divesting yourselves of passion, you will become free. Being free, you will become aware of your liberation and know that you have exhausted rebirth. This will prove that you have lived the holy life, fulfilled what it behooved you to do, and made yourselves subject to this world no longer.

When the Buddha finished his sermon, many of the priests' minds became free from attachment and were delivered of their depravities.[12]

What, though, about ourselves, twentieth-century hearers of the Buddha? Can the Fire Sermon carry across 2500 years? Many Buddhists think it can. After all, we are still possessed of eyes, ears, nose, tongue, and hands eager to touch. We are still the strange animals possessed of minds flowing with ideas, reflex awareness, sensations to drive our days and bedevil our nights. As with the Buddha's contemporaries, unless we have these faculties under control, we are burning with useless passions. If our senses lead us, instead of our leading them, we are bound hand and mind.

Look around you. See how many of your contemporaries rush like lemmings to the sea. Some rush after money. Others rush after pleasure. A third group hustles to gain power. From dawn to midnight, their brains teem with schemes, images of success, numbers adding up to bigger and bigger bank accounts. Do they not seem feverish? Is there not within them a fire wisdom would have to douse?

And how could wisdom go about dousing this fire? Could it not scoop up the old Buddhist verities, the millennial lessons in detachment? "If you want peace," Buddhist wisdom continues to say, "you must gain control over your senses and your mind. To gain control over your senses and your mind, you must detach yourself from their blandishments. Not every image that floats before your mind is profitable. Not every lissome limb or attractive scheme brings you good. Indeed, few images, limbs, or schemes conduce to your peace and freedom. Unless you have conquered your passions, most visitors to your soul will do you harm."

How pressing is this teaching? That depends on how seriously you take human death. If you think your basic task before death is gaining enlightenment, wisdom to free you from death's hold, you will find the Buddha's teaching pressing. If you do not think your basic task is gaining enlightenment, you will let the Buddha's teaching pass by. The Buddha's own criterion for evaluating your state likely would focus on your degree of inner pain. If you find your current circumstances depressing, and you long deeply to change who you are, you are apt to be open to the dharma. The Enlightened One wrested his wisdom from struggles with sadness and discontent; so can you. His wisdom means little to those content with their lot, happy to eat, drink, and be merry. For them the wheel must turn again. They need a deeper experience of life's burning.

The Buddha's preaching won him innumerable converts, men and women alike, many of whom decided to dedicate their lives to following him and his way. A great number entered the *sangha*, or monastic order, assuming a life of celibacy, poverty, and submission to rules of discipline.[13] Other followers decided to practice the dharma while remaining in their lay state, and they frequently gave the Buddha and the

Buddhist community land and money.[14] In both cases people became Buddhists by taking "refuge" in the three "jewels" of the Enlightened One's religion: the Buddha himself, the teaching (dharma), and the community (*sangha* can mean either the monastic community or the entire community of Buddhists, lay and monastic, past and present).[15]

By uttering three times the vow of taking refuge, one became a follower in a strict, official sense. (This act reflects the special, almost magical effect that words had in ancient India. When the Buddha preached, just as when the Vedic priests uttered sacrificial formulas, an active force was believed to be unleashed. When one took refuge, the words effected a binding to the Buddha, the teaching, and the community.)

In time a catechism developed to explain the Buddha's teaching. One of the catechism's most important notions was the "three marks" of reality. Together with the Four Noble Truths and dependent coarising, the three marks have helped countless Buddhists hold the dharma clearly in mind. According to this conception, all reality is painful, fleeting, and selfless. This formula adds something to the insights of the Four Noble Truths. That all life or reality is painful is the first truth: the reality of suffering. By this Buddhists do not mean that one never experiences pleasant things or that one has no joy. Rather, they mean that no matter how pleasant or joyous one's life, it is bound to include disappointment, sickness, misunderstanding, and finally death. Since the joyous things do not last, even they have an aspect of painfulness.

Second, all life is fleeting, or passing. Everything changes—nothing stays the same. Therefore, realistically there is nothing to which we can cling, nothing that we can rely on absolutely. In fact, even our own realities (our "selves") change. On one level, we move through the life cycle from youth to old age. On a more subtle level, our thoughts, our convictions, and our emotions change.

Third, there is no self. For Buddhists, the fleetingness of our own consciousness proves that there is no atman—no solid soul or self. In this the Buddhists directly opposed Hinduism as well as common belief. All people, it seems, naturally think that they have personal identities. Buddhists claim that personalities consist of nothing solid or permanent. We are but packages of physical and mental stuff that is temporarily bound together in our present proportions.

The tradition calls the component parts of all things *skandhas* (heaps), which number five: body, feeling, conception, karmic disposition, and consciousness. Together the *skandhas* make the world and the person of appearances, and they also constitute the basis for clinging to existence and rebirth. To cut through the illusion of a self is therefore the most important blow that one can strike against ignorance. This is done by being open to the flowing character of all life and decisively pursuing nirvana.

The three marks of reality summarize why the wise person does not desire sentient existence, which is the cloth of which nightmares are made. Therefore, the learned and the noble are averse to the works of the senses and the mind, and turn toward what cools the body and the consciousness. In so doing they become free from this painful world. Like the Enlightened One himself, they move with the grace of detachment, the serenity of one who possesses peace.

The early teachers described the realms of rebirth to which humans were subject and in so doing developed a Buddhist version of the Indian cosmic powers and zones of the afterlife. Essentially, the Buddhist wheel of rebirth can occupy any of six realms or destinies. Three are lower realms (hells), which are karmic punishment for bad deeds. The other three are higher realms (heavens) in which good deeds are rewarded. The lowest hell is for punishing the wicked by means befitting their particular crimes. However, these punishments are not eternal; after individuals have paid their karmic debt, they can reenter the human realm by rebirth. Above the lowest hell is the station of the "hungry ghosts," who wander the earth's surface begging for food. The third and least severe realm of the wicked is that of animals. If one is reborn in that realm, one suffers the abuses endured by dumb beasts.

The fortunate destinies reward good karma. The human realm is the first, and in it one can perform meritorious deeds. Since one can only earn merit as a human being, this realm is the most decisive for one's destiny. Even entering nirvana from a heavenly realm above the human is made possible through merit developed in a previous existence as a human.

The two final realms are those of the demigods (Titans) and the gods proper. Both include a variety of beings, all of whom are subject to rebirth. Since even the Buddhist gods are subject to rebirth, their happiness is not at all comparable to the final bliss of nirvana. Better to be a human being advancing toward enlightenment than a divinity liable to the pains of another transmigratory cycle. Perhaps for that reason, the Buddhist spirits and divinities, as well as the Buddhist ghosts and demons, seem inferior to the human being. Apparently Buddhism adopted wicked and good spirits from Indian culture without much thought. In subjecting these spirits to the powers of an *arhat* (one who achieves nirvana), however, Buddhists minimized their fearsomeness.

Despite its sometimes lurid description of the six realms, the dharma basically stated that each individual is responsible for his or her own destiny. The future is neither accidental, fated, nor determined by the gods. If one has a strong will to achieve salvation, a day of final triumph will surely come. As a result, karma is less an enslavement than an encouragement. If one strives to do good deeds (to live by the dharma in wisdom-morality-meditation), one cannot fail to progress toward freedom. At the least, one will come to life again in more favorable circumstances. Thus, Buddhism ousts the gods and the fates from control over human destiny. This is interesting sociologically, because Buddhism has been most appealing to people who have wanted control over their own lives, such as warriors and merchants.

The simpler folk, who might have to spur themselves to such a sober and confident state of mind, drew encouragement from Buddhist art, which illustrates the delights of heaven and the torments of hell. Many renditions of the wheel of life, for instance, show Mara (Death) devouring the material world and those who cling to it. In the center of the wheel are such symbolic animals as the cock (desire), the snake (hatred), and the pig (delusion), who work to keep the wheel turning.[16] "Break with these," the art shouts. "Rise up. You have nothing to lose but your chains."

The dharma, therefore, began as a proclamation of diagnosis and cure. Likening himself to a doctor, the Buddha told his followers not to lose themselves in extraneous questions about where karma or ignorance comes from. Furthermore, he told them not to concentrate on whether the world is eternal or how to conceive of nirvana. To ponder such issues, said the Buddha, would be like a man severely wounded with an arrow who refuses treatment until he knows the caste and character of the man who shot him. The point is to get the arrow out. Similarly, the point to human existence is to break the wheel of rebirth, to slay the monstrous round of suffering, fleetingness, and emptiness.

For about forty-five years after his enlightenment, the Buddha preached variants on his basic themes: the Four Noble Truths, dependent coarising, and the three marks. His sangha grew, as monks, nuns, and laypersons responded to his simple, clear message. At his death he had laid the essential foundation of Buddhism—its basic doctrine and way of life. Thus, his death *(parinirvana)* came in the peace of trance. The physical cause of his death was either pork or mushrooms (depending on which commentator one reads), but in the Buddhist view the more profound cause was the Buddha's sense of completeness. When he asked his followers for the last time whether they had any questions, all stood silent. So he passed into trance and out of this painful realm. According to legend, the earth quaked and the sky thundered in final tribute.

Early Buddhism

After the Buddha's death his followers gathered to codify the dharma, which he had said should be their leader after him. According to tradition, they held a council at Rajagraha during the first monsoon season after the *parinirvana* to settle both the dharma and the Vinaya (the monastic rules). The canon of Buddhist scriptures that we now possess supposedly is the fruit of this council. However, textual analysis suggests that the dharma was transmitted orally for perhaps three centuries. Today the Pali canon (the authoritative collection of materials in the Indian vernacular that the Theravadins use) consists of five *nikayas*, which are collections of discourses (sutras), that the Buddha supposedly preached. Just one of these collections, the middle-length *Majjhima Nikaya*, runs to 1100 pages in modern printing.

In addition to these sutras and the monastic rules, early Buddhists added to the canon the *Abhidhamma* treatises of the early philosophers, who tried to analyze reality by correlating the Buddha's teaching with the experiences of meditation. Therefore, the Buddhist tendency in forming a canon (etymologically, a ruler) by which to measure faith and doctrine was to be as comprehensive as possible.

Because the *Abhidhamma* treatises greatly influenced subsequent Buddhist philosophy, especially in Theravadan countries such as Burma, it is useful to know their general nature. Although they are based on the doctrine attributed to the Buddha in his general discourses, they treat this doctrine in a highly analytic way. This leads to a language that is both technical and abstract, the sort of language scholars use when they are communicating with one another and do not

have to apply their ideas to everyday life. For example, the treatises seldom refer to specific individuals, concrete events, or the daily problems of exercising one's religion in the world. They rather content themselves with schematizing the traditional materials of the philosophical discourses and monastic legislation, for the sake of professionals interested in maps of the main tracts.

Two kinds of questions dominate the *Abhidhamma* treatises. The first deals with consciousness, paying special attention to how we become aware of things, what passes through the mind, the ways that sensations, thoughts, and emotions interact, and similar mentally oriented questions. The second kind of question concerns the relationships among things. This is more outward-looking, and it assumes that reality is a network of interrelations. So, for example, *Y* may exist because of *X*, in a straightforward cause-effect relation. On the other hand, *Y* may only be conditioned by *X*—shaped or influenced, but not caused. The *Abhidhamma* is fascinated by such metaphysical and logical relations. Nonetheless, true to the generally practical slant of Buddhism, *Abhidhamma* scholars tried to justify their work as an aid to liberation. If one knows the map of the mind, they argued, one can more easily liberate the mind.

However, within 100 years of the Buddha's death, dissensions (primarily over doctrine) split the sangha.[17] These were the precursors of the major division of Buddhism into the Theravadin and Mahayana schools, which we shall consider below. The apparent forerunners of the Mahayana schools were the Mahasanghikas, who seem to have favored the laity's interests, while the Sthaviras (Elders), the precursors of the Theravadins, stressed the authority of the monks. About 200 years after the Buddha's death the Pudgalavadins branched off of the Sthaviras; they taught that there is a person or self (neither identical with the *skandhas* nor separate from them) that is the basis of knowledge, transmigration, and entrance into nirvana.

These first schisms prefigured later

Buddhist history. New schools have constantly arisen as new insights or problems made old views unacceptable. As a result, the sangha has not been an effective centralized authority or a successful source of unity. Nonetheless, it has given all Buddhists certain essential teachings (almost all sects would agree to what we have expounded of dharma so far). Also, it has fostered a fairly uniform monastic life, for sects have tended to follow the Vinaya even when they held different doctrines. The monastic order, which has always been the heart of Buddhism (monks have tended to take precedence over laity as an almost unquestioned law of nature), has been a source of stability in Buddhism. We should therefore describe the lives of Buddhist monks and nuns.

Monasticism

A major influence on the Buddhist monastic routine has been Buddha's own life. According to Buddhaghosa, a Ceylonese commentator in the fifth century C.E., the Buddha used to rise at daybreak, wash, and then sit in meditation until it was time to go begging for food. He stayed close enough to a village (wandering from one to another) to obtain food, but far enough away to obtain quiet. Usually devout laity would invite him in, and after eating lightly he would teach them the dharma. Then he would return to his residence, wash, and rest. After this he would preach to the monks and respond to their requests for individual guidance. After another rest he would preach to the laity and then take a cool bath. His evening would consist of more individual conferences, after which, Buddhaghosa claims, he would receive any deities who came for instruction.[18]

The Vinaya established rules that would promote such a steady life of meditation, begging, preaching, and counsel. Originally the monks always wandered except during the rainy season, but later they assumed a more stable setting with quiet lands and a few simple buildings. From the Vinaya's list of capital offenses, though, we can see that a monk's robe did not necessarily make him a saint.

The four misdeeds that merited expulsion from the order were fornication, theft, killing, and "falsely claiming spiritual attainments." Committing any of thirteen lesser misdeeds led to a group meeting of the sangha and probation. They included sexual offenses (intentional ejaculation, touching a woman, speaking suggestively to a woman, urging a woman to gain merit by submitting to a "man of religion," and serving as a procurer), violating the rules that limited the size and specified the site of a monk's dwelling, falsely accusing other monks of grievous violations of the rule, fomenting discord among the monks, or espousing schismatic positions. With appropriate changes, similar rules governed the nuns' lives.

There were hundreds of other things that monks and nuns could not do, and all of them suggest something about the ideals of the sangha. Prohibitions from lying, slander, stealing another's sleeping space, and "sporting in the water" testify to an ideal of honest and direct speech, mutual consideration, and grave decorum. Similarly, prohibitions from digging in the ground and practicing agriculture reflect the ideals of not taking other creatures' lives and of begging one's food. Rules for good posture and table manners indicate that an ideal monk stood erect, kept his eyes downcast, refrained from loud laughter, and did not smack his lips, talk with his mouth full, or throw food into his mouth. The refined *bhiksu* (monk) also could not excrete while standing up or excrete onto growing grass or into the water. Finally, he was not supposed to preach the dharma to monks or laypersons carrying parasols, staffs, swords, or other weapons, or wearing slippers, sandals, turbans, or other head coverings.

The sangha accepted recruits from all social classes, and many of them were youths. From this circumstance and a familiarity with Indian toilet customs, one can understand the concern for the rights of the growing grass and the water. In addition, historians regularly note that the Vinaya is remarkably free from taboos (irrational proscriptions of contact with certain items labeled dangerous, such as menstrual blood, corpses, hair, or fingernails), although Buddhism developed its share of irrationalities. Monks often carried their two principal fears (of taking life or being sexually incontinent) to unjustifiable extremes. Especially regarding matters of sex, the monastic legislation was not always reasonable. (This is also true of Christian monastic legislation.)

The Laity

From earliest times, Buddhism encouraged its laity to pursue an arduous religious life. Though his or her white robe never merited the honor that a monk's colored robe received, a layperson who had taken refuge in the three jewels and contributed to the sangha's support was an honorable follower. Early Buddhism specified morality *(sila)* for the laity in five precepts. The first of these was to refrain from killing living beings. (Unintentional killing was not an offense, and agriculturalists only had to minimize their damage to life.) The second was to refrain from stealing. The third precept dealt with sexual matters. It forbade intercourse with another person's wife, a nun, or a woman betrothed to another man. It also urged restraint with a wife who was pregnant, nursing, or under a religious vow of sexual abstinence. Apparently relations with courtesans were licit, and the commentators' explanation of this precept assumes that it is the male's duty to provide control in sexual matters (because females are by nature wanton). The fourth precept imposed restraint from lying, and the fifth precept forbade drinking alcoholic beverages.

This ethical code was the layperson's chief focus. Occasionally he or she received instruction in meditation or the doctrine of wisdom, and later Mahayana sects considered the laity fully capable of reaching nirvana (in the beginning only monks were so considered). (Nuns never had the status of monks, in part because of legends that the Buddha established nunneries only reluctantly.) The principal lay virtues were to be generous in supporting monks and to witness to Buddhist values in the world. The financial support, obviously enough, was a two-edged sword. Monks who put on spiritual airs would annoy the laity who were sweating to support them. On the other hand, monks constantly faced a temptation to tailor their doctrine to please the laity and so boost their financial contributions. The best defenses against such abuses were monasteries in which the monks lived very simple, poor lives and worked hard at manual tasks.

Other practices that devout laity might take up included regular fasting, days of retreat for reading the scriptures, praying, hearing sermons, giving up luxurious furniture and housing, abstaining from singing, dancing, and theater, and decreasing their sexual activity. Clearly, such practices further advanced the pious layperson toward a monastic sort of regime and often smacked of puritanism.

Scholars suggest that early Buddhism did not develop many new ceremonies or rites of passage; instead it integrated local celebrations and customs into its practices. To this day, birth and wedding ceremonies do not involve Buddhist priests very much, but funeral services do. In early times, the Indian Buddhists likely celebrated the New Year and a day of offering to the ancestors, both of which were probably adopted from Hinduism. In addition, Indian Buddhists commemorated the Buddha's birthday and the day of his enlightenment. Robinson and Johnson suggest that cults of trees, tree spirits, serpents, fertility goddesses, and funeral mounds all came from preexisting Indian religious customs.[19] However, the Bodhi Tree under which the Buddha came to enlightenment prompted many Buddhists to revere trees. Such trees, along with *stupas* (burial mounds) of holy persons, were popular places of devotion.

The worship of statues of the Buddha grew popular only under the influence of

Mahayana theology after 100 C.E., but an earlier veneration of certain symbols of the Buddha (an empty throne, a pair of footprints, a wheel or lotus, or a bodhi tree) paved the way. These symbols signified such things as Buddha's presence in the world, his royal renunciation, and the dharma he preached. The lotus became an especially popular symbol, since it stood for the growth of pure enlightenment from the mud of worldly life.

Meditation

A central aspect of early Buddhist life was meditation, which has remained a primary way to realize the wisdom and to inspire the practice that lead to nirvana. Meditation *(dhyana)* designated mental discipline. For instance, one could meditate by practicing certain devotional exercises that focused attention on one of the three jewels—the Buddha, the dharma, or the sangha. These would be recalled as the refuges under which one had taken shelter, and the meditator's sense of wonder and gratitude for protection would increase his or her emotional attachment. Thus, such meditative exercises were a sort of bhakti.

Indeed, both the saints *(bodhisattvas)* and the Buddha could become objects of loving concentration. However, such devotion was not meditation proper, for *dhyana* was a discipline of consciousness similar to yoga. As is clear from the story of his own life, Buddha's enlightenment came after he had experienced various methods of "mindfulness" and trance. It is proper, then, to consider Buddhist meditation a species of yoga.[20]

The mindfulness of Buddhists was usually a control of the senses and imagination geared to bringing "one-pointed mental consciousness" to bear on the truths of the dharma. For instance, one fixed on mental processes to become aware of their stream and the *skandhas* and to focus on the belief that all is fleeting, painful, and selfless. In addition, meditation masters encouraged

monks to bolster their flight from the world by contemplating the contemptibleness of the body and its pleasures.

Buddhaghosa, for example, proposed lengthy exercises concerning the repulsiveness of food. To help monks eschew it, he suggested that they consider (1) that they have to go get food and thus leave their solitude; (2) that they have to search it out through muddy streets and often suffer abuse from villagers; (3) that chewing food crushes it to a state of repulsiveness, "like a dog's vomit in a dog's trough"; (4) that the four effluvia (bile, phlegm, blood, and pus) go to work on the ingested food; (5) that the food goes into the stomach, which "resembles a cesspool that has not been washed for a long time"; (6) that the food has to pass through this cesspool and its malodorous regions, which are traversed by the stomach's winds; (7) that digested food is not like gold or silver but gives off foam and bubbles, becoming excrement and filling the abdomen like yellow loam in a tube; (8) that digested food brings forth various "putridities," such as hair and nails, and that poorly digested food produces ringworm, itching, leprosy, eczema, and dysentery; (9) that excreted food is offensive and a cause of sadness; and (10) that eating and excreting soil the body.[21]

This master has similarly attractive proposals for meditations on corpses and even beautiful women. A beautiful woman, for instance, is really a bag of bones and foul odors. In a few years she will be a corpse, and like all dead corpses she will be full of worms and maggots. Only a fool would risk nirvana for illusory pleasure with her.

However, wisdom was more than just attacks on hindrances to freedom and nirvana. In careful meditations, Buddhist adepts tried to replicate the Enlightened One's experience during the night of vision, cultivating first his one-pointedness of mind and then his dispassionate heightening of awareness. Adepts also composed meditations focusing on doctrinal points such as the Four Noble Truths or the three marks in order to see their reality directly. This was similar to the insight practices or the way of knowledge *(jnana-marga)* that Hinduism offered, though of course Buddhist beliefs often differed from Hindu.

Mahayana

This last type of meditation clearly brought *dhyana* and wisdom *(prajna)* close together. In the development of Buddhist sects, which reached its most important point in the years 100 B.C.E. to 100 C.E. with the rise of the Mahayana, the wisdom-meditation beliefs were more important than the disputes about morality. The Vinaya was similarly observed by all sects. Also, the laity in the different sects followed the same general precepts. However, the saintly ideal and the place of the laity differed among Theravadins and Mahayanists. Even more, the notion of the Buddha and the range of metaphysics varied considerably. The rise of Mahayana was the first major change in Buddhism.[22] Before its emergence, early Buddhism was fairly uniform in its understanding of Buddha-dharma-sangha and wisdom-morality-meditation. (Theravada has essentially kept early Buddhist beliefs, so the description of Buddhism thus far characterizes Theravada.)

Of course, Mahayana was not without forerunners. We have indicated the lay orientation of the Mahasanghikas, and also the split among the Sthaviras that occurred when the Pudgalavadins advocated the reality of the person. However, the hallmark of Mahayana was its literature, which placed in the mouth of the Buddha sutras describing a new ideal and a new version of wisdom. *Mahayana* means "great vehicle," symbolizing a large raft able to carry multitudes across the stream of samsara to nirvana. *Hinayana* is the term of reproach that Mahayanists used to characterize those who rejected their literature and views. It means "lesser vehicle," symbolizing a small raft able to carry only a few persons across the samsaric stream. Members of the non-Maha-

yana schools refer to themselves not as Hinayanists but as Theravadins, pointing with pride to the antiquity of their traditions and claiming to have preserved the original spirit of Buddhism better than the innovating Mahayanists. Today Theravada Buddhism dominates Sri Lanka, Thailand, Burma, the Khmer Republic (Cambodia), and Laos. Other Asian countries are dominated by Mahayana Buddhism.

Let us deal first with two innovative teachings of the Mahayana schools, emptiness and mind-only, and then consider the Mahayana views of the Buddhist ideal and of the Buddha himself.

Emptiness

Emptiness *(sunyata)* is a hallmark of Mahayana teaching. In fact, the Mahayana sutras known as the *Prajna-paramita* ("wisdom-that-has-gone-beyond") center on this notion. By the end of the Mahayana development, emptiness had in effect become a fourth mark of all reality. Besides being painful, fleeting, and selfless, all reality was empty. Indeed, further rumination on the three marks led Mahayana philosophers to consider emptiness as the most significant mark of all reality. No reality was a substance, having an "own-being." Obviously, therefore, none could be an atman, be constant, or be fully satisfying.

The Heart Sutra, a short specimen of the *Prajna-paramita*, exemplifies the dialectical reasoning with which Mahayana worked on emptiness. We can also perceive the paradoxical result of this reasoning: Nirvana and samsara are one. The sutra begins with an act of reverence (which reminds us that this is religious wisdom, not arid speculation): "Homage to the Perfection of Wisdom, the Lovely, the Holy."[23] "The Lovely" *(Bhagavati)* is feminine, indicating that Buddhism conceives of wisdom as a goddess or maternal figure, out of whom issues the light of knowledge.[24] Next the sutra speaks of the bodhisattva (saint) Avalokitesvara (who in East Asia became Kuan-yin) moving in the course of the wisdom that has gone beyond (that has reached the shore of nirvana) and looking down compassionately on our world. He beheld but five heaps (the *skandhas*), and he saw that they were in their own-being (their substance) empty *(sunya)*.

The word *sunya,* Conze tells us, conveys the idea that something that looks like much is really nothing. Etymologically it relates to the word *swelled.* As a swelled head is much ado about nothing, so things that are *sunya* appear to be full, solid, or substantial but actually are not. The spiritual implication of emptiness *(sunyata)* is that the world around us should not put us in bondage, for it has nothing of substance with which to tie us. Philosophically the word implies *anatman* (no-self), that there is nothing independent of other existents. For the Mahayana, all dharmas (here meaning items of existence) are correlated, and any one dharma is a void.

Dialectics

Having recalled these staples of Mahayana tradition, the Heart Sutra then employs dialectics (the act of playing both sides of an issue) in analyzing the five *skandhas:* Form is emptiness, and this very emptiness is form. Feeling, perception, impulse, and consciousness are all emptiness, and emptiness is feeling, perception, impulse, and consciousness. This identification, the sutra emphasizes, can be seen by anyone "here"—from the viewpoint of the wisdom that has gone beyond. Therefore, reminiscent of Shankara's two levels of knowing Brahman, the *Prajna-paramita* says that there are two ways of looking at ordinary reality. From the lower point of view, feeling, perception, impulse, consciousness, and form are all "something." From the higher viewpoint of enlightenment or perfect wisdom, however, these terms all designate something that is empty, that has no solid core or own-being.

To deal with any dharma as though it were full, therefore, would be to deal with it at least erroneously and possibly desirously—thus, karmically. If, however, we see that *nothing* is pleasant, stable, or full, then we will deal with all things in detachment, moving through them toward nirvana. So, according to the sutra, a bodhisattva sees things without "thought coverings," does not tremble at the emptiness that this attitude reveals, and thereby attains nirvana. That is what all Buddhas (Gautama is not the only one) have done, and it shows that the *Prajna-paramita* is a great spell of knowledge (the sutra concludes with a mantra, a chanting of a wisdom spell: "Gone, gone, gone beyond, gone altogether beyond, O what an awakening, all-hail—this completes the Heart of perfect wisdom").[25]

THE DIAMOND SUTRA

Another good example of the *Prajna-paramita* literature that Mahayana Buddhism developed is the Diamond Sutra, which probably originated in India in the fourth century c.e.[26] This sutra begins by setting the stage for a dramatic discourse. Once when the Buddha was dwelling in the garden of a person named Anathapindika, with a group of 1250 monks, he rose, went on his round of begging, returned, washed his feet, and sat down to meditate. Many monks approached him, bowed at his feet, and seated themselves to await his teaching. One of them, a monk named Subhuti, ventured to ask the Enlightened One how a son or daughter of good family, having set out on the path toward enlightenment, should stand, progress, and control his or her thoughts. The Buddha graciously replied that such a person ought to entertain the thought that although the Enlightened One has led many beings to nirvana, in reality he has led no being to nirvana. How can this be? Because, as any true bodhisattva or enlightened person understands, the notion of "being" or "self" or "soul" or "person" is actually an illusion.

With various subtleties, examples, and further inferences, this is the sutra's main teaching. Thus somewhat later the Buddha repeats the message: Bodhisattvas are those who do not perceive a self, a being, a soul, or a person. They do not perceive a dharma (individual item of reality), or even a no-dharma. They neither perceive nor nonperceive. Why? Because they have reached a realm beyond the dichotomies that perception usually entails, beyond our ordinary tendency to organize things in terms of beings, persons, or selves. Such a tendency seizes on individuals and turns aside from the whole. By concentrating on beings it neglects Being or nirvana. Nirvana is not a thing, not an entity. Those who think in terms of things or entities cannot enter nirvana. Only those who have gone beyond, to the higher knowledge that is unified, intuitive, and comprehensive, can enter nirvana.

To try to jar the hearer from ordinary consciousness, the sutra even moves to outright paradox: "The Tathagata [Buddha] has taught that the dharmas special to the Buddhas are just not a Buddha's special dharmas. That is why they are called 'the dharmas special to the Buddhas.'" If we try to make sense of this, we find ourselves straining at the edge of logical reason. The dharmas—realities or teachings—applying to Buddhas (fully enlightened beings) and making them Buddhas are just not peculiar to Buddhas. They are what enlightenment finds intrinsic to reality, the way things are. For that very reason, however, grasping them makes one a Buddha. In other words, Buddhahood consists in grasping what is so for everyone, for all beings. The special, distinguishing feature of Buddhas is that they *realize* what the rest of us only experience or are. The rest of us, in the final analysis, deal with the same (empty) reality as the Buddhas do. The rest of us are potentially enlightened, potentially bodhi (knowledge) beings. But only the Buddhas realize or actualize this knowledge. Only the Buddhas become what they are, illumine their full selves (which are no-selves) with the light of nirvana or emptiness.

Because he understood this line of discourse, Subhuti could reply to the Buddha in kind.

I am, O Lord, an arhat [saint] free from greed. And yet, O Lord, it does not occur to me, "an Arhat am I and free from greed." If, O Lord, it could occur to me that I have attained Arhatship, then the Tathagata would not have declared of me that "Subhuti, this son of good family, who is the foremost of those who dwell in Peace, does not dwell anywhere; that is why he is called a dweller in Peace."

Once again, the key to moving this statement from the column marked "gibberish" to the column marked "wisdom" seems to be to take it as a paradox, the uneven sort of speech that comes when we have one part of our mind on the level of superior knowledge and the other part on the level of ordinary, worldly knowledge. In terms of ordinary knowledge and discourse, Subhuti is an arhat free of greed. That is how the man in the street rightly would describe him. In terms of ultimate knowledge and discourse, however, this view of the man in the street is seriously flawed, because it assumes that "Subhuti," "arhat," "greed," and the like are solid things. Ordinary discourse tends to reify what it deals with, to invest it with the solidity of a "thing." Forgetting that everything is painful, fleeting, and possessed of no-self, ordinary speech withdraws from the interrelational field of mutual causality, the wheel of conditioned coarising, that, on deeper analysis, shows everything to be without an "own-self."

As one who has passed beyond ordinary speech, Subhuti does not allow himself reifications. Not for him such expressions as "An Arhat am I and free from greed." He would not be dwelling in the peace of enlightenment, the fulfilling realm of nirvana, were he still pervaded by such substantial and dichotomizing thinking. Indeed, for him truly to be an arhat is for him to think in monistic terms, appreciating the omnipresence of emptiness. Arhat and emptiness therefore coincide. Emptiness defines the outlook of an arhat and the outlook of an arhat discloses everything to be empty. How very important, then, are the exercises of meditation that cut below the ordinary mind, the exercises of morality that root out normal egocentricity. Without them, we will never reach the state of wisdom, never will become an arhat (that is a no-arhat).

In some of its literature, then, the Indian Mahayana equated the perception of emptiness with the wisdom that makes a saint. To realize fully how all things are empty was to dispel the spontaneous but illusory view of things that ties one to samsara and rebirth. If things are really empty, then there is nothing to cling to. Then things can move in the coordinated "dance," the flow, that nature invites us to join. Emptiness does not mean that realities have no value, that they do not impinge on our senses, or that we cannot reason over them in the laboratory or excise them with a surgeon's scalpel. For Mahayanists, emptiness means that we should use all realities freely without clinging, letting them go their dancing way. Because nirvana so impressed them, the Mahayana philosophers saw that nothing that is not nirvana is real, is independently existent. In this sense that which is not nirvana is empty, and they would wean us from our naive impression that it is full.

Such weaning, however, is only the first phase of a two-phase task, according to philosophers such as Nagarjuna (around 200 C.E.). The first move in the dialectics of wisdom, described above, is to realize that things are not what they appear to be, and so to distinguish between lower knowledge and higher, between apparent reality (samsara) and full reality (nirvana). However, we must further understand the concepts of emptiness and nirvana themselves. Emptiness is not another kind of thing or quality, and it is thus not full. Nirvana is neither a void nor a plenum (fullness) like Brahman. Rather, it is the ultimate reality present in the relative realities of the samsaric world. Nirvana and samsara thus are one, because neither is a something opposed to other things. Both are qualities (the absolute quality that everything has insofar as it has being, and the relative quality that everything of our direct experience has insofar as its being is always painful, fleeting, selfless, and empty).

All this is very hard to grasp, and Nagarjuna spent much energy reducing all reifying language to absurdity.[27] Perhaps we can best understand what the Mahayana philosophers of emptiness were saying through a Zen notion. Before enlightenment, mountains are mountains, rivers are rivers, and trees are trees. When enlightenment starts to dawn, the world turns over, and mountains, rivers, and trees are no longer what they seemed to be. After enlightenment, though, when we are stable in wisdom, mountains are again mountains, rivers are again rivers, and trees are again trees.

In other words, before one starts out for enlightenment (starts out to imitate the Buddha), one has commonsensical perceptions of things: Mountains are mountains. Then, after one has studied things, meditated somewhat, and purified one's moral habits, things look quite different. One cannot take the mountain for granted. There is a wonder, a mystery in its being. Even though it seems permanent, analysis shows that the mountain is fleeting (for example, it wears away), painful, and without self. It is empty; it is not nirvana. With full illumination, however, the world again turns right side up. The mountain is just a mountain. One is not back at the beginning, however, for the enlightened view of the mountain is different from the commonsensical view. For the enlightened person the mountain is just there, playing its part in the fleeting dance of dharmas, which are all empty in themselves but which combine to give us this world of appearances. In other words, the mountain is nirvana in the midst of samsara, being in the midst of becoming. That is its grandeur and its poverty.

NAGARJUNA

Nagarjuna gained such a lofty reputation in later Buddhism, especially that of Tibet, that he deserves special consideration. He probably lived between 150 and 250 C.E., most likely in South India, and his style of argumentation, as well as his analyses of his opponents' positions, suggests that he was trained as a Hindu brahmin before he converted to the budding movement of Mahayana Buddhism.

Although Nagarjuna is known as the most acute of the Mahayana dialecticians, Tibetan tradition also reveres him as a guru who offered his disciples sound ethical advice. Some verses from "The Staff of Wisdom," a work attributed to Nagarjuna, suggest his ethical style.[28]

First, Nagarjuna insists that the only way to gain the real meaning of the dharma, the Buddhist sciences, and the holy mantras is directly to experience them. Those who merely analyze the meaning of words never come to the core. This insistence expresses the conviction of all Buddhist gurus that words can be deceptive. If we allow words a life of their own, detached from the experiences they are trying to describe, words can distract us from reality. To grasp the dharma or the treatises of wisdom, we must both meditate on the realities to which they point and practice the virtues they extoll. The same with the holy mantras that the tradition urges us to pray. Unless we experience the states from which they flow, the realities to which the saints have spontaneously directed them, the mantras will be but nonsense sounds.

Nagarjuna then reflects on the sort of knowledge that is truly valuable. We only know what this knowledge is in time of need, when we are hard-pressed. Then it is clear that the knowledge contained in books is of little use. Unless we have made an insight our own, it will give us little light or peace. In this, knowledge is parallel to wealth. Time of need shows us that wealth we have borrowed from others is no real wealth. It is nothing on which we can depend, for it can be taken from us at a stroke. Whether it be a matter of knowledge or of wealth, need, pressure, or suffering shows us the stark contrast between what we truly own and what we have merely borrowed. Thus hard times can have a silver lining. If they strengthen our resolve to gain our own wisdom, possess our own (incorruptible) wealth, they can advance us toward fulfillment.

We should consider our work in the same vein. The accomplishments of a teacher of ants, as Nagarjuna describes a person concerned with trivial affairs, are but ways of earning a living. Even the master baker, carpenter, or clerk deserves only the praise we can accord worldly skills. But suppose we meet a person studying liberation. Helping us terminate our earthly incarnation, such a person deals with heavenly affairs, the only things truly necessary. Were we wise, we would turn our admiration from masters of trivial affairs to those few masters who teach the only things truly necessary. Thereby, we would clarify our own essential task, making the study of how to terminate our earthly incarnation *the* great accomplishment to which we can aspire.

Even master-teachers wander off the track at times, and Nagarjuna's next verse seems a tangent to his main line. If you have a chosen truth, a pearl of special wisdom, he says, be careful to whom you give it. Make sure that you scrutinize the character of any person to whom you would impart the dharma. Unscrupulous people can turn the best of teachings to injurious use. Remember the legend of the man who took compassion on a monkey and gave him a small place to live. Before long the monkey had taken over the whole house and the man was out on the street. The same can happen with careless teachers. Unscrupulous disciples can turn the dharma against their teachers, making an act of charity into a shambles.

Bending back to the main stream of his thought, Nagarjuna turns to two kinds of teaching. Some people teach with words; others instruct silently. This is reminiscent of the reed-flower, which has no fruit, in contrast to the walnut, which has both fruit and flower. It is also reminiscent of the kataka tree, the fruit of which clears mud from the water. If you only mention the name of the kataka tree, you will not remove the mud. You must make your teaching bear fruit, make it deal with more than words. You must extend it to the realm of action, instructing by silent deeds as well as wordy lectures. Indeed, if you do not apply your knowledge, you are like a blind man with a lamp. Though you have in hand a source of great illumination, you do not shed it on the road, do not light the way for others to travel.

Stanza after stanza, Nagarjuna tosses out aphorisms like these. Line after line, his advice is poetic, symbolic, image-laden. From deep meditation and reflection, he finds emptiness a font of great illumination. For one who sees, the spiritual life is paradoxical and parabolic. As we come close to enlightenment, the main structures of the holy life stand clear, but these structures (meditation, wisdom, and morality) are capable of endless application. The key is having the experi- ence, grasping the center, knowing emptiness directly. When we realize that reality is a single seamless cloth, we can enjoy all its various designs.

Mind-only

Emptiness was the special concern of the Madhyamika Mahayana school.[29] The second major Mahayana school, the Yogaca- ra, which became influential from about 300 C.E. on, proposed another influential teach- ing on ultimate reality, mind-only.[30] Like the teaching on emptiness, it went beyond early Buddhist teaching, and the Therava- dins rejected the sutras that attributed this teaching to the Buddha. The teaching of mind-only held that all realities are finally products of the cosmic mind. There were antecedents to this viewpoint in the morali- ty literature that Mahayana shared with the Theravadins, such as the *Dhammapada,* and the proponents of emptiness implied it in their belief that all phenomena are illusory (maya), because we do not grasp them in their ultimately empty reality. The *Dham- mapada*'s interest, however, was practical, not speculative: "What we are today comes from our thoughts of yesterday, and our present thoughts build our life of tomorrow: our life is the creation of our mind."[31] The Yogacarins wanted a fuller explanation of mental reality, probably because their intu- itions grew out of meditational or yogic prac- tices (whence their name).

One of the principal Yogacarin sutras, the *Lankavatara*,[32] described a tier of con- sciousnesses in the individual culminating in a "storehouse" consciousness *(alayavij- nana)* that is the base of the individual's deepest awareness, the individual's tie to the cosmic. The storehouse consciousness is itself unconscious and inactive, but it is the repository of the "seeds" that ripen into human deeds and awareness. Further, Yoga- carins sometimes called the storehouse con- sciousness the Buddha's womb. Thereby, they made the Buddha or Tathagata (Enlight- ened Being) a metaphysical principle—a foundation of all reality.

From the womb of the Buddha issued the purified thoughts and beings of enlight- enment. The symbolism is often garbled (and interestingly feminine, suggesting a Buddhist version of androgyny or primal wholeness). Its main point, though, is clear: The womb of the Buddha *(Tathagata-garb- ha)* is present in all living beings, irradiating them with enlightenment. Like the femi- nine *Prajna-paramita*, then, the ultimate reality of the Yogacarins "mothers" the many individual things (that are themselves empty). It is the great mental storehouse from which they issue, the matrix that holds them all in being. It stimulates their dancing flux.

This view has interesting parallels with the Chinese philosophy of the *Tao* that mothers the ten thousand things. For the Yogacarins, though, the dharmas that dance and the *Tathagata-garbha* from which they issue are all mental. There is only mind— material reality is an illusion. When one reaches wisdom and leaves lower knowledge behind, material reality will become almost uninteresting.

Mahayana Devotion

Both major Mahayana schools devel- oped sophisticated philosophies to correlate the many beings of experience with the sim- ple finality of nirvana. It was not philosophy that brought Mahayana popular influence, though, but its openness to the laity's spiri- tual needs, its devotional theology. Early Buddhism held monks in greater regard, con- sidering them the only true followers of Buddha. They were the teachers, the determiners of doctrine, and the guardians of morality. They were the stewards of tradition who made the sangha a jewel alongside the Buddha and the dharma. Consequently, the laity considered themselves to be working out a better karma, so that in their next lives they might be monks (or, if they were women, so that they might be men). The central lay virtue, as we have seen, was giving financial support to the monasteries, and the sangha seldom admitted laity to the higher occupations of philosophy or meditation.

Mahayana changed this view of the laity. Stressing the Buddha's compassion and his resourcefulness in saving all living creatures, it gradually qualified the Theravadin ideal of the arhat and fashioned a new, more socially oriented ideal. Mahayana thereby prepared the way for later schools that were in effect Buddhist bhakti sects, such as the Pure Land sect. Such sects believed that through graceful compassion, a Buddha or bodhisattva only required that one devoutly repeat his name and place full trust in him for salvation. In this "degenerate age," the difficult paths of wisdom and meditation were open only to the few. Therefore, the Enlightened One had opened a broader path of devotion, so that laity as well as monks might reach paradise and then nirvana.

Mahayana did not attack monastic dignity. Rather, it just stressed the social side of the ideal. The Mahayanists saw the Hinayana arhat as too individualistic. To pursue one's own enlightenment and salvation, apart from those of all living creatures, seemed selfish. So the Mahayanists began to talk of a bodhisattva, who postpones entrance into nirvana in order to labor for the salvation of all living things. Out of great compassion (*mahakaruna*), he would remain in the samsaric world for eons if need be, content to put off final bliss so as to help save everything that exists in the cycle of life: humans, birds, plants, and trees.

In Mahayana Buddhism, then, one would finally take a bodhisattva vow, making one's goal not just gaining nirvana for oneself but for all one's fellow creatures.

Mahayanists stressed six great "perfections" (*paramitas*) in becoming a bodhisattva, which effectively summarize Mahayana religious living. First was the perfection of giving: giving material things to those in need, but also giving spiritual instructions, one's own body and life, or even one's own karmic merit. In a life of compassionate generosity, everything could be given over to others. Mahayanists understood the perfections of morality, patience, vigor, meditation, and wisdom in a similarly broad fashion. Thus, they applied the traditional triad of wisdom-morality-meditation in more social ways. Giving, patience, and vigor meant that one became selfless in more than a metaphysical way. For the love of others, for the grand vision of a totally perfected world, the saint would cheerfully donate his goods and talents, suffer abuses, and labor ceaselessly.

Finally, Mahayanists moved away from the early Buddhist view that Sakyamuni was just a man who gained enlightenment. Instead, they began to contemplate his preexistence and the status he had gained as a knowledge being. In this contemplation, his earthly life receded in importance, so much that some Mahayanists began to say that he had only apparently assumed a human body. Then, linking this stress on the Buddha's metaphysical essence with the Indian doctrine of endless kalpas of cosmic time and endless stretches of cosmic space, Mahayanists spoke of many Buddhas who had existed before Sakyamuni and of many Buddhas who presided in other cosmic realms.

In this way the notion of Buddhahood greatly expanded. First it was the quality shared by many cosmic beings of wisdom and realization. Later, in East Asian Mahayana, Buddhahood became the metaphysical notion that *all* beings are in essence enlightenment beings. Enlightenment, therefore, is just realizing one's Buddha-nature. It is the beginning of nirvana, the break with samsara, and the achievement of perfect wisdom all in one.

Buddhahood thus became complex and many-sided. The Buddha came to have three bodies: an apparition body, in which he appeared to perceivers; a dharma body, in which he was the principle of reality or the cosmic presence of nirvana; and a glorification body, in which he manifested his bliss to the heavenly beings. Moreover, the distinction between Buddhas and great bodhisattvas blurred and largely dissolved in the popular mind, giving Buddhist "divinity" a full spectrum of holy beings. Citing the Mahayana understanding of divinity, therefore, is the surest way to refute claims that Buddhism is not a religion. Whatever merit the position that Buddhism is not a religion has rests in the strictly human experiences that *may* have been the core of the historical Buddha's enlightenment. By the fifth or sixth century after the Buddha's death, the hills were alive with chants to a variety of divine figures.

Tantrism

We have seen the Hindu mixture of occult and erotic practices called Tantrism or Shaktism. Indian Buddhism helped create this trend and incorporated many of its notions. Buddhist Tantrism in India seems to have originated around the sixth century C.E., flourishing first in the northwest. From the eighth century on it prospered around Bengal, combining with *Prajna-paramita* philosophy and native magical practices. It later reached Sri Lanka, Burma, and Indonesia.[33] Often it merged with Shaivism, but in Tibet it combined with native Bon (shamanist) practices and became the dominant Buddhist faith.[34]

Tantrism had antecedents in both Buddha's teaching and in the surrounding Hindu Brahmanism. Buddha appears to have allowed magical spells, and the canon contains reputed cures for snakebite and other dangers. *Prajna-paramita* sutras such as the Heart often ended with spells, transferring certain key ideas and words from strictly intellectual notions to mantras. In Brahmanic sacrifices, as we noted, the prayers were understood so literally that they became

Figure 10   Head of Avalokitesvara, from Temple of Prah Khan, twelfth century. Nelson Gallery-Atkins Museum (Nelson Fund).

mantras; if a priest recited a prayer properly, it was sure to accomplish its end.

Buddhist Tantrists took over such sacred sounds as "om," as well as esoteric yogic systems, such as *kundalini*, which associated sacred syllables with force centers *(chakras)* in the body. They also used mandalas (magic figures, such as circles and squares) and even *stupas* (shrines). The Buddhist Tantrists were thus hardly bizarre or innovative, mainly developing ancient Hindu esoteric practices in a new setting.

What novelty the Tantrists did introduce into Buddhism came from their creative use of rites that acted out mandalas and esoteric doctrines about bodily forces. Perhaps under the influence of Yogacara meditation, which induced states of trance, the

Tantrists developed rituals in which participants identified with particular deities. If it is true that many meditation schools, such as the Yogacara, employed mandalas for the early stages of trance in order to focus consciousness, then the Tantrists probably built on well-established practices. In their theoretical elaboration, however, they retrieved certain cosmological notions that were deeply rooted in the ancient religious mind.

For instance, they came to see the *stupas* as replicas of the cosmos. The railings that separated the *stupa* precinct from secular ground divided the sacred from the profane. The edge of the moving mandala that the Tantrist troupe would dance or act out had a function similar to that of the railings. Often Tantrism strove to symbolize the entire cosmic plan. Indeed, the Tantrists tried to draw heavenly worlds (bodhisattva realms) and gods into their meditations and rituals.

A principal metaphysical support of Tantrism was the Madhyamika doctrine of emptiness, which the Tantrists interpreted to mean that all beings are intrinsically pure. Consequently, they used odd elements in their rituals, especially erotic ones, in order to drive home the truths of emptiness, purity, and freedom. For the most part, these ways did not become public, since the Tantrists went to considerable pains to keep their rites and teachings secret. In fact, they developed a cryptic language that they called "twilight speech," in which sexual references were abundant.[35] For instance, they called the male and female organs "thunderbolt" and "lotus," respectively. As with Hindu Tantrism, it is not always possible to tell whether such speech is symbolic or literal. Some defenders of Tantrism claim that it tamed sexual energy in the Indian tradition by subjecting it to symbolization, meditative discipline, and moral restraints. Other critics, however, view Buddhist Tantrism as a corruption of a tradition originally quite intolerant of libidinal practices. For them the Tantrist explanation that, since everything is mind-only, the practice of erotic rites means little is simply a rationalization.

In a typical Tantrist meditation, the meditator would begin with traditional preliminaries such as seeking refuge in the three jewels, cleansing himself of sins (by confession or bathing), praying to past masters, or drawing a mandala to define the sacred space of the extraordinary reality that his rite was going to involve. Then the meditator would take on the identity of a deity and disperse all appearances of the world into emptiness. Next, using his imagination, the meditator would picture himself as the god whose identity he was projecting.

So pictured, he and his consort would sit on the central throne of the mandala space and engage in sexual union. Then he would imagine various Buddhas parading into the sacred space of the mandala and assimilate them into his body and senses. In that assimilation, his speech would become divine, he could receive offerings as a god, and he could perform any of the deity's functions. So charged with divinity, he would then return to the ordinary world, bringing back to it the great power of a Buddha's divine understanding.[36]

Dialectics

Tantrism adopted the Mahayana notion that nirvana and samsara are one and interpreted it to mean that the things of the world of appearances are not ultimate. Thus, classifying them as good or bad or in any other way can prevent one from appreciating their truly empty character. Sutras favored by the Tantrists portrayed the Buddha as having told only "conceited" people that fleeing lewdness, anger, and folly produces liberation. He did not necessarily forbid these things to bodhisattvas. A bodhisattva, then, may appear to be breaking precepts and sinning, but since he is pure of heart, these outward appearances are misleading.

For instance, he may seem to have five wives and concubines yet actually keep his passions free of lust. Like the lotus flowering from the mire, he is purity rising above anything degraded or stained. Working off this model, Tantrists spoke of fighting fire with fire, destroying vice by practicing it with discipline, and rendering poison harmless by small, steady ingestions of it. Using profiles of different character types, the Tantrist masters would also prescribe exercises for different character types, such as the irascible, the timid, or the lusty.

Much in this dialectical development probably was a mixture of self-deception and fascination with the power of imagination and sexual energy. Commenting on the traditional Tibetan texts about the saint Naropa, Herbert Guenther has sketched Tibetan dialectical thought about reality.[37] It moves through the field of the emotions and passions, much as Nagarjuna's dialectic moves through the field of thoughts and judgments, leaving little ordinary understanding upright. For if one seriously considers emptiness and the equation of nirvana and samsara, then everything does indeed overturn for a while. As a result, it is not surprising that the ancient equating of the real with the vividly experienced returns to power. Because imaginative trance can be quite vivid (as can dreams and hallucinations), the space of its mandalas may seem quite real. Then, one can indeed become the god that one's meditation has invoked.

Similarly, the forces of such a god's interactions with a divine spouse, or with alcohol, or with such tabooed objects as skulls can convince the Tantrist that through his rites he is truly tapping divine powers. Mesmerizing themselves in these ways, the Tantrists attributed great religious significance to inner light flashes, heat flashes, and orgasm. They tended to see such events as physical and psychological movements of mystic forces through special bodily columns and centers. All these experiences served enlightenment. If you saw vibrantly colorful images, felt pulsations and rushes, you were approaching success. Of course, meditation masters warned of illusion, but in the jungle of Tantrism, reality and illusion are difficult to differentiate.

The relation of the master (guru) and the disciple was central in Tantrism, because the master represented the tradition. (Zen has maintained this stress on the master but not the Tantrist eroticism.) The

Tantrist gurus forced their pupils to engage in quite bizarre and painful practices to teach them to examine the mirror of their minds, to learn the illusory character of all phenomena, and to stop the cravings and jealousies that clouded their mirror.[38] Often pronouncing the death of old judgments and the birth of new ones of enlightenment, the guru confused the pupil, punished him, and pushed him to break with convention and ordinary vision. When Buddhism had become vegetarian, Tantrist masters urged eating flesh. When Buddhism advocated teetotalism, they urged intoxicating spirits. In such ways, Tantrist wisdom became paradoxical and eccentric.[39] To illustrate the fundamental truths of mind-only and emptiness, the Tantrists would take up each of society's most strongly held prohibitions and violate them. Incest, drinking blood from emptied skulls—every taboo could become a gateway to wisdom. In fact, the stronger the taboo, the more psychic energy it offered.

Tibet

Tantrism was welcomed in Tibet and came to dominate in the region between India and China. Our first historical records date from only the seventh century C.E., when Chinese historians started mentioning it. Under King Srongsten Gampo in 632, Tibet borrowed both writing and Buddhism from Kashmir. Toward the end of the eighth century, two notable Indian figures came to Tibet, Santaraskita and Padmasambhava, who founded a lasting Tibetan sangha. Tradition credits Padmasambhava with inaugurating the influential Nying-ma-pas Tantrist sect, while Santaraskita apparently was responsible for the triumph of Indian traditions over challenges from Chinese schools (especially Ch'an). Since that triumph, Tibet has owed more to Indian scholarship and philosophy than to Chinese.

Stephan Beyer emphasizes that Indian academic structures greatly influenced Tibetan Buddhism.[40] During the Indian Gupta dynasty (320–540 C.E.), great monastic universities became the pillars of Buddhism.

The "curricular Buddhism" of these schools encompassed all the arts and sciences. Further, meditation integrated with scholasticism, which assured that the academic efforts to correlate Buddhist beliefs with existing knowledge never divorced themselves from practical religion. The Tibetan adoption of an Indian rather than a Chinese religious style correlated with this union of study and meditation, for the Indian schools favored a gradual penetration of enlightenment, in which study could play an important role.

One characteristic of Tibetan Buddhism has therefore been its line of scholars based in monastic universities. They have produced voluminous translations and commentaries for the canonical scriptures, as well as a tradition that learning should inform ritualist life. Learning and ritual, in fact, became the primary foci of the Tibetan monastic life. The king and the common people looked to the monastery for magical protection through ritual against evil powers, while individual monks utilized both meditation and ritual in their pursuit of enlightenment.

The typical day of a traditional Tibetan monk began with a private ritual contemplation (Tantrist) before dawn for an hour and a half. During the morning, the monk regularly participated in the community's prayers for two hours and then worked in the monastic library. He devoted the afternoon to more work and public ceremony and again meditated in the evening.

Many monks spent a lifetime in this regime, coming to the monastery at the age of nine or ten and receiving a thorough training in the scriptures, meditation techniques, and ceremonial details. As suggested above, the king supported this life style, because ritual could prop his authority. (Pre-Buddhist Tibetan culture thought of the king in ancient sacred terms, as the tie between heaven and earth. Something of this ancient view continued when monks prayed and conducted rituals for the king's good health.) The common people, whose shamanist heritage emphasized many malevolent spirits of

sickness and death, saw in the ritual spells and ceremonies a powerful defense. As a result, the monasteries were quite practical institutions for them, too.

By emphasizing ritual in both public ceremonies and private meditations, Tibetan Buddhism created its own version of the Tantrist belief that the imagination, senses, and psychological and bodily powers are all potential sources of energy for enlightenment and wisdom. When we discussed Indian Tantrism, we considered how the adept tried to identify with divine forces and gain control over a *cosmion*—a "little world" that represented universal space and time. The Tibetan Tantrist cult acted out many such identifications, so that the common people could indwell something comfortingly universal. The worship of the goddess Tara, for instance, which monasteries and popular festivals promoted, gave the world a motherly and protecting aspect. Monks and laity both prayed personally to Tara for help, while many of Tibet's musical and dancing arts developed through festivals devoted to her.

The success that Buddhism enjoyed in Tibet may also be linked to its ability to capitalize on native shamanist themes and political institutions. The ancient Tibetan Bon ("he who invokes the gods") was a shaman very like the Siberian shaman. Beating his drum, whirling in dance, weaving his spells, he fought against the demons of sickness and death.[41] In addition to developing its own Tantrist rituals to cover these interests of the older religion, Tibetan Buddhism also produced a type of wandering, "crazy" saint who evinced much of the awe and respect that the older shamans had.

The prototype of this ascetic, visionary holy man in Tibet was the much beloved Milarepa (1040–1123).[42] After a harsh initiation by family suffering and a cruel guru, he took to the mountain slopes and gained a reputation for working wonders. In his songs he poetically expressed profound insights into both the nature of dharma reality and the psychology of the ascetic life. Other famous Tibetan saints, such as Tilopa and

Naropa, were similarly poetic. They show that for personal religious life, Tantrism could cast all conventional values and assumptions in doubt so that it could relentlessly pursue enlightenment.

Buddhism capitalized on the demise of the kingship in Tibet in the ninth century to establish a theocratic regime with the monastery at its heart. Despite early persecutions during a period of kings' intrigues and assassinations, by the eleventh century the monasteries were strong. Until the recent Communist takeover, in fact, the monasteries and the Dalai Lamas (religious leaders) dominated Tibetan politics (often with much intrigue and sectarian strife).[43] The Mongol emperor Kublai Khan granted the abbot 'Phags-pa (1235–1280) temporal power over all Tibet, firmly establishing a theocratic rule. By the fourteenth century, however, Tibet was a cauldron of various Buddhist sects vying for power. The Nyingma-pas sect that Padmasambhava founded claimed a certain primacy because of its antiquity, and it also kept close ties with the ancient shamanist loyalties.

Of the sects that developed after the demise of the Chinese T'ang dynasty in the ninth century, the most important was the Ge-lug, which shrewdly employed the idea of reincarnation. Consequently, the Mongols both recognized the Dalai Lama as a spiritual leader and considered him a grandson of the Mongol chief. From the sixteenth century onwards, the Ge-lug wielded great political clout. The Dalai Lamas, for the most part, have been men of considerable spiritual and political acumen, and their rule has meant a vigorous sangha. Presently, the fourteenth Dalai Lama (b. 1935) is in exile from the Chinese Communists, but he is still the spiritual leader of tens of thousands of Tibetan refugees.

Tibetan Buddhism thus stands out for its Tantrist bent and its especially knotted political history. Few cultures have so absorbed one version of Buddhism as Tibet has absorbed the "thunderbolt vehicle" (Tantrism). Perhaps the most famous Tibetan religious text to reach the West is the *Tibetan Book of the Dead*,[44] which purportedly describes the experiences of the deceased during the forty-nine days between physical death and entry into a new karmic state. By employing vivid imagery and specifying rituals designed to help the deceased to achieve nirvana, the *Book of the Dead* exemplifies the Tantrist mentality well. It is a journey through the imagination and unconscious that severely challenges most notions of reality, since it maintains that the period right after death is the most opportune time for liberation.

MODERN TIBET

Much of the Tibetan tradition continued a vigorous life well into the twentieth century, as one learns from travelers such as Alexandra David-Neel, whose *Magic and Mystery in Tibet*,[45] originally published (in French) in 1929, makes fascinating reading. Neel was not long into her travels through Tibet when she had the opportunity to meet the Dalai Lama. Watching him bless a large crowd (one by one), she was struck by the people's manifest belief that physical contact with the Dalai Lama would put them in touch with a magical beneficent power. Indeed, great throngs gathered in Kalimpong, where the Dalai Lama was staying, seeking to benefit from his power.

However, not all the onlookers shared the general credulity, and Neel's contact with one skeptic opened a door to Tibet's Tantrist past. She noticed that a man wearing dirty, much torn monk's robes seemed to be watching the crowd cynically. His matted hair wound around his head like a turban, and he had the small traveling bag of a wandering ascetic. In fact, Neel's interpreter described him as a *naljorpa*, an ascetic possessing magical powers. Upon inquiry, the interpreter found that the man was a wandering monk from

Bhutan, who usually lived here and there—in caves, empty houses, or under the trees. He just happened to be passing through Kalimpong when the crowds gathered for the Dalai Lama's blessing.

Reflecting on the monk's strange behavior, Neel decided to seek him out at the local monastery, where he had said he was headed. She and her interpreter found him finishing his meal in a room containing the holy images before which the monks prayed. When Neel and her interpreter tried to begin a conversation, the monk only grunted through a mouthful of rice. Then he began to laugh and mutter. "What is he saying?" Neel asked. The interpreter was embarrassed, explaining that he did not know whether he should translate the monk's rough speech. Neel urged him to translate accurately, since she was in Tibet precisely to capture the local color. So licensed, the translator said that the monk had asked him, "What is this idiot here for?" To Neel this was the sort of insult Indian yogis frequently threw out, so as to put off or test those who approached them. She told the interpreter to tell the ascetic she wanted to know why he had mocked the crowd that had come to seek the blessing of the Dalai Lama.

The *naljorpa* muttered, "They are insects fluttering in dung, puffed up with their own importance." Once again, this seemed the sort of iconoclasm Neel had witnessed in India. "Are you yourself free of all taint?" she asked. The monk laughed noisily and then launched into a speech worthy of Milarepa, Naropa, or one of the other ancient Tantrist saints. "The person who tries to get out of the dung only sinks in deeper. Therefore I roll in it like a pig. I swallow it, trying to turn it into golden dust, into a brook of clear water. That is the great work: to turn dog dung into stars." He said this with great delight, evidently enjoying himself.

Neel decided to press him. "What was wrong with the people approaching the Dalai Lama? They are simple folk, unable to study the high doctrines. Why should they not take what blessing they can?" The ascetic broke through her little objection. "The only efficacious blessing is that given by a person who truly possesses the power he professes. If the Dalai Lama were genuine, he would not need soldiers to fight the Chinese or his other enemies. He would be able to drive all his enemies out of his country, surrounding Tibet with an invisible barrier no enemy could penetrate. Padmasambhava had such power, and his blessing still reaches those who worship him twelve centuries later, though he now lives in the heavenly land of the sages." The ascetic then suggested that he himself had experienced Padmasambhava's genuine blessing.

Neel tried to extricate herself from the situation gracefully, feeling that the ascetic was perhaps a little crazed, but she made the mistake of having her interpreter offer the ascetic some money. Insulted, he refused the money, and when the interpreter tried to insist, the interpreter was hurled backwards and doubled over in pain, as though he had received a terrible blow in the stomach. He was convinced the monk had loosed a spiritual force against him, and none of Neel's Western, commonsense efforts to explain the incident would appease him.

Throughout her journey, Neel found Tibetan Buddhism undergirt with a great respect for the occult. Ordinary people thought meteorological phenomena were the doing of demons or magicians. A hailstorm, for instance, was one of the demons' favorite ways of preventing pilgrims from journeying to the holy places. It was also the way magicians kept intruders from their hermitages and tested would-be disciples. Many mediums found steady employment communicating with the dead or transmitting messages of the gods. In the Himalayas, the centuries-old tradition that sages and ascetics have to battle powerful forces of darkness was alive and well.

The Demise of Indian Buddhism

Buddhism declined in India after the seventh century, only in part because of Tantrist emphases. Invaders such as the White Huns and the Muslims wrecked many Buddhist strongholds, while the revival of Hinduism, especially of Hindu bhakti sects of Vishnu and Shiva, undermined Buddhism. Mahayana fought theistic Hinduism quite fiercely, not at all seeing it as equivalent to the Buddhist theology of bodhisattvas and Buddhas, but Hinduism ultimately prevailed due to its great ability to incorporate other movements. Indeed, Buddha became one of the Vaishnavite avatars.

By the seventh century the sangha had grown wealthy and held much land—facts that contributed to a decline in religious fervor and to antipathy among the laity. From the time of its first patronage under Asoka (around 260 B.C.E.), Buddhism enjoyed occasional support from princes and kings, and its ability to preach the dharma, to enjoy favor at court, and to influence culture depended on this support. The Kusana dynasty (ca. 78–320 C.E.), for instance, was a good time for Buddhists, while the Gupta age (320–540 C.E.) revived Hinduism. When the Muslims finally established control in India, Buddhism suffered accordingly. Early missionary activity had exported it, however, and Buddhism proved to be hardier on foreign soil than on Indian. So Hinduism, which has largely been confined to India, became the native tradition that opposed the Muslims, while Buddhism became an internationalized brand of Indian culture.[46]

China

Buddhism may have entered China as early as the beginning of the first century B.C.E. and almost certainly established itself by the middle of the second century C.E.[47] Buddhist missionaries traveled along the trade routes that linked northeastern India and China, probably entering at Tun-huang in the west. By 148 C.E., monks such as An Shih-kao had settled at Lo-yang, considerably to the east, and begun translating Buddhist texts. The first interests of these translators and their audiences appear to have been meditation and philosophy, which suggests that the Chinese first considered Buddhism similar to Taoism. However, as the translating progressed through the Han dynasty (ended 220 C.E.), sutras on morality and the Western Paradise of the Buddha became popular, too.

From this beginning, Buddhism slow-ly adapted to Chinese ways. Most of the preachers and translators who worked from the third to the fifth centuries C.E. favored Taoist terminology. This was especially true in the south, where the intelligentsia created a market for philosophy. In the less cultured north, Buddhism made progress by being presented as a powerful magic.[48] By the middle of the fifth century, China had its own sectarian schools, comparable to those that had developed in India. Thus, by that time most of the major Buddhist philosophies and devotional practices had assumed a Chinese style, including the *Abhidhamma* and the Indian Madhyamika and Yogacara schools. In general, Mahayana attracted the Chinese more than Theravada, and so the native schools that prospered developed Mahayana positions.

The Chinese brought to Buddhism an interest in bridging the gap between the present age and the age of the Buddha by constructing a line of masters along which the dharma passed intact. The master was more historical than timeless scriptural texts were, and the authority-minded Chinese were more concerned about history than the Indians had been.

Indeed, conflicts over the sutras were a sore problem for the Chinese, and in trying to reconcile seemingly contradictory positions, they frequently considered one scripture as being authoritative. A principal basis for the differences among the burgeoning Chinese Buddhist sects, therefore, lay in which scripture the sect's founder had chosen as most authoritative. (The notion of sects is distinctly Chinese, since it is based on the old concept of the clan. Chinese culture venerated its ancestors, and each Chinese Buddhist school accordingly had its dharma founder or patriarchal teacher.)

The most popular sects were the Ch'an and Ching-t'u, which devoted themselves to meditation and the Pure Land (a Buddhist heaven), respectively. As we mentioned earlier, the Chinese took to meditation from the beginning of their encounter with Buddhism. There are evidences of yogic practices in the Taoist works attributed to Lao-tzu and Chuang-tzu, and certainly Taoist imagery of what the sage who knows the "inside" can accomplish had made many Chinese eager to tap interior powers. Ch'an capitalized on this interest, working out a simple regime and theory that focused on meditation.[49] (Ch'an is the translation of the Indian *dhyana;* the Japanese translation is Zen.) Its principal text was the *Lankavatara Sutra,* which the Yogacarins also much revered, because that text stressed the mentality of all reality.

According to legend, Bodhidharma, an Indian meditation master devoted to the *Lankavatara,* founded Ch'an in the fifth century C.E. Paintings portray Bodhidharma as a fierce champion of single-mindedness, and he valued neither pious works nor recitations of the sutras. Only insight into one's own nature, which was identical with the dharma-nature of all reality, was of significance; only enlightenment justified the Buddhist life. Tradition credits Bodhidharma with developing the technique of "wall gazing," which was a kind of peaceful meditation—what the Japanese later called "just sitting" *(shikan-taza).*

Probably the most eminent of the Ch'an patriarchs who succeeded Bodhidharma was the sixth patriarch, Hui-neng. According to the *Platform Sutra,* which purports to present his teachings, Hui-neng gained his predecessor's mantle of authority by surpassing his rival, Shen-hsiu, in a demonstration of dharma insight. To express his understanding, Shen-hsiu wrote:

This juxtaposition of the masters' verses reflects the beliefs of the southern Ch'an school, which looked to Hui-neng as the authoritative spokesman for its position that enlightenment comes suddenly. Because all Buddha-nature is intrinsically pure, one need only let it manifest itself. The northern school held that enlightenment comes gradually and thus counseled regular meditation. (Hui-neng himself probably would have fought any sharp distinction between meditation and the rest of life. In wisdom all things are one and pure.) The southern school finally took precedence.[51]

Pure Land Buddhism (Ching-t'u) derived from T'an-luan (476–542). He sought religious solace from a grave illness, and after trying several systems, he came to the doctrine of Amitabha Buddha and the Pure Land. Amitabha is the Buddha of Light, devotion to whom supposedly assures one a place in the Western Paradise. T'an-luan stressed faith in Amitabha and the recitation of Amitabha's name as ways to achieve such salvation. This, he and his successors reasoned, was a doctrine both possible and appropriate in the difficult present age. The Pure Land sect greatly appealed to the laity, and it developed hymns and graphic representations of paradise to focus its imagination. In stressing love or emotional attachment to Amitabha (called Amida in China), it amounted to a Chinese Buddhist bhakti. By chanting "na-mo a-mi-t'o-fo" ("greetings to Amida Buddha"), millions of

---

The body is the Bodhi Tree
The mind is like a bright mirror and stand.
At all times wipe it diligently,
Don't let there be any dust.

Hui-neng responded:

Bodhi really has no tree;
The bright mirror also has no stand.
Buddha-nature is forever pure;
Where is there room for dust?[50]

Chinese found a simple way to fulfill their religious needs and made Amida the most popular god of Chinese history.[52]

These schools dominated Buddhism's rise in China, and during the peak of their influence (900–1300), they shaped the best minds, the art, and much of the imperial policy. Despite periods of persecution, Buddhism held spiritual sway until the fourteenth century. After that time each generation had its eminent monks, but neo-Confucian thought was the prevailing doctrine. Today, under the Communists, the Buddhist physical holdings seem quite devastated. Officially all religion is opposed, but some accommodation may permit Chinese Buddhism to survive.[53]

Japan

Buddhism infiltrated Japan by way of Korea during the second half of the sixth century C.E. It first appealed to members of the royal court as a possible source of blessing and good fortune. Also, it carried overtones of Chinese culture, which had great prestige. The Japanese rulers, in the midst of trying to solidify their country, thought of the new religion as a possible means, along with Confucian ethics, for unifying social life. So, during the seventh century, emperors built shrines and monasteries as part of the state apparatus. In the eighth century, when the capital was at Nara, the Hua-yen (called Kegon in Japan) school established itself and began to exert great influence. The government ideologues expediently equated the emperor with the Hua-yen Buddha Vairocana, and they made the Hua-yen realm of "dharmas not impeding one another"[54] a model for Japanese society. Kegon has survived in Japan to the present day, and it now has about 500 clergy and 125 temples.

At Nara, Buddhism had considerable influence on the arts and crafts, but when the imperial seat moved to Kyoto, it had even more. In the early ninth century, under the monk Saicho, Mount Hiei became an immensely successful center of T'ien-t'ai (Japanese "Tendai"). In its heyday this center had over 3,000 buildings and 30,000 monks.[55] Also in the ninth century the religious genius Kobo Daishi established a school (Shingon) that eventually overtook Tendai in popularity. It was a form of Tantrism that focused on Vairocana as the cosmic Buddha, and it won great favor because of its colorful rituals and Kobo Daishi's political flair.[56] Buddhism of the Heian period (794–1185) finally grew rather corrupt, however, because of the collusion between the monks and the ruling families. When power passed to the military and the court moved to Kamakura, the time was ripe for more popular and native forms of Japanese Buddhism.

Primary among them were the sects of Pure Land Buddhism. As in China, these were devotional schools dedicated to Amitabha. Other sects, such as Tendai, tried in their syntheses to provide for the laity's needs by sanctioning such practices as the chanting of Amitabha's name. However, the Pure Land sects made this practice central. Two great champions of Pure Land were Honen (1133–1212) and Shinran (1173–1262). Honen had considerable success in gaining imperial support for his movement because of his manifest humility and faith. His pupil Shinran felt that the goddess Kwannon (the Indian Avalokitesvara and Chinese Kuan-yin) inspired him to marry, and he received Honen's approval. By this move Shinran made his branch of Pure Land both closer to the laity and a champion of family life. He pushed the chanting of Amitabha's name, the necessity of faith for salvation, and the presence of the gracious Buddha-nature in all living beings.

Still another branch of popular Japanese Buddhism was founded by Nichiren (1222–1282). After considerable time in the Tendai monastery on Mount Hiei, Nichiren became convinced of the need for a purer religion. Tendai at that time had become so diffuse in its efforts to embrace all movements that Nichiren found it hopelessly unclear. So he settled on simply preaching the Lotus Sutra; however, he innovated by chanting a salutation to the sutra that was similar to Pure Land's salutation to Amitabha. By this chanting, one could attain moral virtue, Buddhahood, and paradise. Nichiren was a rather rabid religionist, convinced that other sects were grievously misleading, so he condemned Shingon and Pure Land for neglecting the historical Buddha Sakyamuni in favor of Vairocana. As well, he castigated *Zen* (the Japanese Ch'an sect stressing meditation) for neglecting the eternal Buddha of the Lotus Sutra. For this harshness he narrowly escaped a prophet's reward (martyrdom).

Zen

The Chinese Ch'an sect was present in Japan from the seventh century, but it only gained popularity during the Kamakura period (1185–1333). While the court was in Kamakura, eclecticism fell out of favor and pure single-mindedness was in style. Eisai (1141–1215) was an early Zen master. He began his religious career as a Tendai monk but, dissatisfied, went to China for training in the Lin-chi (Japanese "Rinzai") school of Ch'an. Returning to Japan, he convinced the now influential military class to accept Zen, and he adroitly avoided destructive conflicts with Tendai and Shingon. The link between Zen and the military class has been a hallmark of this school (especially of the Rinzai branch). As a result, Zen has furnished the martial arts and swordsmanship with most of their spiritual rationale. In addition, the Rinzai monk pursues a spartan regime of simplicity and self-discipline, which makes him the most austere of the Japanese warriors of the spirit. Japan also remembers Eisai as the father of tea, for when he returned from China, Eisai brought back some tea seeds and encouraged their planting around Zen monasteries.

A second great figure in the history of Zen is Dogen (1200–1253), who founded the Soto school. After an unsatisfying stay on Mount Hiei, he, too, left in search of a more satisfying regime. Coming under Eisai's influence, he went to China to study and then returned to live a very simple life based on *zazen*—sitting meditation. Zen reveres Dogen as a penetrating thinker who fur-

nished it with some of its deepest metaphysical bases. Analyzing the experiences of *zazen*, Dogen produced a Japanese version of the dialectics of Buddha-nature that we associate with Nagarjuna in India. From experiencing the oneness of all things as it shines forth in enlightenment, Dogen was able to clarify the nature of consciousness and the wonder of simple "is-ness." Contemporary Zen masters such as Yasutani-roshi and Philip Kapleau esteem him most highly.[57]

The fall of the Kamakura rule in the fourteenth century led to great civil strife. The Zen sects were the only ones that held themselves aloof from the fray, their monasteries becoming havens of peace and respite for intellectuals and artists. These monasteries were enterprising and self-sustaining, and often centers of education and culture. During the Tokugawa regime (1600–1867), Buddhism became a bureau of the state.[58] The ethical code (Bushido) that governed both warriors and merchants owed a great deal to Zen discipline, while the devotional sects continued to provide outlets for Buddhist religious emotions. The state kept a close eye on the clergy, tending to tie them to the care of temples, and the general atmosphere was one of stability and stagnation.

Modern Times

Under the Meiji restoration of the emperor, Shinto forces attacked Buddhism. A principal part of the attack was nationalistic: Shinto claimed to be the more ancient and truly Japanese religion. The Buddhists rose to the challenge, however, and modernized considerably. They tried to educate their clergy better for the new times, and they often opened schools for the laity. In fact, Buddhist centers in modern times have taken on many of the features of a Western parish, with organizations for children, small publications, Sunday school, meditation groups, charitable ventures, and so on. Some of the most beautiful Japanese shrines continue to be under Buddhist administration, and Japanese Buddhism has a healthy scholarly life. Along with Tibetan Tantrism,

Zen has had considerable success in the West. In California, for instance, groups of meditators and several monasteries are flourishing.[59]

Two Zen teachers, D. T. Suzuki and Shunryu Suzuki (no relation), have played a large role in this journey of Japanese Buddhism to the West. D. T. Suzuki was a prolific author, who commented especially on the place of Zen in the history of Japanese culture.[60] Since he was fluent in Indian and Western languages, he became the prime ambassador to Western intellectuals of the importance of mind, enlightenment, and nature's oneness. Shunryu Suzuki was a Soto master who wrote only one book but whose personality and simple style have captivated Americans interested in Buddhism.[61] His teaching clarifies the difference between Soto and Rinzai: Where Rinzai tends to strive for enlightenment (satori) directly, trying to break the dualistic mind through intense meditation on koans (paradoxical sayings such as "the sound of one hand clapping"), Soto is more relaxed. It believes that "just sitting" (shikan-taza) is an exercise of one's Buddha-nature and so more important than the peak experience of satori. So Shunryu Suzuki's brief addresses to his meditation groups stress the value of being attentive to each moment of the here and now.

CONTEMPORARY BUDDHIST RITUALS

The austere meditational focus of Zen and the continuing challenge of lofty Buddhist philosophy have captivated most Western observers of Buddhism, perhaps preventing them from properly appreciating Buddhist ritual. To fill out our historical account, let us focus on how contemporary Buddhist piety actually functions in such disparate locales as Burma and California, remembering that a similar ritualism has been important throughout all of Buddhist history.

Melford Spiro's informative anthropological study, *Buddhism and Society*,[62] includes a chapter on the ceremonial cycle of Burmese Buddhism. Of special interest are the devotions that paced the individual through the day. Although participation in these devotions was voluntary, and those who did not participate neither sinned nor lost merit, most Burmese took part (children being observers until they reached their teens).

The pious Burmese Buddhists that Spiro met in the late 1950s and early 1960s began and ended the day with devotions performed in front of a small household shrine. This shrine usually consisted of a shelf for a vase of fresh flowers and a picture of the Buddha. It was always located on the eastern side of the house (the most auspicious side) and placed above head level (to place the Buddha below head level would be insulting). During the time of devotions, householders would light candles and place food offerings before the Buddha.

Coming before this shrine, the householders would begin by saying: "I beg leave! I beg leave! I beg leave! By act, by word, and by thought, I raise my hands in reverence to the forehead and worship, honor, look at, and humbly pay homage to the three gems—the Buddha, the Law, and the Order—one time, two times, three times, O Lord." Then they would petition to be freed from the four woes (rebirth in hell, as an animal, as a demon, or as a ghost), from the three scourges (war, epidemic, and famine), from the eight kinds of unfortunate birth, from the five kinds of enemies, from the four deficiencies (tyrannical kings, wrong views of life after death, physical deformity, and dull-wittedness), and from the five misfortunes, that they might quickly enter nirvana. They would end the morning prayer by reciting the five precepts, pledging to abstain from taking life, from stealing, from drinking intoxicants, from lying, and from sexual immorality.

Clearly, therefore, the Burmese Buddhists sought to orient each day by honoring the Buddha, begging his protection against misfortune, and rededicating themselves to the Buddhist ethical code. In the evening many Burmese, especially the elderly, would conclude a similar session of homage, petition, and rededication by praying a rosary. The Buddhist rosary consisted of 108 beads, one for each of the 108 marks on the feet of the Buddha (which, in turn, represent his 108 reincarnations). While fingering a bead the devotee usually would say either "painful, selfless, fleeting" or "Buddha, dharma, sangha" three times.

In addition to these devotions held in the home, the villagers whom Spiro studied held a public ceremony every evening after sunset in the village chapel. This was located in the center of the village and consisted of a shed open on three sides. The fourth side enclosed an ark containing a statue of the Buddha. Attendance usually was sparse, except in special periods such as the Buddhist Lent, and more sophisticated believers, who thought meditation was the central expression of a mature Buddhist faith, spoke disparagingly of the chapel services as magical or superstitious.

Nonetheless, the village service is interesting because it was led by lay people, rather than monks, and because it used the Burmese vernacular, rather than Pali, the formal liturgical language. Thus, it was a place where common folk and Burmese youth could experience their religion in a form easy to understand.

The ceremony usually began with an invocation of the gods, and then an invocation of the Buddha, before whose image fresh cut flowers had been placed. The worshipers asked permission to reverence the Buddha and prayed that their worship might bring them to nirvana or the higher abodes (the states near to nirvana). Other prayers followed, asking the Buddha to grant the petitioners strength to fulfill the five precepts and understand the three marks.

The central portion of the village ceremony began with an offering of flowers, candles, and water—symbols of beauty, reverence, and purification. Following this, the faithful expressed their veneration of the Buddha, the teaching, the order, their parents, and their teachers. Next came recitations of parts of the scriptures, a profession of love for all creatures, a recitation of the doctrine of dependent coarising, a recitation of the Buddha's last words, a recitation of the five "heaps" *(skandas)* of which human individuality is composed, a prayer to the eight planets, and a confession of faith.

The ceremony concluded with a water libation that called the merit of the worshipers to the attention of an ancient earth goddess, the release of the gods who had been called into attendance, and an enthusiastic "sharing of merit" (of the benefit the participants had gained from the service) with the participants' parents and all other beings. Overall, the ceremony reenforced the main points of Buddhist teaching, reminding the participants how to orient their lives and encouraging them to express both their reverence for the Buddha and the main concerns for which they wanted the Buddha's aid.

Since 1970 there has been a successful Buddhist monastery near Mount Shasta in Northern California. It has seventeen buildings (a Zendo or meditation hall, a founder's shrine, a shrine to the Bodhisattva Kannon, a sewing room, a laundry, a tool shed, a store room, a library, eight residences, and a common room). The monastery was founded by an English woman named Peggy Kennett (Jiyu Kennett-Roshi), who is a guru in the Soto Zen tradition. While maintaining traditional Soto teachings, the Shasta monastery has tried to adapt to American cultural forms. Thus members eat their meals American style at a table rather than Japanese style sitting on the floor, they chant in Gregorian tones rather than Japanese tones, they usually wear Western clerical garb rather than Japanese robes, and they serve English rather than Japanese tea.

The central occupation of the monastery is *zazen*, or sitting in meditation. Most members of the monastery spend two to three hours in meditation each day. Charles Prebish has described the daily schedule of all the monastic duties as follows:

5:45 A.M.	Rising Bell
6:15	*Zazen*
7:00	Morning Service
7:45	Community Tea
8:15	Breakfast
8:45	Community Clean-up
9:15	Trainees' Class
11:00	Community Tea
11:30	Junior Trainees' and Laypeople's Class
1:00 P.M.	Lunch
1:30	Rest
2:00	Priests' Class (Work Period for Others)
3:00	Community Tea

3:30	Work Period
5:00	*Zazen*
6:00	Dinner
6:30	Choir Practice
7:30	Evening Service
7:45	*Zazen*
8:30	Tea
9:00	Return to Residences[63]

During the morning service, the trainees make three bows and offer incense to the celebrant, Kennett-Roshi. The community then intones and recites portions of the Buddhist scriptures. There are three more bows, and then the community processes to the founder's shrine, where they recite more scriptures. During the evening ceremony, in addition to the scripture recitations, there is a reading of the rules for *zazen*. At meals someone recites portions of the scriptures while the food is passed, in order to help community members increase their sense of gratitude for what they are about to receive. Since the meditation hall is closed on any day of the month having a four or a nine (for reasons Prebish does not disclose), six times in most months there is a "closing ceremony." Vespers finish the evening service, and through the day monks say prayers before such activities as shaving their heads and putting on their robes.

If this schedule inculcates the same dispositions that the similar schedules of strict Christian monasteries do, the result is a great focusing of attention. The day passes largely in silence, for speech is allowed only at stated times, and most community members expend much effort in meditation. At Mount Shasta there are regular periods throughout the year when the monks concentrate on meditation almost full-time, making a strong effort to come closer to enlightenment. Yet the Soto conviction that Buddha-nature should emerge peacefully probably keeps most monks from confusing religious intensity with neurotic self-concern.

The recitation of the Buddhist scriptures potentially has the effect of reciting mantras, for when sounds enter consciousnesses that have been purified by discipline and made alert by meditation, they can develop almost mesmerizing cadences. The ritual bows, use of incense, use of flowers, and the like help to engage all the senses and focus all the spiritual faculties, so that the prayer or meditation to be performed can be wholehearted.

A major difference between the monastic ritualism of Mount Shasta and the lay ritualism of the Burmese Buddhism we described is the stress the lay ritualism placed on petitioning the Buddha for protection against misfortune and help with worldly needs. Part of this difference stems from the greater stress that Theravada lay doctrine places on gaining merit. Whereas the monastic doctrine of Soto Zen stresses the enlightenment nature of all reality, the Burmese Buddhists live in a thought-world filled with ghosts and gods that constantly make them aware of a need to improve their karmic state. Consequently, Burmese ritual seems more anxious. While it stresses the merit one must attain for a better future, the Soto ritual stresses the grace, harmony, and peace that enlightenment brings. (Of course, Soto ritual is also an effort to inculcate the dispositions that conduce to enlightenment, such as inner silence, gratitude, and a sense of harmony with all of creation.)

As we saw, Burmese ritual also tends to be a constant reminder of staple Buddhist doctrine. It has an important place for honoring the Buddha, and for expressing the worshipers' needs, but a great deal of its energy goes into reviewing, or trying to deepen the worshipers' hold on, the five precepts, the three jewels, and so on. Mount Shasta appears to take care of doctrine in the classroom.

In both cases, however, Buddhist rituals set believers to worship, the central religious act, as other religions' rituals set their adherents to worship. At worship, members of quite different religious traditions appear to draw much closer to one another. Despite massive doctrinal differences (which, of course, shape what the worshipers understand themselves to be doing), the members of the different traditions are all trying to collect themselves, praise what they take to be ultimate reality, and gain the spiritual aid they need. Not surprisingly, therefore, some of the most fruitful comparative study of religion occurs when we try to enter into the inner dispositions of the different religions' rituals.

STRUCTURAL ANALYSIS

Nature

Stepping back from the historical view of Buddhism, we find that Buddhist attitudes toward nature do not fit together neatly. From its Indian origins, Buddhism assumed much of Hinduism's cosmological complexity. That meant taking up not only a world that stretched for vast distances and existed for immense eons (kalpas) but also the Aryan materialism and yogic spiritualism that lay behind such a cosmology. However, Buddhism came to contribute its own world views. Its numerous "Buddha-fields," for instance, are heavenly realms with which our earthly space-time system shares the boundless universe.

Buddhism has had few equivalents to Vedic materialism, but Buddhism used the doctrine of samsara early in its history to justify acceptance of one's worldly situation and working only to improve it (rather than to escape it for nirvana). On the other hand, the ancient Indian yogic practices impressed the Buddha and his followers deeply. Since Gautama had in fact become enlightened through meditation, and since this enlightenment expressed itself in terms of the antimaterial Four Noble Truths, Buddhism could never settle comfortably in the given world of the senses and pleasure.

Initially, therefore, Buddhism looked on nature or physical reality as much less than the most real or valuable portion of existence. Certainly the belief that all life is suffering reflects a rather negative attitude toward nature, and it indicates that what the eyes see and the ears hear is not the realm of true reality or true fulfillment. Also, to analyze physical reality in terms of three negative "marks" (pain, fleetingness, and selflessness) further devalues nature. At the least, one is not to desire sensory contacts with the world, because such desire binds one to illusory reality and produces only pain. Thus, Indian Buddhists separated themselves from nature (and society and self).

Because the great interest of early Buddhist philosophy was an analysis of dharmas based on probings of consciousness sharpened by intense meditation, the material aspects of the natural realm fell by the way. At best they were background realities and values. The scholastic Abhidhammists did not deny nature, for they were acutely aware of the senses, but they did deflect religious consciousness away from it.[64] Far more impressive than natural phenomena were the states of consciousness that seemed to go below the sensible flux to pure spirituality. They were the places where the Indian Buddhists preferred to linger.

In considering the Buddhist view of nature, we must distinguish between the inclinations of the meditators and scholars, who were interested in nonphysical states of consciousness, and the inclinations of the laity, who saw the world more concretely and less analytically. As we might expect, the laity was more worldly than the monks. When they heard that all life is suffering, they thought of their family burdens, their vulnerability to sickness, and the many ways in which nature and time seemed out of their control. The comforts that they received from Buddhist preaching, therefore, lay in the promise that right living would take them a step closer to the kind of existence where their pain would be less and their enjoyment greater.[65]

Thus, it is no surprise that the most popular Buddhist movements were built on the Indian traditions of bhakti. Just as popular Hinduism fixed on Vishnu, Krishna, and Shiva, popular Buddhism fixed on Amitabha, Avalokitesvara, and Vairocana. These celestial Buddhas or bodhisattvas drew the popular religious imagination away from the historical Buddha and the commonplace world of the here and now to the realm of future fulfillment. In that way, popular Buddhism lay between the deemphasis of the physical realm that the monks and scholars practiced and the simple acceptance of physical life that a worldly or naturalist outlook (such as that of the early Vedas) produced. Emotional Buddhism influenced the sense perceptions of the laity so that this world became just the preliminary to the Western Paradise.[66]

Samsara and Nirvana

As the intellectuals and contemplatives worked further with immaterial consciousness and its philosophical consequences, they changed the relationships between samsara and nirvana. In the beginning, Buddhism thought of samsara as the imperfect, illusory realm of given, sense-bound existence. The Buddha himself exemplified this view when he urged his followers to escape the world that is "burning" to achieve nirvana. His original message regularly said that spontaneous experience makes one ill, and that health lies in rejecting attachments to spontaneous experience. With time, however, the philosophers, especially the Mahayanists, came to consider the relations between nirvana and samsara as being more complex. From analyzing the implications of these concepts, the philosophers determined that nirvana is not a thing or a place. The Buddha realized this, for he consistently refused to describe nirvana in detail. But while the Buddha's refusal was practical (such a description would not help solve the existential problems of being in pain), the refusal of the later philosophers, such as Nagarjuna, was largely epistemological and metaphysical. That is, they thought that we cannot think of such a concept as nirvana without reifying it and that the reality of nirvana must completely transcend the realm of things.

From the viewpoint of the wisdom that has gone beyond (has assumed a transcendent, or epistemologically and metaphysically adequate, point of view), nirvana is the basis and the inmost reality of samsara, so we cannot finally separate nirvana and samsara. They are one, because all the reality of samsara (even the reality of appearances) is grounded in the ultimate reality that we call nirvana.

To follow this line of thought is no easy task, so only the elite grasped the philosophy of the *Prajna-paramita*, with its concepts of emptiness and transcendence. That philosophy influenced the devotional life of Mahayana and the ritual life of Tantrism, however, because even the simple people could grasp its positive implications as presented by the preachers. These positive implications, which blossomed most fully in the East Asian cultures, reduced to seeing that all reality is one. The other side of saying that all dharmas are empty is to say that the Buddha-nature (or nirvana, or the other ways of expressing the ultimate totality) is present everywhere. This belief gave religion a very positive tone. For instance, if all things contain the Buddha-nature, then our world will become glowingly fresh and beautiful as we realize who and what we are.

East Asia

When the message about Buddha-nature came to China and Japan, it was a spark meeting ready tinder. The native traditions of those cultures stressed an ideal harmony of all nature's elements. In fact, both Taoism and Shinto set the individual in a natural whole or pattern (gestalt), inculcating a great reverence for nature and a special sensitivity to natural rhythms (the annual seasons, for instance). Especially in China, the tradition counseled the individual in the landscape of nature to find peace by attunement to the cosmic music, the universal way. Because Buddhism had better techniques (primarily meditative) for sharpening a sense of the oneness of things and their flow, and because it also had a more highly developed system for explaining reality's interconnectedness, serious Chinese and Japanese took it to heart. They could satisfy their native hunger to be at one with nature by following the new wisdom's way. More profoundly and intensely than with their native religious systems, they could enjoy the beauty of emptiness, of fullness, and of Buddha-nature's endlessly creative overflow into trees, mountains, streams, and people.

The East Asian forms of Buddhism, of course, also developed an imaginative or devotional religion for the common people, such as the Pure Land sects. They developed festivals, ceremonies, mythologies of ghosts and helping spirits, and amalgamations of Buddhist lore and native magic.[67] At the heart of the most intense East Asian Buddhist efforts, however, we find that the concept of nature emerges differently than in India. In Hua-yen or Ch'an Buddhism, for instance, aesthetics seem more important than in Indian Madhyamika or Yogacara. That is, the Chinese love of natural beauty makes a stronger impression.

Whereas Indian philosophers love the subtlety of conceptual analysis, Chinese philosophers love the oneness and beauty of the concrete, here-and-now world. Consequently, when the circle of samsara-nirvana relations turns in East Asia, it seems to come back close to a naive starting point. In the beginning, mountains are mountains, and trees are trees. The Chinese and Japanese thinkers accept turning away from this naive starting point, as done by Buddha and then by the Indian philosophers, but they finally bend back to it. For their enlightenment, nature or physical reality just *is*, and such is-ness applies to mountains and trees as much as it applies to the transcendent quality in them that the mind can discern. In other words, after its discernment of nirvana and then its mental reconstitution of nirvana with samsara, East Asian Buddhism placed the ultimate realities and values right back in concrete, here-and-now, visible and audible nature. The landscape paintings, moss and rock gardens, tea ceremonies, and the like exemplify this attitude, as does *shikan-taza.*[68]

Tantrist Buddhism, finally, shares with East Asian schools the belief in the oneness of samsara and nirvana that Indian Mahayana developed but differs in its expression of this belief through ritual magic and imagination. Tibetan practices, for example, are neither intellectual like Indian Buddhism nor nature based and contemplative like East Asian Buddhism. Rather, they play with the world, both loving nature and kicking it away, through sights (mandalas), sounds (mantras), and ceremonies (symbolic intercourse) that engage the participant both psychologically and physically. Insofar as physical nature reaches into the human being through the subconscious and unconscious, Tantrism has most successfully honored and provided for nature's "depth psychology."

Society

The Indian society of the Buddha was divided into castes, which were religiously sanctioned as a way of maintaining social order. Moreover, casteism was part of Vedic India's cosmological myth, since human society's order resulted from the sacrifice of Purusha, according to legend. In Brahmanism, the priests merited their primary status because they derived from Purusha's head.

Buddha, himself a member of the warrior class, brought a message that clashed with this hierarchy. His dharma taught that beings are to free themselves from painful worldly life. Since this invitation was from nature, from what we are, it was more compelling than the call to accept the caste tradition. At least Buddhists could strongly refute the cosmological myth that legitimated casteism. Many warriors and merchants no doubt found Buddhism a convenient weapon in their struggles with the brahmins for power. So they and others who wanted to change the status quo gave Buddhism a close hearing.

There was great liberation potential in the Buddha's message. Indeed, there was considerable radicalism. Buddha did not concern himself very much with politics as such, but his stress on enlightenment, nirvana, and the human calling to conquer karma and samsara challenged the politics of his day, as did the decision to admit persons of all castes into the sangha, including women. This decision was only a logical application of the belief that all humans were in misery.

In application, of course, Buddhism never fully realized these ideals of liberation and radical equality. Caste was too much a part of Indian society to be exorcised without great difficulty. For instance, the *Dhammapada* (vv. 383–423) uses the brahmin as a figure of perfection. The "true Brahmin," it is at pains to show, is not he who is born into a priestly bloodline but he who gains a noble character through morality, meditation, and wisdom. Nonetheless, the *Dhammapada* does not choose to reinterpret the Sudra (lowest class worker). It is the brahmin who continues to denote nobility.

Women's Status

Buddhism offered Indian females considerably more than had been available to them previously.[69] Women were capable of enlightenment and could join the monastic community as nuns. This was in stark contrast to the classical Hindu view, which held that women had to be reborn as men to be eligible for *moksha*. By opening religious life to Indian women, Buddhists gave them an option besides marriage and motherhood—a sort of career and chance for independence. No longer did a girl and her family have to concentrate single-mindedly on gathering a dowry and arranging a wedding. Indeed, Buddhists viewed Hindu child marriage darkly, and they thought it more than fitting that women should travel to hear the Buddha preach. In later times, women could preach themselves, but from the beginning they could give time and money to the new cause.

Moreover, by offering an alternative to marriage, Buddhism inevitably gave women more voice in their marriage decisions and then in their conjugal lives. In fact, Buddhism viewed spouses as near equals. The husband was to give the wife respect, courtesy, faithfulness, and authority, while the wife was to give the husband duties well done, hospitality to their parents, faithfulness, watchfulness over his earnings, skill, and industry. One concrete way in which a Buddhist wife shared authority was in choosing their children's careers. For instance, to enter a monastery, a child needed both parents' consent. Married women could inherit

and manage property without interference. Buddhism did not require or even expect that widows be recluses, while suttee was abhorrent to a religion that condemned animal sacrifice, murder, and suicide. Finally, Buddhist widows could enter the sangha, where they might find religious companionship, or they could stay in the world, remarry, inherit, and manage their own affairs.

Still, Buddhism never treated women as full equals of men. Though the logic of equal existential pain and equal possession of the Buddha-nature could have run to equal political and educational opportunities, it seldom did. Nuns had varying degrees of freedom to run their own affairs in the monasteries, but they were regularly subject to monks. Women never gained regular access to power over males, either in Buddhism's conception of the religious community or in its conception of marriage. Insofar as celibacy became part of the Buddhist ideal, marriage became a second-class vocation and women became a religious danger.[70]

Politics

In its relations with secular political powers, Buddhism had varying fortunes. The Buddha seems to have concerned himself little with pleasing public authorities or worrying how his spiritual realm related to the temporal. By the time of Asoka, however, the importance of royal patronage became clear. Much of Buddhism's influence outside India began when Asoka dispatched missionaries to foreign lands, and his efforts to instill Buddhist norms of ethics and nonviolence in his government became a model for later ages. As Christianity rethought Jesus' dictum about rendering unto Caesar the things that are Caesar's when it found a potentially Christian Caesar in Constantine, so Buddhism after Asoka longed for a union of dharma and kingly authority in the hope that such a union could beget a religious society.

Historically Buddhists tried to gain favor at court.[71] In Sri Lanka, Burma, Thailand, and the rest of Southeast Asia, this effort succeeded, and temporal rulers played a large role in Theravada's victory over Mahayana and Hinduism. In China, Buddhism's fortunes depended on whether it fared better or worse than Confucianism in getting the emperor's ear. During the worse periods, it became the object of imperial persecution. The same was true in Japan, where such persecution had much the same rationale: Buddhism was not the native tradition. Overall, however, Buddhism fared well in East Asia. It had to coexist with Confucian and Taoist cultural forces there, but it regularly dominated philosophy, funeral rites, and art.

For instance, as we have seen, Zen's favor with the ruling classes in Japan after the fall of the Heian dynasty made that sect tremendously influential. Indeed, so long as Japan favored the samurai or warrior ideal, Zen was close to the corridors of power. Finally, Tibet realized the theocratic ideals that Asoka had sparked, for throughout most of its history religious leaders doubled as temporal powers. However, the intrigue, murder, and moral laxity that this binding of the two powers produced during certain periods of Tibetan history necessitated rethinking the relation between the religious and the secular powers.

As with Christianity, a tension is built in between the Buddhist religious community and any temporal state. The sangha and the church both make claims upon their followers that can bring them into conflict with secular powers. Since these claims are made in the name of dharma or God, they carry an aura of sacredness or of coming from a higher authority. To be sure, Buddhism took pains to establish an ethics that urged peaceful citizenship.[72] But the proviso always lurking behind these sincere efforts was that secular rulers not order things unjust, evil, or irreligious. The things that rightly are Caesar's are limited. So long as there is a Christ or a Buddha, a God or a nirvana, Caesar cannot claim everything.

One ploy that Caesar can develop, however, is to claim that he, rather than the priests or monks, is the representative of God or dharma. In other words, employing the aspect of the cosmological myth by which the human ruler is the link between heaven and earth, the king can claim a sacredness of his own. Many Christian successors to Constantine claimed this, and in effect many Buddhist rulers after Asoka did also. Voegelin has sketched the preparation for this sort of claim that a society such as the Mongol had; according to this hypothesis, Kublai Khan gave the Dalai Lama authority over Tibet as an administrative extension of his own sacred power.[73]

Despite its focus on otherworldly matters, then, Buddhism remained knotted in secular-religious controversies. Since it did not clearly establish an authority outside the cosmos (for instance, by coming to a doctrine of creation from nothingness), it was always theoretically liable to attack from kingly Buddhists who wanted to make dharma serve the state.

The Sangha

The sangha alternately raised and dashed hopes for humans living together in harmony and peace. Energetic monasteries, run by learned and holy monks or nuns, were models of what human society could be. Living simply, obeying a common rule and a common authority, such Buddhist professionals acted out a vision of equality and cooperation. When a monastery was in good spiritual fettle, one survived there only if one's motivation was religious. Meditation, hard work, austerity in diet and clothing, long periods of silence, celibacy—these staples of Zen monastic life offered little to the worldling. Monasteries of the devotional sects were quite different. People entered them rather grudgingly and briefly in order to learn the minimal ritual and doctrine necessary to function at the inherited family temple. Early Buddhist monasteries also differed from the pampered, court-favored centers of learning, art, and intrigue that were frequently spawned by Far Eastern Buddhism. So long as the genuine articles existed, Buddhism was alive and well.

The life of Buddhist laity has always reflected the state of the monastic sangha. When the monasteries were spiritually active, the laity tended to support them generously. In return, the monks usually served the laity spiritually. During these periods, the notion that the layperson's vocational obligation was primarily to support the monks evoked no cynicism. On the other hand, when the monks were lax, the reaction of the laity was ambivalent. The laity enjoyed seeing clay feet under yellow robes, but they missed the examples and teachings that might have dissolved some of their own clay. Ideally, then, the monks and nuns and the laity have provided mutual support.[74] Mahayana and Tantra have acted on this ideal by equating nirvana and samsara in such a way that vocational differences between the laity and the clergy were lessened. Even for these schools, however, the monasteries have symbolized places of retreat, meditation, study, and ritual devotion.

BUDDHIST *AHIMSA*

In an appendix to his study of Theravada ethics,[75] Winston King has some interesting remarks about recent Buddhist attitudes toward killing. Perhaps they will somewhat bridge the way from the Indian tradition of *ahimsa* to our present age, with its pressures from nuclear weapons, ecological disorders, and dietary researches to rethink our modern aggression.

Traditionally, Buddhism has laid great stress on the precept of nonkilling, not only because this precept inculcates a respect for all living things, but also because carefully observing it leads to great self-control. For example, if one is to stay away from killing or injuring other creatures, one must control anger, greed, hatred, and the other vices that usually spur our injurious actions.

Nonetheless, in countries such as Burma, where many political figures profess to be faithful Buddhists, the question of how to apply the precept of nonkilling in public policy has grown quite vexed. Thus one candidate in the 1959–60 elections pointed out the difficulty of adhering to strict interpretations of nonkilling while trying to suppress rebel insurgents or run such important government industries as fishing and mutton production. This dilemma differs little from that of the Christian pacifist, but nonviolence probably has been closer to the core of Buddhist tradition than to the core of Christian tradition. Leading Buddhist politicians, such as U Thant, who became head of the United Nations, therefore have had to make some distinctions. Generally they have tried to moderate public policies in the direction of nonkilling but have conceded that a thorough application of *ahimsa* (for example, prohibiting all military action) is not always practical.

Capital punishment is another problem that the precept of nonkilling heightens. Ideally, most Buddhists probably would oppose a law of capital punishment, urging sentences of life imprisonment for capital crimes. This would not only honor *ahimsa*, it would also offer the criminal an opportunity to repent and be converted to Buddhist convictions. Still, through history to modern times most Buddhist countries have practiced capital punishment. This has caused some analysts to speak of a conflict between the mundane morality of the state and the ideal morality of the Buddhist religion. In their view, the state needs capital punishment to maintain order, so one must reluctantly kill the worst social offenders. This might seem to relegate Buddhist ideals to complete impracticality, but further reflection has led some ethicians to a more dialectical notion of nonkilling.

For these dialecticians, there are circumstances in which *not* slaying heinous offenders would be a great violence. Those charged with protecting the common good would seriously fail their charge were they to allow murderers to continue operating without fear of capital punishment. So the dialecticians come to the conclusion that committing the lesser evil is doing a species of good. In other words, they justify capital punishment as a necessary evil, a means public officials must employ if they are to honor the precept of noninjury in more general, far-reaching terms. To prevent great injury to the public at large, one must injure some criminal offenders. Once again, it would not be hard to draw parallels to Western debates over capital punishment.

Still another implication of the precept of noninjury is that one must avoid contributing to the *conditions* that lessen or warp the span of living things, especially human beings. This is parallel to the Latin American theoreticians' discussions of *violencia blanca. Violencia blanca* is the white or invisible violence that an unjust system perpetrates through its inequitable distribution of wealth and power. Thus, when they are accused of corrupting their revolutionary cause by resorting to military violence or violence against the property of the rich, some Latin Americans argue that the prevailing *violencia blanca* in the slums, poverty, shortened life spans, bloated stomachs of little children, illiteracy, and the like, is a greater evil, though of course one to which we have grown accustomed.

The Buddhist parallel quoted by King is quite exact. In it a contemporary Burmese ethician urges his fellow countrymen to apply the precept of nonkilling to "crowded and ill-ventilated buildings, workshops and factories; slum conditions in big cities and towns; the overworking of children as well as adults; careless driving of steam boats, rail engines, planes, motor and other vehicles and engines; sale of spurious and other adulterated foodstuffs; unskilled use of syringes with or without license; treatment of sick people by quacks; sale of foodstuffs not fit for human consumption," and so forth. Anything that violates human health or dignity can be subsumed under the precept of nonkilling. When taken radically, this precept approximates the Christian and Confucian commandment to treat one's neighbor as oneself.

King contrasts this radical social ethics with the fatalistic, somewhat self-centered views of karma that too often obtain in Buddhist countries, offering the radical view as a hopeful sign. Were Buddhism to apply its imagination to developing a social ethics that carried noninjury down to concrete details, it could develop the dharma into a powerful social gospel. Caring for the well-being of all living things, it might make greater strides toward enlightened health care, education, economics, and the like.

The Buddhist thought that most affected society, though, was that the Buddha-nature exists in all beings and makes them worthy of respect and holy living. The bodhisattva vow that Mahayana developed gave this belief solid form, insofar as one aspired to earn the salvation of all living beings. Buddhism has often failed to practice the bodhisattva vow in terms of establishing hospitals, schools, and other charitable institutions as Western religion would do, but the Buddhist record in performing good deeds is not negligible. Buddhist monasteries have not been exclusively places of spiritual retreat, and the bodhisattva's "great compassion" has touched other beings' bodies as well as souls.

Still, the social vision of Buddhism has remained quite spiritual. The bodhisattva's compassion has primarily been directed toward what Buddhism considers the deeper portion of human misery, namely, our living apart from enlightenment in karmic distress. So the ideal society spawned by the Four Noble Truths became similar to the Christian Communion of Saints in that it stretched beyond the temporal world to heaven (the Western Paradise). There all Buddhists might experience how oneness is social.

Self

The practical accent of Buddha's original preaching made the issues related to self paramount. Yet, paradoxically, a capital thesis in that preaching was that self is an illusion, "the most pernicious of errors, the most deceitful of illusions."[76] Consequently, Buddhist religious experience and doctrine concerning the self have been complex. On the one hand, Buddhism has directly addressed individuals, insisting that only the individual can change his or her life. On the other hand, Buddhism has counseled that in order to escape samsara and achieve nirvana, we have to rid ourselves of the notion that we have or are an atman, a soul, or self. This belief has prompted some of Buddhism's central meditation practices and philosophical doctrines.

Historically, the teaching of no-self most distinguished the Buddha's way from that of his Hindu predecessors. As we have seen, a staple of Upanishadic wisdom was that the self is part of the great Atman (the interior aspect of Brahman). In yogic meditation, the Hindu tried to realize this ultimate identity, to experience the oneness of everything in Atman. When Buddha turned away from this teaching, calling human identity just a bundle of elements *(skandhas)* temporarily fused, he laid down a philosophical challenge that Hindu and Buddhist philosophers seldom neglected in later centuries. What motivated this new conception of the human being?

The principal motive, it appears, was Buddha's conviction that the key to human problems is desire. If pain expresses the problem ("All life is painful"), then desire expresses its cause ("The cause of suffering is desire"). These, we have seen, are the first two Noble Truths. The Third Noble Truth ("The removal of desire leads to the removal of suffering") extends the first two, and when Buddhists pondered its meaning and implications, they came to the doctrine of no-self.

The Third Noble Truth itself is psychological. For instance, we may analyze the suffering in human relations in terms of desire. Parents desire their children's success and love. When the children choose paths other than what the parents have dreamed, or when the children demand distance in order to grow into their own separate identities, the parents suffer pain. They feel disappointed or rejected, or that their toil and anxiety have gone for naught. Buddhists would tell such parents that their relations with their children have been unwise or impure. Because they have desired success and love, instead of remaining calm and free, they have set karmic bonds that were sure to cause pain.

But to cut the karmic bonds, the Third Noble Truth implies, one must get to the root of the desire. At this point one must turn psychology into metaphysics—one must realize that the self from which desires emanate is neither stable, fixed, permanent, nor, ultimately, real. In our distraction and illusion, we gladly accept the fiction that we have stable selves. Under the prod of analysis and meditation, however, we start to see what Alfred North Whitehead (the Western philosopher currently touted as the most "Buddhist" of our metaphysicians)[77] called the "fallacy of misplaced concreteness."

In simple terms, the prime reality in our interior lives is flux. At each moment we are different "selves." True, some continuity exists in that we remember past events and project future ones. But this continuity hardly justifies the clinging reliance on a permanent self, which is the substance of desire.

What Buddhists stressed, therefore, was the change and coordination of the "self's" components, just as they stressed the interconnectedness and flux of the entire world (through dependent coarising). They developed a view of both the interior realm of consciousness and the exterior realm of nature that became quite relational. Their metaphysics focused on nature's coordinated interdependencies, its continual movement. The self could not be the exception to such a world view. Humans were too clearly a part of the total natural process to violate the process's fundamental laws. And just as analysis showed all the natural elements to be empty, so, too, analysis showed the self to be empty.

Therefore, Buddhists directly denied what Western philosophers such as Aristotle called a "substance." To live religiously, in accordance with the facts of consciousness, one had to cast off the naive assumption that the human person is a solid something—one had to slide into the flux. In so doing, one could both remove the basis for desire and open up the possibility for union with the rest of coordinated reality.

This movement toward union with the rest of reality became the positive counterweight to the Buddhist negative view of the self. That is, as people advanced in their meditation and understanding, they started to glimpse what Mahayana saw in enlightenment: the realization that all Buddha-nature is one. According to the *Prajna-paramita*, ultimately only Buddha-nature (or Suchness)

existed. All multiplicity or discreteness resulted from a less than ultimate viewpoint. Yogacara texts such as the Chinese *Awakening of Faith*[78] explicitly correlated this viewpoint of ultimate wisdom with meditation. Stressing the centrality of mind, the *Awakening of Faith* tried to lead the reader toward the realization that his or her own consciousness reflected the ultimate oneness. Such a realization, of course, meant the death of the illusion that one was an independent atman.

CONTEMPORARY BURMESE MEDITATION

The Theravada tradition also has stressed the importance of meditation for gaining freedom from the illusions of the self, and this tradition has experienced a vigorous renaissance in contemporary Burma. By and large, most of the recent Burmese meditation masters have emphasized attaining insight into the true nature of reality, in contrast to meditation masters in other eras or lands who have emphasized attaining a formless yogic trance. Since they claim that insight was the original Buddhist emphasis, while trance was the Hindu emphasis, the recent Burmese masters have rather self-consciously striven to give preference to the Buddhist, rather than the Hindu Brahmanistic, influences that Indian history bequeathed them.

For most contemporary Burmese practitioners of meditation, the goal is improving one's karmic state and so gaining a fortunate rebirth. In contrast to the Hindu yogic tradition, which pays close attention to body-mind control, the Buddhist insight tradition is said to pay close attention to *observing* the body-mind unity in its actions, thoughts, and feelings. Control is secondary and less important.

The preferred Burmese focus for observing the body-mind unity is the breath or the body's tonus (feeling). By cultivating a regular breathing that integrates the body-mind components and stressing feeling, the Burmese masters have shifted away from the visual emphasis of the yogic tradition. They urge that one try to grow more sensitive to the touch of the breath at the

nostrils or the rise and fall of the abdomen. Then, with practice, one can expand this tactile awareness to other dimensions of experience, for example, the pleasures or pains one is experiencing. The result should be a heightened attention to what is most real—stimulating, pleasing, or irritating— to the body-mind unity at a given moment. Behind the efforts to gain this heightened attention lies the conviction that the three marks, if vividly experienced, will bring one great progress.

The descriptions of a European Buddhist who learned Burmese meditation may concretize some of these theoretical remarks. The man was in Rangoon, Burma, on a business trip in December of 1952. He had been a practicing Buddhist for eighteen years, had grown interested in meditation while spending a year in monasteries in Mongolia and Tibet, and therefore contacted Guru Sithu U Ba Khin, a prominent Burmese meditation master. Guru Sithu put him on a regime of insight-meditation *(vipassana)*, beginning with two half-hour introductory sessions. These were all the man required to see clearly within himself a remarkable light. He took this light to be the powerful and bright illumination the mind gives off when we free it from disturbances and let it be pure and serene. The basic method the man used to come to this illumination was concentrating on his breath, which allowed him to still and focus his consciousness to "one-pointedness."

The man continued meditating, shifting his concentration to his bodily sensations. The first sensation that preoccupied him was his body's burning or suffering. As he focused on his bodily temperature, a burning within him grew to the point that he felt like steam on the surface of boiling water. As he stayed with this sensation, it expanded to the point that it seemed to envelop the core of his being. The suffering he felt was almost unbearable, since all of him seemed on fire.

> *At the last moment, when I felt myself about dying, it was as if my heart was pulled out of my body and at the same moment—wanting eagerly to be freed from Dukka [suffering]—with a sudden but a small flash of light, I was out of it and felt a refreshing coolness and delight, which words cannot describe. It is an escape and a refuge from all daily trouble, too great to be understood, when not experienced. And the great bliss is that every one can achieve this state; provided he has a pure mind at least for the time of concentration, has the right intentions, attentiveness and concentration, and anyhow tries to live as pure as possible.[79]*

Guru Sithu glossed this account of the man's meditational experiences with the following remarks: (1) He and the European Buddhist had agreed that morality, meditation, and wisdom were the three indispensible steps to Buddhist development. (2) He found the man morally sound and already well advanced in meditation, as the man's quick access to the light of the mind revealed. (3) The man understood theoretically the Buddhist (and contemporary scientific) notion that everything in the universe is in flux. By developing his insight-meditation, he would soon be able to realize the true nature of the forms and names under which everchanging reality appears. (4) The man's experience of heat was a breakthrough on the way to realizing the fluctuating and painful character of all reality. (5) He assured the man that experiencing suffering is one of the best ways to extinguish suffering. (6) The coolness the man experienced was a sort of rebirth, showing that he had burned up a significant portion of the impurities that cause our human suffering.

So, we find in this recent Burmese example the traditional truths of suffering and transiency. Drawing on centuries of meditators' experience, many contemporary Burmese Buddhists are hard at work trying to change their body-mind condition, so that one day, one lifetime, they may experience no-self and be ready for nirvana.

We have belabored this teaching of no-self because it seems most important to the Buddhist attitude toward the individual. It is also the key to the Buddhist view that nature flows to oneness and that society should strive for ultimate reality by means of enlightenment. Because of *anatman* (no-self), the individual could move toward greater intimacy with nature. There were no barriers of separate identity, no walls making him or her isolated. For those who attained enlightenment through the dharma, this oneness of self, nature, and society was a personal experience. As a contemporary account of enlightenment puts it, "The big clock chimes—not the clock but Mind chimes. The universe itself chimes. There is neither Mind nor universe. Dong, dong, dong! I've totally disappeared. Buddha is!"[80]

Buddhism regularly counseled the individual to regard the body, the family, society, and even a spouse or a child with detachment. One was to revere and discipline the body according to the middle way. Clearly, though, the body was a temporary station on the way to nirvana or one's next incarnation. Wealth and pleasure were not, as they were for Hinduism, worthy life goals. The family was a necessary unit, biologically and socially, but frequently it was also an impediment to spiritual advancement, as the Buddha's own life showed. Society would ideally be a context for mutual support in realizing enlightenment. Personal bonds, therefore, could not be passionate and karmic, and even a spouse or a child came under this law.

The love proper to a Buddhist was therefore "great compassion"—desire for the other's good in nirvana. This became no-desire in worldly terms. So alcohol, sex, clothing, and other items affecting the body were governed by the ethical rule of detachment (and came under the "Buddhist economics" that E. F. Schumacher made a cornerstone of his book *Small Is Beautiful*).[81] So business, politics, and art ideally sprang from a free spirit. East Asian painting, poetry, and calligraphy, for instance, ideally occurred in a state of no-mind.[82] Contrary to the regular Western view of the artist, in which the person agonizes through his or her work to produce a vision (and a self), the East Asian artist was to let art flow out of a meditative experience. Its hallmark was to be spontaneity, and the major stumbling block to spontaneity was self-concern.

Tantrism seems to qualify the Buddhist view of the self, since it allowed a more intense connection with food, alcohol, sex, and material ritual items. However, according to its own masters, the watchword in Tantrist rituals was still discipline and detachment. To use alcohol or sex licentiously was just a quick way to attachment and bad karma. The point to Tantrist ritual was to master these items and to retain the energies that would have flowed out to them. In Tantrist sexual yoga, for instance, the male was supposed to discipline himself in order to gain the female *Shakti* power. (That this abused women by making them means to men's ends seems to have been acceptable. Perhaps equal detachment on the females' part was supposed to make the rite equally efficacious for them.) The Tantrists argued that such a detachment "reversed" the spontaneous eroticism of desire, capturing its energy for enlightenment more effectively than avoidance would have.

There were, of course, varying degrees of commitment to the doctrine of no-self and varying understandings of it. The Pudgalava-

dins, as we noted, produced a doctrine of the person that returned the atman.[83] Many Buddhists, laity and monks alike, were strong personalities and so did not take no-self to mean a loss of decisiveness. The Buddhists who settled for improving their karma by meritorious deeds (and who frequently kept close records to detail their progress) must have been hard put not to be intensely self-conscious. The artists who worked in no-mind, overspilling with enlightened union with Buddha-nature, must have numbered relatively few. Therefore, there is substantial historical evidence that no-self was a hard doctrine to live. Like the Christian doctrine of selfless, suffering love *(agape)*, it was not realized just by vowing.

Even if not carried out, the doctrine of no-self shaped Buddhist culture. Wherever Buddhist religion was vigorous, the doctrine of no-self was influential. In fact, we often can sense its effects in the peace and humor of Buddhist texts. Many texts, of course, are complicated and complex. However, some raise serenity, irony, paradox, and wit to a high religious art. For instance, in one story two monks meet a fetching damsel by a rushing river. One charitably hoists her and carries her across. Later the second monk chastises the first for such sensual contact. The first monk replies, "I let the girl down when we crossed the river. Why are you still carrying her?" The Buddhist ideal was to carry nothing, to be utterly free.[84]

Divinity

Debate has raged over the question of whether Buddhism is a theistic religion. For instance, Chogyam Trungpa, a Tibetan master now living in the United States, has complained, "It is especially unfortunate that Buddhism has been presented as a theistic religion, whereas in fact it is a nontheistic spiritual philosophy, psychology, and way of life."[85] On the other hand, there is a good reason why scholars have frequently presented Buddhism as a theistic religion: It has frequently seemed to be such.[86] Devotional Buddhism has venerated a variety of

Buddhas and bodhisattvas, treating them as other religions treat gods and saints. Also, the Buddhist concepts of nirvana, Buddha-nature, and emptiness have on occasion evinced the sacred aura of divinity, generating language that can only be called, by its difference from ordinary language, religious. Therefore, Buddhism frequently has seemed to be both theistic and religious.

To be sure, the Buddha himself does not appear to have claimed divinity. For example, he cast no speeches in the "I am" form that the Jesus of John's Gospel assumed. Rather, Gautama seems to have been a human being who thought that he had found the key to living well. The key was enlightenment, whose expression was the Four Noble Truths. In the enlightenment experience, Gautama encountered ultimate reality. The overtones to this encounter gleaned from the texts are not those of meeting a personal God. Whether that differentiates Gautama's ultimate reality from the God of Western religion is another question, whose answer depends on careful analysis of peak experiences and conceptions of ultimate reality. The personal character of the Western God is not so simple as many Westerners assume, and the impersonal quality of Gautama's encounter with nirvana is less absolute than many assume.[87]

Nonetheless, let us grant that Buddha's enlightenment and preaching do not posit a God. In this we would be agreeing with humanistic interpreters such as Trungpa, dismissing theories (such as Paul Tillich's) which state that one's ultimate concern (in this case nirvana) is one's de facto god. More problematic for the strictly humanistic interpreter of Buddhism is the popular reception that Gautama himself has received through the centuries. First, all Buddhists grant Gautama a special authority in interpreting what human life is. Otherwise, there would be no sense in calling someone a Buddhist.[88]

Second, however, Buddha seems to be divine and related to ultimate reality in less sophisticated, more obvious ways. In Mahayana, the doctrine of Buddha's three bodies has led to the belief that Gautama was a historical form or manifestation of Suchness—the ultimate stuff.[89] In popular Buddhism the faith in the power of the various Buddhas to save, as well as to perform miracles, has been clear evidence that Buddhism for many has been not only a religion but a personal religion. To save, in any profound sense, is to heal and protect life from evil, which only a transcendent being can do. Insofar as Buddhas gave transcendent being personal form, they encouraged people to treat them religiously. For religion is the response to mystery that goes beyond humanistic or scientific resources and reaches out to something more.

When Pure Land founders urged the recitation of Amitabha's name, when Nichiren urged the salutation of the Lotus Sutra, when monks lighted incense and chanted hymns of praise, when the laity prayed for prosperity and against sickness—when Buddhists did any of these things, they engaged in religion.[90] Further, when they gave personal names, faces, and attributes to the objects that their salutations, chantings, or prayers addressed, they evidenced aspects of theistic religion. They put gods, if not God, as partners to their action and petition.

IMAGES OF THE BUDDHA

We may suggest the status of the Buddha by drawing on some of the images in which the sutras have delighted. A first image, of the Buddha as a raincloud, comes from the Lotus Sutra, a scripture very influential in such Mahayana sects as the Chinese T'ien-t'ai and the Japanese Nichiren.

The sutra puts the image of a raincloud in the Buddha's own mouth: "The King of Dharma I am, who arose in the world to crush becoming;

Dharma I teach to beings, after I have discerned their dispositions.... It is like a great cloud which arises above the earth, which covers up everything and overshadows the firmament. And this great cloud, filled with water, wreathed with lightning, resounds with thunder, and refreshes all the creatures."[91]

A few verses later, the Buddha repeats that he has arisen in this world like a raincloud. And when he has arisen, "the World's Savior" speaks, in order to show all living beings the true course they ought to travel. For this he is honored by the whole world, with all its gods. He is the Tathagata, the one who has gone over to enlightenment, a conquerer who has arisen in the world like a raincloud. He refreshes all living beings, whose bodies are withering away because they cling to the lower worlds. The Buddha will ease the pains that are withering them. He will give them pleasures and the final rest of nirvana.

Moreover, he preaches the dharma to all beings, always making enlightenment the foundation of his teaching. This teaching is the same for all hearers. There is no partiality in the Buddha's message, no alteration of voice, for he is beyond hatred and love. Once again, this makes him like a raincloud, which releases its rain evenly on all. Enlightenment applies equally to the noble and the mean. It is the message the Blessed One offers the immoral as well as the moral. The depraved are no different in their need for enlightenment than those whose conduct is good. In all cases, final fulfillment depends on grasping, realizing, the dharma. Thus people who hold false views and people who hold right views, people who hold unsound views and people whose views are pure all stand in need of the Buddha. Prescinding from their merit or demerit, enlightenment presses on all of them as a fierce imperative. Without enlightenment, they are equally needy, equally bereft of the truth that saves. The Buddha is the one doctor dispensing the medicine needed by all the world's sickly souls.

For that reason, the Buddha spends himself, preaching dharma to beings of inferior intellect and beings of superior intellect, to beings whose faculties are weak and beings whose faculties are strong. Setting aside his own fatigue, he rains down dharma on them all. Feeling this rain, the world is well refreshed. Each being who comes under the shower of truth benefits, according to its own capacity. Each finds the well-preached teaching to its taste. In this the dharma is again like the rain, which falls on shrubs and grasses, bushes and smaller plants, trees and great wooded tracts, doing good to each. Throughout all the realms, earthly and celestial, the Buddha's teaching makes beings glow with refreshment and satisfaction.

Thus, the sutra concludes, it is the nature of dharma always to exist for the good of the world, offering a continual refreshment. From this refreshment the world should, like a well-watered plant, burst forth in blossoms of insight, purity, good behavior, and compassion.

If we step back to analyze this imagery, it is clear that the sutra pictures the Buddha and his teaching as the heavenly dew that makes the world green. Without the Buddha's dharma, the world would be a desert, arid and joyless. In the empty wastes of suffering, there would be no cause for hope. But the words of the Blessed One are so powerful and creative they make what was barren burgeon with sturdy growth. Cool, detached, above all the world's tribulations, the Buddha serenely makes the rain of truth fall on just and unjust alike. Only the sun moving in its heavenly circuit, or the clouds drifting high above, can symbolize the Buddha's equanimity and evenhandedness. To him all creatures are in need of the truth, so all have a claim on his enlightened compassion. Whatever their station or disposition, his message is apt and helpful.

The sutra depends on the conjunction of natural imagery with a conviction of Buddha's "skillfulness in means." In this phrase the tradition epitomized its belief that the Enlightened One could find a way into any heart, no matter what that heart's condition. Possessing the light of salvation in all its effulgence, the Buddha knows how to make the light shine into every corner of the world. So deeply does his wisdom go, it is always relevant, always able to clarify the hearer's condition. Just as all creatures need the rain of the skies, so all rational creatures need the heavenly truth. The Buddha was so closely associated with heaven, the supervising powers that rule the world, that the Lotus Sutra instinctively expressed his compassionate aid in terms of heavenly phenomena. Taking up the awe and gratitude human beings have always directed toward the heavens, the sutra focused them on the teaching, the way out of this vale of tears.

Of course, devotional Buddhism developed many other descriptions of the Buddha's status, virtues, and aids. A second Mahayana text[92] will allow us a further glimpse into the fecundity of devotional Buddhism's imagination.

The Buddha possesses no faults and all virtues, so people with any sense go to him for refuge, to praise and honor him, to abide in his region. He is the only protector, for he is the only one all-knowing and without fault. Even people who are spiteful and want to find fault with the Buddha cannot do so. There is nothing to fault in his thoughts, words, or deeds. Therefore we should all give him homage. Wonderful are his works, wonderful his potent and abundant virtues.

Indeed, words fail the task of proclaiming the Buddha's glories. But it brings merit to attempt this task, so we should recall how the Buddha gained preeminence in the world without envying the elite, despising the low, or competing with his peers. (The context seems to be the caste system of Siddhartha's time.) The Buddha made such progress because he focused on the causes of virtue, not on virtue's rewards. Indeed, he accumulated so much merit that even the dust of his feet is now a field of merit, a place where all people can reap benefits.

The only thing to which we can compare the Buddha is the jewel of the dharma. It was by gaining this jewel that he won his great eminence. So now, like the dharma, he is calm yet lovely, brilliant but not dazzling, soft but mighty, able to entrance all who behold him. Whether one has seen his figure once or a hundred times, it never fails to please the eye. Where else would the virtues of a Tathagata house themselves? What other form blazes with Buddha's signs and auspicious marks? Indeed, the world was bound to its defilements so that Buddha might free it. His compassion is so great one doesn't know whether first to praise him or his compassion. Though he knew all the faults of samsara, he lingered in samsara for the sake of the myriads he has helped. When his own taste was for seclusion, his compassion kept him in the crowds.

Thus the recollection of the Buddha's birth gives joy, as the recollection of the Buddha's growth gives delight. Thinking of the Buddha's time among human beings, one feels a great benefit. Thinking of his departure at death, one feels lost. Still, to praise the Buddha takes away all guilt, and to recollect his life lifts up every heart. To approach the Buddha brings good fortune, and to attend the Buddha brings the highest wisdom. If we flee to the Buddha we lose our fear; if we honor the Buddha we find life propitious. For the Buddha is a great lake of merit, pure through his high morality, serene through his lofty meditation, imperturbable through his deep wisdom. He is an island for those swept along by the flood, a shelter to those stricken, a refuge for those terrified by becoming, the great resource of all who desire release.

Fatigue, loss of quiet, having to traffic with people of little worth—what did the Buddha not bear, out of his great compassion? He went hungry, ate bad food, trod uneven paths, slept on mud trampled by cattle. Though master of all, the savior presented himself as a servant all could use for their advantage. No matter how people provoked or abused him, he never transgressed. He studied the welfare of those who meant him harm more than other people study the welfare of those who mean them well. He conquered revilers by his patience, plotters by his blessing, slanderers by his truth, the malicious by his friendliness. Through his skill in means, the harsh became gentle, the niggardly became bountiful, the cruel became tenderhearted.

On and on the litany goes, never tiring of reciting the merits, virtues, and wonders of its beloved object. If this is not religious veneration and theism, those words have lost all significance. Pious Christians would have to change few phrases to apply the litany to Christ. With a few shifts in emphasis, a few accommodations in world view, pious Jews could place the litany in the middle of the psalms that praise the Lord. For the people who wrote sutras such as these (fundamentalist Buddhists would say the Enlightened One spoke them verbatim, as fundamentalist Muslims would say that God dictated the Qur'an verbatim), the Buddha was the pearl of great price, the treasure hidden in a field, for which a person should sell everything she has. In him gathered all virtues, all blessings, all models of sublimity. He was the great refuge, the first of the three jewels, the paradigm of morality, meditation, and wisdom.

Consequently, in our comparative perspective he was the great Buddhist divinity. Although at times bodhisattvas such as Avalokitesvara drew more attention, often because they projected a maternal mercy, the core tenets of Buddhism ran toward placing Gautama, man and primary manifestation of enlightenment, at the center of the bulls-eye. As human, he modeled the pious life. As the primary manifestation of enlightenment, he brought nirvana into the midst of samsara. So his dharma became the Dharma, the teaching that ran the world. So all enlightened persons grew in his lineaments (though Zen masters and others fought any tendency to a literalist aping; for them the essential following of the Buddha was doing what he did, realizing one's own enlightenment-nature). For the common people, reverencing the Buddha was the main way to a better life, in which they might win release from suffering and gain the bliss of nirvana.

Where Buddhism does have a distinctive divinity or ultimate reality is in the identification of nature with nirvana that Mahayana and Tantrism developed. Hinduism, of course, had yogic and philosophical strains that approached this identification. On the whole, though, Indian thought maintained for Brahman a certain otherness. The *nirguna* (unmanifest) Brahman probably did not break the cosmological myth, but it did separate ultimate reality from the here and now.

In East Asian Buddhism, the love of nature native to the civilizations there reduced this separation. While nirvana or the Buddha-nature could have ontological (metaphysical) differences from physical nature, the oneness of that ultimate reality was manifested in rock gardens, in valleys hung with mist, and in floral arrangements. The emptiness and transcendental wisdom related to a solid here and now, for dualistic thinking went against the East Asian grain by frustrating its meditation's quests for unity with Buddha-nature. Even today, a master such as Shunryu Suzuki does not seek the Buddha-nature by flight to a transcendent realm—Buddha-nature is within each moment. Suzuki, however, can speak of God.[93] Whether he equates God with Buddha-nature is not clear, but his regime is sufficiently religious to honor the word *God* and sympathize with its denotations.

The concept of ultimate reality, then, is susceptible to theistic interpretation at most points in Buddhism's history. For Trungpa's own tradition, Tibetan Tantrism, this is also the case. Imaginative identification with deities in meditational exercises, popular celebrations of festivals to the goddess Tara, prayers and spells to deities and such saints as Milarepa and Naropa—these clearly indicate that Tibetan Buddhism has been a religion consorting with gods. Whether by devotion, imagination, meditation, or philosophical exercise, the state to which Buddhism has aspired transcends irreligious, secular reality. It has an aura of the holy, and it has frequently produced holy persons.

Another interesting aspect of Buddhist divinity is its feminine overtones. We have already noted that the *Prajna-paramita* was in effect a mother goddess and that the Yogacara storehouse consciousness was linked with a cosmic Buddhist womb *(Tathagata-garbha)*. Much more influential than these rather abstruse aspects of divinity, however, were the bodhisattva Kuan-yin and the goddess Tara. As Tay's study suggests,[94] Kuan-yin (Figure 11) has been a "goddess of mercy" or a "Buddhist madonna" of a cult occupying half of Asia. In most East Asian homes, a shrine to Kuan-yin focuses the family's desire, even in this life, to rise above karma through the help of a motherly deity who could empathize with human need. In any event, it is clear that very many Buddhists faced life crises by depending on this figure wholeheartedly.

Nirvana has been a help to Buddhists in ages past, it will likely be their hope for years to come, and the careful observer also sees in it aspects of divinity. As a symbol of what life should be, of how human consciousness ought to find fulfillment, it has protected Buddhists against absurdity. In doing so, nirvana has functioned precisely as divinity must. For divinity must be the beyond, the really real. Human beings have a concern for that kind of divinity in their consciousnesses. They are all apt to seek the center, as well as the beginning and the end. When Yeats wrote that the center does not hold, he exposed a horror latent in the modern world. To be without anchors of meaning, cast adrift in a flux going nowhere for no reason, would be the denial of Yeats's very constitution.

Few religions have probed the paradoxes of the center, of empty fullness, more acutely than Buddhism. Few have so focused life on the pursuit of enlightenment. One way, in fact, of interpreting how nirvana conquers karma is to say that it transforms the personality by substituting ultimate concerns for nonultimate ones—that it makes the Buddhist's treasure mystery rather than food, sex, money, or prestige. Nirvana itself is the extinguishing of karmic desire. It is the state of the human flame when it has burned away its oxygen and gone on to purer fuel. Though most of the descriptions of nirvana are in this negative style,[95] Buddhists have added that nirvana is not a void in the sense of a simple nothingness. Rather, it is a source of perfection, fulfillment, and bliss.

To say, then, that nirvana is present in, or even identical with, samsara is to say that present life may carry perfection, fulfillment, and bliss. When Buddhism accents this positive language, it becomes a humanistic religion, correlating divinity with the other three dimensions of reality. For nirvana in the present is what the selfless person

Figure 11   Kuan-yin seated in the "royal ease" position. Courtesy Museum of Fine Arts, Boston, Harvey Edward Wetzel Fund.

seeks in communion, what a dharma-guided society seeks as its preservation from distraction, what nature grasped in enlightenment playfully dances. Thus, Buddhism's negative ultimate can become a center that holds very powerfully, that assures questioners of answers, that tells lovers there *are* objects worthy of their love.

In its own way, therefore, Buddhism has brought home to its adherents one of the final curiosities that human consciousness must admit: We must lose life to find it, we must place meaning in mystery if we are to make it secure.[96] As a result, Buddhism knows that to liberate speech for truth we must go into silence, to gain freedom we must renounce desire, to enhance samsara we must open to nirvana. Each of these religious paradoxes depends on the holding of the Buddhist center. Were there no nirvana, no realm of the really real or holy, none of the paradoxes would make any sense. Insofar as Buddhism does make sense, enlightening minds and enhancing lives, it at least intimates its central force. In sutras, statues of bodhisattvas, lonely mountain retreats, artistic rituals, and ethical codes, that central force is clearly suggested. Empty and gone beyond, as the Heart Sutra says, yet everything's oneness, it has been the treasure behind the three treasures. The Buddha, the dharma, and the sangha—they all live from and for nirvana, from and for Buddhist ultimate reality.

Study Questions

1. What was the essence of Gautama's enlightenment?
2. Is wisdom-morality-meditation a comprehensive, fully adequate religious regime?
3. In what sense was Mahayana both more popular and more speculative than Theravada?
4. How did Tantrist Buddhism concretize the notion that nirvana and samsara are one?
5. What is the relation between Ch'an Buddhism and Pure Land Buddhism?
6. Does Buddhism merge nature and divinity? How?
7. How would you try to persuade your best friend that he or she has no self?
8. Explain the Buddhist symbols of the wheel and the lotus.
9. Why would you like or not like to be a disciple of Nagarjuna?
10. How attractive do you find Burmese Buddhist ritual?
11. Explain the symbol of the Buddha as a raincloud.
12. How practical is a politics that reverses the Buddhist precept of not killing?

Chapter Three

CHINESE RELIGION: TWENTY-FIVE KEY DATES

CA. 3500 B.C.E.	EARLIEST CHINESE CITY
CA. 1600	SHANG BRONZE AGE CULTURE
551–479	CONFUCIUS
520	TRADITIONAL DATE FOR DEATH OF LAO-TZU
403–221	WARRING STATES PERIOD
206	HAN DYNASTY REUNITES CHINA
CA. 200	RISE OF RELIGIOUS TAOISM
CA. 112	OPENING OF "SILK ROAD" LINKS CHINA WITH WEST
CA. 150 C.E.	BUDDHISM REACHES CHINA
304–589	HUNS FRAGMENT CHINA
607	BEGINNING OF CHINESE CULTURAL INFLUENCE IN JAPAN
658	HEIGHT OF CHINESE POWER IN CENTRAL ASIA

Chinese Religion

Buddhism made a permanent impact on Chinese culture,[1] but native Chinese religion always had at least equal influence. In this chapter we consider the history of native Chinese religion and its contributions to the Chinese world view. To begin, we observe Chinese life today in Hong Kong.

APPEARANCE

Most Chinese people today, of course, are behind the "bamboo curtain" that surrounds the People's Republic of China. A few scholars have studied portions of religious life there, but access to the common people and unhindered observation of their daily lives have only become possible since the death of Mao. The studies so far indicate that Mao's campaign against religion and the older, Confucian-based culture was relatively successful. Temples and shrines now have an insignificant role in Chinese life. Still, there is evidence that the older beliefs and customs have not completely died. In rural areas peasants still view the land as being filled with spirits. At times of sickness and death, many people still reach out to unseen powers. Even within the government bureaucracy, Confucian hierarchical thinking, as well as a veneration for leaders that can border on worship, suggest that the Communist Chinese personality has yet to distinguish itself.[2]

In Hong Kong, despite British and Western influences, one can see traditional funeral processions, worship in temples, fortunetellers, and more. Dragon parades wind through the streets on holidays, complete with firecrackers, tumblers, and colored lanterns. They recall the "diffused" operation of religious magic that C. K. Yang found characteristic of Chinese religion.[3] In Hong Kong this mixes curiously with a more apparent dedication to business. The visitor landing at the airport at Kowloon wonders first at the daring of jets dropping between the mountains and the sea dozens of times each day to land on a thin strip of tarmac. Inside the airport terminal, a most efficient hotel service secures for visitors whatever sort of accommodation they desire, and they are then whisked off in trucklike limousines.

As the limousines hurtle through the hilly and crowded streets, stores and signs assault the passengers. Hong Kong is not a Delhi or a Cairo, in which modern building and commerce perch precariously on a poor and ancient physical and human base. It has bicycles and rickshas, but few beasts of burden. Its cars are modern, its people in a hurry. Clothing, electronics, jewelry, and souvenirs are staples. As one gazes across the narrow strait to Hong Kong proper while waiting for the Red Star ferry, the high-rise hotels and banks gleam in the sunlight. On foggy days their tops are obscured by the low-hanging mist. A lot of energy and money went into building them, and a lot of energy and money crackles in the streets. The business of Hong Kong is business.

When one starts to study Hong Kong, though, its Western facade begins to blur. It is not just that tailors work twelve hours a day, seven days a week. Nor is it just that modern containerized shipping goes on in the midst of little junks and sampans. Rather, it is that the emporiums allow aisle space for robed counselors and fortunetellers, who do a thriving business. It is that behind the Hiltons and Intercontinentals is a temple, dark and smoky, with food offerings, burning tapers, and statues of Buddha, Confucius, and Taoist saints. Tablets revealing family lines suggest a long history of ancestor veneration. Fortune slips suggest a continuing interest in divination. In the dark, perfumed air, very old traditions run together. The back streets of Hong Kong are a step back into the millennia of Chinese tradition.

HISTORY

Preaxial Chinese Religion

Philosopher Karl Jaspers has spoken of an "axial period" of human civilization, during which the essential insights arose that spawned the great cultures.[4] In China the axial period was the sixth and fifth centuries B.C.E., and the two most important figures were Confucius and Lao-tzu, whose Confucianism and Taoism, respectively, formed the basis for all subsequent Chinese culture. Before them, however, were centuries, perhaps even millennia, of nature- and ancestor-oriented responses to the sacred, when the ancient mind dominated the Chinese people. As we suggested in our discussion of the ancient mind, some of its oldest features persisted through periods of "higher" culture. In China, for instance, divination mixed with the Confucian ethical code, so that the prime divinatory text, the *I Ching*, became one of the Confucian classics. As the popular Chinese folk novel *Monkey* shows,[5] other ancient attitudes were alive well into the sixteenth century C.E. So the preaxial world view that we now sketch was a constant feature throughout Chinese religious history.

First, though, we must qualify the concept of Chinese religion. China, like most ancient cultures, did not develop religion as a separate realm of human concern. The rites, sacred mythology, ethics, and the like that bound the Chinese peoples were simply their culture. These cultural phenomena were not distinguished from the daily routine. So, what we underscore here for our purposes is not necessarily what the Chinese underscored. Second, the Chinese attitude toward ultimate reality stressed nature—the physical world. Nature was the (sacred) essential context of human existence, and there was no clear creator outside nature.

Of course, nature appeared to be both constant and changing. The cosmos was always there, but it had seasons and rhythms, as well as unexpected activities such as storms and earthquakes. To explain this tension between stability and change, the Chinese thought in terms of a union of opposing basic forces. Yang was the force of light, heat, and maleness. Yin was the balancing force of darkness, cold, and female-ness. The changes in the relations between yang and yin accounted for the seasons, the moon's phases, and the tides.

Another aspect of nature was the mixture or proportions of the five vital forces (water, fire, wood, metal, and earth) at any given time. They were the qualities that activated nature—that gave particular things and events their character. Together, the yin-yang theory and the theory of the five vital forces formed the first Chinese explanation of nature.[6]

Above the system, not as its creator from nothingness but as its semipersonal overlord, was the heavenly ruler. His domain was human and natural behavior. The heavenly ruler probably was the first ancestor of the ruling dynasty. That is, the Chinese first conceived him as the clan head of the ancient ruling house of Shang.[7] Later they modified this anthropomorphic conception to heaven, a largely impersonal force. Then the emperor became the "Son of Heaven," not in the sense that he was the descendant of the first ancestral leader of the ruling clan but in the sense that he represented the force that governed the world.[8]

Another name for the director of the natural system was *Tao*. Essentially, *Tao* meant "way" or "path." The Confucians spoke of the *Tao* of the ancients—the customs or ethos that prevailed in the golden beginning times. Similarly, the Chinese Buddhists described their tradition as the "Way of the Buddha." However, the Taoists most directly appropriated the naturalistic overtones to *Tao* and focused on nature's directing path. For them the *Tao* was an ultimate reality, both within the system and beyond it.

We shall see below how the *Tao* was characteristic of the different Chinese religious traditions. The point here is that they all assumed the ancient view that nature is sufficiently orderly to suggest an overseer and a path. Within the natural system, however, the prehistoric Chinese stressed harmony. That is, they tended to think that trees, rivers, clouds, animals, and humans

Figure 12   *Zoomorphic spiral, western Chou dynasty, probably early ninth century*, B.C.E. *Nelson Gallery-Atkins Museum (Nelson Fund).*

some qualifications that we shall mention, the Chinese have favored long life rather than immortality, enlightenment that polishes worldly vision rather than enlightenment that draws one out of the world. Ch'an's transformation of the Mahayana philosophy of nirvana owed much to Taoist philosophy and this ancient worldliness.

The Peasant Heritage

The preaxial views of nature, therefore, provided the axial thinkers with basic beliefs about nature's patterns, elements, and the consubstantiality (of the same substance) of humans with other forms of life. From these beliefs, the axial thinkers developed prescriptions for both social and individual life. In that way, ancient reflection helped form the rational framework of classical Chinese culture. More influential, though, was the nonrational heritage of the preaxial days. The vast majority of China's billions have been peasants, who, with relatively few changes, continued to stress magic, animistic forces, amulets, and divination rites up to the beginning of the twentieth century (if not right up to the present).

Folk religion is always an effort to explain nature, but it employs a logic that is more symbolic than that of yin-yang, the five dynamic qualities, or *Tao*. Rather, it emphasizes similarities and differences, whether in shapes, sizes, or names. As close to dreaming as to science, folk religion easily allows the subconscious great influence. So, for instance, diviners thought they had a key to nature in the cracks of a baked tortoise shell, or the flight patterns of birds, or the broken and unbroken lines that the *I Ching* interpreted as ratios of yin and yang. It was but a small step to use these interpretational techniques to control nature—to use them as magic.

One functionary who specialized in this symbolic magic was the practitioner of *feng-shui.*[10] *Feng-shui* was the study of winds and water, or geomancy. Essentially, it involved how to position a building most auspiciously. In a convoluted symbolism

compose something whole. As a result, natural phenomena could be portents, while human actions, whether good or evil, influenced both heaven and earth. As the Native Americans identified closely with their forests, so the oldest Chinese were citizens of nature, not a species standing outside and apart from it. Consequently, they did not consider human beings as superior to the other creatures of the cosmos.

When Chuang-tzu spoke of reentering the Great Clod,[9] he spoke from this ancient conviction. To die and return to the material world, perhaps to be a tree or a fish in the next round, was natural and right. With pertaining to dragons and tigers, it tried to make the living forces of nature yield good fortune by figuring out the spiritual lay of the land. What nature disposed, according to *feng-shui*, architecture could oppose or exploit. For instance, straight lines were believed to be evil influences, but trees or a fresh pond could ward them off. Consequently, the basic design of Chinese villages included trees and ponds for protection. Similarly, a winding approach to a house diverted evil forces. The *feng-shui* diviner plotted all the forces, good and evil, with a sort of compass that marked the different circles of power of these forces. *Feng-shui* has prevailed well into modern times, a fact attesting to its perceived importance.

Other important ancient functionaries were the mediums and the shamans. As Waley's translations suggest,[11] the shaman's song frequently called on a personal spirit to come down and enlighten him. Perhaps, then, the Chinese shaman (or shamaness) was less ecstatic than the Siberian, more a subject of possession or a medium than a traveler to the gods.[12] More importantly, the existence of the shaman shows that ancient China believed in a realm of personified spirits.[13] These spirits could come to susceptible individuals with lights and messages or be the spirits of departed ancestors speaking through a medium who was in trance. If one did not revere them, speak well of them, and give them gifts of food, the ancestor spirits could turn nasty.

In later times, ordinary people thought that the ancestor spirits lived in a spiritual equivalent of the human world, where they needed such things as food, clothing, and money. Thus, pious children would burn paper money to send assistance to their departed parents.[14] In fact, one's primary obligation of a religious sort was just such acts of commemoration, reverence, and help. This ancestor veneration so impressed Western missionaries that they fought bitterly among themselves about its meaning. Some missionaries found ancestor rites idolatrous, while others found them praiseworthy expressions of familial love.[15]

Exorcism

Another feature of ancient Chinese religion was the personification and exorcism of evil. In historical times, the Taoist priesthood dominated exorcism, but the roots of exorcism go further back. Peter Goullart has given an eyewitness account of a modern Taoist exorcism,[16] complete with descriptions of weird phenomena like those enacted in the American film *The Exorcist*. The assumption behind exorcism, of course, is that evil forces invade and possess a person. In part, this assumption is just the logical conclusion of a thought world in which shamanism is possible. If the Chinese shaman could be invaded by his helping spirit, and if evil spirits existed, then other persons could be invaded by evil spirits. If we follow another line of logic, demon possession is just the development of ancient fears of evil, while exorcism is just the development of ancient ways of combating such fear.

Goullart's description of the "energumen" (demoniac), however, renders the evil most concrete. The possessing power curses, threatens, and pours out hate (in a terrifying distortion of the demoniac's own voice). It bloats the demoniac's body, pushing the bedspring on which he rests down to the floor. The demoniac howls like an animal, gives off horrid smells, and empties his bladder and bowels repeatedly. Onlookers are terrified, and the Taoist priest strains to the utmost in his spiritual struggles with the evil one. The reader senses something absolutely primitive: human shock before the possibility of naked evil.

In his summary of the religious beliefs of the Chinese Neolithic age,[17] Mircea Eliade sketches the general context for such shock, as well as for shamanism, divination, and other ancient features that we have discussed. There was from earliest times a connection between life, fertility, death, and afterlife that took the form of a regular cosmic cycle and gave rise to annual religious rites. Further, the ancestors were a source of magical and religious power, and all natural forces had an aura of mystery—the mystery of the conjunction of opposites: of life and death, good and evil, rational and irrational. Possession and exorcism, then, are but vivid instances of a generally volatile mix. The ancient Chinese world was thoroughly alive, and one never knew precisely where its power would go.

Confucianism

Confucius (551–479 B.C.E.) became the father of Chinese culture by transforming the ancient traditions into at least the beginnings of a code for directing social life. More than two centuries passed before his doctrine became the state orthodoxy (during the Han dynasty, 206 B.C.E.–220 C.E.), but from the outset it had a healing effect on Chinese society. Confucius lived during a warring period of Chinese history, an epoch of nearly constant social disorder. For Master Kung (another name for Confucius), the way from such disorder toward peace was obtained from the ancients—the venerable ancestors who were closer to the beginning and wiser than the people of the present age. What the ancestors knew, what made them wise, were the decrees of heaven. As we have seen, heaven meant nature's overlord. Thus, Confucius accepted the ancient, preaxial notion that nature has some order. In his view, the way to a peaceful and prosperous society was to adapt to that order. People could do that externally through sacrificial rites and hierarchical social relationships. Internally, one had to know the human mind, and the human mind had to be set in *jen* (fellow feeling or love).[18]

For external order, the emperor was paramount. As the Son of Heaven, he conveyed heaven's will to earth. In other words, the China of Confucius's time held to the cosmological myth. With many other ancient societies, it shared the notion that the king was the sacred intermediary between the realm of heaven and the realm modeled upon it, earth. What the king did for human society, then, was both priestly and exemplary. By officiating at the most important

rites, through which his people tried to achieve harmony with heaven, the king represented society before the ultimate judge of society's fate. By the example that he set at court and by the way that he directed imperial policy, the king not only served as a good or bad model for his followers but also led the state in following or defying heaven's intent. The king achieved his power simply through his close connection to heaven.[19]

Confucius approved of the model leadership of the legendary kings, and he also approved of the notion that ritual makes a sacrament of the vital flow between heaven and earth. One focus of his teaching, then, was historical: He concentrated on how the ancients reportedly acted. Another focus was liturgical. He was himself a master of court ritual, and he thought that proper sacrifice and etiquette were very important. Probably Confucius's most profound impact on Chinese culture, though, was his clarification of human virtues, or spiritual qualities.

Having had little success in public affairs (he never obtained high office or found a ruler willing to hire his counsel), he turned to teaching young men wise politics and the way to private virtue. In other words, he became the center of an academic circle, like that of Plato, which had ongoing dialogues about the good life, political science, private and public morality, and so on. Confucius consistently stressed practicality in his tutoring. The wisdom that he loved intended the good society, the commonweal. It was not a yogic or shamanic regime dedicated to a single individual's spiritual development.

The *Analects* are a collection of fragments from the Master. In them we can see why Confucius impressed his followers, who finally made him the model wise man. (After his death, Confucius gained semidivine status and became the center of a religious cult.)[20] Especially in the third through ninth books, the Confucians preserved sayings that seem to be original, although Confucius himself claimed no originality. In fact, he did not even claim divine inspiration. His way was nothing novel; he only studied the past and then transmitted the ancients' customs. But when Confucius speaks of hearing the Way in the morning and dying content in the evening, we sense how thoroughly he had embraced *Tao*. When he says that at seventy he could do whatever his instincts prompted, we sense that he felt a mystic union with the Way and that the Way dominated his entire personality.

For Confucius, the Way manifests itself as a golden mean. It opens a path between punctiliousness and irregularity, between submissiveness and independence. Most situations are governed by a protocol that will yield graceful interactions if it is followed wholeheartedly. The task of the gentleman is to know that protocol, intuit how it applies in particular cases, and have the discipline to carry it out. The death of a parent, for instance, is a prime occasion for a gentleman to express his love and respect for that parent. According to the rites of mourning, he should retire from public affairs, simplify his living arrangements, and devote himself to grieving (for as long as three years).

As that example suggests, filial piety was a cornerstone of Confucianism. If the relations at home were correct, other social relationships would likely fall in line. The Confucian classic *The Great Learning*[21] spells out this theory, linking the individual in the family to the order of both the state and the cosmos. Moreover, the family circle was the training ground for a gentleman's lifelong dedication to humanity *(jen)* and ritual propriety *(li)*. When a man developed a sincere love for his parents and carried out his filial duties, he rooted himself firmly in both *jen* and *li*. (We consider the place of women below in the section on society.) Confucius's own teaching, therefore, called for a balance between interior goodness and exterior grace. He thought that if people knew their inner minds (grasped at "inwit," in Ezra Pound's translation)[22] and manifested their knowledge through social decorum,

then society would have both the substance and the appearance of humanity.

Different followers developed different aspects of Confucius's teaching. Mencius, for instance, changed the Master's view of *jen*, drawing it down from the almost divine status accorded it by Confucius and making it a real possibility for everyman.[23] For Mencius human nature was innately good. We are only evil or disordered because we forget our original nature. Like the deforested local hill, the typical human mind is so abused that we cannot see its spontaneous tendency toward altruism and justice. If we would stop deforesting it with vice, we would realize that virtue is instinctive. Just as anyone who sees a child at the edge of a well rushes to save the youth, so anyone educated in gentlemanliness will rush to solve civic problems.

Thus, Mencius centered Confucius's teaching on the goodness of human nature. Living two centuries after the Master, Mencius tried to repeat Confucius's way of life. So, he searched for an ideal king who would take his counsel, but he had to be satisfied in having a circle of young students. Mencius, though, somewhat lacked Confucius's restraint in discussing heavenly things (Confucius considered the human realm more than enough to master). According to Lee Yearley,[24] Mencius practiced a disciplined religion to increase physical vigor by acting with purity of heart, and he was willing to die for certain things such as justice and goodness. So, just as one can consider some of Confucius's sayings as quite religious (for example, "It is not better to pay court to the stove than to heaven"), one can view Mencius as having transcendent beliefs. Both Confucian thinkers, we believe, appealed to more than human prudence.

Mencius also proposed an ultimately religious theory that history moves in cycles, depending upon how a given ruling family handles the *te* (the power to govern well) that heaven dispenses.[25] The sharpest implication of this theory was that an unjust ruler might lose the mandate of heaven—

that a revolutionary might properly receive it. Further, Mencius advanced the view that the king only brought prosperity when he convinced the people that the things of the state were their own. This view was in part shrewd psychology: A people who have access to the royal park will think it small even if it is 100 miles square; a people denied access to a royal park one mile square will complain that it is far too vast. As well, however, it brought Confucius's stress on leadership by example and virtue up-to-date: Only if the king demonstrates virtue can he expect the people to be virtuous.

A legalistic wing among Confucius's later followers, led by Hsun-tzu, opposed both Mencius's teaching that human nature is essentially good and the non-Confucian Mo-tzu's doctrine of universal love.[26] Hsun-tzu taught that only strong law can confine human nature to right action; for that reason so many mountains remain bald. Further, Hsun-tzu connected this belief with Confucius's own stress on ritual, arguing that law and etiquette have the pedagogical function of showing the inner spirit what goodness and justice really mean. Unfortunately, later apologists for the state took some of Hsun-tzu's ideas as a warrant for government by compulsion. In themselves, however, his ideas perhaps complemented Mencius's program as much as they opposed it, by clarifying the place for external codes. Arthur Waley, at least, has tried to show that Hsun-tzu mainly reacted against possible abuses of Mencius's views on human nature.[27]

In summary, then, the hallmarks of the original Confucians were a reliance on ancient models, a concern for the golden mean between externalism and internalism, a stress on filial piety, and a deep respect for the ruler's connection with heaven. These socially oriented thinkers emphasized breeding, grace, and public service. Their goal was harmony and balance through a hierarchical social order.[28] They gave little attention to the rights of peasants or women, but they did prize ethical integrity, compassion, and learning. Against the blood and violence of their times, they called for a rule through moral force. This was their permanent legacy: Humanity is fidelity to virtue.

Taoism

The classical, axial-period Taoists responded to the troubled warring period quite differently than the Confucians did. They agreed that the times were disordered and that the way to set them straight was by means of the ancients' *Tao*. But the great Taoist thinkers, such as Chuang-tzu and Lao-tzu, were more imaginative and mystical than the Confucians. In their broad speculation, they probed not only the natural functions of the Way and the interior exercises that could align one with it but also the revolt against conventional values that union with *Tao* seemed to imply. Of the two great Taoists, Chuang-tzu is the more poetic and paradoxical. His stories stress the personal effects of living with *Tao*. Lao-tzu's orientation is more political. For him *Tao* gives a model for civil rule, lessons in what succeeds and what brings grief. Insofar as Chuang-tzu is more theoretical and less concerned with political applications, he enjoys a certain logical priority over Lao-tzu.[29]

Chuang-tzu

What impressed Chuang-tzu most was the influence of one's viewpoint. The common person, for example, can make little of the ancients' communion with nature, unconcern for human opinion, and freedom. Such things are like the great bird flying off where the sparrow has never been. Yet if one advances in the "fasting of the spirit" that the ancients practiced, their behavior starts to make sense. Apparently such "fasting of the spirit" was a meditative regime in which one laid aside distractions and let simple, deep powers of spiritual consciousness issue forth.

Chuang-tzu pictured those powers rather dramatically: They can send the sage flying on the clouds or riding on the winds, for they free the soul so that it can be directed by *Tao* itself. *Tao* is the wind blowing on the ten thousand things, the music of the spheres. With little regard for petty humankind, it works nature's rhythms. The way to peace, spiritual ecstasy, and long life is to join nature's rhythms. But by joining nature's rhythms, one abandons social conventions. *Tao* throws off our human judgments of good and bad, right and wrong. Thus, the true Taoist becomes eccentric with respect to the rest of society, for he (or she, though women seldom participated in Chinese society) prefers obscure peace to troubled power, leisurely contemplation to hectic productivity.

In rather technical terms, Chuang-tzu attacked those who thought they could tie language directly to thought and so clarify all discourse. If *Tao* touches language and thought, he showed, they become highly symbolic. Moreover, Chuang-tzu made his attack on conventional values and language into simple good sense. It is the worthless, cast-off, unpopular trees and people that survive. Those who would be prominent, who would shine in public, often end up without a limb (as punishment for crime or disfavor). When he was asked to join the government, Chuang-tzu said he would rather drag his tail in the mud like a turtle. When his wife died, he sang and drummed instead of mourning: She was just following *Tao*, just taking another turn. Puncturing cant, deflating pomposity, excoriating our tendency to trade interior freedom for exterior position, Chuang-tzu ridiculed the sober Confucians. They, like other prosaic realists, seemed too dull to be borne—too dull for a life of spiritual adventure, for a *Tao* as magnificent as the heavens and as close as the dung.

Lao-tzu

Thomas Merton has published a delightful interpretation of Chuang-tzu that relates him to the contemplative spirit of Western poets and monks.[30] No one has done quite the same thing for Lao-tzu or the *Tao Te Ching*, perhaps because Lao-tzu's style is more impersonal. The *Tao Te Ching (The Way and Its Power)*,[31] like the *Chuang-*

tzu (the book left by Chuang-tzu and his school), is of undetermined origin. Its author's existence is more uncertain than that of the *Analects*. But the book itself has become a world classic, in good measure because of its mystic depth (and vagueness). In it a very original mind meditates on *Tao's* paradoxical qualities to glean lessons about human society. Interpreters vary in the weight they give to the mystical aspects of the *Tao Te Ching*,[32] but in any interpretation Lao-tzu thought that *Tao* holds the secret to good life.

Consequently, a major concern of the *Tao Te Ching* is to elucidate just how nature does operate and how society should imitate it. Its basic conclusion, presented in a series of striking images, is that *Tao* moves nature through *wu-wei* (active not-doing). Three of the principal images are the valley, the female, and the uncarved block. Together, they indicate *Tao's* distance from most human expectations. The valley symbolizes *Tao's* inclination toward the lowly, the underlying, rather than the prominent or impressive. Lao-tzu's female is a lesson in the power of passivity, of yielding and adaptability. She influences not by assault but by indirection, by nuance and suggestion. The uncarved block is human nature before society limits it. These images all show *wu-wei*.

Wu-wei is also shown in the power of the infant, whose helplessness can dominate an entire family. It is in the power of water, which patiently wears away rock. Wryly Lao-tzu reminds us of the obvious: A valley resists storms better than a mountain, a female tends to outlive a male, an infant is freer than a king, and a house is valuable for the space inside it. Such lessons underscore a reality that common sense tends to ignore because it tends to notice only what is prominent. In contrast, *Tao* moves nature by a subtle, elastic power. Were rulers to imitate *Tao*, moving others by *wu-wei* rather than *pa* (violent force), society might prosper.

Wu-wei, it follows, tries to short-circuit the law of the human jungle, the round after round of tit for tat.[33] But to gain *wu-wei*, human nature must become like an uncarved block, which is perhaps the most important of Lao-tzu's symbols. (Holmes Welch, who argues that we can read the *Tao Te Ching* on several levels, makes the uncarved block its key.)[34] It symbolizes the priority of natural simplicity over social adornment. A block of wood or jade, before it is carved, has infinite potential, but once we have made it into a table or a piece of jewelry, its use is fixed and limited.

Impressed by the limitless creativity of nature, Lao-tzu wanted to recover human nature's originality. In his eyes, the Confucians tended to overspecialize human nature. A society with fewer "modern" advances, less technology, and more spontaneous interaction with nature and fellow humans would be much richer than the Confucians'.[35] The Taoists, who took their lead from Lao-tzu and Chuang-tzu, tried to show

how less could be more, how neglect could be cultivation. If people would shut the doors of their senses and thus cut off distractions, how less can be more would be obvious. The good life is not found in having but in being. By being simple, whole, alert, and sensitive in feeling, one finds joy.

Throughout history, many commentators have criticized Lao-tzu and his followers for both naiveté and obscurantism. They have especially jumped on the Taoist precept that a good way to promote peace and simplicity is to keep the people ignorant. Taoists believed that by not knowing and therefore not having many desires, a populace is quite docile. Critics maintain that it is but a short step from such docility to sheephood and being at the mercy of evil rulers. The commentators have a point: The ideas expressed in some of Lao-tzu's sayings invite easy abuse. For instance:

Heaven and Earth are ruthless;
To them the ten thousand things are but as straw dogs.
The sage too is ruthless;
To him the people are but as straw dogs.[36]

However, a close reading of the *Tao Te Ching* shows that *wu-wei* is quite different from mindless docility or even complete pacifism. Rather, it includes the regretful use of force in order to cut short greater evil. As well, *wu-wei* is not sentimental, which further distinguishes it from most Westerners' views of "the people." As easily as nature itself, *wu-wei* discards what is outworn, alternating life with death. Because of this objectivity, Taoism can seem inhumane. For a people close to nature, though, humaneness is a less anthropocentric virtue than it is for ourselves. It is less personal and more influenced by the belief that self-concern is folly.

Religious Taoism and Aesthetics

Two great consequences of the school founded by Chuang-tzu and Lao-tzu had con-

siderable influence through subsequent Chinese history. One consequence was religious Taoism, which was considerably different from the philosophical Taoism of the founding fathers in that it employed their symbolism literally and turned to quests for magical powers and immortality.[37] A second consequence was aesthetic: Chinese art became heavily Taoist.

The religious Taoists formed a "church," generated a massive literature complete with ritualistic and alchemical lore, and earned the wrath of modern educated Chinese, who considered religious Taoism a bastion of superstition. Also, religious Taoists became embroiled in politics and sponsored violent revolutionary groups.[38] Their magic and revolutionary politics went together, because from their magic they derived utopian visions of what human society ought to become.

The religious Taoists sought physical immortality by diverse routes.[39] Some sponsored voyages to the magical islands in the East, where the immortals were thought to dwell. (Sad to say, none of the voyagers ever came back to describe the immortals or their fountain of youth.) Others pursued alchemy, not to turn base metal into gold but to find the elixir of immortality. At one point they thought they had found this elixir in cinnabar (mercuric sulfide), which they persuaded emperors to imbibe so that the rulers could thwart death. On another sad day the religious Taoists discovered that cinnabar is a poison—a powerful elixir of mortality.

A third Taoist interest was hygiene. The two favorite regimes were breathing air and practicing a quasi-Tantric sexual yoga. Along with some dietary oddities, some religious Taoists counseled trying to breathe like an infant in the womb, so as to use up the vital force as slowly as possible. Adepts would lie in bed all day, trying to hold their breath for at first a hundred and eventually a thousand counts. Perhaps some became euphoric through carbon dioxide intoxication. Others went to their reward more quickly than their meat-eating fellows. The yogis of sex practiced retention of the semen during intercourse, thinking that this vital substance could be rechanneled to the brain and thereby enhance one's powers and longevity. Modern physiology says that the semen goes to the bladder, striking another blow against religious Taoism.

Religious Taoism also developed regimes of meditation, which it coupled with a complicated roster of gods. The basic assumption behind this venture was that the human body is a microcosm—a miniature world.[40] Within it, certain gods preside over particular organs and functions. By visualizing one of these gods, Taoists thought, one could identify with its powers of immortality.[41]

Taoism had as strong an impact on Chinese aesthetics as it did on Chinese popular religion.[42] As a guide to creativity, it stressed spontaneity and flow. Largely due to Taoist inspiration, calligraphy, painting, poetry, and music ideally issued from a meditative communion with the nature of things. In what Ch'an popularized as "no-mind," artists worked spontaneously, without calculation or design. Their products were the outflow of a fullness far more comprehensive than logic or method. In fact, the artists were supposed to render both the stream of nature and the way that particular items suddenly focus that stream. So a bird alighting on a tree, a rush of wind, the striking colors of persimmons at daybreak—these were typical themes of poetry and art. Taoist artists owed a great deal to the "retirement" that Taoism advocated as a respite and counterpoint to Confucian "office."[43] Mixed with Buddhist aesthetics, Taoism provided China with most of its artistic depth. Nature, art, and the spirit so came together for the traditional Chinese that they considered their Way superior to that of the rest of the world.

The Popular Amalgamation

By around 350 B.C.E. preaxial folk religion, Confucianism, and Taoism had come together, along with lesser philosophical movements. The major developments from that time until the Christian era were the establishment by the Han emperors of Confucian ideas as a sort of state orthodoxy, the flowering of religious Taoism, and the beginnings of Chinese Buddhism. With influence shifting among the movements, the mixture bubbled and boiled until neo-Confucianism emerged preeminent in the late Sung dynasty (twelfth century C.E.). In this section we try to analyze the effects of the different traditions in the daily life of the Chinese. Since this long stretch of history dominates Chinese culture, we are in effect trying to describe its most representative consciousness.

The Preeminence of Confucianism

In the typical Chinese family religious attention focused on ancestors. The family gained its identity from its clan, so by venerating its dead it constantly reaffirmed who it was. Because Confucianism emphasized filial piety, it suited this clan pattern quite nicely. The most devout thing one could do was to honor one's predecessors. In addition, familial piety involved a broad set of clan obligations whose guiding maxim was "Never bring dishonor on your lineage." Because the Confucians specialized in rites, protocol, gentlemanly bearing, and the like, which gave form to honor, they prescribed most clearly what the typical family wanted to know.

Confucianism was equally important in helping the public articulate the larger, state-centered concern for identity and honor. The emperor was the latest descendant of a most honorable clan, and the emperor's veneration of his ancestors had almost cosmic implications. In addition, the emperor wanted to justify the obedience of and respect from his subordinates. With its sensitivity to rank and its emphasis on a hierarchical social structure to maintain social order, Confucianism buttressed the status quo, which most rulers desired. Thus, the Confucian writings, first informally and later formally, became the basis of a gentleman's education. Further, because gentlemen were obviously the best civil servants, mastering the Confucian writings became a prerequisite to a career in government. As Lawrence Thompson notes, from the middle of the second century B.C.E. to the twentieth century C.E., the canon of Confucian writings influenced the minds of all educated Chinese.[44]

The Non-Confucian Opposition

Thus, Confucianism was the most influential religious tradition for the public functions of the family and the state, and in that sense the most official. For private worship, philosophy, and art, however, Buddhism and Taoism were quite influential. Buddhism and Taoism contended for influence at court and sometimes gained dominance. After the fall of the Han dynasty (third century C.E.), for instance, Confucian influence waned, and Buddhism gained great influence that lasted well into the ninth century. Nonetheless, in most periods the state bureaucracy hewed to the Confucian line.

MEDIEVAL BUDDHISM

"For the first two hundred years of the T'ang, Buddhism flourished as never before. Supported by the lavish donations of the devout, guided by leaders of true piety and brilliance, graced by the most gifted artists and architects of the age, Buddhism was woven into the very texture of Chinese life and thought. These centuries were the golden age of an independent and creative Chinese Buddhism."[45]

The T'ang dynasty (618–907) followed on the Sui (589–618), under which North and South China had been reunited. Buddhism had made steady gains in China even before this reunification, but after reunification it grew by leaps and bounds. A major reason for this growth was the perception of both the Sui and the T'ang rulers that Buddhism could help them knit together the northern and southern cultures. Thus the founder of the Sui dynasty presented himself as a universal monarch who was both a pious Buddhist believer and a generous patron of the sangha. He likened his wars to campaigns to spread the ideals of Buddha, calling his weapons of war incense and flowers offered to the Enlightened One. It is hard to see how this squared with Buddhist nonviolence, but the popularity of Buddhism among the emperor's subjects led him to associate himself with the dharma as much as he could.

On the other hand, both the Sui and the T'ang rulers feared the power of the sangha and took steps to limit its influence. Thus they insisted on regulating the admission, education, and ordination of the Buddhist clergy and on licensing the Buddhist temples. As well, the emperors put pressure on the sangha to enforce the Vinaya strictly, for these rules governing monastic life tended to restrict the clergy's economic enterprises. Such imperial efforts to control Buddhism were only partly successful, for many medieval empresses and wealthy merchants saw to it that temple wealth grew. The merchants' support of Buddhism is an interesting example of fitting a religious rationale to economic goals. For the merchants, the Mahayana notion that money gifts should be put to productive use became a justification for widespread commercial enterprise. Since the prevailing economy was, by imperial design, focused on agriculture, the Mahayana notion in effect buttressed the merchants in their conflict with the state comptrollers.

The government did its best to limit the ways that Buddhist doctrines might become politically subversive, guarding against the revolutionary implications of Mahayana dharma. For example, potential rebels had ready to hand the Mahayana belief that Buddhism would pass through three ages. In the third age, religion would come close to extinction and no government would merit the full allegiance of the Buddhist faithful. A wealthy and powerful sect called the San-chieh chiao seized on this notion and tried to use it to undermine the imperial authority, but the Sui and T'ang rulers reacted vigorously and had the sect suppressed. The Mahayana teaching about Maitreya, the future Buddha, was similarly dangerous. Enough Buddhists believed that the advent of Maitreya was close at hand to present the government a sizeable problem. The popular understanding was that when Maitreya came, a new heaven and a new earth would begin. Thus both the Sui and the T'ang emperors had to battle rebels moving against them under banners of white (the color associated with Maitreya).

Still, the golden age that Buddhism enjoyed in these dynasties flowed from the positive support the emperors gave it. For all their care that Buddhist fervor not become subversive of their own rule, the Sui and T'ang leaders made Buddhist ritual an important part of the state ceremony. Thus the accession of a new emperor, the birth of a prince, and the ceremonies in honor of the imperial ancestors all incorporated Buddhist sutras, spells, and prayers. When the emperor ritualized important occasions, the monasteries and temples received handsome donations, which of course increased their patriotic loyalty and pliability.

At the great capital of Ch'ang-an, Buddhist art dominated a vibrant cultural life. The architecture of the pagodas and temples gracefully blended Indian and native Chinese elements, producing a distinctively Chinese Buddhist appearance. The images and paintings that adorned the temples drew on the full range of sources with which the great Chinese Empire came in contact. Thus there were not only native Chinese art forms but also Indian, Persian, Greco-Roman, and Central Asian. With sufficient freedom married to sufficient imperial support, Chinese Buddhist artists enjoyed a period of great prosperity and created a distinctive new style.

This sort of syncretism—a core of Chinese Buddhist inspiration in touch with many other sources of inspiration—extended to literary art. The T'ang dynasty was a highpoint in the history of Chinese poetry, and the moving forces behind this poetry were the two congenial streams of Buddhist and Taoist philosophy. Thus the celebrated poet Po Chu-i was representative in filling his work with references to the Buddhist rituals and temple grounds that gave him and his contemporaries spiritual nourishment. In one poem he remembers visiting a great hall called the Jade Image, in which rows of white jade Buddhas sat like serried trees. He and his fellow journeyers shook the dust from their clothes and bowed to worship the Buddhas, whose faces were like frozen snow. The Buddhas' white cassocks hung like folded hoarfrost, and their crowns glittered like a shower of hail. So perfect were these white images that the journeying poets scrutinized them in wonder, feeling that here was a work of heavenly spirits, a work more exalted than any earthly chisel could have managed.[46]

Medieval Buddhism also permeated the life of the common people, including the village peasantry, for the government developed a network of official temples that linked the provinces to the capital. On official feast days, ceremonies held throughout the land reminded the people that they shared a uniform religious faith. The provinces also used the Buddhist temple grounds for their fairs, thereby making them the centers of the local social, economic, and artistic life. The great feast days were the Buddha's birthday and the Feast of All Souls, when large crowds would gather to honor the Buddhist deities, listen to the sutras, or hear an accomplished preacher expound the dharma.

When local organizations met for vegetarian dinners, clergy and laity had a fine chance to socialize. Fashioning close bonds of mutual interest, these dinners became a great source of fundraising for the monasteries and blessings for the mercantile and personal interests of the laity. The village clergy usually were not well educated, but they tended to know the laity intimately and to provide them considerable solace at such important times as weddings and funerals. Many of the village Buddhist clergy also functioned as healers and mediums, as well as storytellers and magicians.

The state and the sangha therefore had a symbiotic relationship throughout the Sui and the T'ang dynasties. Whether pulling in the same direction or wanting to go opposite ways, they were mutually influential. One place where Buddhist views considerably modified traditional Chinese customs was the penal codes. The traditional customs were quite cruel, so the Buddhist ideals of compassion and respect for life served as a mitigating influence. Both the Sui and the T'ang rulers granted imperial amnesties from time to time, and when the rulers remitted death sentences they often justified their actions in terms of Buddhist compassion or reverence for life. Specifically, both dynasties took up the custom of forbidding executions (indeed, the killing of any living thing) during the first, fifth, and ninth months of the year, which were times of Buddhist penance and abstinence.

The emperors also converted Buddhist notions of the soul to their own ends, using them for the psychological conditioning of the imperial armies. Whereas the traditional Chinese cult of filial piety had weakened martial fervor, teaching that a good son would return his body to the earth intact, out of gratitude to his parents, the Buddhist stress on the soul (or spiritual aspect of the "person") downplayed the importance of the body. The traditional cult had also taught that immortality depended on being buried in the family graveyard, where one's descendants could come to pay tribute. Thus a soldier buried far from home would have no continuing significance. The Sui and T'ang dynasties made it a practice to build temples at the scene of foreign battles and endow these temples with perpetual services for the souls of those slain in military service. In this way, they lessened the conflict between a generous service in the army and a generous filial piety.

Medieval Buddhism also increased the charitable helps available in Chinese society. Monks were the first to open dispensaries, free hospitals (supported by the T'ang government), and hostels for travelers. They built bridges, planted shade trees, and generally broadened China's ethical sensitivity. Whereas the native ethic seldom took much charitable interest in affairs outside the clan, Buddhism encouraged an interest in the welfare of all living things. For example, it said that giving alms to poor people outside one's clan was a fine way to improve one's karma. This Buddhist universalism never displaced the formative influence of the Chinese clans, but it did move many Chinese to greater magnanimity.

Finally, it was during the medieval flourishing that Buddhist philosophy became fully Chinese. A hallmark of this domestication was the rendering of the abstractions in which Indians delighted into the concrete images the Chinese preferred. For example, the Indian "perfection" became the Chinese "round," while the Indian "essence" became the Chinese "pupil of the eye." Ch'an, the school that most stressed meditation, carried the Chinese spirit to the heart of Buddhist spirituality, distrusting abstract words and stressing metaphors, paradoxes, gestures, or direct, person-to-person intuitions. Ch'an and the other native schools also stressed living close to nature, in the conviction that nature held many of the secrets of enlightenment. This had great appeal to medieval Chinese artists, poets, and philosophers, many of whom would refresh themselves in retreats at Buddhist monasteries.

Buddhism's major impact in the public sphere was its control of burial rites. In time, China associated funerals with monks. Partly out of envy at such influence and partly out of its own searches for enlightenment, Taoism established monastic communities in the fourth century C.E. Along with the rituals of the Taoist priesthood and the Taoist political parties, these communities were strong sources of Taoist public influence.

However, in their struggles against Confucian dominance, Buddhism and Taoism primarily depended upon their greater appeal to individualist and artistic sentiments. In comparison, the sober Confucians offered little to nourish a private, meditative, philosophical, or aesthetic life, although they were not completely lacking resources for nurturing private satisfactions. The Master's love of music, for instance, though he set it in a traditional and public context, could have inspired personal creativity in the arts. However, such inspiration tended to fall to Buddhists and Taoists.

In addition, the Buddhist and Taoist texts seemed richer and more mysterious to middle-aged people seeking meaning in their existence. Few Chinese could live fifty years and not suffer some surfeit from rules, laws, ceremonies, or traditions. At such a point, the lean paradoxes of Chuang-tzu, Lao-tzu, the *Prajna-paramita*, and Ch'an grew very attractive. So did the *Tao* that could not be named, the Buddhist emptiness that one had to attend in silence.

Only the educated upper classes, of course, had the opportunity to immerse themselves in any of the three traditions. For the majority of the population, the influence of these traditions only vaguely affected a world dominated by family loyalties and naturalistic animism, largely because the Chinese population was always overwhelmingly comprised of peasants. Close to nature, these people filtered Buddhist and Taoist ideas through a primal reverence and fear for nature's powers.

For instance, the Chinese peasants incorporated Buddhist demonology, Taoist demonology, and both traditions' concern with saints into their ancient world of ghosts and helpers, which was home to the ancestors. This world was real because it affected the peasants each day, as the family sacrificed or tried to avert bad luck. The magical world of the spirits was alive. Daily the phenomena of the sky and the fields expressed that world's mysteries, and the wind and the sea carried great swans and dragons. The cities and the imperial court had their influence on the hamlets, but real life there confronted nature with little polish or form. What we might call an instinctive Confucianism about family relations blended with an instinctive Taoism about nature and human destiny to produce a curious mixture of formality and magic.

Moreover, the peasants had not separated, either through study or deep meditation, rationality from mythical or pragmatic hopes and fears. Getting enough food, sheltering one's family, warding off sickness, continuing the family line—those were the concerns of the villagers. To meet them, different gods were honored at festivals for the new year and for the changing seasons. As well, the Buddhist goddess of mercy drew those seeking easy births and strong children, and the Taoist cult of the immortals attracted a few who wanted longevity or knowledge of the rulers of their bodily organs. Tradition sanctioned these quests for meaning, but it was a tradition with many cracks. Daily life was largely a fearful effort to avoid the wrath of the ancestors or the evil spirits.

Mercantile Religion

By the fourteenth century C.E., guilds of artisans and businessmen had developed and folk religiosity in China had become more mercantile. The guild became a sort of family or clan and had its patron gods and rituals. People now invoked the spirits who were the patrons of good selling, and a folk mentality affected the examinations that were part of the way to civil office. For instance, masters of the Confucian classics who did well in the examinations and secured good jobs took on an aura of religious power. As well, numerous stories were told of scholars who received miraculous help from a patron deity, and these scholars gave the Confucians their own measure of magic and mystery.[47]

The common people also went to a great variety of shrines and temples to find out their futures. In addition, students prayed for success in their examinations, travelers prayed for safe journeys, and young people prayed for good marriages. Popular Chinese religion thus became almost economic. Gods and powers were the foci of business—a business of getting along well with an unseen world of fate and fortune. Confucianism, Taoism, and Buddhism all were mixed into this economic popular religion, but its base was preaxial superstition. Few Chinese were so far from nature or so safe from adverse fortune that "secularism" was a live option. The state somewhat controlled religion by keeping the Buddhist and Taoist clergy in check, but the religious life of the family and the individual ran all the traditions together in a form that was largely outside the government's control.

Neo-Confucianism

During the Sung dynasty (960–1279 C.E.), the axial Confucian thought that lay in the teachings of Confucius, Mencius, and Hsun-tzu grew into a full-fledged philosophy that included metaphysical interpretations of nature and humanity. That was largely in response to the impressive systems that Buddhism, with its Mahayana doctrines of emptiness and the Buddha's cosmic body (*dharmakaya*), and to a lesser extent Taoism had developed. To Confucius's ethics the neo-Confucians added an explanation of all reality. They accepted the ancient world view, granting an important place to sacrifices for the state and the family. As well, they accepted the moral supremacy of the sage, whose virtuous power might move society or even nature. But they went on and reasoned the sort of reality that nature must be if the sacrifices or the sages were to be efficacious. This neo-Confucian development gave the Sung rulers and their successors a doctrine that buttressed their practical preference for Confucian ethics.

The neo-Confucian philosophy of nature that gained the most adherents involved the interaction of two elements, principle and ether. Ether, or breath, was the basis of the material universe. All solid things condensed out of ether and eventually dissolved back into it.[48] In the dynamic phases of this cycle, ether was an ultimate form of yang. In the still phases, it was the ultimate form of yin. The neo-Confucian view of material nature therefore preserved the tension of dualities—of hot and cold, male and female, light and dark—that had always fascinated the Chinese. One reason for the acceptance of neo-Confucianism, in fact, was that it appeared as just a modern version of the ancient patrimony. The second element in nature's dualism, principle, etymologically related to the veins in jade or the grain in wood. It was the *pattern* running through all material things, their direction and purpose. If you opposed principle (went against the grain), all things became difficult. In terms of cognitional theory, the neo-Confucians invoked principle to explain the mind's ability to move from the known to the unknown. They also used it to ground the mind's appreciation of the connectedness of things. Principle was considered to be innate in human beings—it was nature's inborn guidance. The main task of human maturation and education was to remove the impediments that kept people from perceiving their principle. This task implied a sort of asceticism or moral diligence, sometimes involving meditation and self-denial.

Finally, the neo-Confucians tried to assimilate the folk aspect of Confucianism by finding a place for the spirits. They preferred not to venerate the ancestors' ghosts, but they allowed that *shen* and *kuei* (the two traditional kinds of spirits) could be the stretching and contracting of ether. In that way, they could let the spirits work the planets, the stars, the mountains, the rivers, and so on. Once again, neo-Confucianism was less personal than the earlier traditions, but its new, rather rationalistic system stayed in touch with the old roots.

Chu Hsi (1130–1200 C.E.) was the master thinker who systematized these neo-Confucian ideas.[49] His predilection was sober analysis, a sort of scientific philosophy, and he concentrated on physical nature. Another more idealistic wing of the neo-Confucians took to the Ch'an stress on mind and tended to place principle in the context of a meditative, as well as an analytic, cultivation of reason. Because Chu Hsi's ideas became authoritative in such government-controlled areas as the civil service examinations, neo-Confucianism inculcated in the educated classes a realistic, affirmative view of material nature. However, it accepted meditation enough to stay competitive with Ch'an,[50] and it tried to stay open to such artistic movements as the magnificent Sung dynasty landscape painting.

Despite these metaphysical developments, neo-Confucianism retained a commitment to the traditional Confucian virtues associated with character building. The paramount virtue continued to be *jen*. The ideogram for *jen* represented a human being: *jen* is humaneness—what makes us human. We are not fully human simply by receiving life in a human form. Rather, our humanity depends upon community, human reciprocity.[51] *Jen* pointed in that direction. It connected with the Confucian golden rule of not doing to others what you would not want them to do to you. Against individualism, it implied that people have to live together helpfully, even lovingly. People have to cultivate their instinctive benevolence, their instinctive ability to put themselves in another's shoes. That cultivation was the primary educational task of Confucius and Mencius.

The neo-Confucians also kept the four other traditional virtues: *yi, li, chih,* and *hsin. Yi* meant duty or justice, and it signified what is right, what law and custom prescribe. Its context, therefore, was the Chinese culture's detailed specification of rights and obligations. Where *jen* undercut such formalities, giving justice its heart, *yi* took care of contractual exactitudes.

Li, which meant manners or propriety, was less exact than *yi.* To some extent it depended on learning, so Confucius tried to teach by word and example what a gentleman would do in various circumstances, but it also required instinct, breeding, or intuition. Handling authority over household servants, men in the fields, or subordinates in the civil service involved *li.* So, too, did deference to superiors, avoidance of ostentation, and a generally graceful style. *Li* therefore was the unguent that soothed all social friction. In a society that prohibited the display of hostile emotion, that insisted on a good "face," *li* was very important.

Chih (wisdom) was not a deep penetration of ultimate reality like the Buddhist *Prajna-paramita;* it depended on neither enlightenment nor mystical union with *Tao.* Rather, it was a prudent sense of right and wrong, decent and indecent, profitable and unprofitable that one could hope to gain by revering the ancients and attentive living. *Hsin* meant trustworthiness or good faith. It was related to *jen* insofar as what one trusts in another is his or her decency or humanity, but it pertained more to a person's reliability or dependability. A person of *hsin* was not flighty or capricious.

Some commentators consider these Confucian virtues moralistic or humanistic rather than religious. The virtues amounted to a secular sketch of what right living, living according to *Tao,* entailed. It is true that in neo-Confucian times *Tao,* the Way of Heaven, involved the ancestral clan leader or the overarching seer less than it had in pre-axial or axial times; by the Sung dynasty, *Tao* was for many Confucians just a name for nature's rationality. Still, the difficulty of fully realizing the five virtues remained. So, too, did the character of the Way, if only because Taoists and Buddhists considered the Way sacred. Given our assumption that all ultimate concerns entail religion, neo-Confucian meditation and invocation of the Way and its argument that the five virtues expressed the Way suggest religion.

In summary, neo-Confucianism tried to update the Master's teaching for less anthropomorphic, more rational times. (Until the early twentieth century, though, the neo-Confucians honored Master Kung as a patron saint and endorsed a certain amount of popular ritual.) By acknowledging the power of the Buddhist and Taoist philosophies and incorporating some of their elements into neo-Confucian beliefs, the neo-Confucians expanded what had largely been an ethical code into a full philosophy of nature and humanity.[52]

CONFUCIAN RITUALISM

Although the intelligentsia resisted efforts to deify Confucius, the Chinese people at large reverenced the Master with rituals and cult. To communicate the flavor of this cult, let us briefly describe some of the ceremonies that regularly took place at Confucius's shrines in the southwestern part of Shantung Province. Prior to the communist revolution, such ceremonies were an important part of the Chinese ritual year.

A Western visitor who witnessed the rites at Confucius's ancestral temple in Ch'u-fu in 1903 was first received by the Yeng-sheng Kung ("the Duke who propagates"), as the head of Confucius's clan officially was known. The duke took the visitor around the temple grounds, which covered about thirty-five acres well-wooded with old cypress, yew, and fir trees. Tradition said that one of the trees was planted by Confucius himself and that two others were planted during the T'ang and Sung dynasties. The temple proper was divided into six courts, the innermost of which was venerated as the area where Confucius himself had lived. In front of this innermost precinct were various tablets with inscriptions of praise by various Chinese emperors.

Inside the central area stood an altar, commemorating the spot where Confucius received people who came for his instruction. Behind this altar lay a great hall containing a statue of the Master. The statue was sixteen feet high and portrayed the Master seated on a throne. Near it were screens, embroidered with dragons, that could be arranged as a shield. Magnificent pillars of white and black marble supported the great hall, its floor was lined with black marble, its roof was covered with yellow tiles, and its ceiling consisted of 486 square panels gilded at the edges and ornamented with dragons.

Two of the principal festival days for worshiping at the Confucian temple were the *Ting* days of spring and autumn, when the stems and branches of the foliage were supposed to be flourishing. The minister of music would open the ceremonies, which featured music used in Confucius's own day (but composed even earlier, supposedly about 2000 B.C.E.). The entire ritual employed symbols and artifacts considered to come from the ancient days, when the model heroes whom Confucius revered had led Chinese society wisely by faithfully following the dictates of heaven. The dominant cloth, for instance, was a pure white silk, which ancient chiefs used to give people they wished to take into their employ. Other symbols of the Ting ceremony included the head of an ox (chief of the domestic animals, who leaves broad, permanent footprints); a pig (an animal with a will of its own, as its bristles suggest); and a sheep (plump for food and useful for wool). The incense used suggested the fragrance of virtue, while the wine and food typified the abundance of a virtuous kingdom. The boys performing the ceremonial dance dressed in ancient costumes, bearing in one hand a flute and in the other a pheasant feather. The flute represented the refinement music produces, while the feather stood for the adornment of learning.

Obviously, this ceremony, like most of the others that took place in Confucius's temple throughout the year, was meant to convey elegantly the benefits of virtue and breeding. In tune with the cosmic rhythms, the dancers suggested how any diligent student of virtue might hope one day to live, how any well-ordered state might hope to flourish.

Some of the hymns sung during the sacrifices to Confucius suggest the respect, veneration, and religious need his cult expressed. In one hymn, the choir begins, "Great is Confucius!"

Why is Confucius great? Because he perceives all things accurately, knowing them before they even arise. Because he stands in the realm of heaven and earth, the primal realities, and so can teach the ten thousand ages. Because his power brought lucky portents: The unicorn's horn gained a tuft of silk. Because he unveiled the sun and the moon, making heaven and earth fresh and joyful.

During the offering of the gifts to Confucius the choir members would sing: "I think of thy bright virtue." Never has there been a human being equal to the Master. His teaching is in all respects complete. The vessels people offer today are filled as vessels have been through thousands of years. From time immemorial, the Ting days have been sweet with the smell of sacrifice, adorned with clear wine.

Later in the ceremony, the choir refers to the traditional sounds of the drum and the bell. Echoing as the celebrant offers the ritual wine, the drum and bell express the reverence and harmony at the heart of the ceremony. The rites proceed, the music cleanses the participants' hearts, and the liturgy reaches a point of perfection—let all rejoice!

Then the choir remembers how people have performed these holy rites since antiquity. Even primitive people performed them, wearing rough skin hats. Though these ancient ancestors had only the fruit of the ground to offer, their music was orderly. Only heaven has ever guided any people well, and only a sage of Confucius's stature could have suited his instructions to the needs of any given hour. Following him, we can execute our moral duties properly, reverencing the emperor and our elders. Confucius taught us the link between sacrifice and happiness. Who would dare not be reverent in his hall? In their joy, all who prosper remember him as the source of their culture. Like the mountains of Fu and Yi, the rivers of Chu and Ssu, Confucius's beautiful acts have spread his influence high above and all around. The sacrifice reminds us of his great virtue. He renovates the thousands of the people. He fosters their schools and instruction halls.[53]

As elements of the cult to Confucius suggest, Confucianism built on Chinese customs that long antedated the Master. Indeed, sacrifices such as the one we have described can be traced as far back as the Shang dynasty, which is the limit of current archeological research. Insofar as most emperors gravitated toward Confucianism rather than Buddhism or Taoism, because Confucianism offered a more docile ideology, they found it useful to involve themselves in the Confucian sacrifices. Thus the emperor himself would officiate at the major ceremonies, as clan heads had since earliest times, while Confucian bureaucrats would officiate at lesser ceremonies in the capital and at state occasions in the provinces. This meant that there was no special caste of Confucian priests. In Confucianism, state official and priest merged, becoming but two faces of one public functionary.

Characteristically, the Confucian public functionary opposed innovation, both in the cult and at the government bureau. The party line was that the Confucian literati merely handed on the wisdom and customs of the venerable ancestors, as Confucius had definitively interpreted them. Thus Confucius was in effect the patron saint of the literati. As other clans had their divine protectors, so the literati had Confucius. The difference was that the literati headed the corps of civil servants. Their "clan" staffed the government offices, transmitted the imperial will. As teacher, cult figure, and model, Confucius gave civil servants the sanction of tradition and sober wisdom. Through him came the *Tao* of the ancestors, the basis of good order in his or any time.

By the seventeenth century C.E., the diverse elements of the Confucian tradition had been merged into a rather unwieldy official cult. According to an official list of those to whom imperial worship was due in the seventeenth century, there were three classes of worthies. First came the Empress Earth, the imperial ancestors, and the guardian spirits of the land and the harvest. Second came the sun, the moon, the emperors of the preceding dynasties, the patrons of agriculture and sericulture (raising silk), the spirits of the earth, the planet Jupiter, whose revolution around the sun regulated the Chinese calendar, and Confucius. (In 1907 Confucius was moved up to the first class.) Third came the patron saints of medicine, war, and literature, the North Star, the god of Peking, the god of fire, the dragons of several pools in Peking, the god of artillery, the god of the soil, the patron saint of the mechanical arts, the god of the furnace, the god of the granary, the gods of the doors, and many official patriots.

This list illustrates the amalgamating tendency of the Confucian tradition. On the list's map of reality are the imprints of ancestor veneration, veneration of the deities of the earth, veneration of the patron gods or saints of particular clans, and veneration of Confucius, the mortal whose interpretation of the past was most congenial to the crown. Some of the deities in this list are very ancient, going back to the Shang and Chou dynasties, at the very beginnings of Chinese history.

During the Ch'ing dynasty (1644–1911), the government instructed its officials in the particulars of worshiping the cult figures of the several ranks. The official was to bathe, fast, prostrate himself, and offer prayers. He was to make thanksgiving offerings of incense, lighted candles, gems, fruits, cooked foods, salted vegetables, wine, and other gifts. For special occasions sacrifices of whole oxen, sheep, pigs, deer, or other game were appropriate, as was a burnt sacrifice of a whole bullock. Music and dancing were to accompany these sacrifices. If the sacrifice was to a deity of the first rank, the official had to "fast" for three days prior to it. For sacrifices to deities of the second rank, two fast days sufficed. Fasting meant refraining from flesh, strong-smelling vegetables (such as leeks and onions), and wine.

Moreover, officials were to see to it that during important ceremonial seasons there were no criminal proceedings, no parties, no visits to the sick, and no mourning of the dead. They were especially to forbid entering the chamber of a dead woman, sacrificing to spirits, and sweeping a tomb. The government commissioned inspectors to check on the officials delegated responsibility for the Confucian cult, to make sure that they followed these prescriptions scrupulously. Behind this concern that the officiants be properly prepared lay the Confucian conviction that a province follows the moral character of its officials. If the officials were scrupulous in performing the rites, the people would be orderly. As Confucius was reputed to have said (*Analects*, 2:3): People led by laws and restrained by punishments will avoid laws and punishment without qualm. People led by moral example and restrained by social ritual will develop a sense of shame and become good.[54]

The Communist Era

For over two millennia, the axial ideas and beliefs that we have described prevailed in China with amazing stability and consistency. (Indeed, Hans Steininger has said of Confucianism, "It is these ethics which even today we meet all over East Asia.")[55] Despite new dynasties, wars, changing artistic styles, and even dramatic new religions such as Buddhism and Christianity, the general culture perdured. In the family, the government bureaucracy, and the villages, the folk/Confucian tradition was especially solid.

However, that changed in the early twentieth century. From without, Western science and Western sociopolitical thought dealt it heavy blows; from within, the decay of the imperial government led to the birth of the republic in 1912. Belatedly, China entered the modern world. In the twentieth century, its ancient culture showed cracks and strains everywhere. As a result, Chinese religious traditions, especially Confucianism, came under strong attack. Identified with the old culture, they seemed out of place in the modern world. Since the "cultural renaissance" of 1917, China has tried to cast off its Confucian shackles; since the Communist takeover of 1949, China has espoused a program of ongoing revolution.[56]

The paramount figure in this program, of course, was Mao Tse-tung. Mao was born in 1893 in Hunan (a south-central province) of a "middle" peasant family (that is, not one of abject poverty). His father had little culture or education, and his mother was a devout Buddhist. Mao himself received a traditional primary school education, whose core was memorizing the Confucian classics. (As a result, he developed a profound distaste for Confucius.) He had to leave school when he was thirteen to work the land, but prompted by his desire for more education, he ran away and enrolled in a modern high school. There he first encountered Western authors who challenged traditional Chinese culture. (At that time many educated Chinese felt humiliated by their defeat by the British in the Opium War of 1839–1842, their defeat by the Japanese in 1895, and the repression of their Boxer Uprising in 1900 by a coalition of mainly Western powers. In the opinion of biographer Stuart Shram, Mao probably saw China's need to gain respect in the international community more clearly than he saw its internal needs.)[57]

During his student days in Hunan, Mao gradually came under the influence of socialist and revolutionary writers. He was at Changsha during the revolutionary battles of 1911, but his military participation there was probably slight. In school, though, he had to confront the intellectual turmoil of a country that had abolished its traditional examination system (the backbone of its educational structure) in 1905. Perhaps as a result, from 1913 to 1918 he apparently studied mainly on his own. He read Western authors, did some teaching, and edged toward a career of political activism. The May 4, 1919, demonstrations against the Japanese intensified his commitment to Chinese self-determination, and the news coming out of now-Communist Russia began to color his thought. By 1920 he was a dedicated political activist, engaged in publishing and organizing, although what he was against was clearer than what he was for. He was against a class structure that oppressed peasants, workers, and women and against Chinese lowliness in the world of nations. He was vaguely for a revolution or new regime that would remove these evils.

Slowly Mao adopted a more positive program due to increased engagement with the developing Chinese Communist party, increased knowledge of developments in Russia, and then years as a guerrilla soldier. Before long, Mao was a convert to Marxism-Leninism. He joined the Chinese Communist party in 1921, took part in the Communist collaboration with Chiang Kai-shek's Kuomintang party until 1926, and then led Communist forces that opposed Chiang. By 1935 Mao was in charge of the Communist party and engaged in what became his legendary "long march." Through World War II the Communists and the Kuomintang collaborated uneasily against the Japanese; after the war the final conflict with Chiang led to the Communist takeover in 1949. Throughout this period Mao pursued the twofold career of military general and political theoretician. While gaining power he collaborated with the Russians, but he eventually decided that China had to go its own way. The result was a massive experiment in agrarian reform, enfranchising the lower classes, and trying to control economics by Marxist-Leninist and Maoist dogma.

The reason for this brief biographical sketch of Mao is that he was the most important figure in China's break with tradition and plunge into modernity. Influenced by the Confucian classics and Buddhism, he nevertheless repudiated them both. On the surface at least, Maoism took shape as a secular humanism—a system that referred to nothing more absolute than "the people." Some of its doctrines and programs dramatically changed the life of the people. The women's movement, for instance, and the related changes in the marriage law raised an entire segment of the population from subjection to near equality.[58] By stressing agricultural production, local health care, and "cellular" local government, Chinese Communism has become an even more grandiose socialist experiment than the Russian.

As part of the program instituting these changes, Mao's party denounced religion. Instead of gods and sacrifices, it offered self-reliance, hard work, and the mystique that the people united are invincible. Temples became government property, religious professionals were persecuted, and religious literature was derided or proscribed. The party likewise attacked the Confucian classics, virtues, and traditions. Throughout, its goal was to destroy the old class society and make a new people with one will and one future.

However, as one might expect, religion and tradition died harder than the Communists had hoped. In the rural regions, peasant traditions continued to have great influence. Among the intellectuals, conforming to the party line resulted in rather wooden, if not second-class, philosophy, science, and art. According to R. J. Lifton,[59] Mao himself ruminated on immortality in his last years, for he saw the problem of keeping the revolution "green"—retrieving for a new generation the experiences of the long march and the other peak events that had united the wills of the founding generation.

Something of that concern comes through in the last of Mao's poems.[60] "Two Birds," supposedly written in 1965, contrasts a sparrow, concerned only with beef-filled goulash, with a soaring roc that sees how the world is turning upside down. The options, Mao seems to say, are settling down in material comfort and keeping the revolution green. Many commentators have seen in Mao's sporadic activism (periods of stability followed by upheavals such as the Cultural Revolution) an effort to ward off stagnation.

Whether the constant call to renew revolutionary fervor will continue now that Mao has died is hard to predict. Likely the cult of the leader, which reached impressive proportions under Mao, will diminish. This cult developed prayers and hymns that treated Mao not only as a military and political leader and a great father figure but also as a sort of saviour. Individual needs, nationalistic pride, and other psychic forces can combine to surprising effect. At least, they suggest that religious fires still burn at the Chinese foundation.

STRUCTURAL ANALYSIS

Nature

All ancient societies lived deep in what we have called the cosmological myth, and China was no exception.[61] However, China did not have India's tendency to call sensory experience into question. Throughout its axial period, China's attitude was that nature is utterly real—more primordial than human beings. After the axial period, when Buddhism had a deep effect, native Chinese thought and the dharma were joined in more than a marriage of convenience. For instance, the Ch'an and Hua-yen schools translated the Mahayana philosophy of emptiness into a Chinese version of the theory that nirvana is identical with samsara. Furthermore, although Buddhist devotional sects among the masses drew attention to the heavenly Pure Land, they also described the Pure Land as a present reality. Overall, then, nature bulked large and unquestioned. The vast majority of Chinese doubted neither its reality nor its ultimacy. If there had been a question of subordinating one of the four dimensions of reality (nature, society, self, and divinity), nature would have been the last to go.

Physical reality took form through *Tao*. *Tao* was the most basic force holding nature together. To be sure, the *Tao* most to the fore here is that which humans can name. The nameless *Tao* (which to Lao-tzu was the more real) was too vast, too primordial, too womblike for humans to grasp. It was so unlimited as to be somewhat beyond the world, so full or complete as to be beyond our comprehension.

So, it was the worldly Way—the cause of the seasons, the peculiarities of history, the laws of gravity and the tides—that dominated most Chinese reflection on nature. Most Chinese reflection on nature concerned manifest entities, patterns and forces that affected human beings. The other latent *Tao* was only the intuition of an intellectual, indeed of a mystical, elite. Not only could that *Tao* not be named, it could not be brought under human control. Consequently, it was the best candidate in pre-Buddhist Chinese thought for the mystery whose uncontrollability is our primary indication that something more powerful and basic than what we see is at the origin of things.

Tao, it follows, was both Logos and mother. As Logos, it was the reasonable pattern, the intelligence running through nature. As mother, it was the source of all things. Neither being nor nonbeing, the maternal *Tao* existed in a realm of its own. Yet this transcendent realm was also the basis for all the other realms of nature. The fish, waters, clouds, trees, mud, dung, and other elements of observable reality existed by *Tao*. Both the manner in which they existed and the fact that they existed implied this ultimate. So *Tao* functioned as the within and the without. Not many Chinese reasoned in this somewhat relentless way, but their more poetic and circular descriptions take us to such conclusions. Nature had a sense and a mystery, and this sense finally owed to its mystery. The pregnant word *Tao* signified both.

Throughout Chinese history, *Tao* retained this richness. Confucians and Buddhists used it to express their understanding of nature, as did Taoists themselves. Frequently *Tao* was associated with heaven *(t'ien)*, which often gave it a sacred aspect. Originally heaven was the overseer (a notion that the Chinese shared with Indians and Near Easterners). There was nothing that heaven did not notice and record. Heaven itself, though, never took on personal features among the Chinese. No father with a white beard, no Apollo with a dashing chariot became its emblem. Neither the sun nor the moon solicited reverence as the primary form of heaven. If anything, the sky itself, broad and indistinct, was the focus of Chinese devotion.

Opposite to the sky was the earth. Yet the earth seldom was viewed maternally, as it was by many ancient peoples. The Chinese acknowledged the mysteries of vegetation, seasonal changes, the fallow and the productive, and they touched their newborns to the earth in recognition of their origin. But the maternal aspect of nature's bounty they attributed more to *Tao* than to the earth. Perhaps they were more attuned to pattern and flow than to dirt-bound production. (Or perhaps we are speaking mainly about the beliefs of poets and intellectuals, whose writings shape our impressions overmuch.)

In any event, Lao-tzu, Chuang-tzu, and the Buddhists consistently invested nature with an aura of ultimacy and preferred to bow before *Tao*. For instance, Chuang-tzu's Great Clod is more than mother earth. Returning to the Clod at death keeps one in a universal rhythm. The Great Clod is the material system, the massive lump, that *Tao* turns. Similarly, Buddhist landscapers and gardeners went beyond mother earth to Suchness, Buddha-nature, or emptiness for their inspiration. Although the Japanese developed the aesthetic resulting from this inspiration more fully, it first came from China.

Folk Views

More mundane matters—such as yin and yang, the five dynamic qualities, and the ghosts and helping spirits—absorbed the masses. These concepts rendered Chinese nature lively.[62] Of course, virtually all ancient peoples thought of nature as alive. Although the Chinese stressed the cult of ancestor spirits more than comparable peoples, such veneration was yet present among other peoples. Indian Buddhists, for instance, thought that the dead would turn malevolent unless the living venerated them.

Chinese folk religion is also distinctive (although, again, not unique) in its concern for the compass directions. The geomancy of *feng-shui* is a clear expression of Chinese emphasis on nature's four directions. Of course, other peoples were concerned with directions; Native Americans made a great deal of the four geographic directions, while early civilized peoples such as the Egyptians built their temples with great concern for their orientation toward the sun. However, China carried this concern to a high art. Even for the average person, the angle of the wind or the shape of the terrain was magically influential.

Chinese divination expressed another set of naturalistic assumptions. The *I Ching*, for instance, elaborated upon the belief that yin-yang components shape human participation in nature's course of events. Like the African diviner who studied the patterns of chits in a magical basket, the Chinese fortuneteller believed that numbers and designs expressed nature's coherence. In popular Chinese religion, then, there was a primal sense that nature coordinates with mind. That sense did not develop to the point of control over nature as it would have in science, but for Chinese diviners, astrologers, and even fortunetellers, this sense had great mythic power.

Such a mythic mentality may largely derive from a deep appreciation of what might be. Anything that is not contradictory might be. Therefore, anything noncontradictory can, under the pressure of imaginative suggestion, be accepted as something that is or that soon will be. From Laetrile to the stock market, we can see the same dynamics at work in late twentieth-century America.

In the *I Ching's* patterns of broken and unbroken lines, Chinese diviners were moved by the powerful human tendency to blur the distinction between what might be and what is, between the imaginable and the real. The interest motivating mathematicians, physicists, novelists, and theologians is little different from this tendency. The creative imagination uncovers realities much better than the imagination of the marketplace. The diviners were better in that they made both natural and human events coherent, even elegant.[63]

The place of human beings in Chinese nature, despite the diviners' claims that humans can read the signs of nature's processes, was rather humble. China was not a land where conquerors of heaven were exalted or where intellectuals identified the human spirit with an absolute spirit (exceptions might have existed among the Taoists and Buddhists). Throughout Chinese history humans have been considered rather insignificant compared with nature.

We can feel this mood in Chinese art. The tiny human figures in landscape paintings, for instance, contrast markedly with Western portraiture. In much Western religious art, even when divinity is clearly the paramount power, divinity gathers a people or incarnates a word. When Taoists or Buddhists correlated human beings with *Tao* or Buddha-nature, human beings came out small. The way of the wise, therefore, was indirect and nonassertive. Enlightenment involved losing the self, recognizing the fallacy of "I." In addition to the social forces that predominated over the self, there was a more comprehensive dominance by nature. Whether through Taoist return to the elements or Buddhist transmigration, the self was ever on the verge of slipping back into an unconscious, purely natural process. Since natural processes were the action on center stage, human figures were bound to be of marginal significance.

CLASSICAL CHINESE AESTHETICS

The traditional Chinese notions of beauty were so intimately involved with nature that we can consider both classical poetry and classical painting in a naturalist context. To be sure, classical poetry did not neglect the supernatural world, for one finds poems concerned with God, nature deities, Taoist "immortals," and ancestors. In addition, there were numerous poems concerned with family ties, friendship, love, social justice, war, and other human themes. But nature tended to be the encompassing orbit (for example, "God" was *T'ien*, heaven) and the great source of inspiration.

In the earliest poetry, from the *Book of Poetry* (about 1100–600 B.C.E.), nature often offers analogies to human life. Thus the first poem in this classical collection speaks of the cries of ospreys on an island in a river, which remind the poet of a man longing for the love of a virtuous maiden. As the poem unfolds, the river becomes a backdrop for the shifting emotions of human love.

Another early theme was just the opposite. In poetry from the early centuries C.E., we can read of nature's distance from human ways. Where human beings feel things intensely, hoping and sorrowing, nature goes its way in indifference. Where human affairs are always changing and the human life span is brief, nature goes its way with little alteration, confident in its endlessness. Unlike metal or stone, human beings cannot be expected to endure. The poet finds this contrast poignant, even bitter: Why should human life be so fragile and fleeting?

Still a third theme of classical Chinese poetry is the personification of nature, according it feelings like the poet's own. Thus some lyrics of Li Yu (937–978) describe flowers in the woods losing their red bloom, paling because of chilly rains or strong night winds. The flowers are like rouge-stained tears asking the poet to stay and share nature's sorrow. Other notable Chinese poets indulged in this "pathetic fallacy," as John Ruskin called it. Conventional imagery, for instance, attributed to rivers a great grief, as though their spring rising were the effect of voluminous tears, or their endless flow were a ceaseless lament for the harshness human beings must endure.

A fourth way the classical corpus treats nature is more subtle and sophisticated. Seeming to depict a natural scene objectively, the poet actually evokes almost stylized emotions, through the conventional associations his naturalistic images would stimulate. Thus a ninth-century C.E. poem of Wen T'ing-yun describes a tower backed by a river, a moon gazing down on the sea, and mists along a seacoast punctuated only by two lines of migrating geese. Adding images of frontier sparseness, the poet insinuates the melancholy of the homesick traveler, alone while his family and friends have gathered at night. The Western reader can catch the general mood, but the Chinese reader would have been affected by such details as willows waving along the dyke, because traditionally one gave a willow branch to a friend departing on a journey.

Like artists everywhere, the classical Chinese poets turned their materials this way and that, searching for the best inspiration. They felt little need to be "logical" and treated nature sometimes directly and at other times indirectly. Thus an eighth-century poem of Wang Ch'ang-ling portrays nature subjectively, as a stimulus of emotions. The poem, "A Woman's Complaint," tells of a young wife, hitherto carefree, who first experiences regret when she climbs to the top of a tower on a spring day and catches sight of some willows along the road. They remind her of the gift she gave her husband, when he acceded to her urgings and went off to seek his fortune. Led by the sight of the willows, the woman enters a new land, the domain of regret. For the first time, she wonders whether her impetuous urging was wise. The poet's lesson seems to be that nature can nudge us along the painful passage to wisdom. The timeless powers that move the world can open us to quiet reflection through flowers and sunsets.

Perhaps the most important motif in the classical poets' view of nature, however, was that peace comes from submerging the self in nature. Here the influences of Taoism and Buddhism seem strongest. For example, a work of the eighth-century poet Wang Wei speaks of birds returning home at evening, having traveled the vast void of the sky. At dusk the sky and earth invite the mind, too, to come home from its travels. If the mind would merge with the earth and sky, it would find rest. One feels through the poem the natural whole that birds or the setting sun can reflect. The human spirit finds its best place, the poet seems to say, when it lets birds and sunsets unite it emotionally with nature's mystery.[64]

Classical Chinese painting was equally preoccupied with nature. Prior to the rise of landscape painting, which is probably the most lauded Chinese development, there was a concern with depicting figures, such as impressive Buddhas, and after the heyday of landscape painting there was a concern with birds and animals, grasses and flowers. But landscape painting holds the central panel in the Chinese triptych, so we do well to concentrate on landscape painting.

There is no evidence of landscape painting before the Chin dynasty (265–419). The first specimen of natural scenery, attributed to Ku K'ai-chih, a famous figure-painter of the fourth century C.E., shows a mountain inhabited by wild

Figure 13   Fishermen (handscroll detail) by Hsu Tao-ning, about 970–1051. Nelson Gallery-Atkins Museum (Nelson Fund).

beasts. The animals are disproportionately large, as though they might gobble up the mountain, but for the first time we come upon a Chinese mind able to detach itself from human concerns and contemplate the wilderness. Tsung Ping, who succeeded Ku as the leader of the new movement, wrote an essay entitled "Preface to Landscape Painting," in which he expressed what was to be the guiding philosophy of this school: "The complete form of the mountain cannot be seen when the eye is quite close to it, but from a distance the eye can take in its whole compass, since the size of the mountain diminishes as it recedes from sight."[65] From this bit of common sense, the

landscape artists drew the conclusion that one best deals with naturalistic scenes by stepping back to see them whole.

During the T'ang dynasty landscape painting flourished. Both of its essential components—the composition of the whole and the brushwork detailing the parts—grew more skillful. The northern school favored rugged brush-strokes, leading to a more severe style, while the southern school favored more delicate strokes, leading to a more graceful style. Thus a snow scene by Wang Wei of the southern school is rather misty, with fine bits of snow falling on thin bare branches. A little bridge crosses a cloudy stream, its pilings

and railings whitened by snow. A tiny human figure approaches the door of a house apparently lighted for the evening. The man likely is looking forward to the cheerful fire but regretting having to leave the peaceful winter scene. Such poetic, imaginative emphases were typical of the southern T'ang school.

Landscape painting reached its greatest heights during the Sung dynasty. The fashion of painting richly colored landscapes developed, although a majority of the masters finally favored simple shadings of black ink. Gradually brushstrokes became the distinguishing feature of the great masters, and color faded to insignificance,

but there are some early paintings with beautiful rich colorings. The southern Sung school gained most renown for its fusion of poetry and painting. Not only would the artist usually run a text down the side of the scroll, he would also blend the scene with the poetry so that sight and sound married perfectly. A small snow scene by Liu Sung-nien, for example, perfectly pictures the literary contents of its poem: mountains, a little bridge, lonely pavilions, and a desolate willow tree. The total effect is "poetic" rather than objective, a tug at the heart rather than an analysis by the eye. "Winter is beautiful but bitter," it seems to say. "Much of life's loveliness is bleak and cold." The artist presents the natural forms in considerable detail, conveying a great respect for nature's intricacies.

Later southern Sung landscapes moved away from this detail, preferring a mere hint of nature's intricacies. Thus their canvases grew sparse, with large areas of empty space. The artists would show only the topmost peaks of a mountain or a single spray of flowers. Since this southern Sung development, *space* has dominated Chinese landscapes. Whether one considers this a triumph of Buddhist "emptiness," or a maturation of an inner artistic perception (an indirect way of suggesting nature's mystic whole while emphasizing its striking individual parts), it is singularly effective, pleasing the onlooker in both eye and soul. The eye is drawn to the perfectly executed flower or thin cloud, while the soul delights in vacating details. Communing with the *all* that runs behind, in, and through the details, the soul can aspire to "unknowing" facts and intuiting reality.

Thus a painting of Mi Feng entitled *Pine and Bower* has only several mountain tops, a tree, and a little hut. Half the picture is empty space, which might be clouds obscuring the bottom half of the mountains or a lake behind the little hut. There is no human presence except that suggested by the hut. The entire scene is tranquil: nature perfectly in balance, because left alone. Mi breaks the stereotype of southern delicacy, however, through a predilection for rugged natural features. This squares with a story told of him. Once he was walking along a forest path when he saw a large rock blocking his way. The rock was grizzled and oddly shaped, but his heart went out to it. So he knelt in the dust and embraced the rock, calling it "my elder brother." For this he got the nickname Mad Mi, but any good Buddhist or Taoist could understand his emotion. He developed a technique of "Mi dots" to help him express his love of strong particulars. Thus the mountains of *Pine and Bower* are wonderfully grainy, and the clouds have a thick consistency, as though unknowing were wrapping itself around the mind prior to enlightenment.

Nature in Buddhism

Richard Mather has shown that the concept of nirvana only won acceptance in China after the Buddhists modified it considerably.[66] At the outset, ultimate Buddhist reality seemed wholly contradictory to Chinese concreteness. Thus, Chinese Buddhists accomplished a rather thorough cross-cultural translation. They had predecessors in the Indian Mahayanists, who identified samsara with nirvana, but the Mahayanists were far more abstract than the Chinese. Indeed, Ch'an probably became the most successful of the sects rooted in Mahayana metaphysics because it most thoroughly domesticated nirvana. Little interested in words or speculations, Ch'an focused on meditation, by which one might experience nirvana. It also stressed physical work, art, and ritual that deemphasized dualistic thinking. This deemphasis is more familiar to Western readers in its Japanese form, but it had a Chinese beginning.[67]

So the radical Buddha-nature (whether as emptiness or as mind-only) found in Ch'an a natural form. It could be the essence of all physical things, so present that one need not flee the world nor even close one's eyes to experience it. Since meditation expresses this conviction through the bodily postures that one assumes, one has only to sit squarely in the midst of natural reality and focus on its is-ness. (Not incidentally, one does not close one's eyes. The proper focus is neither a direction within nor a withdrawal to fix on the passing mental stream. In Ch'an it is a gaze with eyes open toward the end of one's nose.) The objective is to see without reasoning the reality that is right here. Such seeing should not focus on particulars, or concern itself with colors and forms. Rather, it should appreciate reality's simple oneness by not making distinctions. When such appreciation flowers, there is enlightenment: "I came to realize clearly that Mind is no other than mountains and rivers and the great wide earth, the sun and the moon and the stars."[68]

Society

Historically, China used Confucianism as its binding social force, and Confucianism thoroughly subordinated individuals to the community. Consequently, the Chinese individual felt inserted not only into a nature more impressive than the self but also into a society greater than its parts. Further, the great Confucian thinkers based their theory of ideal social relationships on legendary rulers of the past. Such rulers embodied the social *Tao*. Their way, then, was a paradigm that ordered society by exemplary morality. Somewhat magically, the virtue *(te)* that went out from the legendary kings and dukes brought those it touched into harmony, at least according to Confucianism.

The Confucian mythic history evidences the common ancient notion of sacred kingship. Because the ruler stands at the peak of the human pyramid, he can conduct heaven's governing power to earth. The Chinese king manifested this holy mediating role by offering sacrifices to the gods of heaven and earth. On occasion, he sacrificed human beings.[69]

The imperial cult, consequently, was the keystone in the Chinese social edifice, and the Confucian notion of *li* (propriety) applied especially to the punctilious execution of its ceremonies. To know the music and ritual appropriate to different occasions was the mark of a high gentleman. In fact, from this cultic center radiated something religious that touched all social relationships. Since human activities related to heaven, they partook of cultic propriety. By maintaining a harmonious family, for instance, individuals contributed to the most important order, that between natural divinity and humanity.

The harmony that the Confucians encouraged, though it extended to all aspects of social life,[70] expressed itself most importantly in its rating of key human relationships. It rated men over women (and so pictured marriage not as a partnership but as the wife's servitude to the husband). It rated children (among whom the eldest son was the plum) distinctly inferior to the parents—so much so that obedience and service toward the parents (most importantly toward the father) dominated the lives of children. Likewise, rulers were rated over subjects, masters over peasants, and, to a lesser extent, elder brothers over younger brothers.

In logical extension of their veneration of the past, the Chinese honored ancient ancestors more than more recent ones, and they rated children according to the order of their birth. Surely some parents loved a younger son more than an elder son or a gracious girl more than a mulish boy, but in determining the important matter of inheritance, age was the sole standard. In these and many other ways, Chinese society looked backwards. The past was the age of paradigms; the elderly were the fonts of wisdom. The axial masters of Chinese political thought give little evidence of celebrating youth or brave new worlds.

Social space was similarly static. From the ruler's key connection to heaven, the social classes descended in clearly defined ranks with little egalitarian or democratic moderation. The Confucians especially felt that the rank of a person was important. One said quite different things to a fellow noble riding in a hunting carriage than to the carriage driver. A person of breeding knew and respected such differences. If Confucius and Mencius themselves are representative, such a person was almost prickly about his social rights.

For example, the master would not visit just anyone, and for a pupil to come into town and not quickly pay a visit of homage was a serious slight. Somewhat like Plato, the Confucian master protected his dignity and honor. Perhaps surprisingly, the Confucians turned their insistence on moral worth into a partial break with the cosmological myth (and with sacred kingship). Implicit in their exaltation of virtue over external station was a turn to the wisdom of the sage—a turn from cosmology to anthropology.[71]

Women's Status

Among the Confucians, a peasant or a woman was unlikely to find honor simply through interior excellence. In fact, of the three Chinese traditions, Confucianism was the most misogynistic. The woman's role in Confucianism was to obey and serve her parents, husband, and husband's parents. She was useless until she produced a male heir, and her premarital chastity and marital fidelity were more important than a man's. In some periods, obsession with female chastity became so great that society insisted upon total sexual segregation.[72]

Since a Chinese woman's destiny was early marriage, childbearing, and household duties, her education was minimal. She was not necessarily her husband's friend, confidante, or lover—males and courtesans could fulfill these roles. A Chinese woman was primarily her husband's source of sons. They were the reason for her marriage—indeed, for her sex. As a result, the ideal Chinese woman was retiring, silent, and fertile. Custom severely curtailed her freedoms, but never more cruelly than through foot binding. Mary Daly recently described this custom in graphic terms: "The Chinese ritual of footbinding was a thousand-year-old horror show in which women were grotesquely crippled from very early childhood. As Andrea Dworkin so vividly demonstrates, the hideous three-inch-long 'lotus' hooks—which in reality were odiferous, useless stumps—were the means by which the Chinese patriarchs saw to it that their girls and women would never 'run around.' "[73] However, there is anthropological evidence that many Chinese women overcame their submissive role by cleverly manipulating gossip so that abusive husbands or mothers-in-law would lose face.[74] Still, until the Communist takeover, women had no place in the political system and did very well if they merely outwitted it.

The Taoists were kinder to women and to the socially downtrodden generally. They were responsible for curtailing the murder of female infants by exposure, and their more positive regard for female symbols as examples of how the *Tao* worked upgraded femininity.[75] This was not an unmixed blessing, since it involved the "strength" of the one who was submissive and the manipulative power of the one who got herself mounted. Still, by bestowing feminine or maternal attributes on the *Tao* itself, the Taoists made femininity intrinsic to ultimate reality.[76]

Further, the Taoist political system, based on *wu-wei*, did not value force. In this Taoists were like the Confucians, agreeing that virtue and example produce social prosperity. (Radical philosophical Taoists, though, challenged the notion of virtue.) Also, the Taoists kept alive the paradox that is important to spiritual vitality. Chuang-tzu observed that many members of the upper class were miserable. By comparison, some poor people lived wholesome lives close to *Tao*. By such an awareness of the paradox of riches and poverty, Taoists prevented Confucian formalism from paralyzing Chinese society. So long as China honored Taoist poetry and Taoist retirement, *life* and *death* remained ambivalent terms.

Buddhist Social Influence

Buddhism downplayed social differences in another way. By teaching that the Buddha-nature is present in all reality, it said that equality is more basic than social differentiation. The monastic sangha institutionalized this equality. It would be naive to think that background or wealth played no part in monks' evaluations of one another, but the sangha was governed by a monastic code that underplayed wealth and severely limited monks' possessions.

Furthermore, during many periods in Chinese history, the sangha was genuinely spiritual. That is, its actual raison d'être was religious growth. In such times, the only "aristocracy" was determined by spiritual insight. For instance, though Hui-neng, who became the sixth Ch'an patriarch, was born poor (and, according to legend, brought up illiterate), his spiritual gifts mattered far more. Because he was religiously apt, a reading of the Diamond Sutra opened his mind to Buddha's light. After enlightenment, his peasant origins became insignificant.

The Buddhist sangha also improved the lot of women. It offered an alternative to early marriage and the strict confinement of the woman's family role. In the sangha a woman did not have full control of her life, but she did often have more peer support and female friendship than she could have in the outside world. In fact, Confucian traditionalists hated Buddhist nuns for their influence on other women. By telling women there were alternatives to wifely subjection, the nuns supposedly sowed seeds of discontent. Besides the jealousy of their Confucian and Taoist rivals, then, and the sometimes warranted outrage at their extensive landholdings, the Buddhists suffered persecution because they offered attractive alternatives to traditional Chinese family and social structures. The government frequently forced monks and nuns back into lay life during a time of purge to force them back into traditional social patterns.

Thus, although persecution was not the norm, Buddhists and other effective religionists often felt the controlling hands of the state. Formally, there was little independent religious authority. In times of peace, Buddhists and Taoists were left to go their own ways. When they perceived any threat, however, the rulers clamped down and made it clear that religion was a function of an integrated Chinese culture, not something outside of the culture that could set itself up as the critic of culture. As the Taoist revolutionary sects showed, the rulers had good grounds for their fears.

Thus, Chinese religion was what Yang has called "diffused."[77] Stronger by far than any institutional achievements was a pervasive sense of the supernatural. In good part because it propped the state against the

potential rebellion that Taoism and Buddhism housed, Confucianism became the state orthodoxy. Taoism and Buddhism, by contrast, were always somewhat heterodox.[78]

Among the common people, an important function of religion was to shore up received culture and authority. Apart from advanced positions in Taoist and Buddhist thought, religion did not liberate the individual. In this sense, Chinese religion broke neither the cosmological myth nor what we might call the social myth (conceiving of the political community as being divine). Both nature and the state (or the local duchy during the many periods of fragmentation) pre-existed the individual and predominated over him or her.

As a result, China had little sense that the human mind makes its own reality—little enlightenment, in the European sense. Neither by revelation nor by reason did Chinese culture gain a sophisticated sense of history (the one human spirit's unfolding through time) or philosophy (life arranged around this spirit's eros). Consequently, it remained closer to nature and more socially unified than later Western religious society did. The Chinese defined themselves by their land and their group. Happy to be the center of the earth, the Chinese Empire regarded all outsiders as barbarians and as less than fully human. This attitude resulted because millennia of living within a shared myth of nature and society had wrought a very strong cultural identity. That was both Confucianism's triumph and its limitation.

Self

The Chinese view of the self has been indirectly indicated by our stress on the primacy of nature and society. Nevertheless, the Chinese experimented with various conceptions of the self, just as they experimented with gunpowder, acupuncture, and pottery. As Donald Munro has shown,[79] axial Chinese thought, both Confucian and Taoist, wrestled with the possibility that human beings are essentially equal (at least male human beings). The effect of this belief on the hierarchical structure of Confucianism is complex, but the Chinese concepts of *jen* and *li* (goodness and propriety) indicate that the Chinese sensed that all persons have something to share as a basis for mutual respect.

In the structure of society, then, the self had some right to acknowledgement. Despite one's subordination to the whole (or, in many cases, one's near slavery), the common person found in such an author as Mencius a champion of the self's essential goodness. Mencius counseled princes to take their people's welfare to heart; his counsel was clearly more than a pragmatic bit of advice about how to avoid rebellions.

Further, the Confucians exercised considerable care on the self's education, at least for the middle and upper classes. Their major motivation seems to have been societal needs (as opposed to the self's intrinsic dignity), but by stressing character formation, the Confucians had to probe what the self's substance and dignity were. They decided, with considerable prodding from Confucius himself, that the paramount human faculty was the inner mind. If one could act from this inner mind with clarity and dispassion, one could act humanely and civilly. The core of the Confucian view of the self, therefore, was a certain rationalism. Confucianism did not stress speculative reason (that which gives rise to abstract theory), since Confucianism was not concerned with the human capacity to illumine or be illumined by the Logos of nature, but it did stress practical reason or prudence. Laying aside passion and prejudice (which required self-control), the good Confucian could hope with experience to discern the appropriate and harmonizing course of action.

Either through reflection on history or further rumination on the mind, the Confucians eventually linked practical reason with the ancients' *Tao*. It is clear from the myths handed down that the foremost ancestors were persons of composed, effective good sense, which enhanced their people's common good and even prosperity.

Because they were not venal or petty, the ancestors were able to lead by example—by radiating the power of *jen*.

On further reflection, the Confucians confirmed that the zenith of human achievement (which Confucius himself later came to epitomize) was such inner-directed action. In other words, the magisterial spirit feared no outer laws or sanctions. It was autonomous—it delighted in the good for its own sake. Though Confucius and Mencius both longed for public office, a major reason that neither ever achieved it was that neither would compromise his standards. Their uncompromising integrity became a lesson to disciples for centuries. When a devout Confucian observed an inhumane ruler, he felt more pity than envy.

The Taoist Self

The Taoists, who paid greater attention to the relationship between human consciousness and the cosmic *Tao*, produced a more paradoxical view of the self. They went against the Confucian standards of sagehood. Their masters were either cryptic eccentrics such as Chuang-tzu or magical "immortals" possessing paranormal powers. The cryptics' suspicion of human reason developed into a strong attack on logic and Confucian prudence. Logically, the *Chuang-tzu*'s chapter on seeing things as equal suggests that the philosophical Taoists found conventional language and morality both arbitrary and relative.[80] Standard terms in Confucian discourse such as *great* and *small*, *good* and *bad* (which were also used in the Chinese linguistic analysis contemporary with Chuang-tzu) turned out to be wholly relative. In fact, the Taoists cast doubt on the entire realm of discursive reason, which plods along from premise to premise and often misses the whole. If one could argue either side of a proposition, as lawyers always have tended to do, one clearly was not in the realm of ultimate concern.

For the philosophical Taoists, the realm of ultimate concern pivoted on *Tao*. They attempted to reach that realm by meditation and *wu-wei.* Consequently, they individualized the self more than the Confucians did. The Confucians, of course, realized that the talents of people differ, including the talent to reach the still inner reason from which humane action emanates. But the Taoists went beyond reason itself, encouraging each person to write his or her own script. What was important was that one write to the tune of the *Tao.* What the specific story was, how one chose to enact *Tao's* inspiration, was secondary.

One of Taoism's greatest influences on Buddhism shows in Ch'an's acceptance of this individualism. Placing little stock in doctrines or formulas, the master determined enlightenment by the pupil's whole bearing. The flash of an eye, the slash of a sword—a single gesture could indicate an enlightened being. One could even "slay the Buddha"—throw off all traditional guidance—if one had reached the goal. To the unenlightened majority, one's actions and life would be strange. Quite literally, one would be eccentric. But if the *Tao* or Buddhanature really became the self's treasure, such eccentricity was but the near side of freedom.

The religious Taoists saw the self as a mortal physical body. Therefore, by the several "hygienic" regimes mentioned, they tried to prolong physical life. As a result, religious Taoists experimented with yogic practices, many of them in the vein of Indian *kundalini* or Tibetan Tantrism, both of which viewed the body as a repository of energy centers.[81] Depending on the particular interest of a religious Taoist group, the self might focus on breath or semen or some other quintessence.

Further, most Taoists regarded the body as a warehouse of tiny gods, each in charge of a particular bodily part. In yogic exercise the adept was to visualize the god in charge of the spleen or the heart, and so gain health or blessing there. By their quests for immortality (in the sense of continued physical existence), then, the religious Taoists simultaneously underscored mortality and suggested that humans can defeat death.

They did not distinguish an immaterial part of the self as candidate for such survival, but they did probe the relations between contemplative ecstasy and nature's apparent immortality.[82]

In such magical concerns, which show numerous shamanist motifs, the religious Taoists exhibited aspects of ancient folk religion. Their "immortals" owed a good deal to the revered ancestors of the clans, who continued on in a real and effective, if indistinct, existence after death. Also, the religious Taoists exploited the folk aspects in the theory of yin and yang (which worked out to a doctrine of two souls—*p'o* and *hun*). Much of the rationale for the ancient burial rites lay in efforts to assure that the yin soul not become an avenging ghost. The yang soul, if survivors treated it well, would become a heavenly source of blessings. In that way, the folk view of the self involved a certain dualism, and when the Taoists spoke of immortality, many of the common people probably understood them as trying to maximize the happiness of the yang soul.

Karma and No-Self

Through Buddhism, China received a heavy dose of belief in karma. That was most effective in the popular Buddhist sects, among which Pure Land headed the list, but it entered the general religious stream, influencing even those who rarely participated in Buddhist rites. Karma, of course, meant that the self was immersed in a system of rewards and punishments. All its actions, good or bad, had their inevitable effects. Past lives pressed upon the present, and the present was but a prelude to a future life. In popular Buddhism, this doctrine encouraged a sort of bookkeeping. Sometimes quite formally, with ledgers and numbers, Buddhists tried to calculate their karmic situation and plan out a better destiny. More generally, the concept of karma prompted the belief that the self's present existence was a trial that would be evaluated at death. How heavily this sense of trial pressed on the average person is hard to say. Combined with the rather lurid popular pictures of the several hells awaiting the wicked, though, karma probably sparked its share of nightmares.

The philosophical and meditative Chinese Buddhist sects accepted the traditional doctrine of no-self. So, the Chinese thinkers who followed Madhyamika or Yogacara speculation agreed that emptiness or mind-only implied an effort to rout the illusion of a permanent personal identity. To become part of the oneness of Buddha-nature and join the dance of the dharmas, the individual had to annihilate samsaric misconceptions about the substantiality of the self. The Chinese appear to have been more concrete than the Indians in such efforts. That is, where the Indians often reasoned over the self very closely, trying by dialectics to understand the illusion of selfhood, the Chinese tried to get the self to see reality's totality. Such seems to be the intent of pictures that T'ien-t'ai and Hua-yen masters drew, as well as the intent of the more radical techniques of Ch'an. Bodhidharma's "just sitting" and "wall gazing," for example, were exercises designed to make clear that only Buddha-nature is real.

Overall, these various Chinese religious views of the self made for considerable confusion and complexity. Despite Buddhist philosophical influence, the average person through Chinese history apparently did not doubt the reality of his or her self. The educational and governmental establishments in most periods were shaped by the Confucian ideal of a sober, restrained, altruistic personality. One aimed at discipline and grace, at becoming a source of wisdom. The force that shaped the Confucian self was political in the sense that living together with family members and fellow citizens rather than in isolation was the norm. Only the few artistic and religious professionals seem to have broken this pattern. For them Taoist or Buddhist contemplative solitude stressed the mystery of the self insofar as the self was where the *Tao* or Buddha-nature most directly manifested itself. According to Lao-tzu, one would find *Tao* by shutting the "doors" (the senses) and going within.

The conceptions of the self that were presented in the three high traditions blurred when they entered the common culture. Most of the people came to Confucianism, Buddhism, or Taoism from its superstitious or magical side. So the Confucian scholar became a sort of wonder worker, the Buddhist bodhisattva glamorized holiness, and the Taoist "immortal" represented victory over death. From the ancient spirit world, ancestors and ghosts said that being conscious meant participating in a cosmos that was alive, a system of heavens and hells that impinged on the present.

WOMEN WARRIORS AND SHAMANS

In Maxine Hong Kingston's *The Woman Warrior*,[83] one glimpses how the Chinese sense of the supernatural lived on in the twentieth century. As a child, Kingston heard from her mother innumerable stories about Fa Mu Lan, the woman warrior. Stretching the imagination that would later make her a fine writer, she pictured what it would be like to be Fa.

It would be like a little girl coming upon a little hut in a forest and having the door open. An old man and woman would come out carrying bowls of rice, soup, and a branch of peaches. They would offer the little girl a share of their meal, she would refuse out of politeness, but they would press her to honor them with her presence. After lunch the three would go for a walk, the little girl enjoying the lovely mountains and pines, the old couple walking so lightly their feet would not disturb so much as a pine needle. The old couple would invite the little girl to spend the night and she, fearing the ghosts of the forest, would thankfully agree. Being tucked into a little bed just her width, the little girl would hear the old woman say, "Breathe evenly, so that you do not fall out."

The old couple would then raise the roof over the girl's bed, and she would fall asleep watching the moon and the stars.

The next day, the old couple would invite the girl to stay with them, so that they could train her as a warrior. "What about my family?" the girl would ask. Stirring the water in a drinking gourd, the old man would show the little girl her family discussing the honor of their daughter being invited to become a warrior. So she would agree, and begin her strict training.

First, she would learn to be quiet. The couple would leave her by streams, that she might watch the animals that came to drink. If she were not absolutely quiet, she would scare them away. With time the squirrels would come and bury their hoardings near the hem of her skirt, taking her for part of the landscape.

Next would come years of strengthening. With time her body would be strong enough to run with the deer, to leap twenty feet into the air, to control even the dilation of the pupils of her eyes. Then she would be ready for her first test, surviving alone in the forest. Fasting, she would find out how much her body could endure, how sharp her senses could become, the energy that comes when the body grows pure. She would grow so intimate with the forest a rabbit would toss himself into her fire, making himself her meal. The trial in the forest would end with a vision of a man and woman made of gold dancing together, like the axis of the earth's turning. They would be lion dancers, all light. They would be angels with high white wings. They would become so bright they would make the girl's head swim, and she would faint. Later she would be able to see ordinary people as golden dancers, understanding all the meanings of their movements. When she awoke, the old couple would feed her hot soup and ask for an account of her adventures. They would be satisfied, and so set her onto the next phase of her training.

This would involve learning all about dragons. Tigers convey adolescent power, but dragons are the source of a mature wisdom. The mountains are but the heads of dragons. A person climbing a mountain is like a bug moving along the forehead of a great beast. The quarries in the mountain show the dragon's veins and muscles.

The minerals are its teeth and bones. The soil is its flesh and the trees are its hairs. One can hear its voice in the thunder and feel its breath in the winds.

The girl's training would conclude with the martial arts, and then she would return home to her family, whose need of a champion would have grown desperate. Indeed, so strong would be their desire for revenge on their enemies, they would carve in the girl's back a whole series of oaths. When she recovered from this operation, she would get ready for battle. A white horse would come into the courtyard, as a magical sign the drama was to begin. Donning her armor and mounting the horse, the girl would begin gathering her army. When her troops met marauders and gangs of criminals, she would lead them forward, screaming a mighty scream and swinging two great swords over her head. From her mouth would come rousing songs urging her troops to victory. Wherever they went order would be restored.

Finally they would come to the capital in Peiping and prepare to face the wicked emperor who had caused all the hardship in the provinces, all the hunger and conscription of sons. So quickly that it would be anticlimactic, the woman warrior and her husband (she would have married during the campaign and brought forth a child) would behead the emperor, clean out the palace, and set on the throne a peasant who would preside over a new social order. Then they would journey along the Long Wall, chasing back the Mongols.

Still, the woman warrior would not yet have avenged her brother, whose conscription had caused her family's great sorrow. To gain this revenge she would have to slay the fat baron who had led her brother away. Finally she would confront the baron, tearing off her shirt and showing him the oaths inscribed in her back. While he stared at her breasts, shocked that the famous warrior was a woman, she would slash him across the face and cut off his head. Then she would ride back to her family, and the whole village would celebrate a great festival.

Kingston's girlhood fantasies drew on a great treasury of Chinese folk tales. The dragons, tigers, golden dancers, and warriors with which her brain seethed had delighted Chinese children for centuries. However, she wanted to draw closer to actual history and began to collect stories of her mother's life; but all her efforts seemed only to tie her more tightly to myth.

Her mother had trained as a doctor in China in the 1920s. Before the family's flight in 1939, her mother had been a person of prestige. The laundry the mother ran in San Francisco's Chinatown was a great comedown from her previous station. At night she would tell the children stories of her training to be a doctor, which involved much more than battles with textbooks. It involved battles with ghosts, for even in her time Chinese doctors kept one foot in the shamanist tradition. Though the medical schools were opening to Western science, they had not completely closed the door on ghosts.

Kingston's mother was older than the other medical students, having lied about her age. She therefore made fun of their reports that a ghost had occupied an abandoned dormitory room. When the other students challenged her for affecting unconcern, she offered to spend the night in the ghost's room. Her account of that night burned itself into her daughter's mind, and so was reconstructed years later, as a young Chinese-American author tried to fix herself and her mother to paper. The ghost of her mother's medical training came to stand for all the ghosts transplanted people must exorcise. To become American and modern, Kingston felt she had to conquer the incubi of her unconscious, which said that in Chinese scales no female, no matter how glorious a warrior, could ever balance a male.

Her mother was reading in the ghost's lair, slowly making herself sleepy. Her eyes drooped and she turned out the lamp. The darkness was so black it shocked her awake. All her nerves grew taut, like the time she had been caught in a snowstorm on a mountain. A rushing came at her from under the bed. Fear seized the soles of her feet, as something alive climbed the foot of the bed, rolled over her, and sat on her chest. It pressed against her, sapping her breath. "It is a sitting ghost," her mother thought. The more she pushed against it, the heavier it became. She grabbed the ghost's thick hair, which was like an animal's coat. She pinched its skin and tried to gouge its flesh with her fingernails. She searched for its eyes, to stab them, but it seemed to have no eyes. So she grew discouraged. The more she fought, the more her strength oozed away.

If only she could reach the knife lying on the lampstand. The ghost sensed her thoughts and spread itself over her arms. Rallying her spirit—the spirit that her daughter later found so indomitable—she began to hector the ghost:

You will not win, greedy ghost. There is no pain I cannot endure. This school has big jars of alcohol. I will get some alcohol, put it in my bucket, spread it across the floor, set fire to it, and burn you out. You have made a big mistake, greedy ghost. I will track you all over the school and burn you out. What an ugly ghost you are. You must be one of the lower spirits. Now I am going to chant tomorrow's lessons. There are no such things as ghosts.

When she awoke in the morning, Kingston's mother told her classmates of her adventure. After class she gathered them all in the ghost's room and began the great burnout. In twos and threes, they arranged their buckets and jars of alcohol. Down poured the alcohol, up flared the flames, across went the rows of fire. Back and forth, they burned the room free of its ghost. "I told you, stupid ghost. Your end has come. There is no place for you in this school of medicine. You have to go—back to your dark haunts, back to the old villages, back to the depths of our minds."

When the smoke cleared and the mops stood idle, the room rested in peace. Under the bed where Kingston's mother had slept was a piece of wool, dripping with blood. They burned it in a bucket, and the stench was like a corpse exhumed for its bones.

In her inner rites of passage, Kingston could not tell which ghosts to laugh at, which ghosts to accredit. Her mother was a fabulous woman, a creature from a different age. Storyteller and shaman, warrior and healer, her mother was the tip of a mythic iceberg. How could a child of the new world manage such a mother's psyche? What could women's liberation say to a dragon ironing sheets?

We are not only the person our social

group reflects back to us. We are also the person our imagination conjures: the hero riding forth in dreams of the day, the ghost-slayer battling in dreams of the night. Taoists like Chung-tzu who rode the winds knew much about the spirit of fancy. Healers who tapped pulses and drove off devils imagined a better balance for bodies and souls. Writing her way through the labyrinth to her self, Kingston put Chinese characters on American paper. Her fingers typed an IBM Selectric, but her mind reproduced images of tattered scrolls. Our character and our images imprint one another. Much more than what we eat, we are what we imagine.

Divinity

China was only vaguely aware of sacred powers and ultimate reality, lacking a monotheistic or even a henotheistic tradition. At most, certain high points of Buddhist and Taoist speculation, and to a lesser extent of Confucian speculation, indicated a monism—a single, impersonal principle that is the inmost reality of all beings. As we have seen, the first stirrings of religious consciousness probably apotheosized (deified) the clan founder, making him the "face" of over-watching Heaven. As nature became better understood, however, heaven became less personal as the general symbol of the vast sky. Earth, in association with a maternal *Tao*, took on overtones of a Great Mother, but with less of the humanity and intimacy that other cultures developed.

For most Chinese throughout history, nature has been the effective divinity. In other words, nature and divinity ran together. The physical world itself was something sacred and mysterious. This world intimated something beyond itself that was grasped by those who saw nature with mystic clarity, but the majority at best sensed this something beyond only vaguely. To sense clearly the *Tao* that cannot be named, one must reject the adequacy of all things nameable. Realizing that water, air, fire, wood, earth, yang, yin, and so on do not explain the totality of heaven and earth, the mind senses that the ultimate is of a different order. It is without the limitations that characterize all the primal elements. As such, it must dwell in obscurity, too full or great or bright for mere human intelligence. Philosophical Taoism

and Buddhism but intimate that line of thought.

A muted reference to ultimacy probably plays in Confucius's laconic references to heaven. For the most part, the Master refrained from speculating about heavenly things. Like Alexander Pope, he believed that "the proper study of man is man." But Confucius's reverence toward the sacrifice to heaven suggests that, had such a modern Western notion been available to him, he would not have explained the sacrifice as a humanistic means of social bonding. Rather, he probably saw a link between the ancients' *Tao* and the way of sacred nature, and so viewed the sacrifice as humanity's chance to align itself with the power that most mattered, the power behind all life and all things.

Confucius made heaven the ultimate sanction for his ethical program. He believed that those who pay full court to the stove have no recourse when they fail. The true judge of success and failure must be more stable than a human creation. Against the Taoist belief that heaven treats all creatures as straw dogs, Confucius believed that heaven is the great champion of *yi* (justice). We go well beyond Confucius himself if we work this commitment to heaven into a theology or a theodicy (a vindication of God's justice). Clearly, however, the Confucians justified their calls to virtue by appealing to suprahuman standards.

Buddhism, of course, addressed ultimacy more squarely. In the philosophical mainstream, an impersonal ultimate (whether nirvana, Buddha-nature, Suchness, or emptiness) held sway. This mainstream

Figure 14   Lohan (arhat), Liao-Chin dynasty, tenth to thirteenth century, C.E. *Nelson Gallery-Atkins Museum (Nelson Fund).*

to the rather worldly point of the wisdom-that-has-gone-beyond. By contrast, those who followed Yogacara idealism stayed apart from the physical world mentally.

All Buddhist schools, however, characterized ultimate reality indirectly. By the Buddha's own teaching, talk about the nature of nirvana was useless. Nirvana was not a void, not a nothingness. Chinese Buddhists could equal Hindus in calling nirvana being, bliss, and awareness. But they stressed its "otherness," even when they loved that otherness as something near and dear. Because of its great value, nirvana functioned as the philosophical Buddhists' divinity. Mainstream philosophy did not conceptualize it as a God or as something personal, although it did relate it to the holy power that makes things be. That power, Van der Leeuw has shown, is a constant in human conceptions of divinity.[84]

Buddhism also tends to speak of ultimacy as the Buddha's "body." In addition to the body of Sakyamuni, there were the dharma-body and the bliss-body. The dharma-body was an equivalent of Suchness, or the final metaphysical principle. It connoted a teaching (dharma) prescriptive of all reality itself—a sort of cosmic Logos. However, because this dharma-body had some connection with the physical body and the teaching of Sakyamuni, it somewhat personalized the Buddhist divinity. That did not make it a God, but it does indicate that Buddhism is not a strictly impersonal monism (let alone an antireligious humanism) as many interpreters conclude.

In popular Buddhism, such as Pure Land, some divinities had quite precise features. The Buddha of Light, Amitabha, had a "personality" rather like that of an Apollo or a Krishna. The reliance on such Buddhas as Amitabha, like the reliance on bodhisattvas or the goddess of mercy Kuan-yin, was definitely a theistic bhakti. Between devotee and divinity a personal bond of love grew up. Just as the goddess Tara personalized Tibetan Buddhist divinity, Kuan-yin gave Chinese Buddhists a motherly figure of comfort and

tended to be monistic. That is, it suggested that the ultimate is the single, really real existent. For the idealists, the accent was on the mentality of the ultimate. In their view, the many things that we perceive by sense are fraudulent because only spirit or mind finally makes something be. For the less idealistic schools, material things and ideas were equally fraudulent. To accept the apparent plurality of either physical nature or consciousness was the folly of an unenlightened mind. The idealists were less concerned with physical nature than the nonidealists. By calling all dharmas empty, the followers of Madhyamika went directly mercy. (C. N. Tay, as we noted in the previous chapter, has described Kuan-yin as the cult of half Asia.)[85]

But if people rely on a mother goddess, they have a theistic deity at hand, even if they do not clearly distinguish it from other deities or from an impersonal natural force. In its popular religion, then, Chinese Buddhism offered an access to aspects of ultimate reality that Confucianism barely indicated. (Taoism is more complicated: The *Tao* was a mother, and religious sects made Lao-tzu into a cosmic principle.) The cult of Confucius himself qualifies this judgment somewhat, but overall the Buddhists offered the most personal concepts of divinity.

The beliefs of philosophical and religious Taoists, of course, must be distinguished. As we have seen, the philosophical Taoists, following Chuang-tzu and Lao-tzu, fixed on the cosmic Way. Often they seem to have invested it with divine attributes. For the philosophers, *Tao* was the source, the ultimate power, the model, and the prime value of the world. Inspiration from it, communion with it, and direction by it were the ways to wisdom, wholeness, and fulfillment.

Nonetheless, despite intuitions in Lao-tzu that *Tao* is beyond the physical world, philosophers tended to equate *Tao* with nature. The naturalistic symbolism they preferred suggests this, as does their unconcern with immortality or an afterlife. If *Tao* had been independent of nature, union with *Tao* should have generated thoughts about escaping the cycle of birth and death. In India, for instance, the *nirguna* (unmanifest) Brahman and the Buddhist ultimate led to doctrines of *moksha* and nirvana as human release. For Chuang-tzu and Lao-tzu, natural harmony in the present was all-important, and they paid little heed to future enjoyment of some otherworldly states. Consequently, the divinity of *Tao* was preeminently the undergirding and direction it gave cosmic nature.

Reaching back to prehistory, the religious Taoists conceived of a pantheon of divine forces, often giving them picturesque names and features. Furthermore, the goal of religious Taoist practices was to prolong life, and so religious Taoists ventured into alchemy and yoga, as well as voyages to the Lands of the Blessed (the Immortals). What they shared with their philosophical counterparts, however, was a characteristically Chinese concern with the body. Their ideal was not an extinction of suffering humanity in nirvana, not a release in *moksha*, but a consolidation of vital powers so as to resist death. Their divinities, consequently, were gods who could help this process, or "immortals" (who probably spanned the often narrow gap between saints and gods) who had successfully accomplished such consolidation. In either case, they offered followers encouragement and models.

How did Chinese divinity appear in the popular amalgamation? Through ritualistic, emotional, and shamanic points of entry.[86] The prevailing magic in the popular mind, which was primarily interested in warding off evil fortune and attracting good, and the great importance of ancestor veneration gave ultimate reality a rainbow of colors. Ceremonies at the family hearth reaffirmed the clan by acknowledging the reality of its ancestors. Ceremonies in the fields, for building a new dwelling, or for curing someone seriously ill brought people face to face with spooky forces of life, luck, and disease. Shamans and mediums were the key figures, contacting spirits and ancestral souls. Diviners gave advice and told fortunes. The average person gathered talismans and totems, but also Buddhist and Taoist saints. The educated people patronized Confucius, but even they were open to other sacred figures who offered help. To say the least, then, the Chinese religious mind was syncretistic, and the study of folk religion, as recent studies suggest,[87] has to be very comprehensive.

However, most characteristic of China is its commitment to physical nature. It shares this with Japan and with many ancient peoples, but China most directed its various intimations of divinity toward na-

Tao, the Chinese Buddha-nature, of spirits—these far outweighed personal qualities. At least as much as the American Indian Wakan Tanka, the Chinese divinity was the arc of the sky, the pulse of the earth, the life force itself.

Study Questions

1. Can one sketch the outline of axial Chinese religion in terms of *Tao*? How?

2. What are the positive aspects of Chinese ritual propriety *(li)*?

3. What are the negative aspects of *wu-wei*?

4. Why were the ancestors such a potent symbol in popular Chinese religion?

5. Explain some of the likely assumptions and dynamics in Chinese divination.

6. If you meditate on the practice of foot binding, how do you picture Chinese social arrangements?

7. Why did philosophical Taoism long exist alongside religious Taoism, and how can one reconcile their different views of immortality?

8. What was the function of music in Confucian ritualism?

9. What was the perception of space in Chinese landscape painting?

10. What did the woman warrior teach you about the Chinese imagination and the Chinese self?

Chapter Four

JAPANESE RELIGION: TWENTY-FIVE KEY DATES

CA. 4500–250 B.C.E.	JOMON PERIOD: HUNTING AND GATHERING
CA. 660	JIMMU, TRADITIONAL FIRST EMPEROR
CA. 250 B.C.E.–250 C.E.	YAYOI PERIOD: BLENDING OF ETHNIC GROUPS
5 C.E.	BUILDING OF NATIONAL SHRINE AT ISE
285	CONFUCIANISM INTRODUCED
CA. 550	BUDDHISM INTRODUCED
594	BUDDHISM PROCLAIMED STATE RELIGION
645	TAIKA REFORM REMODELS JAPAN ON CHINESE LINES
712–720	COMPLETION OF SHINTO CHRONICLES
805–806	INTRODUCTION OF TENDAI AND SHINGON BUDDHIST SECTS
890	CULTURAL RENAISSANCE: NOVELS, LANDSCAPE PAINTING, POETRY
1175–1253	INTRODUCTION OF PURE LAND, ZEN, AND NICHIREN BUDDHIST SECTS

Japanese Religion

To complete our survey of religions in East Asia, we move from China to Japan. Actually, much of what we have seen in China appears in Japan. We have already noted this, for instance, regarding Buddhism. In the main, the schools that the Chinese developed took root in Japan; furthermore, Confucianism had a strong impact. Nonetheless, Japan was never a passive recipient of Chinese culture. In religion, as in other spheres, it adapted the imported ideas so that they could grow on Japanese soil.

The major influence in the native Japanese tradition that forced such adaptations was Shinto, which was an aboriginal nature religion that became more clearly defined under the impact of Buddhism. Consequently, our historical survey focuses on Shinto and indicates how the traditions imported from China and later from the West transformed the Shinto tradition into the syncretistic religion that has characterized Japan through most of its history. In reviewing Japan's history, we will divide it into the major periods delineated by H. Byron Earhart: the ancient-formative, the medieval-elaborative, and the modern-reformative.[1]

APPEARANCE

In steamy mid-July we were sitting on a park bench in Tokyo, reflecting on how the Meiji shrine there compared with the Shinto shrines we had seen in Kyoto and Ise, when an elderly man, dressed in a kimono, approached to chat. He was a retired businessman come for his daily walk and swim in a pool near the shrine. We offered a chance for him to indulge his curiosity, practice his English, test Japanese-American relations (he had been in World War II), and, as it turned out, inform us what the Japanese way in religion really is. "You have one God," he rather incautiously pronounced. "We have thousands—eight hundred thousand, according to tradition. In this park many gods dwell. We come to enjoy the beauty and honor them." With much warmth and good cheer, he questioned us about our trip, and

then rambled off for his swim. Had we met a living Shintoist?

Perhaps, but answering this question exactly would require defining some terms. The man had not called himself or his people Shintoists, Buddhists, or anything else. He just used the pronoun *we.* The *we* indicates an ethnic solidarity which even traveling Japanese manifest. Despite the evidence that today's Japanese people are comprised of at least three racial strains, there has been enough time and isolation for those strains to merge into something distinctive. What these people hold in common overshadows their sects and individual religious traditions.

The 800 thousand gods conjure the Shinto *kami* (spirits or gods), but through history the Japanese have also honored a plethora of Buddhist divinities. Perhaps the most significant line in the man's little speech was: "We come to enjoy the beauty." In counterpoint to its industrial development, Japan retains a great love of natural beauty. Its gardens, parks, and pools are not merely props to sanity in the midst of bustle and smog. As places for aesthetic, religious, and recreational experience, they remain central in the people's spiritual life. At the Shinto (and Buddhist) shrines one glimpses the earliest Japanese Way that even today has its effect.

HISTORY

The Ancient-Formative Period

According to ethnologists, the people we now call the Japanese are a mixture of an indigenous people (the Ainu) and peoples from the Asiatic mainland and the southern islands. This mixture is one clue to the composite character of Japanese religion as well as to the general tolerance that has historically marked Japanese culture. The native religion goes back to the Japanese prehistoric period, which lasted until the early centuries C.E. Clay figurines that archeologists have excavated from this earliest Jomon period indicate a special concern with fertility.[2] As the hunting and gathering culture of the earliest period gave way to agriculture and village settlement, religious practices came to focus on agricultural festivals, revering the dead, and honoring the leaders of the ruling clans. According to the primitive mythology, which existed long before the written versions that date from the eighth century, such leaders were descendants of the deity— once again a version of sacred kingship.

However, the mythology and cult surrounding the ruling family were but part of the earliest Japanese religion. Research suggests that in the villages outside the leading families' influence, people probably conceived of a world similar to that of Siberian shamanists. That world has three layers. The middle is the realm of humans, where we have a measure of control, but the realms above and below, which spirit beings control, are far larger. The kami dwell in the high plain of heaven and are the objects of cultic worship; the spirits of the dead live below, condemned to a filthy region called Yomi.[3] (In some versions, the dead go to a land beyond the sea.) Apparently Yomi was especially important for the aristocrats' cult, which suggests not only a connection between folk and imperial religion but also the reason why Shinto came to stress ritual purification, especially from polluting contacts with the dead.

The Kami

The kami represented the sacred power involved in the principal concerns of prehistoric Japanese religion (kingship, burial of the dead, and ritual purification).[4] They were rather shadowy figures or spiritual forces who were wiser and more powerful than humans. From time to time, kami would descend to earth, especially if a human called them down and helped them assume a shape (in their own world the kami were shapeless). They were called down by means of *yorishiro*—tall, thin objects that attracted the kami. Pine trees and elongated rocks were typical *yorishiro*, and they suggest that the kami had phallic connotations. To a lesser extent, rocks of female shape also attracted the kami, and relics from the great

tombs of the third and fourth centuries—a profusion of mirrors, swords, and curved jewels—suggest that these artifacts also drew the kami. (Such objects became part of the imperial regalia.)

Because the kami held key information about human destiny, it was important to call them down into human consciousness. That occurred through the kami's possession of shamans or mediums. Most of the early shamans *(miko)* were women, and they functioned in both the aristocratic and the popular cults. Ichiro Hori has shown that female shamans persisted throughout Japanese history.[5] The *miko* were quite important to society. They tended to band together and travel a circuit of villages, primarily to act as mediums for contact with the dead but also to serve as diviners and oracles. They also ministered to spiritual and physical ills, which popular culture largely attributed to malign spirits. As a result, the *miko* developed both a poetic and a pharmacological lore. In composing songs and dances to accompany their ministrations, they contributed a great deal to the formation of traditional Japanese dance, theater, balladry, and puppetry.

Essentially, the kami were the forces of nature. They impressed the Japanese ancient mind, as they impressed the ancient mind elsewhere, by their striking power. Sensitive individuals could contact them, but the kami remained rather wild and unpredictable. Later, Shinto shrines stressed natural groves of tall trees and founders of religious cults were often possessed by spirits. As the early mythology shows, however, the kami remained in charge.

As the eighth-century chronicles, the *Kojiki* and *Nihon-shoki*, have preserved it, Japanese mythology adapted to Chinese influences early on. For example, redactors regularly changed the Japanese sacred number 8 to the Chinese sacred number 9,[6] and they were influenced by the Chinese cosmogonic myths. The result was a creation account in which the world began as a fusion of heaven and earth in an unformed, eggshaped mass that contained all the forces of life. Gradually the purer parts separated and ascended to heaven, while the grosser portions descended and became the earth.

Shinto Mythology

Chinese influence disappears when the chronicles come to the myths of the kami's origin and to the related question of how the Japanese islands came to be. The first kami god was a reed shoot that formed between heaven and earth; he established the first land. Six generations later, the divine creator couple, Izanagi and Izanami, arose by spontaneous generation. They married and produced the creations that followed.

For instance, heaven commanded Izanagi and Izanami to solidify the earth, which hitherto had been only a mass of brine. Standing on a bridge between heaven and the briny mass, they lowered a jeweled spear and churned the brine. When they lifted the spear, drops fell, solidified, and became the first island. The couple descended to this island, erected a heavenly pillar (the typical shamanistic connector to heaven), and proceeded to procreate. The account of their interaction is both amusing and revealing:

Now the male deity turning by the left, and the female deity by the right, they went around the pillar of the land separately. When they met together on one side, the female deity spoke first and said: "How delightful! I have met with a lovely youth." The male deity was displeased, and said: "I am a man, and by right should have spoken first. How is it that on the contrary thou, a woman, should have been the first to speak? This was unlucky. Let us go round again." Upon this the two deities went back, and having met anew, this time the male deity spoke first, and said: "How delightful! I have met a lovely maiden."[7]

In tortuous logic, the myth describes the fate of the first two. Izanami died giving birth to fire, and Izanagi followed her to the underworld. Izanagi then produced many deities in an effort to purify himself of the pollution of the underworld. By washing his left eye he produced the sun-goddess Amaterasu, and by washing his right eye he produced the moon-god. When he washed his nose he produced the wind-god Susanoo. In this story of descent to the underworld and divine creation, scholars see an expression of the aboriginal Japanese fears of death and rites of purification. The sun-goddess, who became the supreme being of the Yamato clan, a powerful Japanese family, and the focus of the clan's cultic center at Ise, presided over the land of fertility and life. Opposing her was the domain of darkness and death. Rituals were performed to keep darkness and death from afflicting sunny fertility—harvests, human procreation, and so on. As Izanagi purified himself of death by plunging into the sea, the Japanese throughout their history have used salt as a prophylactic. People still scatter it around the house after a funeral, place it at the edge of a well, set a little cake of it by a door jamb, and even scatter it before the bulging sumo wrestler as he advances toward his opponent.[8]

In subsequent myths, Amaterasu and Susanoo have numerous adventures arising from the antagonism between the life-giving sun and the withering wind. These figures also demonstrate the trickster and noble sides of natural divinity. Susanoo, the trickster, committed "heavenly offenses" that later became a focus of ritual purification: He broke the irrigation channels for the imperial rice field that Amaterasu had set up; he flayed a piebald colt and flung it into the imperial hall; and, worst of all, he excreted on the goddess's imperial throne. Unaware, she "went straight there and took her seat. Accordingly, the Sun Goddess drew herself up and was sickened."[9] These offenses reflect practical problems of an agricultural society (respecting others' fields), cultic problems (a sacrificial colt was probably supposed to be of a single color and not be flayed), and speculation on the tension between divine forces of nature.

From these and other materials in the earliest chronicles, it is clear that the ancient-formative period of Japanese history centered on natural forces, some of which were anthropomorphized. In the background were the kami, whom we may consider as foci of divine power. Anything striking or powerful could be a kami. To relate themselves to the natural world, the early Japanese told stories of their love for their beautiful islands (worthy of being the center of creation) and of the divine descent of their rulers. The fact that Amaterasu is a sun-goddess suggests an early matriarchy, as does the fact that kingship only came with the

Taika reforms of 645 C.E. Shinto maintained the divinity of the emperor until the mid-twentieth century, when the victorious allies forced the emperor to renounce his claims.

Buddhism sometimes eclipsed Shinto, but the native tradition always lay ready to reassert itself. Whenever there was a stimulus to depreciate foreign influences and exalt native ones, Shinto quickly bounced back. Also, Shinto only defined itself in the seventh century, when Buddhism, Confucianism, and Taoism started to predominate. In crystallizing, it acquired Buddhist philosophy, Confucian ethics, and Taoist naturalism. The result was a nature-oriented worship with special emphasis on averting pollution. Shinto domesticated Buddhism as a religion of kami-bodhisattvas, and it topped Confucian social thought with the emperor's divine right.

SHINTO SHRINES[10]

To set off places where people might venerate the kami, the Japanese have long fashioned wooden shrines with encompassing groves. They have not designed the shrines for communal worship, but rather as simple sites where people might recite ritual prayers and make offerings to the kami. Unlike the Buddhist temples, the Shinto shrines originally did not contain statues. The official focal point of veneration usually was an old sword or mirror, which was considered to be the kami's resting place or "body." However, these ritual objects were seldom seen, even by the Shinto priests, so the general impression most visitors received was of a simple wooden pavilion where one might make a personal petition or venerate the kami in the course of a village celebration.

Usually the encompassing grove was almost as important as the wooden pavilion. The grove typically was of rectangular shape, and one entered it through a sacred archway or *torii*. At the entrance stood a well, where the visitor was to take some water in a wooden dipper and purify his hands. At the entrance to many Shinto shrines two stone lions stood guard. Even today the tall trees create an atmosphere of quiet, which the trees' association with the kami turns in the

direction of religious respect. The general appearance of both the grove and the shrine buildings is unadorned. Thus the grove's vegetation burgeons almost wildly and the shrine buildings usually are of rough wood. Exceptions occur, as in the red-painted Heian shrine of Kyoto, but even there the total effect is subdued, in flight from anything fancy or garish. The roofs of the large Heian buildings are shingled with natural materials, and the gardens behind the buildings are understated. As with the great shrine at Ise, the grove keeps a fairly dense appearance, probably so that the natural influences of the kami can seem to outweigh the cultural influences of human beings.

When visitors approach a main shrine, they usually clap their hands and ring a suspended bell to attract the gods' attention. They then bow, in reverence or prayer, and deposit their offerings in a money chest. Another building, at the innermost part of the shrine, is a sort of holy-of-holies, where the deities actually dwell. Laity have no access to this building, and the popular attitude has been that to peek into it, and observe the ritual objects that attract the kami, would be to court blindness or death. Buddhist influences caused some Shinto shrines to erect pictures of human beings or images of gods, but generally the "bodies" of the kami have been impersonal objects. In addition to the old swords and mirrors, stones, sacred texts, ancient scrolls, jewels, and balls of crystal have predominated. All these objects have associations with natural forces (or, on occasion, heroic human figures) thought to embody the kami. When the influence of Buddhist bodhisattvas came to color the Shinto notion of the kami, and so led to deifying especially loyal subjects of the emperors, the headgear, batons, weapons, clothing, writing implements, and other possessions of such deified subjects also became "bodies" of the kami.

Prior to the disestablishment of Shinto after World War II, the government classified shrines on twelve levels. At the head of the list was the Great Imperial Shrine at Ise. Below Ise came the various large government or national shrines, such as the Heian Shrine in Kyoto and the Meiji Shrine in Tokyo, and then the smaller local shrines. Not even on the list were the tens of thousands of little village or domestic shrines, at which a great deal of Shinto worship actually occurred. Before World War II there were about 111,000 official shrines and about 15,500 Shinto priests.

From accounts of pilgrims who have journeyed to shrines such as Ise in a spirit of devotion, one can sense the religious emotions that Shinto-ism tended to arouse. The huge groves of pines, contrasting with the few wild flowers, tended to inculcate a sense of the sacredness, the specialness, of the shrine precinct. It was not ordinary space but divine space. The straight crossbeams of the *torii* could symbolize the divine rectitude of the kami, while the rough reed-thatch of the shrine eaves could recall the primitive days, when roofs were not trimmed. (Shinto priests at great shrines such as Ise tended to keep Buddhists from the innermost areas, to emphasize the distinction between the aboriginal Japanese tradition and the relative newcomer.) The outer purifications, such as washing with sea water, would prepare the pilgrim for an inner purification, such as washing the mind free of injurious thoughts.

Thus two major themes sound in most pilgrims' accounts. One is the holiness of nature, and nature's superiority to our cultural gewgaws. If not interfered with, nature offers us a lush growth and quiet that can reorient our souls. The second major theme is the antiquity of the Shinto shrines and their traditions. Ancestors have come to shrines such as this, prayed prayers such as these, for hundreds of years. Shinto has been the native Japanese way, the tradition that has made us who we are. Coming close to nature, doing as our ancestors have always done, we approach the sacred center of reality, where things work as they should.

The Medieval-Elaborative Period

During the Taika period (645–710), Japan experienced its first extensive contact with a literate, highly organized foreign culture—China's.[11] It quickly took up Chinese writing and Confucian bureaucracy. As well, it accepted the influence of the Buddhist, Confucian, and Taoist religious figures who accompanied the Chinese traders and politicians. Reacting to those influences, the native religion strove to assert itself. Hitherto, it had been diffuse and unstructured. As *Shinto* ("the way of the kami"), it began to compete with the ways of the Buddha, the Tao, and Confucius. However, at this early period and throughout subsequent times, such competition produced more syncretism than warfare.

By the end of the Nara period (710–784), Japan had a fairly elaborate court life. A class of nobles emerged that was distinct from the common farmers, and a native literature arose, which identified a Japanese culture. Buddhism had established its major schools, and the government loosely organized the many religious temples. By such organizing, the government in effect proclaimed a state Buddhism, but the common people cottoned to the new religion less than the emperor and the nobles did. Nonetheless, Buddhism quickly started to affect Jap-

Figure 15   Torii (sacred gateway) to National Shinto Shrine at Ise. Photo by J. T. Carmody.

anese culture, offering it a philosophy far more penetrating than the native tradition. Japanese political thinkers accepted Confucianism as the rationale for good government, and Confucian formality encroached on social interactions. Religious Taoism had its biggest impact on Japanese rituals and folk beliefs. It impressed the common people as a source of blessings, and they took to its immortals and gods of the body.

Earhart defines the medieval-elaborative period of Japanese history, when these religious traditions were adopted, as being the years 794 through 1600.[12] This stretches from the Heian era, when the court at Kyoto had a glorious culture, through the Kamakura and Muromachi eras, and ends with the fall of the Momoyama dynasty. During the Heian era, court life developed a sophisticated aesthetic sense; by the Kamakura era the warrior estates had assumed power and

made the emperor merely a puppet. As we noted earlier, the Buddhist sects of Shingon and Tendai, which dominated the Heian era, were esoteric, comprehensive systems that tried to accommodate a variety of interests. Though they later lost influence to Zen and Pure Land, they began Buddhism's penetration of the lower classes. For its own part, Shinto kept pace with Buddhism by organizing itself.

In the Kamakura period (1185–1333), Buddhism responded to the increasing importance of the warrior class. Zen especially became a central part of the warrior's discipline, furnishing spiritual resources for his ideal of fearlessness and spontaneous action. Among the common people, devotional Buddhism—Pure Land and Nichiren—gained favor. They effected the final domestication of Buddhism, making it serve the lower classes in their search for prosperity and a good afterlife. In this period Shinto became highly eclectic, as we shall see more fully below, for by then it had fully combined with popular Buddhism.

The Muromachi (1333–1568) and Momoyama (1568–1600) eras were periods of great civil strife. Agriculture developed, towns and marketing grew, and military rulers (shoguns) gained power. Japan was first exposed to Western religion in the sixteenth century, at which time its own religious traditions were tightly controlled by the government. Shinto experienced a considerable revival, as the government used it to buttress the imperial family line. Overall, the religious situation was confused.

Japanese Buddhism

Francis Cook has summarized the Japanese innovations of traditional Buddhism.[13] First, the Japanese tended not to adhere to traditional codes of conduct, whether for laity *(sila)* or for monks *(vinaya)*. Eventually, priests were able to marry, eating meat and drinking alcoholic beverages were allowed and monks could have more than a spare robe. Second, Japanese Buddhism tended to move religious activity from the temple to the home. As a result, emphasis was shifted to the laity, and monks or priests were relegated to the care of temples and the performance of ceremonies (especially funerals). Caring for temples frequently came to be a family affair, as fathers passed a priesthood on to their sons.

Third, after the Kamakura period several sects promulgated the notion that one practice summarized Buddhism. In that they were to a degree reacting against the syncretism of the Shingon and Tendai sects. For instance, Honen made chanting Amida's name (a practice known as *nembutsu*) the only way to be reborn in the Pure Land. Dogen, the founder of Soto Zen, thought that *zazen* (meditative sitting) summarized everything essential. Nichiren, finally, insisted that chanting "homage to the Sutra of the Lotus of the True Law" was the way to identify with the Buddha. What these sects shared was a strong stress on faith. The personality would only come to enlightenment, they argued, if one engaged all of one's will and emotion.

KAMAKURA BUDDHISM[14]

In many scholars' opinion, the rise of the Pure Land, Nichiren, and Zen Buddhist sects during the Kamakura dynasty (1185–1333) produced one of Japan's most distinctive religious achievements. Pure Land Buddhism, which focused on Amida, the bodhisattva of light, became the most influential form of devotional Buddhism. It was popularized by evangelists such as Ippen (1239–1289) who encouraged songs and dances in honor of Amida. Ippen taught that devotion to Amida and the holy realm where Amida presided was "the timely teaching" suitable for a degenerate age. By practicing the *nembutsu* or recitation of "homage to Amida Buddha," followers could gain great merit or even full salvation (entry to the Pure Land). This prescription was simple, practicable, and available to all. It did not require deep philosophy or meditation, simply faith. The laity found Ippen's message very appealing.

As one of Ippen's devotional works makes clear, he encouraged followers of Pure Land with a steady stream of moralistic advice. Verse after verse, the work tells devotees to adore the glory of God, not ignore the Buddha's virtue, revere the three jewels, not forget the power of faith, devoutly practice the *nembutsu*, forget other religious practices, trust the law of love, not denounce the creeds of other people, promote a sense of equality, and avoid discriminatory feelings. They were to awaken a sense of compassion, be mindful of the sufferings of other people, cultivate amiability, not display an angry countenance, preserve a humble manner, and not arouse a spirit of arrogance. It is as though Ippen found all the traits of a good character to flow from faith in Amida. Were the faithful to yearn for the bliss of the Pure Land and not forget the tortures of hell, they would lead wonderfully meritorious lives.

Honen (1133–1212) was more insistent on the singularity of the *nembutsu*, in effect separating Pure Land Buddhism from other sects and making the *nembutsu* the be all and end all of the middle way. Honen personally suffered persecution for his position and for his success in winning converts. In a letter written to the wife of the ex-regent Tsukinowa, Honen described the essentials that a convert to Pure Land would have to embrace. The gist of his exposition is that the *nembutsu* is the best way to rebirth in the Pure Land, because it is the discipline described in Amida's own vow to become a bodhisattva and open salvation to all creatures. Indeed, the earthly Buddha Sakyamuni entrusted the *nembutsu* to his disciple Ananda, that Ananda might make it Sakyamuni's main bequest to posterity. Finally, all the Buddhas of the six quarters of the world endorse the *nembutsu*. So while other religious practices, such as meditations or ritual ceremonies, have considerable value, only the *nembutsu* has the highest stamp of authority. What does it matter that some critics claim the *nembutsu* is too easy, fit only for simpletons? Amida and Sakyamuni have endorsed it; would one rather stand with earthly critics or heavenly masters?

Shinran (1173–1262), Honen's most successful disciple, came to feel that the successful propagation of the *nembutsu* depended on the clergy's closer identification with the laity. He therefore urged breaking with the tradition of clerical celibacy and he himself took a wife. So strong was his conviction that salvation depends purely on the grace of Amida that he rejected practices such as monastic vows and disciplines as possible impediments to genuine faith. Whereas some conservative Pure Land preachers urged a continuous recitation of the *nembutsu*, Shinran thought that a single invocation of Amida Buddha, if filled with loving faith, would suffice for salvation. Shinran's hymns ring with this loving faith: Amida endlessly sends forth his pure, joyous, wise, universal light. It is brighter than the sun and the moon, illumining numberless worlds. Sakyamuni came into the world only to reveal Amida's vow and the primacy of faith in Amida's grace. By faith even the worst of sinners will come to Amida's mercy, as surely as all mountain water finally comes to the ocean.

Pure Land has the effect of providing Japan a very appealing form of Buddhist bhakti. The mercy of Amida rang true to the Japanese tendency to seek a God who shows signs of maternal

kindness. Nichiren (1222–1282) agreed with the Pure Land Buddhists that simple devotional forms like the *nembutsu* were desirable, but he found their stress on Amida unwarranted. For Nichiren the be all and end all of Buddhist faith was the Lotus Sutra. He considered this scripture the final teaching of Sakyamuni, in which his three bodies (historical, doctrinal, and blissful) came together in a marvelous unity. Other schools had overlooked one or more of these three aspects, slighting either the historical life of the Buddha, his existence as the dharma giving all reality its true form, or his existence as the perfection of salvation (the center of the abode of the blessed). Devotion to the Lotus Sutra assured that a balance would be restored. Thus Nichiren urged the practice of chanting homage to the Lotus Sutra. In rather uncompassionate style, he called Amida Buddhism a hell and Zen a devil. Today there are many subsects of Nichiren Buddhism that together make this school second only to Pure Land in popularity.

Two of the great pioneers who launched Ch'an on its illustrious career in Japan were Eisai (1141–1215) and Dogen (1200–1253). Eisai studied Ch'an in China and then established himself in Kamakura, the new center of Japanese political power. His teaching won special favor among the hardy warlords who were coming to dominate Japan, and from his time Zen and the samurai code had close bonds. For Eisai mind was greater even than heaven. Buddhism, which concentrated on the mind, had known great success in India and China. Among the different Buddhist schools, the one founded by Bodhidharma especially riveted onto mastering the mind. From Bodhidharma's missionary ventures in China, Zen had made its way to Korea and Japan. Now it was time for Japan to capitalize on Zen's great potential.

By studying Zen, one could find the key to all forms of Buddhism. By practicing Zen, one could bring one's life to fulfillment in enlightenment. To outer appearances, Zen favored discipline over doctrine. Inwardly, however, it brought the highest wisdom, that of enlightenment itself. Eisai was able to convince some of the Hojo regents and Kamakura shoguns to become patrons of Zen, and so he planted it solidly in Japan.

If Eisai proved to be a good politician, able to adapt to the new Kamakura times and benefit from them, Dogen proved to be the sort of rugged, uncompromising character Zen needed to deepen its Japanese roots and gain spiritual independence. After studying at various Japanese Buddhist centers without satisfaction, he met Eisai and resolved to follow in his footsteps and visit China. After some frustration in China, Dogen finally gained enlightenment when he heard a Zen master speak of "dropping both mind and spirit" (dropping dualism). Returning to Japan, he resisted the official pressures to mingle various forms of Buddhism and would only teach Zen. Nonetheless, within Zen circles Dogen was quite flexible, teaching, for example, that study of the Buddhist scriptures (scholarship) was not incompatible with a person-to-person transmission of the truth (the guru tradition).

Within Zen circles, Dogen also distinguished himself for his worries about the use of koans. The Rinzai school of Ch'an that Eisai had introduced to Japan stressed the use of these enigmatic sayings as a great help to sudden enlightenment. In Dogen's opinion, the Chinese Soto school was more balanced and less self-assertive. He therefore strove to establish Soto in Japan, teaching a Zen that did not concentrate wholly on the mind but rather on the total personality. This led him to a practice of simple meditation (zazen) that ideally proceeded without any thought of attaining enlightenment and without any specific problem in mind. Disciplining the body as well as the mind, Dogen aimed at a gradual, lifelong process of realization.

In some of his "conversations," Dogen movingly expressed his great faith in the power of Zen Buddhism. Quoting Eisai, he spoke of a monk's food and clothing as gifts from heaven. The teacher is but an intermediary between the pupil and heaven. Heaven gives each of us what we need for our allotted life span, and we should not make a fuss over these things. The student should direct his gratitude to heaven, much more than to his master, opening himself to all of heaven's gifts. The greatest of heaven's gifts is truth, and it is the good fortune of monks to be able to pursue truth full time. The difficulties monks or any of us face in securing life's practical necessi-

ties should not obscure this central point. Such difficulties should merely make us serious, willing to sacrifice for being able to pursue the truth. If monks lived utterly leisurely lives under full patronage, they likely would grow lazy and selfish. If, on the contrary, they live in poverty, begging for their food or working the land, they likely will grow hardy in spirit.

Dogen's compassion was equal to his faith, for he also liked to tell his disciples the story of Eisai's decision to give some copper to a destitute man who had come to the monastery begging help for his wife and children. The copper had been destined to make a halo for a statue of the Buddha. When some of Eisai's monks complained that he had forgotten this lofty destination, Eisai agreed that ideally the copper would have gone into a halo for the Buddha's statue. But Buddha's own example of spending himself for the sake of needy human beings had urged Eisai to be generous, sacrificing some of the monastery's goods for the lives of fellow human beings.

Both Pure Land and Zen made their great impressions on Japanese culture largely in terms of the goodness they encouraged. From its deep faith in the goodness of Amida Buddha, Pure Land taught the Japanese people Shinran's concern for sinners, outcastes, men and women tending to doubt their own worth. From its deep experiences of self-realization, Zen matured a gratitude for all of creation that easily became a great compassion for all creatures suffering pain. Situating themselves within the common Buddhist tradition, the Kamakura schools suggested that faith and insight, devotion and practical charity, are not antagonistic but complementary. If one goes deeply enough into faith, one reaches a gratitude that is almost identical with the gratitude that rushes forth in enlightenment. If one goes deeply enough into meditational insight, one reaches a gratitude that is almost identical with the wholehearted faith that Amida Buddha is utterly trustworthy and good. The legacy of the Kamakura schools, finally, was their depth. Shinran and Dogen were such heroes of the spiritual life that all subsequent Japanese aspirants to sanctity or wisdom saw in them clear models of the way.

Overall, the Japanese gave Buddhism a strong aesthetic aspect. This ranged from a general emphasis on a simple, direct style in speech and bearing to haiku (seventeen-syllable poems calculated to give a fleeting glimpse of reality), the martial arts (swordsmanship and archery), and the use of incense, flowers, candles, and music. The tea ceremony, which concerned not only the tea itself but also the architecture of the teahouse and the style of the utensils, became a religious and aesthetic way of life. In the twelfth century, the monk Saigyo fused nature, religion, and art through his exquisite poetry.[15] In the seventeenth century, the poet Basho wrote such haiku as the following:

April's air stirs in
Willow-leaves . . .
A butterfly
Floats and balances[16]

White cloud of mist
Above white
Cherry-blossoms . . .
Dawn-shining mountains[17]

Even recent literature, such as that by the Nobel laureate Yasunari Kawabata, employs this aesthetic. The tea ceremony has a central place in his *Thousand Cranes;*[18] his *The Master of Go*[19] shows how a game can symbolize existence and be the basis of an entire life style; and *The Sound of the Mountain*[20] pivots on nature symbolism.

Figure 16   Amida Nyorai (Amitabha Buddha), twelfth to thirteenth century. Nelson Gallery-Atkins Museum (Nelson Fund).

Shinto and Christianity

While Japan worked its changes on Buddhism, Shinto was liberally borrowing from the foreign traditions. Since it represented the oldest native traditions, the result was a great enrichment, or at least a great complication, of what constituted Shinto. From Buddhism, Shintoists developed the notion that the kami were traces of the original substances of particular Buddhas and bodhisattvas. As a result, Buddhist deities were enshrined by Shintoists (and kami by Buddhists). So thoroughly did Buddhism and Shinto combine that Dengyo Daishi and Kobo Daishi, the founders of Tendai and Shingon, thought it natural to erect shrines to honor the kami of the mountains of their monastic retreats.

From Shingon, Shintoists absorbed certain esoteric practices, such as using mandalas to represent the basic dualities of mind-matter, male-female, and dynamic-static.[21] Because of such dualism, people began to call Shinto "Ryobu," which means "two parts" or "dual." In one of its most dramatic actions, dualistic Shinto gave the Ise shrine an inner and outer precinct to make two mandalas that would represent the two sides of Amaterasu. She was the sun-goddess of the ancient traditions, but she was also Vairocana, the shining Buddha of Heaven.

Later in the medieval period, a number of Shinto scholars took issue with syncretism.[22] Some of them just wanted to upset the evenhandedness that had developed, so that the kami would predominate over the bodhisattvas or so that Amaterasu would predominate over Vairocana. Others wanted to rid Shinto of its syncretions and return it to its original form. The most important of these medieval Shinto reformers were Kitabatake and Yoshida, who worked in the fourteenth and fifteenth centuries. They drew from writings of Ise priests, who wanted to give Shinto a scripture comparable to that of the Buddhists. Another step in the consolidation of Shinto's position was the organizing of its shrines, which began in the tenth century and continued through to the twentieth. The resulting network provided every clan and village with a shrine to represent its ties with the kami.

In the mid-sixteenth century Christianity came to Japan in the person of the charismatic Jesuit missionary Francis Xavier. It flourished for about a century, until the Tokugawa rulers first proscribed it and then bitterly persecuted it. The first Western missionaries made a great impact because Japan was used to religions of salvation. Pure Land Buddhism, for instance, was then popular among the common people. By impressing the local warrior rulers (often by holding out prospects of trade with the West), the Christians gained the right to missionize much of Japan and made some lasting converts. Western artifacts fascinated the Japanese as well, and for a while things Western were the vogue.

However, before the missionaries could completely adapt Christianity to Japanese ways, the shoguns became suspicious that they had political and economic designs. The shogun Ieyasu (1542–1616)

killed many who had converted to Christianity, and after his death Christianity's brief chapter in Japanese history came to a bloody close. Shusaku Endo's recent novel about the Christians' persecution, *Silence*,[23] caused a stir among the contemporary Japanese Christian community because of its vivid description of the trials (in faith as well as body) that the missionaries underwent.

At the end of the medieval period of elaboration (around 1600), then, five traditions were interacting. Buddhism brought Japan a profound philosophy that stressed the flux of human experience, the foundation of is-ness, and death. In return, it was revamped to suit Japanese tastes. Confucianism furnished a rationale for the state bureaucracy and for social relationships. It stressed formality and inner control, which especially suited merchants and government officials, and one can see its imprint in the Bushido Code, which prevailed during the Tokugawa period.[24] Taoism most influenced folk religion, while, as we have seen, Shinto developed a rationale for the kami and a strong shrine system. Christianity came to represent foreign intrusion, but since it converted perhaps 500,000 Japanese, it also satisfied a hunger for other ways to salvation. Probably the average person mixed elements from these traditions with folk superstitions in order to fashion a family-centered religion that would harmonize human beings with the forces—kami, bodhisattvas, and evil spirits—that presided over good fortune and bad.

The Modern-Reformative Period

During the Tokugawa shogunate (military dictatorship), which lasted from 1600 to 1867, Japan experienced peace and stability. The Tokugawa rulers expelled the Christian missionaries and severely limited contacts with the West. The biggest shift in the social structure was the rise of the merchant class, which went hand in hand with the growth of cities.

Regarding religion, the Tokugawa shoguns made sure that all traditions served the state's goals of stability. In the beginning of the seventeenth century those goals had popular support because the preceding dynasties had allowed great civil strife. Buddhists had to submit to being an arm of the state. Neo-Confucianism eclipsed Buddhism in state influence, largely because it was less likely to stir thoughts of independence or individualism. Shinto suffered some decline in popular influence but retained a base in folk religion. As well, Shinto generated a clearer rationale for separating from Buddhism.

Finally, during the Tokugawa period the first new religions arose. They were eclectic packagings of the previous, medieval elements, and they drew their success by contrasting favorably with the highly formal, even static, culture that prevailed in the early nineteenth century. The new religions usually sprang from a charismatic leader who furnished a connection with the kami—indeed, whom his or her followers took to be a kami. By personalizing religion and addressing individual faith, the new religions stood out from the dominant formalism and offered something attractively dynamic.

The Bushido Code provides a good summary of the religious and ethical values that formed the Japanese character through the late medieval and early modern period. John Noss says of Bushido:

Bushido did not consist of finally fixed rules. It was a convention; more accurately, it was a system of propriety, preserved in unwritten law and expressing a spirit, an ideal of behavior. As such, it owed something to all the cultural and spiritual forces of the feudal era. Shinto supplied it the spirit of devotion to country and overlord, Confucianism provided its ethical substance, Zen Buddhism its method of private self-discipline, and the feudal habit of life contributed to it the spirit of unquestioning obedience to superiors and a sense of honor that was never to be compromised.[25]

Bushido was the "way of the warrior," whether he be a samurai (warrior) in fact or only in spirit. For Japanese women, the Bushido concern for honor focused on chastity. Manuals instructed young girls who had been compromised how to commit suicide (with the dagger each girl received when she came of age), including details of how, after plunging in the blade, she should tie her lower limbs together so as to secure modesty even in death. When a powerful lord would not stop his advances, the noble Lady Kesa promised to submit if he would kill her samurai husband first. The lord agreed, and she told him to come to her bedroom after midnight and kill the sleeper with wet hair. Then she got her husband drunk, so that he would sleep soundly, washed her hair, and crept under the covers to await her fate.[26]

From the close of the Tokugawa period in 1867 to World War II, Japan was in transit to modernity. It abolished the military dictatorship and restored the emperor. It also changed from a largely decentralized feudal society into a modern nation organized from Tokyo. Japan made astonishing strides in education and culture, assimilating Western science and again opening itself to the outside world (at first under duress, due to Admiral Perry and the U.S. gunboats during 1853 and 1854, then voluntarily). Success in two major wars with China and Russia between 1895 and 1905 gave the Japanese great confidence, and the first third of the twentieth century was a time of increasingly strident nationalism.

During this period Buddhism lost its official status as a branch of the government, Shinto was established as the state religion, and Christianity was reintroduced. In addition, more new religions appeared, which, like Buddhism and Shinto, took on nationalistic overtones.

For our interests, the modern period, beginning with the Meiji Restoration (of the emperor) in 1868, is most significant because of the revival of Shinto. This was largely a political operation, designed to glorify the imperial family and to unify the country around its oldest traditions. Edwin Reischauer has described the widespread changes in secular life that the Meiji leaders introduced.[27] Japanese cities were revamped, and Western ideas of individual rights and responsibilities that are part of a modern state were brought in. H. B. Earhart provides documents of the propaganda that Meiji leaders generated to link the nation with religion and reestablish Japan's sense of divine mission.[28] "The Imperial Rescript on Education" (1890),[29] for instance, explicitly linked the imperial throne ("coeval with heaven and earth") with filial piety to make nationalism the supreme personal virtue. To bring their tradition up-to-date and do what their revered ancestors had done, the modern Japanese had only to be utterly loyal to the emperor. In fact, Joseph Kitagawa has argued that the Japanese notion of national community *(kokutai)* "incorporates all the major thrusts of individual and corporate orientation of the Japanese people to a sacral order of reality."[30]

The New Religions

Since the government was pushing Shinto, the new religions tended to join the nationalistic trend. Tenrikyo and Soka Gakkai both owe as much to Buddhist as to Shinto inspiration, but other new religions found it useful to shelter under the nationalistic umbrella. Tenrikyo sprang from a revelation that its founder, Nakayama Miki, had in 1838.[31] She had been a devout Pure Land Buddhist, but while serving as a medium in a healing ceremony for her son, she felt a kami possess her—the "true, original kami Tenri O no Mikoto" ("God the Parent"). Miki embarked on a mission to spread her good news, healing sick people and promulgating the recitation of "I put my faith in Tenri O no Mikoto." The Tokugawa authorities harassed her somewhat, but in time a large number of followers accepted her as a living kami. Her writings became the Tenrikyo scripture, her songs became its hymns, and her dances shaped its liturgy. Recalling the creation myth of Izanagi and Izanami, she built a shrine "at the center of the world," where the first parents had brought forth the land. The shrine had a square opening in its roof and a tall wooden column—ancient symbolism for the connection to heaven.

Miki's teachings stress joyous living. In the beginning God the Parent made humans for happiness, but we became self-willed and gloomy. By returning to God the Parent and dropping self-concern, we can restore our original joy. The way to return is faith in God the Parent and participation in Tenrikyo worship. Earhart has suggested that Tenrikyo's success comes in part from its return to peasant values.[32] By stressing gratitude for (sacred) creation, social rather than individual good, hard manual work, and the like, this sect has generated great popular enthusiasm. By the end of the nineteenth century, Tenrikyo claimed over two million members, testifying to the power of combining old, shamanistic elements with new organizational forms and liturgies. Tenrikyo even revived the ancient Shinto concern for purification by focusing on an interior cleansing of doubts and untoward desires.

Soka Gakkai derives from Makiguichi Tsunesaburo (1871–1944), who preached a new social ethic based on three virtues: beauty, gain, and goodness.[33] Makiguichi found Nichiren Buddhism attractive, so he worked out his ethics in terms of the Lotus Sutra: Beauty, gain, and goodness came from faith in the Lotus. During World War II the leaders of Soka Gakkai refused the government's request that all religionists support the military effort, arguing that compliance would compromise the truth of the Lotus Sutra (by associating Soka Gakkai with other Buddhist sects and with Shintoists). For this they went to prison. Makiguichi died in prison, but his movement revived after the war through the efforts of Toda Josei. By 1957 Toda had reached his goal of enrolling 750,000 families, largely through his fine organizational abilities and his shrewd use of enthusiastic youths. As well, Soka Gakkai capitalized on the frustration of Buddhists committed to the Lotus Sutra but alienated by the bickering among the various Nichiren groups. In a time of national confusion, Soka Gakkai's absolutism (all other religious options were held to be false) held great appeal. According to Soka Gakkai, commitment to the Lotus Sutra (and to itself) would dissolve all ambiguities.

Many observers have criticized Soka Gakkai for its vehement missionizing and its political involvement. It offers a "cellular" structure like that of communists, a simple program for daily devotion, pilgrimages to the National Central Temple near Mount Fuji, and an extensive educational program. Under the name Nichiren Shosu, it has exported itself to the West, and though Soka Gakkai has separated from its political arm (Komeito), the party continues to have considerable political effect.

Recent History

Japan's defeat in World War II produced great national trauma, prompting the success of hundreds of new religions. Culturally, defeat meant a shattering of national pride; religiously, it meant a body blow to state Shinto. The Western conquerors, led by Douglas MacArthur, force-fed the Japanese democracy and the concept of individual liberties. On its own, Japan rebuilt with incredible speed, soon becoming the economic giant of Asia. The new constitution disestablished Shinto and allowed complete individual religious freedom. The older traditions, which people identified with the national

self-consciousness of prewar times, were shattered, and the new religions rushed in to fill the void. In the past fifteen years or so, the older traditions have regrouped, especially Buddhism, but the dominant trend has been secularism. Caught up in its technological spurt, Japan has seemingly put aside nationalistic and cultural issues, preferring to let the traumas of the war heal by benign neglect.

Today the Japanese religious picture is quite complicated. The culture is secularistic, at least outwardly, but in the alleyways Buddhism and Christianity struggle to revive themselves. Confucian and Taoist elements remain part of the Japanese psyche, but in rather muted voice. Strangely, perhaps, it is Shinto—the ancient version rather than the state—that is the strongest religious presence. Divinity in nature, which Japanese religion has always stressed, continues in the shrines that connect present times to the aboriginal kami.

STRUCTURAL ANALYSIS

Nature

From its earliest beginnings, Japanese religion has been enraptured by nature. Y. T. Hosoi has detailed prehistoric Japan's focus on the sacred tree;[34] Waida has described the rich mythology that surrounded the moon;[35] and ancient mythology, as we have seen, featured the sun-goddess Amaterasu and the wind-god Susanoo. Further, we best describe the kami as nature forces (though they could also possess human beings), and the Japanese Buddhists' love for nature, which poets such as Saigyo and Basho dramatize, developed from a pre-Buddhist base. A closeness to nature, a love of natural beauty, an aesthetic geared to flowers and trees, seasons and vistas—these have been Japanese characteristics.

Japanese folk religion, which exerted a hardy influence, viewed nature with a peasant's eye. Nature was fertile and fickle, nourishing and devastating. The early myths

Figure 17   Moss Temple grounds, Kyoto. Photo by J. T. Carmody.

reflect this paradoxical quality. The sun-goddess was benevolent—a source of warmth, light, and the power to make things grow. The wind-god was unpredictable, often destructive. Susanoo's punishment for his misdeeds belies a peasant hope that nature's order and benevolence will prevail. However, Susanoo and his like might have destructive outbreaks at any time: Japan has been a land of earthquakes, volcanoes, floods, and typhoons. Japan is a very beautiful land, but rugged and not easily tamed, and controlling the effects of nature has been a herculean task. Perhaps that accounts for the Japanese delight in gardens and groves—places where they have brought peace to nature.

As we noted in describing the Japanese innovations of Buddhism, this sort of delight showed in the Japanese embellishment of religious ceremonies. Not only do most temples have some sort of grounds, often quite lovely, but their liturgies employ flowers, incense, candles, and other adornments. Along with the Japanese stress on order and cleanliness, which goes back to ancient concerns for purification, a desire has grown to make living graceful. Buddhism has benefited from this desire, as the breathtaking Moss Temple and the Rock Garden Temple grounds show. In Shinto shrines, such as Ise, Heian, and Meiji, gardens, pools, fields of flowers, and lofty trees also reflect this desire.

The mode in which the Japanese have received these nature lessons, we suggest, has been "religio-aesthetic." Japan is not very concerned with a philosophy of nature in the Western sense. It does not analyze "prime matter" or the nature of nuclear particles. Its religion appears to move by a sense of harmony. If the folk interest is nature's agricultural energies (and the powers responsible for sickness), the higher-class interest is nature's ability to soothe. Sensing that the groves and gardens represent something primal, the warrior, merchant, and bureaucrat have returned to it to escape the human concerns that threaten to swamp them. By communion with nature, the samurai warrior could collect his spirit for a single-minded attack. By slipping away from his accounting, the merchant could anticipate a "retirement," which, in Japan as well as China, allowed more poetic, Taoist preoccupations. The same applies to the bureaucrat. Even today's emperor, who is merely a figurehead, specializes in marine biology. Somewhat inept in social situations, he comes alive in his pools and gardens.

This interest in nature is religious in the sense that nature has regularly represented to the Japanese something ultimate. Thus, concern for nature has often been an ultimate concern—a stance before the holy. This stance seldom involved violent beliefs. The major prophetic figures do not tell tales of burning bushes or theologize out of mysteriously parted seas. Rather, the predominant mood has been peaceful and unitive.[36] Japanese religion tries to gain access to the core of the personality, where the personality touches nature's flow. It tries, probably semiconsciously, to let the moss and rocks work their influence. These objects can summarize existence, giving messages from mind-only. Such Buddhist ideas suggest emptiness—the strangely satisfying "nothing-ness" that the spirit disgusted with ideas, the spirit more holistically inclined, often finds in open space or the sea.

The religious veneration of nature, or even the religio-aesthetic use of nature for soothing the soul, implies an impersonal ultimacy. Further, it implies that humanity, as well as divinity, is more at one with nature than over or against it. Religion based on nature, in fact, tends to collapse humans and gods into nature's forces or nature's flows. As a result, Japan has not seen the world as created by a transcendent force. Rather, Japan has let nature somewhat suppress knowledge and love of divinity, subordinating them to energy and flow. Human beings have been encouraged not to exploit nature (though recent technological changes qualify this statement). Through most of Japanese history, one would prune or rake nature rather than lay waste to it, at least in part because human beings did not have a biblical writ to fill the earth and subdue it.[37] Rather, they had a call to live with nature. Today we might hear that as a call to be ecological, grateful, and thus graceful.

This emphasis on nature relegated intellectual concerns to second place. Many monks have lived in mountain fastnesses, while relatively few have been theoreticians of divinity's word. The reasoning of theoreticians tends to be sharp, attacking, and dialectical. The reasoning of contemplative monks tends to be poetic, symbolic, and expressive. Those who ponder the "feminine" intelligence of Eastern cultures come upon this contemplative mind. Generally, Japan has sought the whole rather than the part, the movement rather than the arrest, the beauty as well as the utility. These are feminine characteristics only if *masculine* refers to only one sort of logic (the shortest distance between two points). If a culture moves more circuitously, Western men will likely call it feminine. We are fortunate to live in a time that challenges such stereotypes.

Society

Women's Status

It is ironic that a culture that has been considered feminine has been almost oppressively male dominated. Although there are traces of an early matriarchy and strong influences from female shamans and their successors in the new religions, women have regularly occupied a low position in Japanese society. Of course, women's influence in the traditional home and even the modern office is stronger than superficial sociology suggests.[38] Expert in the very refined Japanese tact, wives and mothers have found ways of influence despite their institutionalized powerlessness. Officially, however, Japan accepted Confucian notions of social relationships (no doubt because they fit traditional predilections), so the female was almost always designated as the underling.

The important religious roles played by females in Japanese history should be further discussed. Perhaps their phallic overtones made it fitting that the kami should possess females. Or perhaps shamanism offered the powerless a chance to gain attention and influence. Whatever the reasons, women were the prime contact with divinity in folk Shinto, despite strong menstrual taboos. As well, they were the prime contact with the spirits of the dead and so were central in maintaining the clan. The figurines from the prehistoric Jomon period suggest that women were originally considered awesome because of their power to give birth. The almost complete failure of the women's liberation movement in contemporary Japan suggests that the powers of women represented by these former roles have long been suppressed.

For reasons of psychological convenience as well as self-interest, the men dominating Japanese society have found it advantageous to place religion and femininity in opposition to warfare and business. As the recourse to nature (retirement) has been in contrast to things official, so the recourse to monasteries, female shamans, and even geishas has been in contrast to workaday life. In part, of course, this contrast links religion with recreation, art, and family life. (In modern Japan a man identifies as much with his job and company as with his family.) Thus, nature, religion, and women are considered surplus commodities and yet especially valuable ones: surplus in that they do not figure much in modern work, but valuable in that work alone does not constitute a complete existence.

Clan Emphasis

The modern stress on a man's work, identifying him with his corporation, is the result of the group structure of Japanese business. Consequently, the typical businessman takes much of his recreation with his fellow workers apart from his family. Considered in the context of Japanese religious history, this situation is somewhat anomalous. Earhart, for instance, has gathered documents that testify to the religious significance of family life,[39] showing the sense of clan that has predominated. (In fact, the modern corporation exploits this sense of clan loyalty.)

Moreover, a characteristic of the traditional family was concern with the dead. As in China, ancestor veneration was a significant portion of the average person's religious contacts with ultimate powers. Originally, the Japanese probably believed that the departed continued to hover around the places where they had lived. The Japanese tended to associate their ancestors with kami and bodhisattvas after these figures were introduced by Shinto and Buddhism. Therefore, in its petitions and venerations, the clan reminded itself of its own identity (the function that some sociologists, such as Durkheim, have considered the main rationale for religion) and kept attuned to the natural forces of life and death.

Thus, the family tended to be the locus of daily worship, and the family shrine tended to predominate over the village or national shrine. Still, there was not a sharp division between the family clan and the national clan. The emperor was often considered the head not only of his own line but also of the entire Japanese people; the gods of Shinto mythology were the gods of the collective Japanese group; and national shrines such as Ise were the site of ceremonies performed on behalf of the entire nation. Kitagawa's study,[40] referred to above, underscores the Japanese idea of a national community. Alan Miller has shown that in some periods the state functioned as a liturgical community.[41] Waida augments these studies with data suggesting that both the national community and the national liturgy are rooted in the concept of a sacred kingship,[42] while Davis has recently detailed the complicated dynamics of myth and ritual that bind a typical new religious community.[43]

These studies all spotlight the manifold cohesiveness of Japanese religious society. Japan is not a place where Whitehead's definition of religion (what a person does with his or her solitude) is very helpful.[44] Although standing alone before the Golden Pavilion has shaped for many Japanese a sense of ultimacy,[45] group activities—at home, in war, or at work—have been the crucial factors in developing such a sense.

Ethics

This historical sense of clan was accompanied by certain ethical assumptions that were immensely influential in shaping the Japanese conscience. The small boy trudging off to school would hear his mother call after him, "Don't come home if you disgrace us by failing your examination." The medieval samurai felt that his life belonged to his feudal lord. If he failed his lord, by being defeated or less than fully successful, he was expected to offer to commit ritual suicide—to petition his lord for this "favor," so that he might mend the honor he had violated. In contemporary Japan, the individual worker is supposed to promote the honor of his bosses above all. He is to assume any failures by his group and to attribute any successes to the group's leader. Thus, the boss (or at most the group as a whole) always gets credit for a bright idea or increased productivity. If the worker does not rock the boat, the corporation will take care of all his needs until he dies.

Buddhism offered an alternative to the Japanese group orientation. Though the

Buddha's own thought was quite social, as manifested by the sangha, his original message stressed the uniqueness of each individual's situation. It is true that each being possessed the Buddha-nature (at least according to Mahayana Buddhism, which introduced the Buddha to Japan), and that this belief coupled with the doctrine of no-self led to a conception of the oneness of reality. Practically, however, the Buddha made the existential personality the religious battleground. Only the individual could remove the poison of karma and rebirth; only the individual could pronounce the Buddhist vows for himself or herself, let alone live them out. So, at the beginning, Buddhism offered little to a clan or state seeking to make itself the center of the world.

In Japan Buddhism both kept some of its individualism and suffered a socialization. As Zen perhaps best shows, the sangha could gear itself to making free spirits. Its discipline could be odd, even cranky. At least, the Zen masters brim with spontaneity, venerating their tradition but often in iconoclastic ways. Yet Japan acculturated Buddhism. Indeed, Buddhism became a government agency, propping war lords and nationalistic ideology. Ultimately, Japan decided that Shinto served nationalism better than Buddhism, but that was not for Buddhism's lack of trying.

Self

Theoretically in Buddhism there was no self and so no barrier (for the enlightened) to union with nature or the group. Shinto defined the self less clearly than it defined nature or the group. Thus, when Confucianism brought an elaborate social protocol, the sense of self in Japanese religious consciousness was bound to be deemphasized.

In fact, Japanese religion does not emerge as a champion of freethinking. Compared with religion elsewhere, Japanese religion does not support individual initiative or responsibility to a significant degree. Except for Zen, Japan has told the individual that fulfillment is a matter of harmonizing with nature and society. For instance, the traditional Japanese artist did not agonize in the creative process like Western artists do. Japanese art has not been primarily for working out a self. We may doubt, therefore, that many Japanese artists have thought of their lives or work in terms of Patrick White's "vivisection" (of experience).[46]

More prominent has been the Taoist notion that the artist goes to the center of nature, where the Way rules, and from union with the Way spontaneously expresses a fleeting glimpse of reality.[47] The fall of a cherry blossom, the pattern of a scarf, the rumble of a mountain—those are the subjects that seize a Basho or a Kawabata. In the tea ceremony, the No play, archery, or swordsmanship, the ideal is selflessness. Such activities, in fact, are but active forms of what the meditator pursues in *zazen*. Cast off the dichotomizing mind, the culture has said. Distinguish no more between your self and the world. Distinguishing makes for multiplicity and illusion. Buddha-nature is one. Full attainment, in the Japanese aesthetic religion, is the unitive mind, the mind lost in Mind.

JAPANESE AESTHETICS[48]

Much of the Japanese effort to gain the unitive mind has expressed itself aesthetically, in artistic pursuits. Classical Japanese painting, for instance, tended to portray the physical world realistically, with great attention to details. It was not abstract or surrealistic. On the other hand, classical painting also was not photographically objective, but tended to use a flat, undistanced surface to express subjective perceptions of reality. A good example is a series of screens by Kano Naizen from the Momoyama period (1568–1600). The screens portray the arrival of Portuguese merchants and the conversion of some Japanese citizens by Christian missionaries. In one street scene the foreground presents the foreign priests and merchants mingling with the Japanese natives. In the background, a local shop and a pine grove are portrayed without depth, covered by golden mists. The effect is a standoff between time and eternity. The busy street scene with the newly arrived foreigners argues that times are always changing, novelty is nearly rampant. The golden mists, pine grove, and stylized shop argue that the more things change the more they stay the same. Novelty is but a small wrinkle on the surface of an ancient culture and a timeless nature.

Some of the oldest Japanese ceramics, the *haniwa* figurines from the fifth and sixth centuries, C.E., display what became an almost standard Japanese love of simple, austere presentations. The *haniwa* figurines tend to have oval eyes and tiny mouths, as though they were timeless masks, suitable for the ceremonial dances that take us out of profane time. They are sober and archetypal, yet poised on the brink of motion (for the sacred dance is always occurring, always inviting us to join in). Some historians find Chinese influences in these early ceramics, but they express qualities that Japan soon made wholly its own.

Buddhist influences brought an increased concentration on portrait sculpture, in order to represent the Enlightened One. In the best of these representations, artists captured the Buddha's humanity, giving him the slightest trace of a smile, a bit of warmth and playfulness. Portrait sculpture of the Nara period (710–794) included monks among its subjects. Thus the sculpture of the famous blind monk Ganjin shows a holy man deep in meditation. The smile lines at the mouth and the corners of the eyes help to heighten his attractiveness. Though physically blind, he probably had great insight into human nature. Though concentrating on the timeless dharma, he probably had been molded to a timely humaneness, becoming a person we would like to know.

Zen masters of the Muromachi period (1392–1568) were instrumental in Japan's appropriation of the landscape techniques developed during the Chinese Sung dynasty. This led to the *suiboku* (ink on paper with splashed-ink wash). The conventions of the *suiboku* landscapes called for a vertical perspective, featuring craggy mountains or deep basins with lakes and canyons. Clouds or empty spaces tended to divide the pictures into three realms, reminiscent of the doctrine of the Buddha's three bodies. The lower level of the painting usually dealt with earthly and human concerns: a lake, a hermit's hut, several fishermen. The middle of the picture would have temples or pagodas suggesting paradise. At the top the picture would portray icy mountain peaks, to symbolize the perfection beyond all human imagining.

Working within this conventional form, a Zen master such as Sesshu (1420–1506) was able to introduce some striking originality. His *Winter Landscape*, for example, shows jagged mountain tops lost in clouds, a temple in the middle range, and near the base a traveler in a broad-brimmed hat. The traveler is lost in the immense landscape, quite vulnerable as he picks his way. Though this is all quite conventional, Sesshu has invested the painting with an electric energy. Using short, ragged lines, he has expressed the Zen sense that nature is tremendously alive. Thus the impression is not of a soft, misty nature but of sharp angles, well-defined particulars. That this effect at the bottom is in tension with empty space at the top, with a white, heavenly vagueness, makes the picture an epitome of Zen philosophy. Emptiness accents particulars. Mystical absorption at the top should lead to vitality and decisiveness at the bottom.

Another interesting Japanese art form was the *ukiyo*, which means a picture of the "floating world." The hallmark of this style was the changeableness of things, the world's transiency. Yet whereas transiency had traditional Buddhist overtones of sadness, the *ukiyo* artists tended to be gay. The excitement of the latest gossip, the fun of seizing the day, run through their work. One of their favorite subjects was Kabuki actors. In the celebrated series of portraits done by Toshusai Sharaku in 1794–95, the arresting feature is the actors' facial expressions. They show brilliant rage, triumph, coyness, defeat—all the emotions required on the Kabuki stage. The faces are heavily made up, and the total effect is to drive home the energy and pathos of the actor's life.

Japanese aesthetics also led to notable architecture, gardens, and rituals such as the tea ceremony. The traditional Japanese house was a model of simplicity, even austerity. It had straw-mat floors, sliding-screen walls, and very little furniture. The custom of removing one's shoes on entering the house suggested coming into a new, venerable space. The screen walls offered minimal protection against nature, but they were flexible enough to accommodate to quick changes of mood. In summer the screens easily opened to the elements, eliminating the barriers between the family and nature.

During the Muromachi period Zen monastic influence made the style of the abbot's quarters attractive for lay people's houses. The main room therefore came to center around a floor-level writing desk, and there would usually be an alcove for arranged flowers. A scroll usually would hang in the corner, the floors would be covered with *tatami* (straw mats), and the walls would be sliding paper doors and screens. Among the wealthy, who could afford large houses with many screens, there would be special arrangements for viewing the moon or the snow to best advantage. The Katsura imperial villa on the edge of Kyoto is a good model of such large houses designed for beautiful views.

For many Japanese, the most beautiful views have opened onto exquisite gardens. The Shinto roots of the gardening tradition stressed gnarled old trees and large rocks in places set aside for the kami. When Chinese culture began to shape Japanese tastes, Taoist and Buddhist influences became important. Traditional Chinese gardens sought to reproduce the islands and grottoes of the Taoist immortals or the beauty of the Buddha's Pure Land. Chinese geomancy set many of the stylistic ideals, and harmony between yin and yang forces was a high requirement. Thus a large yang boulder would be counterbalanced by a low yin pool. Waterfalls represented life and bamboo represented strength.

Once again, Zen was the native Japanese development that most directly varied the Chinese model. In the case of gardening, Zen pushed the designs in a more abstract and asymmetrical direction. In the Zen scheme, gardens were not so much places for leisurely strolling as places for meditation. Translating many notions from Sung landscape painting, the Zen gardeners stressed emptiness and the lack of human or emotional

Figure 18   Rock garden, Kyoto. Photo by J. T. Carmody.

touches. So the Zen gardens tended to have no benches or wine cups. Instead of showy flowers they stressed moss or rocks. The Ryoanji or Rock Garden Monastery of Kyoto, built around 1500, epitomizes this abstract style. There are no ponds or streams, only white gravel raked to resemble eddies—phenomenal reality playing on the surface of emptiness (see Figure 18).

The tea ceremony was one of several rituals the Japanese developed to beautify each part of daily living. Often it would take place in the teahouse of a shrine garden. Indeed, many Zen Buddhists came to consider the tea ceremony a sort of sacrament, symbolizing the grace, austerity, and concentration that good living requires. While the core of the ceremony was simply making and sipping whipped green tea, the teahouse, the utensils, and the manner of serving all played important parts. Ideally there would be lovely surroundings: a garden of great beauty, flowers, a *suiboku* painting or a scroll of elegant calligraphy. Afficionados paid special attention to the bowl in

which the tea was served, and master potters often strove to produce simple, elegant tea vessels. Although the upper classes sometimes embellished the tea ceremony with ostentatious displays, the protocol developed by Sen no Rikyu, the greatest of the tea masters, stressed "poor tea": absolute simplicity and ordinariness.

Flower arrangement *(ikebana)* brought aesthetic refinement home to many Japanese family circles. In a sense, the goal of flower arrangement was to make a miniature garden, and so a miniature, domestic paradise. Like the tea ceremony, flower arrangement became a "way": an avocation both refreshing and disciplining. In flower arrangement the great virtues were simplicity, asymmetry, and form (color was secondary). The preferred forms were understated rather than obvious, subtle rather than bold. The ideal was to hint at a mysterious meaning and suggest old, somewhat formal ways. During the Tokugawa period (1600–1868) a threefold style developed. A high and a low branch on one side would represent heaven and human beings. A middle branch on the opposite side would represent earth. One would gain variety by changing the flowers, grasses, leaves, sticks, and other elements placed in these three positions. The result was a timeless pattern varied by new materials.

Throughout all their arts, the Japanese have tried to express and develop their sense of emptiness, form, the changeableness of human beings, and the primacy of nature. Rarely did a Japanese art form flourish without close ties to religion. In the tea and flower ceremonies, for instance, one is hard-pressed to say where art leaves off and religious contemplation begins. A certain blankness signals the touch of Buddhist emptiness. A certain austerity signals the touch of Shinto antiquity, when life was close to nature, unemotional and strong.

As a consequence of selflessness, the individual Japanese may appear ethically underdeveloped to the Westerner. Such a description can provoke confusion, as well as misperception and offense. Still, a Western student has to begin with existing Western categories, even if they prove inappropriate. In Western ethics, the individual person judges right and wrong, largely because Greek philosophy and Israelite religion, the bases for Western culture, made the individual an intellectual and moral subject of revelation—in the Greek case, revelation from a logical being; in the Israelite, revelation from a willful God. By the time of the Enlightenment (the eighteenth century), the West had developed this patrimony to the point that the individual could be autonomous and ethics a matter of individual reasoning. Even though recent thought has found this view to be inadequate, it remains influential and at least partially true.

For instance, Western scholars of Shinto such as Bownas[49] and Blacker[50] go out of their way to underscore that its persistent concern with pollution had little to do with morality. Pollution did not pertain to the intentions of the actor, and no distinctions were made between accidental and deliberate violations. Merely to shed blood or encounter death was polluting. Consequently, the polluted person did not have to assume responsibility, to repent, or to renew the self morally. Essentially, both the pollution and the purification were external to the violator and amoral. Polluting acts occurred in the context of rather physical forces, akin to electricity or the shark's response to blood.

In the medieval period, the warrior or serf let his master be his will. The master held the power of life and death over the servant; morality was more a matter of loyalty to the master than loyalty to conscience. This deemphasis on conscience in personal life has persisted even in the modern period. As the honor accorded ritual suicide suggests, the individual has been subject to the social code in nearly all matters.

The corporation dominates modern Japanese life. The individual favors working in a group, where both responsibility and success are shared. The worst thing that can befall an individual is the need to step out of the group and speak up in his own name. Shame is the force that sustains the Japanese social code. Whether an act is right or wrong is not as important as whether it will bring shame to the family, the company, or the country. Thus, the uproar over the disclosures of widespread bribery among government officials doing business with American aircraft companies, as reported in the Japanese press in 1976, centered less on dishonesty than on disgrace. These officials tarnished the good name of the government and of the Japanese people in the world community. That the actions were instances of gross self-aggrandizement—or simply modern theft—was secondary. Similarly, when the Japanese retreated from Hong Kong at the end of World War II, the emperor's statements contained no acknowledgement of defeat, let alone any indication of wrong in Japan's original aggression. They read like a communique from a bureaucratic agency announcing a change from the use of green memo paper to blue.

Of course, the Japanese ways have a logic and a morality of their own. We are not concerned here with the difficult, though crucial, business of working out a transcultural ethics, rooted in the essential human drives to know and love, that would apply everywhere.[51] Rather, the present purpose is descriptive: trying to characterize for a Western audience the Japanese sense of self. The Japanese self appears unwilling to stand up and take personal responsibility as well as uncommonly polite and helpful. Further, what Japanese may lack as individuals they compensate for as groups. Japanese groups are quiet, clean, helpful, and cooperative; indeed, as their productivity shows, few peoples can match their discipline and output.

From medieval times, as we suggested earlier, an individual's proper bearing toward the group was loosely codified in Bushido, the warrior's way. Bushido was a sort of chivalry, expressing how the gentleman or person of honor would act. It smacked of Shinto devotion to country, Confucian propriety, and Zen self-discipline, rounding these concepts together to create a spirit of obedience and loyalty. The loyalty was primarily to the emperor and secondarily to one's immediate overlord. However, there were other Bushido virtues, and describing them will flesh out the Japanese sense of ethics.

For instance, the honorable person was grateful: for goods that others (especially parents and superiors) gave him or her, for life, for the beautiful Japanese land, and for all the boons of the kami. Another Bushido virtue was courage. The Japanese gymnast in the 1976 Olympics who did his routine with a broken leg (finishing with a ten-foot somersault from the rings) demonstrated Bushido courage to millions of homes the world over. In the warrior ideal, life itself was secondary to loyalty or honor. As Ignatius Loy-

ola described Christian commitment to Christ in terms of a Spanish hidalgo's willingness to die for his commander, Bushido held as virtuous the courage to die for one's military leader or emperor.

Justice, truthfulness, politeness, and reserve were other Bushido values, inspiring the young person to develop a stern self-discipline. Most of all, he or she was to keep emotion in check, never revealing anger or small-mindedness. Robert Bellah's study of Tokugawa religion suggests that Bushido discipline is largely the basis for the vitality of the modern Japanese economy, serving a similar purpose as Protestant worldliness did to Western capitalism.[52]

The watchwords for the individual in Japanese religious history, then, were discipline and self-effacement. Fulfillment would come from submission to nature and service to the group, not from self-development or personal contact with God. The religious traditions, consequently, tended to help satisfy society's need for good workers and compliant citizens. Although this is true of religious traditions in most places, it stands out in Japan. The happy life that a new religion such as Tenrikyo holds out to its faithful is the result of reviving ancient concepts, including the submersion of the individual in the group; Soka Gakkai and other politically active religions stress service to the group.

Just as radical and Marxist political groups in the West offer their faithful a cause in which to lose themselves, the Japanese new religions have capitalized on the security that an individual feels in being part of a large group. In the clan, the nation, or the religious group, the Japanese individual has felt secure—safe from meaninglessness and partner to something large and compelling. All the beauty in Japanese culture, all the intelligence in Japanese technology, ought to incline us to study such "belonging" carefully.

Divinity

Japanese divinity, though complex, is essentially an impersonal collectivity of natural forces. Although devotion to a particular kami, Buddha, or Taoist god qualifies this assertion somewhat (the people who place offerings at the "baby shrine" of the Goddess of Mercy in Tokyo no doubt pray to an individual figure), the sharply defined personage that we associate with the God of Western religion hardly appears in Japan. The gods of Shinto mythology, for instance, have a quite finite knowledge, love, and power; they have not separated from the cosmos to make particular demands. (Particular kami do take over individuals such as Miki, the foundress of Tenrikyo, so we must qualify that statement, too.)

In the course of Japanese history, there have been personal claims to divinity such as Miki's. In the thirteenth century, Nichiren was confident enough of his success in propagating Buddhist dharma to proclaim himself "Bodhisattva of Superb Action."[53] In his case, a strong imagination took advantage of the common doctrine about the Buddha-nature residing in all living things. For the common populace, though, divinity did not reflect individual humanity. Its best representations were nature or the clan. Yet insofar as people always conceive of divinity through their sense of perfection or power (and through their revelatory experiences), even impersonal Japanese divinity occasionally touched the human qualities of knowledge and love.

The Buddhists best showed divine knowledge to Japan—the ultimate reality that shone in enlightenment. Insofar as Japan deified the Buddha, it deified glorious understanding. From enlightenment, further, one could reason that the Buddha-nature was the basis for the world's intelligibility. It was what makes things be and what gives things meaning. It was also an active source, issuing all things from its womb. The generation of all things from Buddha-nature was not the same as the "logical" creation that Hellenized Western religion developed, but it did equate Buddhist ultimate reality with mind and understanding.

Love was another matter. The bodhisattva vow, of course, included great com-

passion, and all East Asia best loved the bodhisattva Kuan-yin, the goddess of mercy, to whom it looked for motherly care. In keeping with the injunction to stop craving, though, love or compassion was not to stir desire, however noble. So one could work for the salvation of all beings in good cheer, believing that their present sufferings were no cause for raging against divinity's or even society's injustices. So the love of the bodhisattva, even when it entailed suffering, was of a different sort than the redemptive love (agape) in Western religion.[54] For Japan evil is more an illusion than a disordered love or an idolatry. In the eons of time, in the vastness of *ku* (emptiness), present problems are but fleeting. If we abandon thinking about them and loose our attachment to them, we can meld into the One. Then death loses its sting and suffering has no fangs.[55]

The Buddhists were by far the most acute Japanese philosophers; the conceptions of divinity in the other traditions were far less generalized. For Japanese folk religion, which touched all but the most intellectual, divinity was quite piecemeal. Its representation was the local shrine or the house altar; neither negated the other, and neither denied the divinity of the shrines in the neighboring villages or of the altars in the next block. Folk religiosity therefore was quite tolerant—and quite confusing. It was relatively happy to multiply divinities without seeming necessity. A Shinto wedding, a Buddhist funeral, and a good many charms in between were the common custom. The gods of Shinto mythology, Taoist magic, and popular Buddhism but varied a sacredness felt to be quite near. For the few who hungered after simplicity, nature or the Buddhist void sufficed. Either could anchor spirituality in the present. Either could rouse wonder and make any time or space profound.

The times and spaces that were most wonderful, though, were the folk festivals and the popular pilgrim shrines. As the diary of a pilgrim to Ise puts it: "One does not feel like an ordinary person any longer but as though reborn in another world."[56] At special festivals or shrines, one passed a threshold *(limen)* and went from the ordinary to the sacred world. The diary of the Ise pilgrim describes this liminal experience in the aesthetic manner noted above: The pine groves have an unearthly shadow; the rare flowers that survived the frost carry a delicate pathos; most of the adornments in the shrine recall the ancient days, when religious life was honest, simple, and rough. The pilgrim notes the spray over the hills, the solitary woods that beckon to the meditative. He washes in the sea to gain outer purity and strives for a clean Shinto worship (with no Buddhist interference) to gain inner purity. Throughout, the physical beauty of Ise engrosses him.

There is something fresh and clean in such Japanese perceptions of divinity. Scholars of Shinto stress that most of the kami were forces of good, but Japanese cleanliness and goodness were astringent, dealing more with mountain streams than with human persons. Indeed, the Japanese divinity differs from ordinary persons by assuming the simplicity of streams and rocks. Far from the madding crowd, it booms in the surf, arches in the pines. As we may analyze Indian yoga in terms of a desire to return to a primal state below busy consciousness, so we may analyze Japanese naturalism as a search for relief from social complication, individual tension, and even the busy world of blessings and spells. Probably this search was seldom fully conscious, but it breathes in the pilgrim's account. He feels released into a new world, reborn, because the Ise grove dwarfs him with the peace that nature had before humans arrived.

If so, the divinity that Japan called upon to sanction its special place in the sun was beyond all social arrangements. The pilgrim in the grove does not concern himself with his clan. His country and people are present indirectly (Ise is their national holy place), but something else is to the fore—the mystery behind or in the is-ness of things.

Study Questions

1. In what sense is Shinto a fertility religion?
2. Can you explain the Buddhist philosophy behind the two Basho poems given in the text?
3. What seem to have been the primary psychodynamics of the new religions?
4. Analyze the feminine and masculine components in native Japanese culture.
5. How does the Japanese sense of shame differ from the Western sense of sin?
6. Does Japan make any hard distinctions between aesthetics and religion?
7. What is the function of the *nembutsu?*
8. Contrast the two Zen practices of working on a koan and *zazen.*

Conclusion

THE ANCIENT RELIGIOUS MIND: TWENTY-FIVE KEY DATES

4.6 BILLION YEARS AGO   FORMATION OF THE EARTH

3.6 BILLION YEARS AGO   RISE OF LIFE

---

4 MILLION YEARS AGO   *AUSTRALOPITHECUS*, ADVANCED HOMINID IN AFRICA

---

2 MILLION YEARS AGO   *HOMO HABILIS;* STONE TOOLS

1.5 MILLION YEARS AGO   *HOMO ERECTUS;* MORE SOPHISTICATED TOOLS

500,000 YEARS AGO   USE OF FIRE

100,000 YEARS AGO   *HOMO SAPIENS;* RITUAL BURIAL

75,000 YEARS AGO   MOUSTERIAN CAVE DWELLERS; CLOTHING TO SURVIVE NORTHERN WINTERS

40,000 YEARS AGO   *HOMO SAPIENS SAPIENS,* "MODERN MAN," FULL HUNTING CULTURE

35,000 YEARS AGO   CLOTHING ADEQUATE FOR LIFE IN SIBERIA

30,000 YEARS AGO   PREHISTORIC PAINTING AND SCULPTURE

30,000–25,000 YEARS AGO   MIGRATIONS ACROSS BERING STRAIT TO NEW WORLD

Summary Reflections

20,000 YEARS AGO	COLONIZATION OF EUROPE, JAPAN
15,000 YEARS AGO	EXTENSIVE CEREAL COLLECTING
10,500 YEARS AGO	HUMANS THROUGHOUT SOUTH AMERICA
9,500–6,500 YEARS AGO	CEREAL CULTIVATION, DOMESTICATION OF ANIMALS
8,000 B.C.E.	FULL WITHDRAWAL OF GLACIERS
8350–7350	JERICHO, FIRST WALLED TOWN (10 ACRES)
6250–5400	CATAL HUYUK (TURKEY), LARGE CITY (32 ACRES)
CA. 6000	RICE CULTIVATION IN THAILAND; POTTERY AND WOOLEN TEXTILES IN CATAL HUYUK
CA. 5000	IRRIGATION OF MESOPOTAMIAN ALLUVIAL PLAINS
CA. 4000	BRONZE CASTING IN MIDDLE EAST
CA. 3500	MEGALITHS IN BRITTANY, IBERIAN PENINSULA, BRITISH ISLES; INVENTION OF WHEEL
CA. 3100	PICTOGRAPHIC WRITING IN SUMER
CA. 3000	SPREAD OF COPPER WORKING

A t the outset, we postulated that the religious life of humanity is a vast and diversified spectacle. Perhaps you now find that postulate only too well verified. The ancient religious mind, the wisdom religions of the East, the prophetic religions of the West all combine to make a tapestry of unmanageable proportions. We have tried to discern some of this tapestry's principal patterns. We have tried to present the information and the themes that might make such terms as *Hinduism* or *Buddhism* intelligible. Our final task is to review the whole and suggest its implications.

UNITY AND DIVERSITY

The unity of the phenomena we have studied is religion—the common quest for a way to the center. The diversity of the phenomena makes the religions—the distinctive traditional ways in which sizable numbers of people have worked at this quest together.

The quests are all deeply humanistic. For instance, according to C. G. Jung,[1] the American Indian or African who greets the sun as a daily miracle performs deep psychic work. The Hindu who makes *puja* (worship) or whom bhakti carries to Krishna constructs a world that makes sense and provides emotional comfort. The same is true of Buddhists who ponder koans, Taoists who try to confect the elixir of immortality, and Hasidic Jews who learn diamond cutting to preserve what they can of the old Jewish life. In most times and places, the religions have supported or developed meaning unpretentiously, unobtrusively. For most people the traditions have worked subtly as sets of largely unquestioned assumptions.

Still, the traditions have varied in their subtleness. People who ate bean curd sensed the world differently than people who ate roasted lamb. The Prophet who recited, "There is no God but God," oriented Arabs away from the world that the Greek philosopher Thales saw ("The world is full of gods"). The recent introduction of social sci-

entific and critical historical methods has made religious studies more empirically minded and so more sensitive to such variety. Thus, the differences among the religions have been in the spotlight. Increasingly scholars debate whether there is a common quality among all the traditions, a common religion at the traditions' cores.

We believe that there is such a common quality or unity, and at various points we have described it as a common attraction toward mystery. Relatedly, we believe that the empiricism that misses such unity and mystery is at least an unwitting reductionism—an insistence that humanity is no more than as it behaves. Usually, that insistence indicates an impoverished imagination and interiority—an inability to intuit how two different behaviors (for example, shamanic ecstasis and yogic enstasis) might be directed toward the same goal: sacredness, the really real.[2]

The tricky thing about meaning, which extroverted observers tend to miss, is that ultimacy or mystery is always but a step away. Still, distraction and lack of reflection on the part of either the people under scrutiny or the scholars who are scrutinizing are defenses that mystery easily breaks down. As Brahman, nirvana, *Tao*, and Buddha-nature, ultimacy broke down the defenses against deep meaning in the peoples we have studied. Whether they wanted it or not (and usually they did), sacred mystery defined their world.

If one can see the sacred, it breaks through the Iron, Bamboo, and other curtains that divide our world today. Perhaps the only traces of the sacred we can see are the anxieties on which the aspirin industry trades. Or perhaps we are able to appreciate it in the Nobel Prize–winning efforts of outstanding scientists and writers. Either way, with or without overt theology, ultimacy is always at hand. We may choose not to embrace it, not to call mystery our inmost vocation. However, as surely as we suffer and die, it will embrace us. All people by nature desire to know, Aristotle declared. Our mortal condition makes Aristotle's dog-

Figure 19   *Taj Mahal: Islam on Hindu soil. Photo by J. T. Carmody.*

ma existential: All people by nature desire to know the mystery from which they come and to which they go. All people are by nature set for religion.

Religion

The word *religion* refers to the inmost human vocation. By empirical fact as well as theoretical interpretation, *religion* pertains to all life that is reflective, that heads into mystery. Largely for that reason, the word *religion* was seldom uttered by the great teachers.[3] They rather spoke of meaning, the way to "walk," the traditional wisdom, the balance called justice, and the fire called love. Because they were embodied spirits speaking to other embodied spirits, they used familiar figures: mountains, rivers, widows giving alms. Further, their speech led to common action: rhythmic prostra-

tions, gutsy resistance to the emperor, dancing with the Scripture, helping a friend. All of these actions, though, were religious.

People organized communities around the great teachers' speech and actions. The communities expressed their religion (their venture after meaning into mystery) in ways that Joachim Wach has labeled theoretical, social, and active.[4] That is, they made theologies, brotherhoods and sisterhoods, and liturgies and laws. Regularly, the communities lost the spirit of their founders, as succeeding generations regularly prized order more than charisma, control more than inspiration, and orthodoxy more than creativity. Just as regularly, reformers tried to find their way back to the original vision. In China it was "Back to the ancients." In the West it was "Back to the Word."

The various traditions have shaped

191

their peoples in endless ways. Some have spoken rather simply—Judaism and Islam, for instance. Others have made strange bedfellows and cultures more complex, such as the religions of China and Japan. Still, all traditions have used the past to decipher the present and to prepare for the future. All have received and handed on.

That handing on is what we mean by *tradition*.[5] None of us fashions meaning free of external influences. All of us receive a cultural inheritance, meager or rich, to which we add. We do this willy-nilly—by having children, teaching students, working with colleagues, supporting friends. Original sin is the dark side of such a sense of tradition. According to this concept, we all take our first breath in air that is polluted, in a game that is tilted against us. How polluted or tilted the world is has been a matter of vigorous debate. The only consensus seems to be that evil is a sad fact and that there is sufficient good to justify hope. The handing on therefore leads all the religions to revile evil and to buttress hope—a process that can be called a concern for salvation.

For instance, ancient peoples banded together for evolutionary salvation—against the evil of extinction and in hope that the race would go on. Close to the earth, they thought in concrete terms, undifferentiatingly, telling stories of life and death. Life came from the fatherly sky and the motherly earth. Life was as possible, as renewable, as heavenly water and productive dirt. Death was breathtakingly near, but perhaps the dead were as seed falling in the ground. Perhaps they were but a link in the chain of generations. Or, maybe they passed to a new form of life. As smoke passes from burning wood, so perhaps the subtle part of a human, the part that thinks and travels in dreams, could pass to a new state. In those ways, perhaps, ancient peoples fought for hope, tried to block out absurdity.

To suffer, lose, rejoice, or trust—such acts know no religious, ethnic, or national bounds. We all walk a way (if only a way to death) that we cannot name. We all seek (if only covertly) a path that is straight, a path

that mystery blesses. If some of our predecessors have been Nordic berserks, who heated up to feel mystery boil, others have been Eastern yogis, who so slowed themselves that they could be buried alive. If some of our predecessors have been erotics, convinced that the force of the way is sexual *shakti*, others have been lonely ascetics, convinced that meat clouds the spirit. There are few roads that no one has taken, few options that no one has tried. Though the options make all the difference for the individual, we can see from others where we might have gone. Indeed, that is a major reason why we study the humanities. There would be no basis for studying the humanities were there no unity called human nature. Likewise, there would be no religious studies were there no unity called religion.

Contending with nature, society, the self, and whatever ultimacy they have known, all human beings have mused about their sunrise and sunset. For all of them, the cosmos and the group have had effects, the self and ultimacy have beguiled. Without and within each person, the world has taken shape, changed, occasionally threatened to slip away. Since we are "synthetic" beings, whose incarnate spirits include the lowest matter and the heights of thought, we cannot escape religion's full span. Madness comes when the span tilts and the synthesis comes unglued. Boredom comes when we lose the span's tension, when imagination goes stale. In health, we find nature, society, and the self fascinating. In health, science, politics, and art are all essential, all deeply humanistic. If they become so specialized, so arcane, that their essential humanity is not apparent, we must speak of disease—of dysfunction, pathology, alienation.

Though disease has terrible power in our time, as the arms race and the prison systems show, it has always written arguments for despair. Parents who wept over dead children heard despair at Stonehenge, Gettysburg, and My Lai. Every woman raped, every man tortured, has heard counsel to abandon hope. Amazingly, though, human beings will not live by despair alone. Their very sense that the times are out of joint is a cry that there ought to be health.

Until we give up completely, we label health as normal. Disease, we say, is the lack of health. Evil, we say, is the lack of good— of proper order, right being, justice, and love. Indeed, so deep is our drive toward health that we cannot think of nonbeing and evil directly. They are irrational, absurd, and void. In their hope, then, the religions uncover more religion. In their hope, Buddhists and Christians can dialogue.

Meaning and Idiosyncrasy

The themes above are some of the constants that all the traditions carry. If they are general, it is because they pertain to all of humanity. In religious perspective, our human characteristics comprise a common condemnation (or consecration) to meaning. Thus, the differences among traditions are simply *how* their peoples have sought, conceived, and enacted meaning. That affirms, of course, that differences do differentiate.[6] It affirms that a Buddhist is not a Hindu and a Christian is not a Jew.

Because he or she is always dealing both with religion as a whole and with the individual religions, the student of religion must develop a peculiar balance. If she or he is blind to the unity behind all religions, the student will miss the deep humanity that the traditions can offer us. On the other hand, if the student sweeps all the information together, making all Buddhists anonymous Christians or all Christians renegade Jews, he or she will miss the texture that religion always has in people's lives. As is often the case, the ideal involves a duality: *both* cutting to the heart of the matter, where all humans are siblings, *and* respecting the idiosyncrasies that differentiate people as nations, tribes, sexes, individuals, and traditional religionists.

The idiosyncrasies are mysterious. Why should the Buddha have proposed no-self? A first answer might be because no-self answered the question of suffering that Bud-

dha's personal life and the life of his Indian culture posed. Fine, but this is hardly an end to the matter. Why should death, disease, and putrefaction have troubled this particular prince so deeply? Presumably many other princes saw corpses without deciding to leave their palaces, wives, and children to adopt a life of asceticism; similarly, many other cultures experienced suffering. Why, then, did the Indians penetrate the psychology of suffering so profoundly? Why not the Babylonians, Chinese, Aztecs, or Mayans?

As those questions show, there is a limit to historical analysis. It can explain some of the differences among individuals or cultures, but their real origin lies beyond it. For the real origin of differences is the incomprehensible world order.[7] We did not set the cosmic dust spinning. We don't know why it wove the combinations it did. Therefore, when we respect differences, we respect the totality of history and its mystery. We respect the ultimacy behind the facts, the often very brutal facts, that just this universal drama has played and no other.

Let us again try to be concrete. The Australian dream world, as scholars imperfectly reconstruct it from artifacts and interviews, reflects the peculiar landscape of the Australian continent. The aboriginal myths are similar to those of other areas that explain how the ancestors or demiurges fashioned the world, yet the aboriginal world is unique. The Australian use of the *tjurunga*, the sacred wooden boards, for instance, is distinctive. Other ancient peoples painted and carved, but none (that we know) with just the Australian concern for totemic ancestors. Again, the Chinese divination practice of *feng-shui* (geomancy) is like the complex basket divination of the Africans, yet they differ greatly. The two types of divination have the same purpose (to determine what will happen in nature and time), but they express it differently. *Feng-shui* would not seem appropriate in the Congo.

Differences, then, are real. We could develop that theme for Hinduism contrasted with Jainism or Buddhism, for Catholics contrasted with Orthodox or Protestants.

How great differences are, how divergent they make their adherents' realities, is difficult to determine. Often it seems as much a matter of the analyst's temperament as of the adherents' realities. In the terms of a recent debate,[8] the analyst who has an "esoteric" (inner) personality tends to stress the unity in the traditions, while the "exoteric" (outer) personality tends to stress the diversity.

Esoteric types respond to innermost notions and innermost realities. For them, a common mystery is as real as distinctive facts, even more real. Therefore, esoteric types tend to the negative way—the Hindu *"neti, neti"* ("not this, not that"). They may downplay or even disparage the diverse ways that people have chosen to pursue the supreme value. In contrast, exoteric types respond to outer phenomena—to the actual births, hungers, murders, orgasms, and deaths that make people's lives colorful, intense, palpably real. They fear that moving away from such realities ignores the way things are.

Beside exoteric blood, sweat, and tears, God does seem esoteric, pale and abstract. Looking closely, though, we find that esoterica have given religions most of their life. Hindu bhakti festivals make no sense without a Krishna to play the flute, a Kali to wield the sword. Buddhist meditation depends completely on karma and nirvana. In the West, circumcision, the Eucharist, and the Muslim *haji* (pilgrimage to Mecca) depend on the covenant, the redemption, and the eternal Word. In the lives of religious people, the exoteric is a body for the esoteric. It should be the same in the writings of religion scholars.

METHODOLOGICAL ISSUES

In this book we have tried to present the exoteric and esoteric sides of the Asian religions by stressing history and structural analysis. Our historical sections have tended to report on the events, personalities, and ideas that shaped the "outside" of the tradition in question, its "body," while our structural analyses have tended to reflect on the "inside" of the tradition in question, probing for its "soul." If we have succeeded at all, you now have a beginning sense of both how "Hinduism" evolved and what "Hinduism" connotes as a world view, a perspective on reality.

There are other ways of presenting the Asian religions, of course, and it would be good for you to be aware of them. Although we have not followed these other ways, except as brief detours from our main approaches, other scholars have shed considerable light on Asian religions by employing them. W. Richard Comstock once offered beginning students a list of five basic methodological perspectives,[9] and our describing these five should fill out your map.

First, there is the *psychological* perspective. Since the time of Freud (1856–1939), who was quite interested in religion's parallels with neurosis, Western scholars have been sensitive to the inner drives that set people to work, parenting, religion, and the many other aspects of human culture. For example, sexual satisfaction, acceptance by our peers, and a sense of control all play a part in our development of human culture. C. G. Jung (1875–1961) broke with Freud over the interpretation of sexual and religious drives. For Jung the second half of life tends to be a pursuit of meaning (giving one's time and experience coherence). Often the symbols people use in pursuing meaning are religious, so even today the psychoanalyst probing his patients' dreams can come upon archetypal symbols reminiscent of ancient religious mythologies.

If we generalize the sensitivity that recent psychological studies sharpen, the main point seems to be that we must stay alert to the complexity of human motivation. For example, in studying a holy man from the Hindu tradition, such as Mahatma Gandhi, we should realize that his asceticism had a basis in his adolescent sexual traumas and that his political ambitions were forged by his experiences of racial discrimination in young adulthood. At these formative times in his life cycle, Gandhi was tested to an unusual degree. He found himself unready for the erotic aspects of marriage, and his experience as a "colored" person in South Africa told him he had to champion India's oppressed.

If we so focus on psychological issues such as these that we neglect the history, sociology, economics, politics, and other aspects of Gandhi's life and times, we become reductionists, trying to squeeze all of reality onto the psychoanalyst's couch. On the other hand, if we neglect such inner demons and angels, we divorce ourselves from a powerful tool of understanding (probably because we do not want to face the similar demons and angels warring in our own souls). As usual, a balanced use is the ideal.

Just as scientific psychology is a fairly recent development, not available to scholars of religion a century ago, so is *sociology*. And just as the pioneer psychologists were quite interested in religion, so were pioneer sociologists such as Max Weber (1864–1920) and Emile Durkheim (1858–1917). In both cases, their interest was religion's role in making a group cohesive. The religious ideas of a tribe, or even a large culture, are always in part a projection of the tribe's or the culture's sense of its own identity. For example, Hindus have been people stratified by Vedic wisdom into four main social classes. Chinese have been people living at the center of the world in accordance with the *Tao* of nature and the ancient men of wisdom. Americans have been high-minded refugees come to make a place of justice and freedom in a new world. Thus neither Hindu caste nor Chinese misogyny nor American racism could be the patent inhumanity an outside observer might think it. Sacralizing the way they talked about themselves, all three peoples wrote their customs' heavenly approbations.

Recently cultural anthropologists such as Clifford Geertz and Victor Turner have tuned the interests of the classical sociologists more finely. Living in the midst of the societies they would interpret, they have sought the deep structures and threshold moments through which a people reveals how it constructs its world view. Geertz's study of the Balinese cockfight,[10] for example, is a marvel of sophisticated participant-observation. Sensitive to the drama of what he calls "deep play," Geertz makes the cockfight a microcosm of the Balinese thought-world.

A third methodological orientation popu-

lar in recent religious studies is the *historical*. One of the drawbacks of the psychological and sociological approaches is that they can seem to bracket time past (and time future), as though their analyses were moved by an Archimedean lever standing outside the flowing stories of either their subjects or themselves. But such ahistoricism obviously is fallacious. The self always enacts a story, a unique version of the common life cycle, and a society is always being pushed by its past and lured by its future. Since the modern discovery of evolution, and the rise of modern retrieval techniques such as archeology, the study of religion has become more historical, and so more faithful to the traditions' ongoing changes. Even the most conservative tradition alters in at least small ways, generation by generation. Though they perform the same rituals and tell the same myths, a people of any era understand themselves somewhat differently than their forebears did or their children will.

The good historian's goal is telling the story of these changes. Representing the past as most likely it was, the good historian brings her reader from point alpha to point omega. In the beginning, at the earliest point we can reconstruct, Buddhists understood Gautama in such and such a way. A thousand years later, when controversies inside the sangha had caused much debate, there were the three following major interpretations. Today, in Japanese Buddhism, the third of these interpretations prevails, due to such and such factors.

One thinks, then, of a continuum or a map. In the image of the continuum, the historian grants all centuries a certain equality, showing how Buddhism changed century by century. In the image of a map, the historian plots the journey from the Buddha's India to modern Japan, showing the geographic and cultural routes the dharma traveled. The result should be a sense of perspective and interrelationship. Alpha led on to beta, because of factor alpha prime, just as today omega seems to be leading on to omega-plus-one, because of factor omega prime.

Comstock's fourth methodological perspective is *phenomenological*. Referring to the work of scholars such as Geradus van der Leeuw (1890–1950), who have concentrated on the different *forms* that many religious traditions seem to share, we can emphasize the concern many phenomenologists have to find *typical* patterns that show up repeatedly across the full range of religious data. So, for example, sacred persons appear in most traditions. East and West, monks or ascetics or yogis have generated great veneration. One can distinguish among these three categories of holy persons, but they share an orientation away from worldly affairs, toward contemplation and self-discipline. The typical Hindu holy man fits the pattern of withdrawal, as does the typical Buddhist monk. In China and Japan, both Buddhism and Taoism prized withdrawal from worldly affairs, seclusion in order to grow better attuned to the dharma or the *Tao*.

Phenomenological studies therefore tend to stress the sameness of certain structural features, providing a basis for discussing how Hindu yogis differ from Buddhist monks, or how Eastern ascetics differ from Western ascetics. By grouping them together in general terms, we are stimulated to ask how they differ in particulars. The results of such inquiries can seldom be iron-clad, since there are usually exceptions to general trends, but the inquiries are very stimulating. (They are also very useful for orienting beginning students, so long as they remain flexible and open to exceptions. Our own categories of nature, society, self, and divinity owe more to a philosophical analysis of the constants in human experience than to a phenomenological description of how the religious traditions present themselves, but in part we have used these structural categories because they facilitate comparisons.)

Comstock's fifth methodological perspective is *hermeneutical*. If anything, this perspective has increased in importance since the time he made his survey. Hermeneutics is the study of interpretation. It concerns processes such as that by which a teacher from Massachusetts tries to explain to a student from Kansas what it was like to live in medieval China or India. In one sense,

hermeneutics applies to all parts of this communication. Even the gap between Massachusetts and Kansas can be significant. But the gap between twentieth-century America and medieval China or Japan is enormous. Thus, hermeneutics tends to be most concerned with how we can tease from texts or artifacts reliable interpretations of past or foreign cultures. The cultural anthropologists we mentioned have come to the forefront of the hermeneutical debates, but historians, psychologists, sociologists, and philosophers of language have also been prominent. These debates tend to get very technical, generating schools such as structuralism and subdisciplines such as semiotics, as well as a lot of bad writing. The scholarly end of the hermeneutical "turn" is not yet in sight, so its overall significance is still emerging.

For undergraduates, though, the gist of the hermeneutical perspective is clear enough: Try to be quite sensitive to the sources and ranges of the meanings you are studying. Above all, realize that in studying a text, or any other cultural artifact, you are involved in a two-way conversation. A text is not a brute object whose meanings are obvious to any beholder. Physically, a text is simply some marks on a piece of paper or some impressions in clay. To convey meaning, these marks have to "speak" from the mind of the person who set them down to the mind of people like you who are trying to pick them up. Thus, the languages and assumptions of both minds come into play, your own as much as the author's. You can assume that you and the author share a great deal, since you are both human, but you must be careful about how you deploy this assumption. The death of a child in T'ang China was both very like the death of a child in contemporary America, and very different. Thus, you are back to balancing the esoteric and the exoteric. Boiled down, hermeneutics is but walking the tightrope between sameness and difference.

THE USES OF RELIGION

The study of world religions suggests that religion has served several uses. Historically, most people have groped after meaning through a religious tradition. Even when they came to conclusions that differed from those of fellow traditionists (fellow Jews or fellow Christians, for instance), a tradition set before them their major questions. For example, Maimonides and Halevi evaluated reason differently, but their common Jewish tradition set them the question, How does reason relate to faith? Similarly, Aquinas and Bonaventure evaluated love differently, but their common Christian tradition set them Paul's dictum that love is the greatest of God's gifts. In those cases, unity probably predominated over difference, though when partisanship flamed, the difference generated great heat.

Jews, Christians, Hindus, and Buddhists also tried to be faithful to the unity that they glimpsed in diverse peoples. They all met peoples who did not accept their tradition—did not accept the Torah, Jesus, the Vedas, or Buddha. Such peoples sought a living, wept when they were in pain, and hoped for a happy future. They might have had funny customs, but they, too, worried about doing what was right. Sometimes they even came through with a surprising act of kindness. Even when they did not—when they were abrupt traders or harsh rulers—they expressed qualities one already knew from home: Fellow Hindus profiteered, fellow Christians kicked the dog.

Thus, the fact that people were members of particular religions and members of the human race made people aware that their cultures were both many and one. The notion of a universal humanity[11] may only have come to consciousness clearly in the ecumenical age, but people knew it instinctively long before that time. When sexual relations with a foreign slave begot a half-breed, people instinctively knew the falsity of racist biology. When a foreigner performed an act of kindness, prejudice had to loosen.

Because religion has been at the historical center of people's meaning systems, religion has played a key role in this dialectic of unity and difference, and this dialectic has played a key role in religion. When Francis Xavier met the Japanese, he thought that they were the most moral people in the

world. As a result, his notions of sin, grace, paganism, and hell were challenged. Centuries later, his fellow Jesuit Karl Rahner, building on experiences such as Xavier's, developed a theory he called the "supernatural existential."[12] Simply, it meant that no people live apart from grace.

A first value of religion, then, is that it prompts people to broaden their horizons. When it deals with a genuinely mysterious ultimate, religion makes all fellow humans brothers and sisters. (When it does not deal with a genuinely mysterious ultimate, we may infer, religion makes fellow humans slaves, victims, and enemies.)

A second value of religion is educational. From its station at the core of people's quests for meaning, religion can teach students of humanity behavior that reality can be both/and. For instance, religious wars have shown that faith can be *both* demonic *and* sanctifying. In Jewish, Christian, and Muslim faith, it has made for demonic faith a special symbol: holy war. Thus, Psalm 137 told Israelite soldiers to smash the heads of enemy babies against the wall. Thus, the Qur'an (8 : 68) instructed Muslim soldiers to slaughter and reap booty. Thus, American "Christian" soldiers found it fitting to destroy Vietnamese towns in order to save them. Muhammad, David, Saint Louis—they are all ambiguous warrior saints.

To be sure, religious battle is not monochromatic. In its time, the theory of a just war made much sense. There is an ambiguity about war, as there is an ambiguity about pacifism. Sensing the latter, Gandhi gave the opinion that it was better to fight than to choose pacifism out of cowardice. Films of British and Indian soldiers felling Gandhi's *satyagrahis* with clubs and rifle butts show that his opinion came from experience.

A similar both/and attends marriage, celibacy, the treatment of women, and the treatment of slaves. For instance, though slavery is almost wholly a stigma, some Muslim and Christian owners treated their slaves compassionately. The same is true of polygamous husbands—traditional African,

Muslim, and Mormon alike. For example, as Islam improved the lot of slaves at its outset, so it improved the general lot of wives.

Thus, a knowledge of religion stimulates a respect for human variety—for the wide spectrum between good and evil. As the religious philosophers who reflect on ultimate mystery find human beings quite alike, so the religious historians find that religious peoples are nearly equal in their diversity and complexity.

COMPARING THE ASIAN TRADITIONS

When we discussed some of the methodological perspectives scholars are using to study religion today, we tacitly assumed the diversity and complexity of the world religions. In principle, most contemporary methods are supposed to be "value-free," assuming that all traditions are equally human. In our view, this does not mean a scholar must refrain from all value judgments. We see no need to pass by Hindu caste, Chinese footbinding, or American racism with nary a discouraging word. We do see a need to explain how the traditions in which they occur see such phenomena and to make no assumptions that Indians or Chinese or Americans are more or less virtuous than other human tribes.

In this spirit, we shall attempt a summary comparison of the four traditions we have studied, assuming that they are equally human, equally complex, but trying to distill the unique character, advantages, and liabilities of each. This distillation is bound to reflect biases we do not fully appreciate, but so would any other comparison, as well as the decision not to make a comparison at all.

Placed side by side, Hinduism, Buddhism, Chinese religion, and Japanese religion are four asymmetrical traditions. Although each is dizzyingly complex, and arguably is complete unto itself, their dependencies upon one another are unequal. Hinduism generated a great deal of Buddhism, and continues to share a great deal with it, because of their common Indian roots. It shares much less with Chinese and Japanese religions. Buddhism shares much more with Chinese and Japanese religions, because of being transplanted to China and Japan. In the case of China, Buddhism set its seal very deeply, but in turn was influenced deeply by Taoism, and to a lesser extent by Confucianism. In Japan, Buddhism interacted with Shinto, receiving a further stimulus to focus on nature, and giving the Japanese love of nature a more profound philosophical underpinning. China and Japan themselves interacted, China having more cultural influence on Japan than Japan on China. Neither China nor Japan had a great cultural influence on India, but the lands between India and China often melded characteristics of the two. Thus Tibet, Burma, and Thailand sometimes seem to be mid-countries, whose scripts, architectures, and religions have creatively blended Chinese and Indian elements.

Generally, India has been the great land of interiority and speculation. China has been the great land of exteriority and practicality. That does not mean India did not farm, fight, and organize political units. It does not mean China did not meditate, worship, and philosophize. It just means that when one searches for that elusive thing called a country's peculiar "genius," one does not point to India's political organization, nor to China's metaphysics. Despite all its wars and internal divisions, China has been the land of order and bureaucracy. Despite all its trade and kingdoms, India has been the land of karma and transmigration. Where China fingered the world like a piece of fine cloth, something to be delicately appreciated, India thought about the world like a mathematical problem or a dramatic plot, something to be grasped mentally. "Planting our feet solidly," the Chinese said, "let us make here a family structure, a cuisine, an aesthetic, a technology that allows us to live harmoniously with nature and one another." "Since the world of the senses is doubtful," the Indians said, "let us plant our feet lightly, and keep our spirits free. Pleasure and wealth are legitimate life-goals, but duty and salvation are higher."

Of course, these are simplistic comparisons—almost caricatures. In venturing to make them, we do not deny they can be terribly abused. Indeed, we are reminded of the Western "negative" tradition, which taught that God is more unlike than like even our true statements about him (or her, or it). There is a cultural analogue: If one could get down to specific villages and individuals, our comparisons might prove more untrue than true. From the Goodyear blimp, however, the cultural contrasts we have made seem valid. India has been the more esoteric cultural basin, China the more exoteric.

The religious poles in this comparison would be philosophical Hinduism and Buddhism, on the esoteric side, and Confucianism, on the exoteric side. Devotional Hinduism and Buddhism, Taoism, and Shinto would occupy the intermediate ground. The cutting edge of Indian philosophy has been idealism—the priority of mind over matter. The cutting edge of Confucianism has been social realism—the priority of public affairs over private thoughts. In between, devotional Hinduism and Buddhism have worked the emotions and the imagination that mediate between human mentality and materiality. Taoism and Shinto have worked the nature spirits and human aesthetics that mediate between nature-centered humanity and political humanity. This does not mean Indian philosophers did not have to consider economics and statecraft. It does not deny Confucians made a place for meditation. It simply paints with the broad brush "summary reflections" suggests, responding to those students who come to "summary reflections" hoping their teachers finally will risk a few generalizations.

Of the Asian traditions, to which should you go for a penetrating theory of nature? You should go to Hinduism or Buddhism for an analysis of how "nature" comes to us through the senses, and to Chinese or Japanese religion for directives on how best to enjoy natural beauty. For the foundations of natural science, you should go outside the Asian orbit, to Greek philosophy and Western revelation, for they were the main sources of the confidence in nature's intelligibility necessary for what we have come to call "natural science."[13]

To which Asian tradition should you go to for a penetrating theory of society? You should go to Confucianism and Taoism. Confucianism taught that only moral virtue will make any political unit healthy. The great Confucian key is the quality of a village's or a country's rulers. If such rulers are learned and good, the village or country will prosper. To be learned, they must know the ways of the ancients, the giants who first saw the lay of the political land. To be good, they must attune themselves to the *Tao* of reality, disciplining selfishness, vanity, greed, and the other vices that keep us from walking the Way. The Way to social prosperity is "there," objectively available. If we have eyes to see and ears to hear, we can find it. But self-interest or seeking material profit so regularly blinds our eyes or deafens our ears that most of our social units wobble along in the ditch. Until inner goodness *(jen)* joins with gracious protocol *(li)*, our social relations will continue to go badly.

Taoism agreed with much of this deeper Confucianism, but Taoism was appalled by the Confucian tendency to make stuffed shirts. When lesser spirits trumpeted the Confucian tunes about inner goodness and outer protocol, legalism and bureaucracy multiplied like cancers. For the Taoists, imagination was the crucial difference. Unless we stay creative, our societies will bumble into dead ends or become impossibly boring. Only free spirits can keep the bureaucrats from driving us all to drink. Only wit, irony, satire, and creative musing can keep our politics free to see the point. The point is justice, fair-dealing, and the way to justice is *we-wei*: indirection, not-doing, the wink that's as good as a nod. Heavy-handedness, aggression, the lawyers' obsession with jots and tittles are the sure and rocky road to political disaster. People must be lured, seduced, beguiled into cooperation. Unless you have won their hearts and minds, you have lost the long-range game. Because we will not grasp these rather obvious truths, we get generation after generation of wars and fatuous politicians.

To which Asian tradition should you go for a penetrating theory of the self? You should go to Hinduism or Buddhism. Their common font of wisdom is the centrality of detachment. If the human self is to become free, it must detach itself from layer after layer of illusion. Although Hinduism and Buddhism disagree about the final layer, Hinduism tending to retain a "self" and Buddhism tending to deny it, they agree that the individual is wrongly situated until he connects himself with the All. Whether the All is Brahman or nirvana, it is the only adequate context for human self-understanding. If we do not understand the mysterious envelope in which we are sealed, we do not understand our most basic characteristic.

In Western terms, the analogue that comes to mind is Danish philosopher Sören Kierkegaard's view that the self is a relation relating itself to the Absolute. As a relation, my "I" is both a subject and an object: I can think about, reflect on, move myself. As a relation relating itself to the Absolute, my "I" moves its complex self toward God, whether it realizes this or not. For Kierkegaard, the great prod to grasping the human situation is sin, which shows itself in depression and despair. For Hinduism and Buddhism, the great prod is death, which shows itself in suffering and disease. Either way, the only solution is to realize, actualize, achieve what we are. Christian, Hindu, and Buddhist salvation all come from uniting the self with the All that lets the self be.

The Chinese and Japanese theories of the self have been more social and less profound. Behind that judgment, of course, is our conviction that social relations are less profound than the ontological (being) relation of the self to the Absolute. Many contemporary scholars would dispute this thesis, either speculatively or practically (either in their theories or the ways they choose to do their work). For them "the social construction of reality" makes all our selves intrinsically

dependent on the cultures in which we live, move, and have our being. We have no language without our culture, no economics or politics. Language, economics, and politics more shape religion or metaphysics than they derive from religion or metaphysics.

There is a lot to be said for this thesis, but we do not think it finally wins the day. For all the massive influence of our cultures, we remain people who can move from language to language, religion to religion, economic system to economic system. Contrariwise, we can never move away from our relation to Brahman, nirvana, or God, because this relation is constitutive, built into the depths of reflective intelligence (selfhood).

To which Asian tradition should you go for a penetrating theory of God? To devotional Hinduism or Zen. Devotional Hinduism, focused on Krishna or Shiva, spotlights the centrality of love. Binding the devotee to divinity with reasons of the heart, it makes religion a consuming passion. Zen Buddhism, pivoted on realizing one's union with nirvana, one's intrinsic knowledge-nature, unites the self with the divinity that is impersonal, the "God" that goes beyond our human tendency to limit the ultimate to what we can imagine or conceive. In silence, Zen sacramentalizes our ultimate, self-constituting relation. The result can be a wonderfully gracious living, cool, serene, and artistic. Such living says that God dances, paints, speaks herself forth in poetry. It says that God is art, science, and ineffable light.

THE SAGE AS EASTERN ARCHETYPE

If asked to paint a picture of the ideal product the Asian traditions were trying to develop, we would entitle it *The Sage*. Whereas the nonliterate traditions have tended to pivot on the shaman and the Western traditions have tended to pivot on the prophet, the Asian traditions have tended to pivot on the sage. To be sure, there have been shamans and prophets in India and East Asia, just as there have been sages in the West. But Buddha, Confucius, and Lao-tzu—the three most influential

Asian personalities—have all been more sagacious than prophetic. It will be useful, therefore, to reflect on the differences in the Asian traditions' understandings of sagehood and then on the message the Eastern sage offers students of the world religions today.

The Indian sage, Buddhist or Hindu, has tended to be a yogi. The *rishis* whose visions lay behind the Vedas, the Mahavira, and the Buddha all disciplined the flesh and the mind in order to win enlightenment and liberation. The Indian archetypal figure won his great wisdom by penetrating the veil of maya or samsara, by intuiting the reality of Brahman or Suchness. The popular tradition might embellish this victory with miracles and myths, but its core was yogic meditation. Meditation was the method, wisdom was the substance, and morality was the fruit. Archetypally, intuition *(jnana)* or trance *(dhyana)* were the principal yogas. *Karma yoga* (acting without attachment) and *bhakti yoga* (devotion) were accommodations, perfectly valid and effective for salvation, but spun off from the quieter core.

In East Asia, the sage had a more social inclination. For both Confucius and Lao-tzu, union with the *Tao* was a font of political order. One might say, therefore, that the East Asian sage was more prudent or ethical, the Indian sage more ontological. For example, there is little evidence that the Buddha aspired to political office. The world was burning; it would have been folly to plunge into worldly affairs. By contrast, Confucius greatly aspired to political office, or at least political counselorship. Like Plato, Confucius thought that good social order was the prime requisite and that good social order would only come when kings had sages for brains. From the demands of good social order, Confucius worked his way back to gentlemanliness, and then to *jen*, the heart of human nobility. By the time he was seventy, he could move nobly in all situations, letting his *jen* be the Way's embodiment. Thus a certain mysticism shines through Confucius's last relations with the Way. He could hear the Way in the morning and in the evening die content because the Way had become his meat and drink, the other half of his heart and soul.

Lao-tzu is initially more mystical than Confucius, but eventually just as political. For Lao-tzu, all power *(te)* comes from union with the Way, for the Way runs nature and society alike. Therefore, the sage shuts the doors of the senses and places his spirit in the Way. Therefore, the sage advocates *wu-wei*, reveres the uncarved block. Backing away from social conventions and hackneyed speech, the sage is alert, poetic, and paradoxical. To the ordinary run of people, he is an eccentric, always trying to see the world afresh. Chuang-tzu pushed this eccentricity further than Lao-tzu, delighting in affronting the sobersided Confucians. Soaring with the great birds, he was not surprised that the little birds found him very odd.

The deeper Confucians and Taoists joined with the East Asian Buddhist philosophers to make the sage's wisdom worldly. In the final frames of the Zen teaching pictures called *Herding an Ox*, the enlightened person comes back into the market place, able to enjoy nirvana in the midst of buying and selling, eating and drinking. Empty and gone beyond, the *Prajna-paramita* is as near as a blooming cherry blossom, as full as the rugged rocks. Wisdom swirls in the master's whipped green tea, whistles in the flight of the archer's arrow. The enlightened life is graceful, integrated, at home in the world. By the time the dharma reached the Pacific, the world was no longer burning. It had cooled in the mountains of the Sung landscapes, lost its fever in the Shinto pools. So pacified, it looked outward as much as inward, found rest on the keen edge of body-mind. It grew to love subtlety and indirection, tactfulness and play. "There is no good and evil," the Zen disciple heard. "All jobs are worth doing well." What is is what is in front of us. After enlightenment, mountains are mountains and trees are trees.

It is hard to imagine Indian Buddhists and Hindus comfortable with this East Asian worldliness. In Delhi, Bombay, and Calcutta, life remains very steamy, burning with misery. The grass around Hindu shrines is seldom immaculate. The water buffalo behind the Taj Mahal intrude an instructive dung and mud. Along with the blazing summer sun, they mock the sultan who thought the Taj would immortalize his lovely queen. The Taj will have crumbled long before the queen's soul has found rest.

Does the Eastern sage have a distinctive message for students of the world religions today? Perhaps so. If the students come from the West, they likely have been touched by the West's loss of confidence in wisdom. Western people who speak authoritatively about enlightenment, persuasively incarnate the *Tao*, are few and far between. So, an increasingly influential argument has arisen. "Since so few wise people appear in our midst," the argument runs, "wisdom must be an endangered species, going the way of the dodo. Evolution must be in the hands of the technicians, the marines shouting 'can do!' " Swiftly and surely, the Eastern sages rebut this argument. Let Lao-tzu occupy your mind a half-hour and the marines will lie high and dry. "What can you do?" Lao-tzu politely asks. "What is the end of all your technique? If your graphs do not bring you beauty, your tanks do not win you peace, why all your plotting and piloting?"

The Eastern sages are sufficiently concerned with technique—in meditation, painting, ritual, and many other things—to make it clear that they are not opposed to engineering. They are merely opposed to calling a spade a pearl. A spade should be called a spade: an instrument for digging. With a spade, you may dig in the earth and come up with a goodly treasure. If you want a pearl, especially one of great price, you will have to dive into the sea, go down deep to rebirth. It is his deep intelligence, his midmost mind, that gives Confucius his clout. Were he only to work the surface, to push and pull his facts, we could read Confucius like a newspaper. Similarly, it is *samadhi*, the deepest consciousness, that gives the yogi his freedom. Were he merely to sense or reason, we could watch him like daytime TV.

For the Indian and East Asian sages, the way up remains the way down. If you want to glimpse the heavenly *Tao* or consort with the glorified Buddha, you will have to return to yourself, find who you are, see your face before your parents were born. It is your inner space, your emptiness, that will make your house useful. To focus attention on your walls or roof is to miss your house's meaning. Similarly, it is its spiritual drama that makes your community significant. To focus on your community's moving and shaking is to miss what your people might be.

You do not like these quirky phrases? Paradoxes put you off? Ah well, no Eastern sage ever promised you a garden of platitudes. If you want a good guru, an abbot who knows his business, you will have to knock and knock and knock again. Easy admittance means superficial discipline. Superficial discipline means shallow learning. Shallow learning means specious enlightenment, and so the dharma's sickening. It is not cruelty that makes good gurus demanding. It is unusual kindness. In the spiritual life, you become what you do. In the spiritual life, outer persona and inner self must come closer and closer together.

"Consider yonder Bald Mountain," the sage Mencius said. "You know, once it was thick with trees. The mind of men is much the same. If they would nurture it, it would grow lush and very useful. But they neglect it, or abuse it, or hack it away without care, so it becomes barren and ugly, useless and an eyesore."

The *Dhammapada* begins: "Yesterday's thoughts make the self of today, and today's thoughts make the self of tomorrow, our life is the creation of our mind." Is the *Dhammapada* passé? Have we found shortcuts to beautiful selfhood on our way to the mushroom cloud?

No. Many people in many nations now lament the lack of vision, the venality, the smallsouledness in which they drown. But few Western people know that therapy is as near as the *Mencius*, as simple as the *Dhammapada*. You cannot have political vision if you never open your mind. You are bound to be venal and pusillanimous if you never feed your soul.

What doth it profit a person if she can assemble any stereo and never hears the music of the spheres? What doth it profit a person to place all his energies in the stock market? Stereos and the stock market have their place—all the Eastern sages allow them. What the Eastern sages do not allow them is primacy of place. If the *Tao* is in urine and dung, the *Tao* is in stereos and the stock market. But to hear the *Tao* in the morning or in the evening to die content, one must vacate assembling and selling. The business of life is not business. The business of life is being. If we want to prosper significantly, we must be open, collected, and disciplined—"one-pointed" in soul and mind. It does not matter that many of our schools know nothing of such Eastern wisdom. The college catalogue is seldom a great book. Real learning occurs in dark nights and painful passages. Wisdom to live by goes far below figures and facts.

"Leave off, Buddha and Chuang-tzu," you may be saying. "Confucius, give us a break." "So sorry," the sages respectfully answer. "We thought you were asking Asia to try to gladden your heart."

If our hearts are ever to gladden, we must give them something to love. If we listen to the Eastern sages, we will give them natural beauty, social order, and personal depth. Day by day, one day at a time, we will try to make time graceful, to empty space for landscapes of peace. In emptiness we may possess our souls. In graceful time, the *Tao* may sing. If today you would possess your soul, you must empty it of what is tawdry. If today you would hear the *Tao*, you must attune your inner ear.

Sagacious Politics

When Gandhi went looking to buttress *satyagraha*, his politics of truth-force, he settled on the fourth of the *Gita*'s yogas. Most useful to him was karma-yoga discipline—grasping ultimacy through selfless labor. He found it a high art, a trick hard to master. Can we engage in politics today as though spinning thread carelessly? Can an effective action not be concerned with the fruits of success? To Western ears, those are strange questions. On the other hand, is there any effective action that is attached, that is concerned with success? Don't we see again and again in the West that success mottles our work, that ego corrodes our politicians?

Thus, Gandhi's work dialectic sharpened his religion, honing it to a paradox. To become an instrument of truth, he saw, he had to lose self, ambition, concern. Bone weary with service, he had to count all his service as nothing. Yet, marvel of marvels, self-loss was energizing. It sent him on long marches to the sea, on long terms in prison. In his depths it evoked love for his enemies, help for those who persecuted him. Indeed, in his depths it did away with enemies and made his persecutors brethren.

If Gandhi had not freed a modern nation, we would count his *satyagraha* as so much hot air, but India used *satyagraha* to gain home rule (and then abused it to produce the Hindu-Muslim partition). Thus, we have to consider *satyagraha* quite real. In fact, we have to be humble enough to see in *satyagraha* one of Western religion's own truths about action: Work as though everything depended on God, and pray as though everything depended on yourself.

In the past few pages, we have taxed your patience, getting more than a little oracular in order to conjure how living religions actually speak. Such language perhaps shows a final utility that shamans, sages, and prophets have offered humankind— their capacity to shock sleepy humanity awake. The paramount religious figures have forced humanity to be more than animal by insisting that life is more than food and the body more than clothing. They above all have underscored the strange play of life and death that prompts deep reflection.

What is genuine living? What riches are valuable? Such questions can be cultural dynamite. For instance, if it is easier for a camel to pass through the eye of a needle than for a rich person to enter the kingdom of God, what happens to Judaism's blessing for wealth, Hinduism's permission for *artha*, the Mormon Tabernacle, and St. Peter's in Rome? Similarly, if it were better for Chuang-tzu to drag his tail in obscurity, like a turtle in mud, what happens to ambition, even to service, let alone to Chinese bureaucracy?

Seers, founders, and saints all qualify our instinctive values. Instinctively we all tell the mirror, "Prosper, fill your barn, appease your loins." The saints answer, "You fool! This night God may require your soul." Because of saints, we have been prompted to think that money, sex, and fame are not all. Confucius kept China aware that it might be better to pay court to heaven than to the stove.

But is this shock really useful? Does it do anything more than upset the slothful majority and tempt the upsetters to pride? Our answers to that question say a great deal about our own values. If there is nothing but cradle to grave, religious persons are of all the most to be pitied. If there is no nirvana in samsara, Zen bipeds are of all the most wingless. The merit in teasing the mind over paradoxes, in disciplining the heart to search out reasons, stands or falls by whether the examined life is more than sound and fury. At bottom, there are just the two ways that Deuteronomy foresaw. One is death to humanity—to reflection, making a self, freedom, and love. It is the way that denies the examined life, that denies faith. The other way—reflection, freedom, love—makes real life.

The choice between the two ways, between death and life, is inalienable: No one can make it for you. Even not to choose is a choice—a choice to drift. There is a time to drift, as there is a time to come ashore. To drift too long, though, is to choose against the deeper spirit, against the deeper life. Religion has the (painful) utility of forcing us to hear that we are not what we eat. We are what we choose to be. In Augustine's terms, we can choose love of self unto contempt of divine mystery, or love of divine mystery unto contempt of self. In the *Dhammapada*'s terms, we can choose thoughts that form our selves to suffering or that form our selves to joy.

The contempt in the second half of Augustine's dichotomy is not self-hatred. It is not tearing the psyche to keep the ego important. Rather, it is letting go, opening up, saying yes to a world one did not make and does not finally control. At the end of the life cycle, Erik Erikson says, the "virtue" (power) we most need is wisdom. Wisdom, then, is the ability to love life in the face of death, to say yes in the face of nature's no. Before old age, wisdom often is the ability to say yes in the face of the senses' no. Accordingly, we are hardly wise if the senses have been our only tutors.

The religions say that the senses are splendid—when they serve the spirit, the mind, and the heart. Then, a tree is just a tree in a quite different way. In enlightenment, all trees are sacramentals. In the illuminative way, basic human acts (eating, intercourse, washing, anointing) are sacraments. They make life good enough to merit a profound love in the face of death. They make

the golden mean, the Aryan middle way. The final utility of religion is that it can teach us how to die and how to live. For Plato, the love of wisdom was the art of dying. Plato was everything we require a religious sage to be. For Chuang-tzu, Taoism was the art of living. Chuang-tzu was everything we require a religious sage to be.

ON BEING AN AMERICAN CITIZEN OF THE RELIGIOUS WORLD

The first lesson that the world religions offer Americans is that America is not as important as Americans tend to think. Our 400 years of religious experience are not much beside India's 5,000. If our 6 percent of the world's population and almost 40 percent of the consumption of the world's raw materials are disproportionate, we need all the help we can get to help us become less important.

We are not advocating the suppression of patriotism. Few existing cultures are very old. Europeans or Asians who sniff because their cultures go back more centuries than ours are hardly less ridiculous than we. All nations need a perspective on world history. All nations need to see things "under the aspect of eternity."

For most Americans, religion has been Christianity, and Christianity has often pivoted on Jesus and the founder of one's own sect. In some cases the dark ages between those two personages stretch 1,800 years. For such sects, Catholics are not considered Christians, and Orthodox are beyond the pale. True, Americans modified this intolerance by coexisting with their neighbors. Almost all Americans, though, need a deep breath of cosmopolitan air.

The root of provincialism is what Erik Erikson calls "pseudospeciation"—pretending that we are the only true human beings. In the past, that "we" has been Chinese, Japanese, and Eskimos. It has been Boston Brahmins and Oklahoma dirt farmers. It has been Catholics who would never darken a Protestant church door, Orthodox who would

*Figure 20   The Underground Railroad, Charles T. Webber, courtesy of
The Cincinnati Art Museum.*

never visit a synagogue. Fortunately, we now know enough about the psychodynamics of pseudospeciation, largely through analyses of prejudice, to show that it has little to do with religion as such. In fact, we now know that genuine religion directly opposes pseudospeciation.

In most cases, pseudospeciation stems from a combination of fear and self-interest. We fear the universal humanity, the radical equality, that a pluralistic world implies. It would force us to shed our shells; it would snatch away our platform for boasting. Similarly, we fail to grasp notions such as the Christian Church because it is to our advantage that "in Christ" there be male and female (Gal. 3 : 28). We fail to enact the notion of a union of all nations, because it is to our advantage to dictate prices to the

world. Few of us are magnanimous willingly, textbook writers included.

If we Americans are to gain stature in religion's golden eye, we will have to become more realistic about time and space than we have tended to be. Throughout all time, most people have not been Americans, Christians, or whites, and any true God has blessed more lands than just ours. By today's standards, the colonial Puritans' "errand in the wilderness" was terribly naive. Those who launched it simply did not have our facts about human prehistory and human diversity. It was largely ignorance, then, that led them to locate salvation in New England. The same is true of those who proposed that America be God's new Israel. Sober students of American history wonder to what extent such notions were used to justify ravaging the Indians. Historians of religion stumble over the obvious fact that God's old Israel was perfectly well.[14]

If we deflate our egos, we may see things in better perspective. From the vantage point of the sun goddess Amaterasu, Americans have never been *the* holy people. Long before the whites, reds revered every striking American locale. Shortly after the whites, blacks became America's suffering servants. Unbeknownst to our pioneers, peoples in Asia were living lives of grace under pressure.

The only holy people, in religious perspective, are of the single race, the single species. All divisions make but partial stories. There is a dictum in religious studies that he or she who knows just one religion knows no religion. By that dictum Americans urgently need to study world religions; if only to determine our own identity, we need to know what others have been, what alternatives there were.

We have become used to speeches telling us that our government has only to be as good as its citizens for America to prosper. In too many political assemblies, churches, and synagogues, that is a palliative. It brings no health or distinction to the speaker or the audience. To a religious guru, it shows that the speaker ignores the human condition—the beginner's mind, the nature of enlightenment. Unreflective, unmeditative, the speaker cannot be terse, poetic, evocative; he or she can only pour forth the old, stale, placating language. Ignorant of ignorance and sin, the speaker sees no tragedy. Lacking rigor, stupid in the reasons of the heart, the speaker thinks hope is found in good cheer.

Much the same is true of the audience, of ourselves. Not having gone down in spiritual death, we do not fly to the gods. Not set for spiritual combat, we do not resent that the seats are plush, the rhetoric easy. In part, that is because our culture tells us that only eggheads knit their brows and ponder. In part, it is because we are too lazy to live. It is a major accomplishment for us to endure ten minutes of silence.

From a religious perspective, the economics of American popular culture—the money we pay entertainers, athletes, and business executives—is obscene. Compared to what we pay the people who shape our nation's soul—the artists, scientists, nurses, teachers, and mothers—it is what Aeschylus called *nosos*—spiritual madness. Compared to how we treat the world's starving, it is beyond expression. Two thousand years ago, the *Book of Mencius* began by condemning profit. Wise persons would have taken that lesson and banked it. We, however, have built a culture on profit. It is what makes our Sammy and Sally run. When will we see that they are running in circles?

People who say things that others do not want to hear, no matter how true such things may be, will suffer for their indiscretion. Socrates stands as the paradigm of their fate, and Socrates shows that in the political realm, prophets and sages are one. He also shows that prophets and sages cannot live for audience applause. They must do what they have to do, say what they have to say, because it is their truth, their good, their charge. Shamans, for instance, must sing—because it relieves their sadness, because it makes them whole. Plato's "Seventh Letter" says that the philosophical soul must live by a love of the Good, that it can only deny the Good by denying its self. Religious people, creative people, humanity's benefactors—they have all found something more precious than human praise. Better, they have all been found by something more precious.

That something is the sacred, the numinous, the holy, the really real. It is Wakan Tanka, the *Tao*, Buddha-nature, God. Commonly, it is the essence of any conviction significant in the ultimate order, in the world as it finally is. The world as it finally is is the one place where you get what you are. It is where someone may finally tell you, "If you do not believe in mystery, God, or the *Tao*, be honest about it." By doing so you will reap two benefits. First, you will not bring those realities into further disrepute. Second, you will take the first step in the pilgrimage toward wisdom—simple honesty.

A second step is no less simple or heroic. It is to love the truth that you see. That may be the truth that mystery is beautiful or the truth that the religions often cant. It may move you to sound the ram's horn or to void at the flag. The point is not so much the content as the act. The dynamic of human consciousness, on which any genuine wisdom takes its stand, is a movement from one's present light to wherever that light leads. "Lead kindly light," Cardinal Newman and others have prayed. Go to your light's source, Augustine and others have counseled. Your light shines in the darkness, and the darkness cannot overcome it—so long as you want to be human, so long as samsara is not your all.

Whatever is noble, whatever is good, whatever is honest—think on it, Paul said. Whatever is your current belief about American religion, face it and start to love it. If it is a solid truth, your personality will ripen, your social circle will take fire. If it is a rotten pseudotruth, you will hear a call to turn and change your heart. In the spiritual life, the only disaster is avoidance. Because they will not face their own beliefs, whether solid or rotten, many stay half-asleep.

Thus, human consciousness becomes intrinsically religious by pursuing the light to where it is love. Worthy religious traditions and patriotism have nothing to fear from this pursuit. The pursuer does have some things to fear, but they pale in comparison with what there is to gain. In Eastern terms, the pursuer learns about ignorance: how much is samsaric in his or her starting "truth." In Western terms, the pursuer learns about sin: how difficult it is to follow only the light. Why we do not know the good we should know, why we do not do the good we should do—they are among our deepest mysteries. Only when you ponder them can you call yourself mature, let alone wise. Still, understanding these mysteries is the major therapy that any self needs. Understanding them is the heart of traditional political science.

However, the religions' dharma and prophecy illumine more than ignorance and sin. Ultimately they lead to enlightenment and grace. Enlightenment happens: It is an empirical fact. Light floods some people, bringing them inexpressible joy. Similarly, grace happens: There are marvelous saints. They love God with whole mind, heart, soul, and strength. They serve sisters and brothers more than themselves.

In a dark and troubled time (that is, in any historical time), saints and enlightened people save our beleaguered hope. Just one of them is stronger than all the rubbish, all the valid ground for cynicism. For a single really holy, really religious, really humane person says that what we want and need is possible. We want and need light and love. Light and love are possible. By definition, light and love are Buddha-nature and God, our center.

Study Questions

1. To what extent do the religions share a common attraction toward mystery?

2. Explain the following: "The final utility of religion is that it can teach us how to die and how to live."

3. Write a brief definition of *religion* that takes into account the traditions' unity and the traditions' diversity.

4. What do you think is the most profitable methodological perspective for studying the world religions? Explain your choice.

5. Why did East Asia no longer find the world to be on fire?
6. What are the major assets and liabilities of the Eastern archetypal personality?
7. Why is religious language bound to be paradoxical?

Appendix A
One Hundred Key Dates in World Religious History

4.6 billion years ago	Formation of the earth	800–400	Upanishads
		750	Homer and Hesiod written down
500,000 years ago	Homo erectus using fire	750–550	Hebrew Prophets
		ca. 628–551	Zoroaster
100,000 years ago	Homo sapiens: ritual burial	599–527	Mahavira, founder of Jainism
		586	Fall of southern kingdom (Judah)
50,000 years ago	Homo sapiens in Australia	551–479	Confucius
		536–476	Buddha
30,000 years ago	Prehistoric painting and sculpture; Mongoloid peoples cross Bering Strait	525	Persian conquest of Egypt
		525–406	Aeschylus, Sophocles, Euripides
8,000–6,000 B.C.E.	Agriculture, domestication of animals, rise of towns	500–200	*Mahabharata, Ramayana, Bhagavad Gita*
4500	Early Jomon period of hunting and gathering in Japan	427–347	Plato
		350	*Tao Te Ching*
4000	Casting of bronze	331	Alexander conquers Palestine
3500	Invention of wheel; Megalith cultures in Britain and Iberia	273–236	Asoka
		200	Rise of religious Taoism
3100	Unification of Egypt; Invention of writing in Sumer	80	Buddhist decline in India
		50	Formation of Buddhist canon
3000	Farming in central Africa	5 C.E.	Building of Japanese National Shrine at Ise
2750	Growth of civilization in Indus Valley	30	Death of Jesus of Nazareth
1600	Shang Bronze Culture in China	50–95	New Testament writings
1570–1165	New Kingdom in Egypt	70	Romans destroy Jerusalem
1500	Vedas, Rise of Iranian-speaking peoples	80–110	Canonization of Hebrew Bible
1200	Exodus of Hebrews from Egypt	220–552	Buddhist missions to China and Japan
1000	Colonization of Arctic	304–589	Huns fragment China
900	Nubian kingdom of Kush		

325	First Ecumenical Council at Nicaea
400	Fall of Indian Gupta dynasty
451	Council of Chalcedon
500	Compilation of Babylonian Talmud
570–632	Muhammad
637	Islamic invasion of Persia
645	Taika reform—Japan takes Chinese model
650	Canonization of Qur'an
700	Golden Age of Chinese poetry
712–720	Shinto Chronicles
749	First Buddhist monastery in Tibet
750–1258	Abbasid caliphate
762	Foundation of Baghdad
787	Second Council of Nicaea
788–820	Shankara
800–900	Rise of Hindu orthodoxy
845	Persecution of Chinese Buddhists
966	Foundation of Cairo
1054	Mutual anathemas of Rome and Constantinople
1058–1111	Al-Ghazali
1130–1200	Chu Hsi, leading Neo-Confucian
ca. 1135	Maimonides
1175	First Muslim empire in India
1175–1253	Introduction of Pure Land, Zen, and Nichiren schools in Japan
1225–1274	Thomas Aquinas
1453	Ottoman Turks capture Constantinople
1469–1539	Nanak, founder of Sikhism
1473–1543	Nicolaus Copernicus
1492	Expulsion of Jews from Spain
1517	Luther's ninety-five theses
1526–1707	Islamic Mogul Dynasty in India
1549	Francis Xavier in Japan
1565	Roman Catholic colony at St. Augustine
1585	Matteo Ricci in China
1619	Beginning of black slavery in colonial America
1620	Mayflower Compact
1654	Jewish settlement at New Amsterdam
1734	First Great Awakening in New England
1801	Beginnings of revivalism in western United States
1809–1882	Charles Darwin
1818–1883	Karl Marx
1856–1939	Sigmund Freud
1868–1871	Meiji persecution of Buddhism
1869–1948	Mahatma Gandhi
1879–1955	Albert Einstein
1880–1913	Partition of Africa by Western powers
1893	World Parliament of Religions in Chicago
1893–1977	Mao Tse-tung
1894–1905	Japanese victorious in wars with China and Russia
1910	Beginning of Protestant ecumenical movement
1933–1945	Nazi persecution of Jews
1945	Japanese surrender; Disestablishment of Shinto
1947	Partition of Pakistan from India
1948	Creation of state of Israel
1954–1956	Sixth Buddhist Council, Rangoon
1962–1965	Second Vatican Council
1964	Civil Rights Act in United States

Notes

Introduction

[1] This story is adapted from the Dutch Catholic bishops' work, *A New Catechism* (New York: Herder and Herder, 1967), p. 3.

[2] See Michael Polanyi, *Personal Knowledge* (New York: Harper Torchbooks, 1964); Stephen Toulmin, *Human Understanding* (Princeton, N.J.: Princeton University Press, 1977). For a discussion of Western religion and the distinctive rise of Western science, see Stanley L. Jaki, *The Road of Science and the Ways to God* (Chicago: University of Chicago Press, 1978).

[3] Philip Kapleau, *The Three Pillars of Zen* (Boston: Beacon Press, 1967), pp. 189–291.

[4] For example, Heinz Robert Schlette, *Toward a Theology of Religions* (New York: Herder and Herder, 1966).

[5] Another view of theology, geared to its easier practice in the university, is Shubert Ogden's "Theology and Religious Studies: Their Difference and the Difference It Makes," *JAAR*, 1978, 46(1):3–17.

[6] John Carmody, "Faith in Religious Studies," *Communio*, 1976, 3(1):39–49.

[7] Mircea Eliade, *Shamanism* (Princeton, N.J.: Princeton University Press, 1964), pp. 3–13.

[8] Odd Nordland, "Shamanism as an Experiencing of the 'Unreal,'" in *Studies in Shamanism*, ed. Carl-Martin Edsman (Stockholm: Almquist and Wiksell, 1967), pp. 166–185.

[9] Arthur Waley, *The Nine Songs* (London: Allen & Unwin, 1955).

[10] Ichiro Hori, *Folk Religion in Japan* (Chicago: University of Chicago Press, 1968), p. 181.

[11] I. M. Lewis, *Ecstatic Religion* (Middlesex, England: Penguin, 1971).

[12] John Neihardt, *Black Elk Speaks* (Lincoln: University of Nebraska Press, 1961), p. 20.

[13] Napoleon Chagnon, *Yanomamo: The Fierce People* (New York: Holt, Rinehart and Winston, 1968), p. 52.

[14] Some of the usual methods of structural analysis are surveyed in Frederick J. Streng, *Understanding Religious Life*, 2nd ed. (Encino, Calif.: Dickenson, 1976). More directly influential on this work is Eric Voegelin, *Anamnesis* (Notre Dame, Ind.: University of Notre Dame Press, 1978).

[15] This cognitional theory is most fully elaborated in Bernard J. F. Lonergan, *Insight: A Study of Human Understanding* (New York: Philosophical Library, 1958).

Chapter One

[1]Troy Wilson Organ, *Hinduism* (Woodbury, N.Y.: Barron's, 1974), p. 40; see also Thomas Hopkins, *The Hindu Religious Tradition* (Encino, Calif.: Dickenson, 1971), pp. 3–10; A. L. Basham, *The Wonder That Was India* (New York: Grove Press, 1959), pp. 10–30.

[2]R. N. Dandekar, "Hinduism," in *Historia Religionum, II*, ed. C. J. Bleeker and G. Widengren (Leiden: E. J. Brill, 1971), p. 241; see also Wendy Doniger O'Flaherty, *Asceticism and Eroticism in the Mythology of Shiva* (New York: Oxford University Press, 1973), pp. 8–11.

[3]On the earliest history and religion of the Indian Aryans, see Mircea Eliade, *A History of Religious Ideas*, vol. 1, *From the Stone Age to the Eleusinian Mysteries* (Chicago: University of Chicago Press, 1978), pp. 186–199.

[4]Organ, *Hinduism*, p. 51.

[5]See Edward C. Dimock, Jr., et al., *The Literature of India: An Introduction* (Chicago: University of Chicago Press, 1978), pp. 1–2. Also Satsvarupta dasa Gosvami, *Readings in Vedic Literature* (New York: Bhaktivedanta Book Trust, 1977), pp. 3–4. For an overview of Vedic literature, see James A. Santucci, *An Outline of Vedic Literature* (Missoula, Mont.: Scholars Press), 1976.

[6]Most youths who received the classical training were male. However, there are some indications that in early Hinduism young women could be well educated. For a general view of women in Hinduism, see Denise Lardner Carmody, *Women and World Religions* (Nashville, Tenn.: Abingdon, 1979), pp. 39–65.

[7]On the polarity of the *asuras* and *devas* in Vedic religion, see F. B. J. Kuiper, "The Basic Concept of Vedic Religion," *HR*, 1975, 15(2):111.

[8]Stella Kramrisch, "The Indian Great Goddess," *HR*, 1975, 14(4):235–265. As an introduction to the complexity of the Hindu order of the gods, see J. Bruce Long, "Daksa: Divine Embodiment of Creative Skill," *HR*, 1977, 17(1):29–60.

[9]See Organ, *Hinduism*, p. 66.

[10]See Eliade, *History of Religious Ideas*, vol. 1, pp. 213–214; see also O'Flaherty, *Asceticism and Eroticism*, p. 83; J. Gonda, *Visnuism and Sivaism* (London: Athlone Press, 1970), pp. 1–17.

[11]Hopkins, *Hindu Religious Tradition*, pp. 19–35.

[12]Mircea Eliade, *Histoire des croyances et des idées religieuses*, vol. 2, *De Gautama Bouddha au triomphe du Christianisme* (Paris: Payot, 1978), p. 194.

[13]Robert Ernest Hume, *The Thirteen Principal Upanishads* (New York: Oxford University Press, 1971), pp. 5–13.

[14]Organ, *Hinduism*, p. 102.

[15]See R. C. Zaehner, *Hinduism* (New York: Oxford University Press, 1966), pp. 57–79; see also K. Sivaraman, "The Meaning of *Moksha* in Contemporary Hindu Thought and Life," in *Living Faiths and Ultimate Goals*, ed. S. J. Samartha (Maryknoll, N.Y.: Orbis, 1974), pp. 2–11.

[16]See Robert Ernest Hume, *The Thirteen Principal Upanishads*, 2nd ed., rev. (New York: Oxford University Press Paperback, 1971), pp. 362–365.

[17]For a comparison of the Vedic and Upanishadic mystiques, see S. N. Dasgupta, *Hindu Mysticism* (New York: Frederick Ungar, 1959), pp. 3–57.

[18]Max Weber, *The Religion of India* (New York: Free Press, 1967), pp. 3–54.

[19]See Eliade, *Histoire des croyances*, vol. 2, pp. 151–153.

[20]Heinrich Zimmer, *Philosophies of India* (Princeton, N.J.: Princeton University Press, 1969), pp. 227–234.

[21]For a brief summary of Jainism, see Carlo Della Casa, "Jainism," in *Historia Religionum, II*, ed. C. J. Bleeker and G. Widengren (Leiden: E. J. Brill, 1971), pp. 346–371; see also A. L. Basham, "Jainism," in *The Concise Encyclopedia of Living Faiths*, ed. R. C. Zaehner (Boston: Beacon Press, 1967), pp. 261–266.

[22]See Dasgupta, *Hindu Mysticism*, pp. 113–168.

[23]Organ, *Hinduism*, p. 150; see also David R. Kinsley, *The Sword and the Flute* (Berkeley: University of California Press, 1975), pp. 1–78.

[24]See John Stratton Hawley, "Thief of Butter, Thief of Love," *HR*, 1979, 18(3):203–220.

[25]See Kinsley, *Sword and the Flute*; see also Basham, *Wonder That Was India*, pp. 304–306.

[26]Franklin Edgerton, *The Bhagavad Gita* (New York: Harper Torchbooks, 1964), p. 105; see also R. C. Zaehner, *The Bhagavad-Gita* (New

York: Oxford University Press, 1973), pp. 1–41; Ann Stanford, *The Bhagavad Gita* (New York: Seabury, 1970), pp. vii–xxvii; Juan Mascaró, *The Bhagavad Gita* (Baltimore: Penguin, 1962), pp. 9–36; Gerald James Larson, "The *Bhagavad Gita* as Cross-Cultural Process," *JAAR*, 1975, *43*(4): 651–669.

[27]O'Flaherty, *Asceticism and Eroticism*, pp. 83–110. For specimens of later Dravidian devotional Shaivism, see R. K. Ramanujan, *Speaking of Siva* (Baltimore: Penguin, 1973).

[28]See Roy C. Amore and Larry D. Shin, eds., *Lustful Maidens and Ascetic Kings* (New York: Oxford University Press, 1981), pp. 74–76.

[29]See ibid., pp. 166–168.

[30]Dimock et al., *Literature of India*, p. 2.

[31]Organ, *Hinduism*, p. 182.

[32]See Cornelia Dimmitt and J. A. B. van Buitenen, eds., *Classical Hindu Mythology* (Philadelphia: Temple University Press, 1978), pp. 38–41.

[33]Zaehner, *Hinduism*, pp. 57–79.

[34]Selections in Sarvepalli Radhakrishnan and Charles A. Moore, eds., *A Sourcebook in Indian Philosophy* (Princeton, N.J.: Princeton University Press, 1957), pp. 184–189.

[35]On the "tripartite Indo-European ideology" (priests-warriors-farmers) that Georges Dumézil has found at the root of Aryan society, see Eliade, *History of Religious Ideas*, vol. 1, pp. 192–195.

[36]See Radhakrishnan and Moore, *Sourcebook in Indian Philosophy*, pp. 193–223.

[37]Sudhir Kakar, "The Human Life Cycle: The Traditional Hindu View and the Psychology of Erik H. Erikson," *Philosophy East and West*, 1968, *18*:127–136; see also Basham, *Wonder That Was India*, p. 158.

[38]Basham, *Wonder That Was India*, pp. 177–188.

[39]On the six orthodox schools, see Radhakrishnan and Moore, *Sourcebook in Indian Philosophy*, pp. 349–572; Zimmer, *Philosophies of India*, pp. 280–332 (Samkyha and Yoga), 605–614.

[40]Rudolf Otto, *Mysticism East and West* (New York: Macmillan, 1970).

[41]See Zaehner, *Hinduism*, pp. 36–56; see also R. C. Zaehner, *Hindu and Muslim Mysticism* (New York: Schocken, 1969), pp. 41–63.

[42]Charles S. J. White, "Mother Guru: Jnanananda of Madras, India," in *Unspoken Worlds: Women's Religious Lives in Non-Western Cultures*, ed. N. A. Falk and R. M. Gross (San Francisco: Harper & Row, 1980), p. 23.

[43]Ibid., p. 27.

[44]See Dimmitt and van Buitenen, *Classical Hindu Mythology*, pp. 59–146.

[45]Glenn E. Yocum, "Shrines, Shamanism, and Love Poetry," *JAAR*, 1973, *61*(1):3–17.

[46]See Zaehner, *Hindu and Muslim Mysticism*, pp. 64–85.

[47]On the Puranic Shiva, see Dimmitt and van Buitenen, *Classical Hindu Mythology*, pp. 59–146. On Shiva in the Tamil literature, see Glenn E. Yocum, "Manikkavacar's Image of Shiva," *HR*, 1976, *16*(1):20–41.

[48]Organ, *Hinduism*, p. 288.

[49]See Zimmer, *Philosophies of India*, pp. 560–602; see also Kees W. Bolle, *The Persistence of Religion* (Leiden: E. J. Brill, 1965); Mircea Eliade, *Yoga: Immortality and Freedom* (Princeton, N.J.: Princeton University Press, 1970), pp. 200–273.

[50]Ernest Wood, *Yoga* (Baltimore: Pelican, 1962), pp. 140–147; see also Eliade, *Yoga*, pp. 244–249.

[51]For a brief survey of Sikhism, see Kushwant Singh, "Sikhism," in *Historical Atlas of the Religions of the World*, ed. I. al Faruqi and D. Sopher (New York: Macmillan, 1974), pp. 105–108; see also John Noss, *Man's Religions* (New York: Macmillan, 1974), pp. 226–235.

[52]However, see Cyrus R. Pangborn, "The Ramakrishna Math and Mission," in *Hinduism: New Essays in the History of Religions*, ed. Bardwell L. Smith (Leiden: E. J. Brill, 1976), pp. 98–119.

[53]See Organ, *Hinduism*, pp. 319–325.

[54]Nervin J. Hein, "Caitanya's Ecstasies and the Theology of the Name," in *Hinduism: New Essays in the History of Religions*, ed. Bardwell L. Smith (Leiden: E. J. Brill, 1976), pp. 15–32; Joseph T. O'Connell, "Caitanya's Followers and the Bhagavad-Gita," in *Hinduism: New Essays in the History of Religions*, ed. Bardwell L. Smith (Leiden: E. J. Brill, 1976), pp. 33–52.

55See Edward C. Dimock, Jr., and Denise Levertov, trans., *In Praise of Krishna* (Garden City, N.Y.: Doubleday, 1967).

56Following are some representative works: Swami Prabhupada, *The Nectar of Devotion* (Los Angeles: Bhaktivedanta Book Trust, 1970); *Krishna: The Supreme Personality of Godhead*, 3 vols. (Los Angeles: Bhaktivedanta Book Trust, 1970). On the Hare Krishna movement, see J. Stillson Judah, *Hare Krishna and the Counterculture* (New York: Wiley, 1974).

57Radical feminist Mary Daly has recently exposed the full horror of suttee; see Mary Daly, *Gyn/Ecology* (Boston: Beacon Press, 1979), chap. 3.

58For brief selections from the leading Indian voices of the past century, see Ainslee T. Embree, *The Hindu Tradition* (New York: Vintage, 1972), pp. 278–348.

59See Walker G. Neevel, Jr., "The Transformations of Sri Ramakrishna," in *Hinduism: New Essays in the History of Religions*, ed. Bardwell L. Smith (Leiden: E. J. Brill, 1976), pp. 53–97.

60Joan Bondurant, *Conquest of Violence*, rev. ed. (Berkeley: University of California Press, 1965).

61Erik H. Erikson, *Gandhi's Truth* (New York: Norton, 1969).

62See Mohandas K. Gandhi, *An Autobiography: The Story of My Experiments with Truth* (Boston: Beacon Press, 1957).

63See Adrian C. Mayer, *Caste and Kinship in Central India: A Village and Its Region* (Berkeley: University of California Press, 1960), pp. 99–102.

64Gerald D. Berreman, *Hindus of the Himalayas: Ethnography and Change*, new extended ed. (Berkeley: University of California Press, 1972), p. 89.

65James M. Freeman, "The Ladies of Lord Krishna: Rituals of Middle-Aged Women in Eastern India," in *Unspoken Worlds* (note 42), pp. 110–126.

66Eliade, *Yoga*, pp. 47–100.

67Dasgupta, *Hindu Mysticism*, pp. 3–30, 33–57, 141–168.

68Basham, *Wonder That Was India*, pp. 74–231.

69Kuiper, "Basic Concept of Vedic Religion"; see also Bruce Lincoln, "The Indo-European Myth of Creation," *HR*, 1975, *15*(2): 121–145.

70Basham, *Wonder That Was India*, p. 153.

71Zaehner, *Hinduism*, p. 102.

72Vern L. Bullough, *The Subordinate Sex* (Baltimore: Penguin, 1974), pp. 230–231.

73See Basham, *Wonder That Was India*, pp. 186–188.

74Noss, *Man's Religions*, p. 188. On the role model that the *Mahabharata* described for women in Draupadi, see Nancy Auer Falk, "Draupadi and the Dharma," in *Beyond Androcentrism*, ed. Rita M. Gross (Missoula, Mont.: Scholars Press, 1977), pp. 89–114. For a sensitive fictional treatment of the modern Indian woman, see Kamala Markandaya, *Nectar in a Sieve* (New York: Signet, 1954).

75Bullough, *Subordinate Sex*, p. 232.

76Reference in Organ, *Hinduism*, p. 387.

77Basham, *The Wonder That Was India*, p. 160.

78Reference in Organ, *Hinduism*, p. 29.

79For example, Gandhi, *Autobiography*, p. 8.

80See Basham, *Wonder That Was India*, pp. 324–325.

81A popular version is that by Swami Prabhavanada and Christopher Isherwood, *How to Know God* (New York: Mentor, 1969). The commentary is from the viewpoint of Vedanta, whereas Patanjali's own philosophy was Samkhya.

82Wendy Doniger O'Flaherty, *The Origins of Evil in Hindu Mythology* (Berkeley: University of California Press Paperback, 1980), p. 5.

83Ibid., p. 375.

84See David Kinsley, "The Portrait of the Goddess in the Devi-mahatmya," *JAAR*, 1978, *46*(4):489–506.

85A good reminder that most Hindus have not directly known or followed the high literary tradition is found in Philip H. Ashby, *Modern Trends in Hinduism* (New York: Columbia University Press, 1974), pp. 7–24.

[86]See Rita M. Gross, "Hindu Female Deities as a Resource for the Contemporary Rediscovery of the Goddess," *JAAR*, 1978, *46*(3):269–291. On the methodological aspects, see Gross's "Androcentrism and Androgyny in the Methodology of History of Religions," in *Beyond Androcentrism*, ed. Rita M. Gross (Missoula, Mont.: Scholars Press, 1977), pp. 7–21.

[87]Kinsley, *The Sword and the Flute* (note 23), pp. 111–112.

Chapter Two

[1]Phillip Kapleau, *The Three Pillars of Zen* (Boston: Beacon Press, 1967), pp. 10–11.

[2]Richard H. Robinson and Willard L. Johnson, *The Buddhist Religion* (Encino, Calif.: Dickenson, 1977), p. 13; see also Trevor Ling, *The Buddha* (London: Temple Smith, 1973), pp. 37–83; Mircea Eliade, *Histoire des croyances et des idées religieuses*, vol. 2, *De Gautama Bouddha au triomphe des Christianisme* (Paris: Payot, 1978), p. 174.

[3]Edward Conze, *Buddhist Scriptures* (Baltimore: Penguin, 1959), p. 34; see also Eliade, *Histoire des croyances*.

[4]Conze, *Buddhist Scriptures*, pp. 48–49; see also Lowell W. Bloss, "The Taming of Mara," *HR*, 1978, *18*(2):156–176.

[5]Robinson and Johnson, *Buddhist Tradition*, p. 28.

[6]Ibid., p. 31; see also Edward J. Thomas, *The History of Buddhist Thought* (New York: Barnes & Noble, 1951), pp. 58–70; Henry Clarke Warren, *Buddhism in Translations* (New York: Atheneum, 1973), pp. 202–208.

[7]See William Theodore de Bary, ed., *The Buddhist Tradition* (New York: Vintage, 1972), pp. 15–20; see also Edward Conze, *Buddhism: Its Essence and Development* (New York: Harper Torchbooks, 1959), pp. 43–48; I. B. Horner, "Buddhism: The Theravada," in *The Concise Encyclopedia of Living Faiths*, ed. R. C. Zaehner (Boston: Beacon Press, 1967), pp. 283–293.

[8]See Winston L. King, *In the Hope of Nibbana: Theravada Buddhist Ethics* (LaSalle, Ill.: Open Court, 1964).

[9]Texts on wisdom, morality, and meditation are available in Stephen Beyer, *The Buddhist Experience* (Encino, Calif.: Dickenson, 1974); see also Conze, *Buddhist Scriptures*.

[10]Edward Conze, *Buddhist Meditation* (New York: Harper Torchbooks, 1969); see also Nyanaponika Thera, *The Heart of Buddhist Meditation* (London: Rider, 1969).

[11]John Bowker discusses this rather creatively; see John Bowker, *The Religious Imagination and the Sense of God* (Oxford: Clarendon Press, 1978), p. 244; see also Willis Stoesz, "The Buddha as Teacher," *JAAR*, 1978, *46*(2): 139–158.

[12]We have adapted H. C. Warren's presentation of the Fire Sermon. See his *Buddhism in Translations* (note 6), pp. 351–353.

[13]See I. B. Horner, "The Teaching of the Elders," in *Buddhist Texts through the Ages*, ed. Edward Conze (New York: Harper Torchbooks, 1954), pp. 17–50. Also Warren, *Buddhism in Translations*, p. 392; Charles S. Prebish, ed., *Buddhism: A Modern Perspective* (University Park: Pennsylvania State University Press, 1975), pp. 16–26, 49–53; Conze, *Buddhism: Its Essence and Development*, pp. 53–69; Beyer, *Buddhist Experience*, pp. 65–73.

[14]On the laity, see Conze, *Buddhism: Its Essence and Development*, pp. 70–88.

[15]See Conze, *Buddhist Scriptures*, pp. 182–183.

[16]See Robinson and Johnson, *Buddhist Religion*, pp. 34–38; on early Indian Buddhist folk religion, see Lowell W. Bloss, "The Buddha and the Naga," *HR*, 1973, *13*(1):36–53.

[17]See Prebish, *Buddhism: A Modern Perspective*, pp. 29–45; see also Edward Conze, *Buddhist Thought in India* (Ann Arbor, Mich.: Ann Arbor Paperbacks, 1967), p. 121; Janice J. Nattier and Charles S. Prebish, "Mahasamghika Origins: The Beginnings of Buddhist Sectarianism," *HR*, 1977, *16*(3):237–272.

[18]Robinson and Johnson, *Buddhist Religion*, p. 77; see also John S. Strong, "Gandhakuti: The Perfumed Chamber of the Buddha," *HR*, 1977, *16*(4):390–406.

[19]Robinson and Johnson, *Buddhist Religion*, p. 81.

[20]Mircea Eliade, *Yoga: Immortality and Freedom* (Princeton, N.J.: Princeton University Press, 1969), pp. 162–199; see also S. N. Das-

gupta, *Hindu Mysticism* (New York: Frederick Ungar, 1959), pp. 85–109.

[21]Conze, *Buddhist Meditation*, pp. 100–103.

[22]For general overviews of Mahayana, see Edward Conze, "Buddhism: The Mahayana," in *The Concise Encyclopedia of Living Faiths*, ed. R. C. Zaehner (Boston: Beacon Press, 1967), pp. 296–320; *Buddhist Texts*, pp. 119–217.

[23]Edward Conze, *Buddhist Wisdom Books* (New York: Harper Torchbooks, 1972), p. 77.

[24]See Joanna Rodgers Macy, "Perfection of Wisdom: Mother of All Buddhas," in *Beyond Androcentrism*, ed. Rita M. Gross (Missoula, Mont.: Scholars Press, 1977), pp. 315–333.

[25]Conze, *Buddhist Wisdom Books*, pp. 101–102.

[26]Our exposition depends on Edward Conze's translation and study in *Buddhist Wisdom Books* (note 23).

[27]See Frederick J. Streng, *Emptiness* (Nashville: Abingdon, 1967), pp. 139–152.

[28]See Nagaruna and Sakya Pandit, *Elegant Sayings*, trans. Tarthang Tulku (Emeryville, Calif.: Dharma Publishing, 1977), pp. 38–39.

[29]See Conze, *Buddhist Thought in India*, pp. 238–244; see also Prebish, *Buddhism: A Modern Perspective*, pp. 76–96; T. R. V. Murti, *The Central Philosophy of Buddhism* (London: Allen & Unwin, 1955).

[30]See Conze, *Buddhist Thought in India*, pp. 250–260; Prebish, *Buddhism: A Modern Perspective*, pp. 97–101; Thomas, *History of Buddhist Thought*, pp. 230–248.

[31]Juan Mascaró, trans., *The Dhammapada* (Baltimore: Penguin, 1973), p. 1.

[32]D. T. Suzuki, trans., *The Lankavatara Sutra* (London: George Routledge, 1932).

[33]Conze, *Buddhist Thought in India*, pp. 270–274; Robinson and Johnson, *Buddhist Tradition*, pp. 116–127; Thomas, *History of Buddhist Thought*, pp. 245–248; David Snellgrove, "The Tantras," in Edward Conze, ed., *Buddhist Texts through the Ages* (New York: Harper Torchbooks, 1954), pp. 221–273; Conze, *Buddhism: Its Essence and Development*, pp. 174–199.

[34]Hellmut Hoffmann, *The Religions of Tibet* (London: Allen & Unwin, 1961); Herbert V. Guenther, *Treasures of the Tibetan Middle Way* (Berkeley: Shambhala, 1976).

[35]Beyer, *Buddhist Experience*, pp. 258–261; Eliade, *Yoga*, pp. 249–254.

[36]Robinson and Johnson, *Buddhist Religion*, p. 120.

[37]See Herbert Guenther, trans., *The Life and Teaching of Naropa* (New York: Oxford University Press, 1971), pp. 112–249.

[38]Guenther, *Naropa*, p. 43; see also W. Y. Evans-Wentz, ed., *Tibet's Great Yogi Milarepa* (New York: Oxford University Press, 1969), p. 93.

[39]See Beyer, *Buddhist Experience*, pp. 174–184, 225–229, 258–261.

[40]Stephan Beyer, "Buddhism in Tibet," in *Buddhism: A Modern Perspective*, ed. Charles Prebish (University Park: Pennsylvania State University Press, 1975), pp. 239–247.

[41]Hoffmann, *Religions of Tibet*.

[42]Evans-Wentz, *Milarepa*.

[43]On modern times, see David L. Snellgrover, "Tibetan Buddhism Today," in *Buddhism in the Modern World*, ed. Heinrich Dumoulin (New York: Macmillan, 1976), pp. 277–293.

[44]W. Y. Evans-Wentz, *The Tibetan Book of the Dead* (New York: Oxford University Press, 1960).

[45]Alexandra David-Neel, *Magic and Mystery in Tibet* (New York: Dover, 1971), pp. 5–9.

[46]There are major qualifications to this statement, of course. On Hinduism in Southeast Asia, see Robinson and Johnson, *Buddhist Tradition*, pp. 129–136; on Hinduism in Indonesia, see Clifford Geertz, *Islam Observed* (Chicago: University of Chicago Press, 1968), pp. 29–43.

[47]For overviews, see R. H. Robinson, "Buddhism: In China and Japan," in *The Concise Encyclopedia of Living Faiths*, ed. R. C. Zaehner (Boston: Beacon Press, 1967), pp. 321–344; C. Wei-hsun Fu, "Mahayana Buddhism (China)," in *Historical Atlas of the Religions of the World*, ed. I. al Faruqi and D. Sopher (New York: Macmillan, 1974), pp. 185–194. Space forbids consideration of the history of Buddhism in the many other Asian lands that it influenced. For treatments on this subject, see Prebish, *Buddhism: A Modern Perspective*. On contemporary issues, see Heinrich

Dumoulin, ed., *Buddhism in the Modern World* (New York: Macmillan, 1976).

[48]On Buddhist beginnings in China, see Arthur F. Wright, *Buddhism in Chinese History* (Stanford, Calif.: Stanford University Press, 1959), pp. 21–41. Also Kenneth K. S. Ch'en, "The Role of Buddhist Monasteries in T'ang Society," *HR*, 1976, *15*(3):209–230.

[49]See Heinrich Dumoulin, *A History of Zen Buddhism* (Boston: Beacon Press, 1969), pp. 52–136.

[50]Robinson and Johnson, *Buddhist Religion*, p. 161. For a full discussion of this sutra, see Philip B. Yampolsky, *The Platform Sutra of the Sixth Patriarch* (New York: Columbia University Press, 1967); see also Wing-Tsit Chan, *The Platform Sutra* (New York: St. John's University Press, 1963). Interesting background is Alex Wayman, "The Mirror as a Pan-Buddhist Metaphor-Simile," *HR*, 1974, *13*(4):251–269.

[51]Dumoulin, *History of Zen Buddhism*, p. 88; Yampolsky, *Platform Sutra*, pp. 23–121.

[52]Beatrice Lane Suzuki, *Mahayana Buddhism* (New York: Macmillan, 1969), pp. 63–65; T. O. Ling, *A Dictionary of Buddhism* (New York: Scribner's, 1972), pp. 15–16.

[53]Holmes Welch, "Buddhism in China Today," in *Buddhism in the Modern World*, ed. Heinrich Dumoulin (New York: Macmillan, 1976), pp. 164–178; see also Donald E. MacInnes, *Religious Policy and Practice in Communist China* (New York: Macmillan, 1972).

[54]For an introduction to Hua-yen metaphysics, see Francis H. Cook, *Hua-yen Buddhism* (University Park: Pennsylvania State University Press, 1977).

[55]Robinson and Johnson, *Buddhist Religion*, p. 175.

[56]Francis H. Cook, "Heian, Kamakura, and Tokugawa Periods in Japan," in *Buddhism: A Modern Perspective*, ed. Charles S. Prebish (University Park: Pennsylvania State University Press, 1975), p. 223.

[57]See Kapleau, *Three Pillars of Zen*, pp. 295–299.

[58]See H. Byron Earhart, *Japanese Religion: Unity and Diversity* (Encino, Calif.: Dickenson, 1974), pp. 85–92; see also Robert N. Bellah, *Tokugawa Religion* (Boston: Beacon Press, 1970).

[59]See Emma McClory Layman, *Buddhism in America* (Chicago: Nelson-Hill, 1976), pp. 52–80.

[60]See, for example, D. T. Suzuki, *Zen and Japanese Culture* (New York: Pantheon, 1959).

[61]Shunryu Suzuki, *Zen Mind, Beginner's Mind* (New York: John Weatherhill, 1970).

[62]Melford Spiro, *Buddhism and Society* (New York: Harper & Row, 1970), pp. 209–214.

[63]Charles S. Prebish, *American Buddhism* (North Scituate, Mass.: Duxbury Press, 1979), p. 164.

[64]See Lama Govinda, *The Psychological Attitude of Early Buddhist Philosophy* (New York: Samuel Weiser, 1969), pp. 77–142.

[65]For instance, Spiro found that the goal of Burmese Buddhists was not nirvana but a better rebirth; see Melford E. Spiro, *Buddhism and Society* (New York: Harper & Row, 1970).

[66]On the Buddhist shaping of Chinese folk religion, see Daniel L. Overmyer, "Folk-Buddhist Religion: Creation and Eschatology in Medieval China," *HR*, 1972, *12*(1):42–70.

[67]Laurence G. Thompson, *The Chinese Way in Religion* (Encino, Calif.: Dickenson, 1973), pp. 77–129; see also Arthur Waley, trans., *Monkey* (New York: Grove Press, 1958); Daniel L. Overmyer, "Boatmen and Buddhas," *HR*, 1978, *17*(3–4):284–302. For Japan, see H. Byron Earhart, *Religion in the Japanese Experience* (Encino, Calif.: Dickenson, 1974), pp. 37–64; Ichiro Hori, *Folk Religion in Japan* (Chicago: University of Chicago Press, 1968), pp. 83–139.

[68]On the relation between Buddhism and the Japanese love of nature, see William LaFleur, "Sagyo and the Buddhist Value of Nature," *HR*, 1973–74, *13*(1,3):93–128, 227–248.

[69]Denise Lardner Carmody, *Women and World Religions* (Nashville: Abingdon, 1979), pp. 45–52; I. B. Horner, *Women Under Primitive Buddhism* (New York: Dutton, 1930).

[70]See Nancy Falk, "An Image of Woman in Old Buddhist Literature: The Daughters of Mara," in *Women and Religion*, rev. ed., ed. J. Plaskow and J. A. Romero (Missoula, Mont.: Scholars Press, 1974), pp. 105–112.

[71]Frank Reynolds, "The Two Wheels of Dhamma," in *The Two Wheels of Dhamma*, ed. Bardwell L. Smith (Chambersburg, Pa.: American

Academy of Religion, 1972), pp. 6–30; Bardwell L. Smith, "The Ideal Social Order as Portrayed in the Chronicles of Ceylon," in *Two Wheels of Dhamma*, ed. Smith, pp. 31–57.

⁷²King, *Hope of Nibbana*, pp. 176–210.

⁷³Eric Voegelin, *Anamnesis: Zur Theorie der Geschichte und Politik* (Munich: R. Piper, 1966), pp. 179–222. This portion is not available in Gerhart Niemeyer's recent translation of *Anamnesis* (Notre Dame: University of Notre Dame Press, 1978). However, it first appeared under the title "The Mongol Orders of Submission to European Powers," in *Byzantion, Vol. XV* (1940/41), pp. 378–413.

⁷⁴See Jane Bunnag, *Buddhist Monk, Buddhist Layman* (Cambridge: Cambridge University Press, 1973); see also Spiro, *Buddhism and Society*, pp. 396–421. On the more spiritual ties among members of the community, see Richard Gombrich, " 'Merit Transference' in Sinhalese Buddhism," *HR*, 1971, 11(2):203–219.

⁷⁵King, *In the Hope of Nibbana*, pp. 277–284.

⁷⁶G. P. Malalasekera, "Theravada Buddhism," in *Historical Atlas of the Religions of the World*, ed. I. al Faruqi and D. Sopher (New York: Macmillan, 1974), p. 172.

⁷⁷John B. Cobb, Jr., "Buddhist Emptiness and the Christian God," *JAAR*, 1977, 45(1): 11–25.

⁷⁸Yoshito S. Hakeda, trans., *The Awakening of Faith* (New York: Columbia University Press, 1967).

⁷⁹Winston L. King, *Theravada Meditation: The Buddhist Transformation of Yoga* (University Park: Pennsylvania State University Press, 1980), pp. 126–127.

⁸⁰Kapleau, *Three Pillars of Zen*, p. 207.

⁸¹E. F. Schumacher, *Small Is Beautiful* (New York: Harper Colophon, 1973), pp. 50–58.

⁸²D. T. Suzuki, *Zen Buddhism* (New York: Anchor Books, 1956), pp. 157–226. On the Taoist influence, see Chang Chung-yuan, *Creativity and Taoism* (New York: Harper Colophon, 1970).

⁸³Conze, *Buddhist Thought in India*, pp. 122–134.

⁸⁴The famous Zen ox-herding pictures display the progress toward this freedom. See Kapleau, *Three Pillars of Zen*, pp. 301–313.

⁸⁵Chogyam Trungpa, "Foreword," in *Buddhism: A Modern Perspective*, ed. Charles S. Prebish (University Park: Pennsylvania State University Press, 1975), p. ix.

⁸⁶John Bowker has recently discussed this matter in the illuminating context of information theory; see Bowker, *Religious Imagination*, pp. 244–307.

⁸⁷This point is discussed further in John Carmody, "A Next Step for Roman Catholic Theology," *Theology Today*, 1976, 32:371–381.

⁸⁸On the broader question of hermeneutics, see Robert A. F. Thurman, "Buddhist Hermeneutics," *JAAR*, 1978, 46(1):19–39; on the devotional implications of the Buddha's hermeneutical status, see Nancy Falk, "To Gaze on the Sacred Traces," *HR*, 1977, 16(4):281–293.

⁸⁹Alex Wayman, "Buddhism," in *Historia Religionum, II*, ed. C. J. Bleeker and G. Widengren (Leiden: E. J. Brill, 1971), pp. 393–395; see also Frank E. Reynolds, "The Several Bodies of the Buddha," *HR*, 1977, 16(4):374–389; B. L. Suzuki, *Mahayana Buddhism*, pp. 52–63.

⁹⁰For a discussion of Chinese Buddhism as religion, see C. K. Yang, *Religion in Chinese Society* (Berkeley: University of California Press, 1970). For a discussion of Zen as religion, see Kapleau, *Three Pillars of Zen*, passim.

⁹¹*Saddharmapundarika*, V:1, 5, 6; in *Buddhist Texts through the Ages*, ed. Edward Conze (note 13), p. 139.

⁹²*Matrceta, Satapancasatkastotra*; in *Buddhist Texts through the Ages*, pp. 190–194.

⁹³Suzuki, *Zen Mind, Beginner's Mind*, pp. 65–67.

⁹⁴C. N. Tay, "Kuan-yin: The Cult of Half Asia," *HR*, 1976, 16(2):147–177.

⁹⁵Thomas, *History of Buddhist Thought*, pp. 119–132.

⁹⁶On the history of mystery, see Eric Voegelin, *Order and History*, vol. 4, *The Ecumenic Age* (Baton Rouge: Louisiana State University Press, 1974), pp. 316–335.

Chapter Three

¹See E. Zürcher, *The Buddhist Conquest of China* (Leiden: E. J. Brill, 1972); Kenneth K. S. Ch'en, *Buddhism in China* (Princeton, N.J.: Princeton University Press, 1964).

[2]Laurence G. Thompson, ed., *The Chinese Way in Religion* (Encino, Calif.: Dickenson, 1973), pp. 231–241; Donald E. MacInnes, *Religious Policy and Practice in Communist China* (New York: Macmillan, 1972).

[3]C. K. Yang, *Religion in Chinese Society* (Berkeley: University of California Press, 1970), pp. 294–340.

[4]Karl Jaspers, *The Origin and Goal of History* (New Haven, Conn.: Yale University Press, 1953), p. 2.

[5]Arthur Waley, trans., *Monkey* (New York: Grove Press, 1958).

[6]Laurence G. Thompson, *The Chinese Religion: An Introduction*, 2nd ed. (Encino, Calif.: Dickenson, 1975), pp. 3–15; Joseph Needham, *Science and Civilisation in China*, vol. 2 (Cambridge: University Press, 1969), pp. 216–345.

[7]David N. Keightley, "The Religious Commitment: Shang Theology and the Genesis of Chinese Political Culture," *HR*, 1978, 17(3–4):213.

[8]Hans Steininger, "The Religions of China," in *Historia Religionum*, II, ed. C. J. Bleeker and G. Widengren (Leiden: E. J. Brill, 1971), pp. 479–482.

[9]*Chuang Tzu*, sec. 6; see Burton Watson, trans., *Chuang Tzu: Basic Writings* (New York: Columbia University Press, 1964), pp. 76, 81.

[10]Thompson, *Chinese Religion*, pp. 21–23; Needham, *Science and Civilisation*, pp. 354–363.

[11]Arthur Waley, *The Nine Songs: A Study of Shamanism in Ancient China* (London: Allen & Unwin, 1955).

[12]Eliade, however, stresses the Chinese shaman's magical flight. See Mircea Eliade, *Shamanism* (Princeton, N.J.: Princeton University Press, 1972), pp. 448–457.

[13]On the ritualistic side of early Chinese shamanism, see Jordan Paper, "The Meaning of the 'T'ao-T'ieh,'" *HR*, 1978, 18(1):18–41.

[14]Anna Seidel, "Buying One's Way to Heaven," *HR*, 1978, 17(3–4):419–431.

[15]Donald W. Treadgold, *The West in Russia and China*, vol. 2 (Cambridge: University Press, 1973), pp. 20–26.

[16]Quoted in Thompson, *Chinese Religion*, pp. 30–32.

[17]Mircea Eliade, *Histoire des croyances et des idées religieuses*, vol. 2, *De Gautama Bouddha au triomphe des Christianisme* (Paris: Payot, 1978), pp. 11–12.

[18]Arthur Waley, trans., *The Analects of Confucius* (New York: Vintage, 1938), pp. 27–29.

[19]A. C. Graham, "Confucianism," in *The Concise Encyclopedia of Living Faiths*, ed. R. C. Zaehner (Boston: Beacon Press, 1967), p. 367.

[20]Thompson, *Chinese Way*, pp. 139–153.

[21]Wing-Tsit Chan, *A Source Book in Chinese Philosophy* (Princeton, N.J.: Princeton University Press, 1963), pp. 84–94.

[22]Ezra Pound, *Confucius* (New York: New Directions, 1969), p. 219.

[23]W. A. C. H. Dobson, trans., *Mencius* (Toronto: University of Toronto Press, 1963), p. 131.

[24]Lee H. Yearley, "Mencius on Human Nature," *JAAR*, 1975, 43:185–198.

[25]See Eric Voegelin, *Order and History*, vol. 4 (Baton Rouge: Louisiana State University Press, 1974), pp. 272–299.

[26]On Hsun-tzu, see Chan, *Chinese Philosophy*, pp. 115–135; Sebastian de Grazia, *Masters of Chinese Political Thought* (New York: Viking, 1973), pp. 151–181. On Mo-tzu, see Chan, *Chinese Philosophy*, pp. 211–217; de Grazia, *Chinese Political Thought*, pp. 216–246.

[27]Arthur Waley, *Three Ways of Thought in Ancient China* (Garden City, N.Y.: Doubleday, 1956), p. 205.

[28]On this period, see Werner Eichhorn, *Chinese Civilization* (New York: Praeger, 1969), pp. 43–85; H. G. Creel, *The Birth of China* (New York: Reynal and Hitchcock, 1937), pp. 219–380.

[29]H. G. Creel, *What Is Taoism?* (Chicago: University of Chicago Press, 1970), pp. 37–47.

[30]Thomas Merton, *The Way of Chuang Tzu* (New York: New Directions, 1968).

[31]Arthur Waley, trans., *The Way and Its Power* (New York: Grove Press, 1958).

[32]Waley stresses the mystical; Wing-Tsit Chan's *The Way of Lao Tzu* (Indianapolis, Ind.: Bobbs-Merrill, 1963) stresses the pragmatic.

[33]Denise Lardner Carmody, "Taoist Reflec-

tions on Feminism," *Religion in Life*, 1977, 44(2):234–244.

[34]Holmes Welch, *Taoism: The Parting of the Way* (Boston: Beacon Press, 1966), pp. 35–49.

[35]For a sketch of a utopia that is Taoist in spirit if not in origin, see Ernest Callenbach, *Ecotopia* (New York: Bantam, 1977).

[36]*Tao Te Ching*, chap. 5, in *The Way and Its Power* (New York: Grove Press, 1955), p. 147; Chan, *Lao Tzu* (Indianapolis, Ind.: Bobbs-Merrill, 1963), p. 108, note 2, says: "Straw dogs were used for sacrifices in ancient China. After they had been used, they were thrown away and there was no more sentimental attachment to them."

[37]Current scholarly opinion, however, associates religious Taoism with preaxial religion. See *Encyclopedia Brittanica*, 15th ed., s.v. "Taoism," "Taoism, History of"; N. Sivin, "On the Word 'Taoist' as a Source of Perplexity," *HR*, 1978, 17(3–4):303–330.

[38]Werner Eichhorn, "Taoism," in *The Concise Encyclopedia of Living Faiths*, ed. R. C. Zaehner (Boston: Beacon Press, 1967), pp. 389–391; Welch, *Taoism*, pp. 151–158.

[39]Welch, *Taoism*, pp. 130–135; K'uan Yu, *Taoist Yoga* (New York: Samuel Weiser, 1973).

[40]Kristofer Schipper, "The Taoist Body," *HR*, 1978, 17(3–4):355–386.

[41]Edward H. Schafer, "The Jade Woman of Greatest Mystery," *HR*, 1978, 17(3–4): 393–394.

[42]Chang Chung-yuan, *Creativity and Taoism* (New York: Harper Colophon, 1970), pp. 169–238; Albert C. Moore, *Iconography of Religions* (Philadelphia: Fortress, 1977), pp. 170–180; Raymond Dawson, *The Chinese Experience* (New York: Scribner's, 1978), pp. 199–284.

[43]C. Wei-husn Fu, "Confucianism and Taoism," in *Historical Atlas of the Religions of the World*, ed. I. al Faruqi and D. Sopher (New York: Macmillan, 1974), p. 121.

[44]Thompson, *Chinese Religion*, p. 123.

[45]Arthur F. Wright, *Buddhism in Chinese History* (Stanford, Calif.: Stanford University Press, 1959), p. 70.

[46]See ibid., p. 72.

[47]Yang, *Religion in Chinese Society*, pp. 265–272.

[48]Graham, "Confucianism," p. 370.

[49]See Chan, *Chinese Philosophy*, pp. 588–653.

[50]This appears in Rodney L. Taylor, "The Centered Self: Religious Autobiography in the Neo-Confucian Tradition," *HR*, 1978, 17(3–4):266–283.

[51]Thaddeus Chieh Hang T'ui, "*Jen* Experience and *Jen* Philosophy," *JAAR*, 1974, 42:53–65.

[52]For an absorbing depiction of the tradition from 1661 to 1722, see Jonathan Spence, *Emperor of China: Self Portrait of K'ang-hsi* (New York: Knopf, 1974). As a link to the communist era, see Dawson, *Chinese Experience*, pp. 285–292.

[53]Adapted from Thompson, *Chinese Way in Religion*, pp. 144–153.

[54]Adapted from Thompson, *Chinese Religion: An Introduction*, 3rd ed. (1979), pp. 75–78.

[55]Steininger, "Religions of China," p. 468.

[56]See Thompson, *Chinese Way in Religion*, pp. 231–241; MacInnes, *Religious Policy and Practice*. See also Yang, *Religion in Chinese Society*, pp. 341–404.

[57]Stuart Shram, *Mao Tse-tung* (Baltimore: Penguin, 1967), p. 23.

[58]Elisabeth Croll, ed., *The Women's Movement in China* (London: Anglo-Chinese Educational Institute, 1974).

[59]Robert Jay Lifton, *Revolutionary Immortality: Mao Tse-tung and the Chinese Cultural Revolution* (New York: Vintage, 1968).

[60]Mao Tse-tung, *Poems* (Peking: Foreign Language Press, 1976).

[61]N. J. Giradot, "The Problem of Creation Mythology in the Study of Chinese Religion," *HR*, 1976, 15(4):289–318; see also his "Myth and Meaning in the *Tao Te Ching*: Chapters 25 and 42," *HR*, 1977, 16(4): 294–328.

[62]Alvin P. Cohen, "Concerning the Rain Deities in Ancient China," *HR*, 1978, 17(3–4):244–265.

[63]See Helmut Wilhelm, *Change: Eight Lectures on the I-ching* (New York: Pantheon, 1960).

[64]This section is adapted from James J. Y. Liu, *Essentials of Chinese Literary Art* (North Scituate, Mass.: Duxbury Press, 1979), pp. 4–24.

[65]Chiang Yee, *The Chinese Eye: An Interpretation of Chinese Painting* (Bloomington: Indiana University Press, 1964), p. 152. We are indebted to Chiang throughout this section.

[66]Richard Mather, "Buddhism Becomes Chinese," in *The Chinese Way in Religion*, ed. Laurence G. Thompson (Encino, Calif.: Dickenson, 1973), pp. 77–86.

[67]Heinrich Dumoulin, *A History of Zen Buddhism* (Boston: Beacon Press, 1969), pp. 52–136.

[68]Philip Kapleau, *The Three Pillars of Zen* (Boston: Beacon Press, 1967), p. 205.

[69]Steininger, "Religions of China," pp. 482–487; Creel, *Birth of China*, pp. 204–216.

[70]See Arthur F. Wright, ed., *Confucianism and Chinese Civilization* (New York: Atheneum, 1964).

[71]This is a major theme in Peter Weber-Schafer, *Oikumene und Imperium* (Munich: P. List, 1968).

[72]Vern L. Bullough, *The Subordinate Sex* (Baltimore: Penguin, 1974), p. 249.

[73]Mary Daly, *Gyn/Ecology* (Boston: Beacon Press, 1979), chap. 4. The reference to Dworkin is to her *Woman Hating* (New York: Dutton, 1974), p. 103.

[74]Magery Wolf, "Chinese Women: Old Skills in a New Context," in *Woman, Culture, and Society*, ed. M. Z. Rosaldo and L. Lamphere (Stanford, Calif.: Stanford University Press, 1974), pp. 157–172.

[75]Denise Lardner Carmody, *Women and World Religions* (Nashville: Abingdon, 1979), pp. 66–72.

[76]Ellen Marie Chen, "Tao as the Great Mother and the Influence of Motherly Love in the Shaping of Chinese Philosophy," *HR*, 1974, 14(1):51–63.

[77]Yang, *Religion in Chinese Society*, p. 294.

[78]Max Weber, *The Religion of China* (New York: Free Press, 1968), pp. 173–225.

[79]Donald J. Munro, *The Concept of Man in Early China* (Stanford, Calif.: Stanford University Press, 1969).

[80]A. C. Graham, "Chuang Tzu's Essay on Seeing Things as Equal," *HR*, 1969, 9:137.

[81]Chung-yuan, *Creativity and Taoism*, pp. 123–168.

[82]In her article "Is There a Doctrine of Physical Immortality in the Tao Te Ching?" (*HR*, 1973, 12(3):231–249), Ellen Marie Chen argues that Lao-tzu did not propose immortality. She also argues against the Taoist character of *The Secret of the Golden Flower* because it is Confucian in emphasizing the yang principle (p. 246, note 22). For the psychodynamics of *The Golden Flower*, see C. G. Jung, "Commentary," in Richard Wilhelm, trans., *The Golden Flower* (New York: Harcourt, Brace & World, 1962), pp. 81–137.

[83]Maxine Hong Kingston, *The Woman Warrior: Memories of a Girlhood among Ghosts* (New York: Knopf, 1977).

[84]G. Van der Leeuw, *Religion in Essence and Manifestation*, vol. 1 (New York: Harper & Row, 1963), pp. 23–187.

[85]C. N. Tay, "Kuan-yin: The Cult of Half Asia," *HR*, 1976, 16(2):147–177.

[86]On the original peasant mentality, see Marcel Granet, *The Religion of the Chinese People* (New York: Harper & Row, 1975), pp. 37–56.

[87]David C. Yu, "Chinese Folk Religion," *HR*, 1973, 12:378–387. On the complexity of so small an item as a Taoist talismanic chart, see Michael Saso, "What Is the *Ho-t'u?*" *HR*, 1978, 17(3–4):399–416.

Chapter Four

[1]H. Byron Earhart, *Japanese Religion: Unity and Diversity*, 2nd ed. (Encino, Calif.: Dickenson, 1974).

[2]Johannes Maringer, "Clay Figurines of the Jomon Period," *HR*, 1974, 14:128–139.

[3]Carmen Blacker, "The Religions of Japan," in *Historia Religionum*, II, ed. C. J. Bleeker and G. Widengren (Leiden: E. J. Brill, 1971), p. 518.

[4]Earhart, *Japanese Religion*, pp. 11–16.

[5]Ichiro Hori, *Folk Religion in Japan* (Chicago: University of Chicago Press, 1968), pp. 181–251. See also Carmen Blacker, *The Catalpa Bow* (London: Allen & Unwin, 1975).

[6]G. Bownas, "Shinto," in *The Concise*

Encyclopedia of Living Faiths, ed. R. C. Zaehner (Boston: Beacon Press, 1967), p. 349.

[7]Ryusaku Tsunoda et al., *Sources of Japanese Tradition,* vol. 1 (New York: Columbia University Press, 1964), pp. 25–26.

[8]Bownas, "Shinto," p. 357.

[9]Ibid.

[10]This section adapts materials from *Religion in the Japanese Experience: Sources and Interpretations,* ed. H. Byron Earhart (Encino, Calif.: Dickenson, 1974), pp. 19–26.

[11]Chinese culture began to penetrate Japan at least as early as 57 C.E. See Arnold Toynbee, ed., *Half the World* (New York: Holt, Rinehart and Winston, 1973), p. 184.

[12]Earhart, *Japanese Religion,* pp. x–xi.

[13]Francis H. Cook, "Japanese Innovations in Buddhism," in *Buddhism: A Modern Perspective,* ed. Charles S. Prebish (University Park: Pennsylvania State University Press, 1975), pp. 229–233.

[14]The section adapts materials from *Sources of Japanese Tradition,* vol. 1, compiled by Ryusaku Tsunodu et al. (New York: Columbia University Press, 1964), pp. 184–260.

[15]William LaFleur, "Saigyo and the Buddhist Value of Nature," *HR,* 1973–74, 13:93–128, 227–248.

[16]Peter Beilenson, trans., *Japanese Haiku* (Mount Vernon: Peter Pauper Press, 1956), p. 11. Reprinted by permission.

[17]Ibid., p. 13. Reprinted by permission.

[18]Yasunari Kawabata, *Thousand Cranes* (New York: Berkley Medallion, 1968).

[19]Yasunari Kawabata, *The Master of Go* (Rutland, Vt.: Tuttle, 1973).

[20]Yasunari Kawabata, *The Sound of the Mountain* (Rutland, Vt.: Tuttle, 1971).

[21]Earhart, *Japanese Religion,* p. 73.

[22]See Tsunoda et al., *Sources of Japanese Tradition,* pp. 261–276.

[23]Shusaku Endo, *Silence* (Rutland, Vt.: Tuttle, 1969).

[24]Robert N. Bellah, *Tokugawa Religion* (Boston: Beacon Press, 1970), pp. 90–98.

[25]John B. Noss, *Man's Religions,* 5th ed. (New York: Macmillan, 1974), p. 324.

[26]Denise Lardner Carmody, *Women and World Religions* (Nashville: Abingdon, 1979), p. 84.

[27]Edwin O. Reischauer, *Japan Past and Present,* 3rd ed. rev. (Tokyo: Tuttle, 1964), pp. 108–141.

[28]H. Byron Earhart, *Religion in the Japanese Experience* (Encino, Calif.: Dickenson, 1974), pp. 201–210; see also Ryusaku Tsunoda et al., *Sources of Japanese Tradition,* vol. 2 (New York: Columbia University Press, 1964), pp. 131–210.

[29]Earhart, *Religion in the Japanese Experience,* p. 204.

[30]Joseph Kitagawa, "The Japanese *Kokutai* (National Community): History and Myth," *HR,* 1974, 13:209–226.

[31]See Blacker, *Catalpa Bow,* pp. 130–132.

[32]Earhart, *Japanese Religion,* p. 112.

[33]Ibid., pp. 114–117.

[34]Y. T. Hosoi, "The Sacred Tree in Japanese Prehistory," *HR,* 1976, 16:95–119.

[35]Manabu Waida, "Symbolisms of the Moon and the Waters of Immortality," *HR,* 1977, 16:407–423.

[36]See Blacker, *Catalpa Bow,* and Hori, *Folk Religion in Japan,* for the shamanistic exceptions to this statement.

[37]See Lynn White, Jr., "The Historical Roots of Our Ecological Crisis," in *Ecology and Religion in History,* ed. David and Eileen Spring (New York: Harper Torchbooks, 1974), pp. 15–31. The other articles in this volume suggest the sort of qualifications one would expect in discussing Japanese ecology. See especially Yi-Fu Tuan, "Discrepancies between Environmental Attitude and Behaviour," pp. 91–113.

[38]On contemporary professional and business life in Japan, see Ichiro Kawasaki, *Japan Unmasked* (Rutland, Vt.: Tuttle, 1969); Nobutaka Ike, *Japan: The New Superstate* (Stanford, Calif.: Stanford Alumni Association, 1973).

[39]Earhart, *Religion in the Japanese Experience,* pp. 145–159.

[40]Kitagawa, "The Japanese *Kokutai.*"

[41] Alan Miller, "Ritsuryo Japan: The State as Liturgical Community," *HR*, 1971, *11*:98–124.

[42] Manabu Waida, "Sacral Kingship in Early Japan," *HR*, 1976, *15*:319–342.

[43] Winston Davis, "Ittoen: The Myths and Rituals of Liminality," *HR*, 1975, *14*:282–321; 1975, *15*:1–33.

[44] Alfred North Whitehead, *Religion in the Making* (New York: Meridian, 1960), p. 16.

[45] Yukio Mishima has brought this lovely Zen temple into recent Japanese religious consciousness. See his *The Temple of the Golden Pavilion* (Rutland, Vt.: Tuttle, 1959).

[46] Patrick White, *The Vivisector* (New York: Viking, 1970).

[47] Chang Chung-yun, *Creativity and Taoism* (New York: Harper Colophon, 1970).

[48] This section adapts materials from Robert S. Ellwood, Jr., *An Invitation to Japanese Civilization* (Belmont, Calif.: Wadsworth, 1980), pp. 95–125.

[49] G. Bownas, "Shinto."

[50] Carmen Blacker, "Religions of Japan."

[51] We would begin that business with Bernard Lonergan's *Insight* (New York: Philosophical Library, 1958), pp. 595–633.

[52] Bellah, *Tokugawa Religion*, pp. 107–132, 178–197.

[53] Mircea Eliade, *From Primitives to Zen* (New York: Harper & Row, 1967), pp. 452–454.

[54] Considering Shinran as a bodhisattva would force us to alter this judgment. See Robert N. Bellah, "The Contemporary Meaning of Kamakura Buddhism," *JAAR*, 1974, *42*:7–9.

[55] See Shunryu Suzuki, *Zen Mind, Beginner's Mind* (New York: John Weatherhill, 1970), pp. 92–95, 102–104.

[56] Earhart, *Religion in the Japanese Experience*, p. 25.

Conclusion

[1] C. G. Jung, *Memories, Dreams, Reflections* (New York: Vintage, 1963), p. 235.

[2] In our view, Mircea Eliade shows that persuasively; see his *Shamanism* (Princeton, N.J.: Princeton University Press/Bollingen, 1972); *Yoga* (Princeton, N.J.: Princeton University Press/Bollingen, 1970).

[3] See Wilfred Cantwell Smith, *The Meaning and End of Religion* (New York: Mentor, 1964); on the rise of the term *religio* with Cicero, see Eric Voegelin, *Order and History, IV* (Baton Rouge: Louisiana State University Press, 1974), pp. 43–48.

[4] See Joachim Wach, *The Comparative Study of Religions* (New York: Columbia University Press, 1961).

[5] Three recent works that illumine tradition are Huston Smith, *Forgotten Truth: The Primordial Tradition* (New York: Harper & Row, 1976); E. F. Schumacher, *A Guide for the Perplexed* (New York: Harper & Row, 1977); Peter Slater, *The Dynamics of Religion* (New York: Harper & Row, 1978).

[6] This is a theme in John Bowker, *The Sense of God* (Oxford: Clarendon Press, 1973).

[7] See Voegelin, *Order and History*, pp. 330–335.

[8] Huston Smith, "Frithjof Schuon's *The Transcendent Unity of Religion*: Pro," and Richard C. Bush, "Frithjof Schuon's *The Transcendent Unity of Religion*: Con," *JAAR*, 1976, *44*:715–719, 721–724.

[9] W. Richard Comstock, *The Study of Religion and Primitive Religions* (New York: Harper & Row, 1971), pp. 13–17.

[10] See Clifford Geertz, *The Interpretation of Cultures* (New York: Basic Books, 1973), pp. 412–453.

[11] Voegelin, *Order and History*, pp. 300–335.

[12] See Karl Rahner and Herbert Vorgrimler, *Theological Dictionary* (New York: Herder and Herder, 1965), pp. 308–309.

[13] See Stanley Jaki, *The Road of Science and the Ways to God* (Chicago: University of Chicago Press, 1978).

[14] On religious interpretations of American destiny, see Conrad Cherry, ed., *God's New Israel* (Englewood Cliffs, N.J.: Prentice-Hall, 1971).

Annotated Bibliography

The following books ought to appeal to undergraduates, and we recommend them for further reading. Adventurous students may pursue other, often more specialized resources given in the chapter notes.

Introduction

Carmody, Denise Lardner. *The Oldest God: Archaic Religion Yesterday and Today.* Nashville: Abingdon, 1981. A study of the ancient religious mentality from prehistoric times to the present.

Carmody, Denise Lardner. *Women and World Religions.* Nashville: Abingdon, 1979. A survey of female images and roles in the major religious traditions that describes what being religious as a female has meant in the past and means today.

Carmody, John. *The Progressive Pilgrim.* Notre Dame, Ind.: Fides/Claretian, 1980. An extended essay on the religious life, stressing its expression in education, prayer, play, marriage, and other primary zones.

Comstock, W. Richard. *The Study of Religion and Primitive Religions.* New York: Harper & Row, 1971. A somewhat dry approach that surveys recent approaches to world religions and then treats religious symbol systems.

Dunne, John S. *A Search for God in Time and Memory.* New York: Macmillan, 1969. A meditation on the autobiographical aspects of religion, stressing insights of Sören Kierkegaard, Bernard Lonergan, and C. G. Jung.

Eliade, Mircea. *The Sacred and the Profane.* New York: Harcourt, Brace & World, 1959. A concise statement of Eliade's view that human beings try to find meaning by making sacred the primary realities of their lives.

Ellwood, Robert S., Jr. *Introducing Religion: From Inside and Outside.* Englewood Cliffs, N.J.: Prentice-Hall, 1978. A readable introduction that stresses social scientific approaches to the world religions and tries to relate them to contemporary Western life.

Lewis, I. M. *Ecstatic Religion.* Baltimore: Penguin, 1971. An anthropological study of spirit possession and shamanism that shows their function in modern peoples' social lives.

Novak, Michael. *Ascent of the Mountain, Flight of the Dove.* New York: Harper & Row, 1971. An exposition of religious studies as a personal exploration of the self, society, culture, and religious organizations.

Chapter One: Hinduism

Basham, A. L. *The Wonder That Was India.* New York: Grove Press, 1959. A readable and comprehensive study of Indian life before the coming of the Muslims.

Embree, Ainslie T., ed. *The Hindu Tradition.* New York: Vintage Books, 1972. A good selection of original sources, readable and covering the whole span of Hindu religious history.

Erikson, Erik H. *Gandhi's Truth.* New York: Norton, 1969. A psychoanalytic study of the modern founder and theory of militant nonviolence.

Hopkins, Thomas J. *The Hindu Religious Tradition.* Encino, Calif.: Dickenson, 1971. A brief and solid survey of the major religious developments.

Kinsley, David R. *Hinduism: A Cultural Perspective.* Englewood Cliffs, N.J.: Prentice-Hall, 1982. A brief overview of the whole, stressing the interplay of belief, worship, and social structure.

Kinsley, David R. *The Sword and the Flute: Kali and Krishna.* Berkeley, Calif.: University of California Press, 1975. An intriguing study of the origins and rituals of these two important Hindu deities.

Markandaya, Karmala. *Nectar in a Sieve.* New York: Signet, n.d. (originally 1954). A simple novel of Indian women caught in the crumbling of traditional culture.

Organ, Troy Wilson. *Hinduism: Its Historical Development.* Woodbury, N.Y.: Barron's Educational Series, 1974. A clear, useful survey of the major Hindu doctrinal and devotional developments, from earliest times to the twentieth century.

Stanford, Anne, trans. *The Bhagavad Gita.* New York: Seabury, 1970. A fairly readable verse translation of India's most influential book.

Zimmer, Heinrich. *Philosophies of India.* Princeton, N.J.: Princeton University Press/Bollingen, 1969. A thorough, rather scholarly survey of the major Indian philosophical schools, stressing the Indian views of the highest good, of time, and of eternity.

Chapter Two: Buddhism

Conze, Edward. *Buddhism: Its Essence and Development.* New York: Harper Torchbooks, 1959. A compact treatment of the major sects of Buddhism.

Conze, Edward, ed. *Buddhist Texts through the Ages.* New York: Harper Torchbooks, 1964. A good selection of primary sources from the Theravada, Mahayana, Tantrist, and East Asian schools.

de Bary, William Theodore, ed. *The Buddhist Tradition in India, China and Japan.* New York: Vintage Books, 1972. Primary texts, with commentaries, that show the development and spread of the Buddha's dharma.

King, Winston. *In the Hope of Nibbana: Theravada Buddhist Ethics.* LaSalle, Ill.: Open Court, 1964. A solid study of the framework and content of Theravada ethics, both individual and social.

Ling, Trevor. *The Buddha: Buddhist Civilization in India and Ceylon.* Baltimore: Penguin Books, 1976. An illuminating study of the Buddha's time and the impact of his message on Indian society.

Nyanaponika, Thera. *The Heart of Buddhist Meditation.* London: Rider, 1969. A thorough study of the Buddha's way of mindfulness that reflects Theravada traditions.

Paul, Diana Y. *Women in Buddhism: Images of the Feminine in Mahayana Tradition.* Berkeley, Calif.: Lancaster-Miler, 1979. A comprehensive overview of women's position, paths to salvation, and images, with important primary texts.

Robinson, Richard H., and Johnson, Willard L. *The Buddhist Religion.* Encino, Calif.: Dickenson, 1977. A comprehensive survey of Buddhist religion throughout the world.

Streng, Frederick J. *Emptiness: A Study in Religious Meaning.* Nashville: Abingdon, 1967. A demanding but rewarding study of Nagarjuna's philosophy, with translations of two key texts.

Suzuki, Shunryu. *Zen Mind, Beginner's Mind.* New York: Weatherhill, 1970. A lovely and penetrating vision of Zen by a contemporary master.

Chapter Three: Chinese Religion

Chan, Wing-Tsit. *A Source Book in Chinese Philosophy*. Princeton: Princeton University Press, 1963. A fine collection of primary sources, with interpretations, that document the rise of the different Chinese philosophical schools.

Creel, H. G. *Confucius and the Chinese Way*. New York: Harper Torchbooks, 1960. A standard introduction to Confucius the man and to the tradition that arose from his teaching.

Gernet, Jacques. *Daily Life in China: On the Eve of the Mongol Invasion 1250–1276*. Stanford, Calif.: Stanford University Press, 1962. An interesting description of city, family, and cultural life in late medieval China.

Grousset, Rene. *The Rise and Splendour of the Chinese Empire*. Berkeley, Calif.: University of California Press, 1953. A straightforward historical account of China from earliest times to the brink of modernity.

Pound, Ezra. *Confucius*. New York: New Directions, 1951. An idiosyncratic but stimulating translation of major Confucian texts.

Thompson, Laurence G. *The Chinese Religion: An Introduction*. 3rd ed. Belmont, Calif.: Wadsworth, 1979. An overview of the major components of Chinese religious culture.

Thompson, Laurence G. *The Chinese Way in Religion*. Encino, Calif.: Dickenson, 1973. A good collection of original sources that represent the span of Chinese religion.

Waley, Arthur, trans. *The Way and Its Power*. New York: Grove Press, 1958. A readable version of China's most beguiling classic.

Welch, Holmes. *Taoism: The Parting of the Way*. Boston: Beacon Press, 1957. A stimulating interpretation of the *Lao-tzu*, with a good sketch of the religious Taoism that followed on it.

Wright, Arthur F. *Buddhism in Chinese History*. Stanford, Calif.: Stanford University Press, 1959. A straightforward survey of Buddhism's fortunes in the major historical periods.

Chapter Four: Japanese Religion

Bellah, Robert N. *Tokugawa Religion*. Boston: Beacon Press, 1970. A somewhat demanding sociological analysis of Japanese religious culture on the verge of modernity.

Earhart, H. Byron. *Japanese Religion: Unity and Diversity*. 2nd ed. Encino, Calif.: Dickenson, 1974. An exposition of Japanese religious development from prehistoric times to the present.

Earhart, H. Byron. *Religion in the Japanese Experience*. Encino, Calif.: Dickenson, 1974. A good collection of texts that represent the many aspects of Japanese religion.

Ellwood, Robert S., Jr. *An Invitation to Japanese Civilization*. Belmont, Calif.: Wadsworth, 1980. A brief and readable survey of Japanese history, religion, art, and modern culture.

Hori, Ichiro. *Folk Religion in Japan*. Chicago: University of Chicago Press, 1968. A somewhat specialized study whose richness of detail, especially on shamanism, makes it of interest to the nonspecialist.

Kapleau, Phillip, ed. *The Three Pillars of Zen*. Boston: Beacon Press, 1967. A clear view of the practice of Zen in modern Japan.

Kitagawa, Joseph. *Religion in Japanese History*. New York: Columbia University Press, 1966. A comprehensive account of the whole, rather factual and dry.

Ono, Sokyo. *Shinto: The Kami Way*. Tokyo: Bridgeway Press, 1962. A systematizing view that organizes Shinto into a world view comparable to those of the other religious traditions.

Ouchi, William. *Theory Z: How American Business Can Meet the Japanese Challenge*. Reading, Mass.: Addison-Wesley, 1981. A fascinating view of Japanese social traditions in the context of contemporary corporate life.

Tsunoda, Ryusaku, et al., eds. *Sources of Japanese Tradition*. New York: Columbia University Press, 1964. Two volumes of primary sources, with commentaries, that cover the entire historical span.

Conclusion: Summary Reflections

Bowker, John. *The Religious Imagination and the Sense of God.* Oxford: Clarendon Press, 1978. A stimulating study of several religious traditions, including Buddhism, that shows the great yield that sympathetic and imaginative scholarship can produce.

Foy, Whitfield, ed. *Man's Religious Quest.* New York: St. Martin's Press, 1978. A good general sourcebook on the world religions, offering many primary texts (but curiously lacking East Asian sources).

Johnston, William. *The Inner Eye of Love.* New York: Harper & Row, 1978. Shows the contemplative foundations of religion, with special reference to Christianity and Buddhism.

Krim, Keith, ed. *Abingdon Dictionary of Living Religions.* Nashville: Abingdon, 1981. The best single-volume resource for the main concepts, people, and events of the world religions.

Ling, T. O. *A Dictionary of Buddhism.* New York: Charles Scribner's Sons, 1972. Brief explanations of key Buddhist notions, people, and events.

Pannikar, R. *The Intra-Religious Dialogue.* Ramsey, N.J.: Paulist Press, 1978. Stimulating ground rules for comparative religious studies and dialogue, by an eminent practitioner.

Pannikar, Raimundo. *The Unknown Christ of Hinduism.* Maryknoll, N.Y.: Orbis, 1981. A revised edition of a stimulating work by a scholar of Christian-Hindu heritage.

Slater, Peter. *The Dynamics of Religion.* New York: Harper & Row, 1978. A rather conceptual but rich theory of how the religions configure and can best be analyzed.

Streng, Frederick. *Understanding Religious Life.* 2nd ed. Encino, Calif.: Dickenson, 1976. An analysis of methodology in religious studies, traditional ways of being religious, and the varieties of religious expression.

Waldenfels, Hans. *Absolute Nothingness.* Ramsey, N.J.: Paulist Press, 1980. An interpretation of Buddhist philosophy in the context of Buddhist-Christian dialogue.

Glossary

aesthetic: concerning the beautiful or artistic

ahimsa: Hindu nonviolence or noninjury

Allah: Muslim God

anatman: Buddhist no-self

animism: ancient tendency to assume spirits in all things

anthropomorphism: personification; treating something nonhuman as though it were human

archaic: old; premodern and prescientific

arhat: Buddhist term for saint; perfected one who has reached nirvana

asceticism: discipline; abstinence from self-indulgence

atman: Buddhist and Hindu term for self or substantial entity

bhakti: Hindu term for devotion

bodhisattva: Mahayana Buddhist term for saint or enlightened one

Brahman: Hindu term for ultimate reality

brahmin: Hindu member of upper, priestly caste

caste: inheritable Hindu social class

cosmos: the universe conceived as an orderly system

dharma: the teaching of the Buddha; Buddhist doctrine and truth; Hindu social theory

dharmas: the ultimate constituents of phenomena

divination: art of discerning future events

enlightenment: Buddhist term for realization of the truth or attainment of the goal

ethics: study or teaching concerned with morality or right and wrong

faith: belief; commitment or assent beyond factual surety or proof

fetish: object believed to have protective powers

God: the Supreme Being; usually considered personal in the West

god: a being of more than human power

grace: divine favor or free help

henotheism: worshiping one god without denying others

Hinayana: older Buddhist sects that arose in India in the first four centuries after Buddha's death; "smaller vehicle"

holy: set apart and dedicated to the worship or service of the divine

jen ("run"): Confucian virtue of humaneness

jnana-marga: Hindu term for the way of knowledge

kami: Shinto gods or spirits

karma: Hindu and Buddhist term for the physical law of cause and effect

li: Confucian term for propriety and ritual protocol

magic: attempts to control divinities for one's own use

Mahayana: branch of Buddhism that arose in the schism of the second century after the Buddha's death and that came to dominate East Asia; "greater vehicle"

meditation: Hindu and Buddhist interior exercises aimed at liberation

metaphysics: philosophical study of underlying causes

moksha: Hindu term for release or liberation

mystery: something that has not been explained or cannot be explained

mysticism: experience of direct communion with ultimate reality

myth: explanatory story, usually traditional

nature: physical reality in its totality; whatness or character

nirvana: Buddhist goal of liberation or fulfillment

ontology: the study of being or existence

oral peoples: those peoples whose cultures had or have no writing

prajna: Buddhist term for wisdom

Prajna-paramita: Mahayana literature concerned with the perfection of wisdom

prehistoric: prior to written history

priest: religious functionary who performs sacrifices, rites, interpretations, and so on

primitive: original or underived; undeveloped

prophet: spokesperson for God or a divinity

religion: communion with, service of, or concern for ultimate reality

revelation: disclosure (of sacred truth)

ritual: prescribed, formalized religious action or ceremony

sacrament: sacred, empowering action, such as Christian baptism or Eucharist

sacrifice: an offering that "makes holy"; oblation of something of value (such as an animal) to God or sacred powers

salvation: saving from sin; making whole and healthy

samadhi: Indian term for highest state of meditation or yoga

samsara: Hindu and Buddhist term for the state of continual rebirths

sangha: Buddhist term for the community (especially of monks)

secularism: worldly view of life that tends to depreciate religion

shaman: ancient specialist in techniques of ecstasy

sin: offense against God; moral (culpable) error or misdeed

skandhas: Buddhist term for the "heaps" that temporarily comprise the "person"

sunyata: Buddhist term for emptiness

sutra: Buddhist text or discourse, especially from the Buddha himself

tantra: Hindu and Buddhist term for ritual manual; approach to liberation through ritualistic, symbolic, or magical means

Tao ("dow"): Chinese term for cosmic and moral "Way" or "Path"

theology: study or teaching about God or the gods

Theravada: older, conservative school of Pali Buddhism, in contrast to Mahayana; survivor of Hinayana branch

tradition: teaching and practice that have been handed down

transcendence: going beyond the usual limits, often out to the divine

transmigration: the passing of the life force from one entity to another

Trimurti: Hindu divinity as Brahma-Vishnu-Shiva

Vinaya: the code of Buddhist monastic discipline

wu-wei: Taoist notion of active not-doing

yang: Chinese principle of nature that is positive, light, and male

yin: Chinese principle of nature that is negative, dark, and female

yoga: Hindu and Buddhist term for discipline, especially that which is interior and meditative

Zen: Japanese school of Buddhism that stresses meditation

Index of Names and Places

Index of Subjects